ALONE TOGETHER

Alone Together

Poetics of the Passions in Late Medieval Iberia

HENRY BERLIN

UNIVERSITY OF TORONTO PRESS
Toronto Buffalo London

Toronto Buffalo London
utorontopress.com

ISBN 978-1-4875-0967-5 (cloth)
ISBN 978-1-4875-0969-9 (EPUB)
ISBN 978-1-4875-0968-2 (PDF)

Library and Archives Canada Cataloguing in Publication

Title: Alone together : poetics of the passions in late-medieval Iberia / Henry Berlin.
Names: Berlin, Henry, author.
Series: Toronto Iberic ; 59.
Description: Series statement: Toronto Iberic ; 59 | Includes bibliographical references and index.
Identifiers: Canadiana (print) 2021020656X | Canadiana (ebook) 20210207302 | ISBN 9781487509675 (hardcover) | ISBN 9781487509699 (EPUB) | ISBN 9781487509682 (PDF)
Subjects: LCSH: Emotions in literature. | LCSH: Sentimentalism in literature. | LCSH: Spanish literature – To 1500 – History and criticism. | LCSH: Portuguese literature – To 1500 – History and criticism.
Classification: LCC PQ6058 .B47 2021 | DDC 861/.209353–dc23

This book has been published with the help of a grant from the Federation for the Humanities and Social Sciences, through the Awards to Scholarly Publications Program, using funds provided by the Social Sciences and Humanities Research Council of Canada.

University of Toronto Press acknowledges the financial assistance to its publishing program of the Canada Council for the Arts and the Ontario Arts Council, an agency of the Government of Ontario.

Canada Council for the Arts
Conseil des Arts du Canada

Funded by the Government of Canada
Financé par le gouvernement du Canada

"Love should be put into action!"
screamed the old hermit.
Across the pond an echo
tried and tried to confirm it.

–Elizabeth Bishop, "Chemin de Fer"

Contents

Acknowledgments

Alone Together explores how the works of single authors may nevertheless instantiate collective modes of composition, and it bears the mark of the many colleagues and friends who have helped me think through both the problems I study in it and my way of presenting them. From the beginning, Simone Pinet encouraged me to pursue my scholarly interests with sincerity and helped me to do so with conceptual rigour; our more recent collaborations have continually pushed me to rethink and refine my approach to medieval studies. Josiah Blackmore has been a model of intellectual and professional generosity, and an inspiring reader of poetry. Cynthia Robinson showed how scholarly boundaries can only be pushed by the most scrupulous work. Cary Howie sparked my interest in literary theologians and critical poetics.

I am grateful to colleagues at Transylvania University, Miami University of Ohio, the University of Chicago, Harvard University, and the University of Massachusetts Amherst for their insightful questions and comments at presentations of material that would become part of this book, and also to the many colleagues who listened carefully and responded to conference presentations. It is my sincere hope that the critical acumen of Jean Dangler, Emily Francomano, Ryan Giles, Albert Lloret, Sol Miguel-Prendes, David Nirenberg, and Julian Weiss is in some way reflected in my analysis.

At the University at Buffalo, I am grateful for the support and intellectual community afforded by all of my colleagues in the Department of Romance Languages and Literatures and the Humanities Institute's Early Modern Research Workshop. I am particularly indebted to David Castillo, both for early feedback that led to a substantial restructuring of the book's argument and for focused comments on a completed draft. Hal Langfur offered thoughtful encouragement at key moments. A graduate seminar on Petrarch and Petrarchism taught in collaboration with Paola Ugolini offered a space to re-examine important aspects of the poetry of Ausiàs March and other authors included in this study. I have also benefitted from the curiosity and good humour reliably exhibited by my undergraduate and graduate students over the last several years.

Essential research for this book was supported by a National Library of Portugal and Luso-American Development Foundation Short-Term Research Grant, as well as a Kenan Research Grant from Transylvania University. An earlier version of chapter two appeared in *Hispanic Review* (spring 2016) under the title "Alfonso de Madrigal, *el Tostado*, on the Politics of Friendship." Copyright © 2016 University of Pennsylvania Press. All rights reserved. The epigraph is from "Chemin de Fer" from POEMS by Elizabeth Bishop. Copyright © 2011 by The Alice H. Methfessel Trust. Publisher's Note and compilation copyright © 2011 by Farrar, Straus and Giroux. Reprinted by permission of Farrar, Straus and Giroux. All rights reserved.

Many friends have contributed in ways large and small to the shape this book would eventually take. Among them are Beth Bouloukos, Robert Davidson, António and Kathryn de Ridder-Vignone, Wilson Dickinson, Juan Manuel Espinosa, Peter Northup, Ben Novotny Owen, Jeremy Paden, Juan Sierra, Daniel Stifler, Daniel Tonozzi, William Viestenz, and Zac Zimmer.

Throughout the publication process, the advice and support of Suzanne Rancourt have been indispensable. In addition to her work on the index, Carla DeSantis provided excellent editorial assistance. The comments of the manuscript's anonymous readers helped me to focus and clarify the main threads of my argument and also to eliminate some historical imprecisions. Any remaining errors are my own.

In writing a book on medieval attempts to shape and control the passions, I discovered some of my own limitations in this respect. I am grateful for the support of my mother, Joan Berlin, my aunt Sharon Lapkin Matenko, and my late grandmother Lena Winesanker, and I can only hope one day to repay the patience that my daughter Rosa Aurelia Negrete Berlin has shown me over the past four years. Finally, this book would never have been completed without the love and critical attention of my wife, Fernanda Negrete, who has made the difference in my life since the day we met. *Alone Together* is dedicated to her.

ALONE TOGETHER

Introduction

Courtly Conflict and the Passions

Tenho tanto sentimento
Que é frequente persuadir-me
De que sou sentimental,
Mas reconheço, ao medir-me,
Que tudo isso é pensamento,
Que não senti afinal.

– Fernando Pessoa

The turn of the fifteenth century throughout Iberia saw an explosion of literature that was not just sentimental but about sentiment as such. This explosion was among the most important of the substantial changes in intellectual and literary culture taking place in the crowns of Portugal, Castile, and Aragon as new dynasties took and consolidated power.[1] The fact that these changes were concurrent implies no special relationship among them, and this is particularly true when one considers that the cultural changes were hardly uniform: as Portugal underwent the retreat of courtly lyric in favour of ethico-political treatises and increasingly robust official chronicles, that same lyric tradition underwent an unprecedented revival in Castile and a decisive process of linguistic change in Aragon.[2] It is nevertheless the central thesis of this book that these cultural and political changes were related; that, furthermore, they developed in constant relation to one another; and that what they shared was a renewed and urgent attention to the passions as an ethically stigmatized, but poetically and rhetorically powerful, field of intellectual debate. In particular, it was perceived that pressing questions of sociopolitical unity and disunity, harmony and discord, could be addressed through discourse (lyrical and otherwise) about the passions. Across the three crowns and their affiliated territories, a loose network of vernacular writers – many, although not all, situated at the highest levels of the nobility – explored textual strategies for freeing the passions from their politically stultifying, but philosophically and theologically authorized, opposition to reason. That they did so across a wide and rapidly evolving variety of genres – lyric poetry and sentimental fiction, but also ethical, political, and theological treatises, magisterial lectures, and translations of classical material from Cicero and Seneca to Ovid – only reveals the urgency and vitality they brought to bear on what was perhaps, ultimately, an impossible task.

I do not claim that these writers coordinated their efforts explicitly, or even that they expected the same local consequences from the rehabilitation of the passions. There nevertheless exists substantial textual evidence that they understood their writing, no matter how apparently personal, frivolous, or conventional, not just as a shared pastime and rite of communal belonging but rather as a response to the ongoing factional conflict whose violent burden they often bore. Broadly speaking, these conflicts arose from a power struggle between nascent national monarchies and nobles seeking to regain, retain, or even expand their traditional privileges (Ruiz, *Spain's Centuries of Crisis* 93).[3] At the same time, because Iberian nobles travelled from court to court, "their interests, connections, and political agendas transcended the confines of emerging 'national' kingdoms" (115). That such political agendas should be expressed in literature comes as no surprise: to give one initial, well-known example, Juan de Mena, in his celebrated *Laberinto de Fortuna* (1444), repeatedly laments that vicious discord among the Castilian nobility is impeding the progress of the "virtuosa, magnífica guerra" against the Islamic kingdom of Granada (lines 1209–16; cf. lines 657–8, 1169–76, 2017–40). Mena's poem is explicitly "national" in its viewpoint, however (*Obras completas* 24); it is less clear that apparently inward cultural products, such as amatory poetry, should respond to political circumstances. The initial basis for such a claim lies in two proleptic passages in letters sent between 1444 and 1449 by the renowned poet (and subject of Mena's 1438 panegyric the *Coronación*) Íñigo López de Mendoza, Marquis of Santillana.

Courtly Conflict and Lettered Reticence

On 15 January 1444, Santillana wrote to his friend Alfonso de Cartagena, bishop of Burgos and one of Castile's leading intellectuals, with a question about a chivalric oath mentioned, but not explained, in Leonardo Bruni's *De militia*. Having articulated the question, Santillana anticipates Cartagena's surprise – tinged, perhaps, with disapproval – at his apparently idle curiosity:

> Podredes vos agora, señor mío, con asaz aparente razón dezir cómmo la voluntat mía se puede mover a pensar nin entender en tales cosas, esguardado e visto este tienpo trabajoso, donde tantos escándalos, debates e bolliçios son movidos, e todos días por pecados nuestros cresçen e se aumentan tanto que ya las soberviosas flamas de la yra paresçe que llegan al çielo. (Gómez Moreno, "La *Qüestión*" 348)[4]

> You may now ask, my lord, with quite apparent justification, how my will can be moved to think about or try to understand such things, in view of this arduous time, in which so many scandals, debates, and tumults arise, growing and increasing each day by our sins so much that the raging flames of anger seem to reach the sky.[5]

In his response, dated 17 March of the same year, a sympathetic Cartagena first dismisses the concerns foreseen by Santillana as excessively corporeal – "commo si fuéramos nasçidos para comer e bever" (350; "as if we were born to eat and drink") – and then, turning to the historical and practical, asks his own rhetorical question: "E dezidme, yo vos ruego, si esperamos a que la fortuna nos dé tranquilidat e quiete, e en tanto que dura el tienpo turbado tenemos la péñola queda ¿non temeremos con grand razón que por ventura pase nuestra vida oçiosa, syn dexar de sí escriptura durable?" (350; "And tell me, I beg of you, if we wait for fortune to give us peace and quiet, and hold our quill still as long as the troubled time lasts, will we not quite rightly fear that our life may pass by idly, leaving behind no lasting piece of writing?"). True idleness, Cartagena suggests, would be to refrain from writing, and Santillana, situated at the heights of the Castilian nobility, runs this risk more than most:

> E este temor más le devedes tener los grandes que en esta provinçia bevides, donde siempre ovo, e temo que avrá, torvellinos e vientos que en las alturas suelen ferir. E recoligid, si vos plaze, en vuestra memoria los tienpos que pasaron de aquel don Pelayo silvestre, en quien començó la real poliçía, so cuya sonbra en este çiterior España bivimos, ca ante dél era la monarchía más larga e extensa, e a la presente non tan semejable, e claramente veredes muy poco aver durado el sosiego quando contra enemigos guerra non era; porque tanta es la animosidat e brío de la nobleza d'España que si en guerra justa non exercita sus fuerças, luego se convierte a las mover en aquellas contiendas que los romanos çibdadanas llamavan, porque sobre el estado del regimiento de su çibdat se movían, aunque después se estendían por diversas partes del mundo; *e nos propiamente fablando podemos llamar cortesanas, pues sobre el valer de la corte se mueven, aunque se estienden por las más provinçias del regno.* (350–1; emphasis added)

> And you most of all should fear this, the great nobles who live in this province, where there always were, and I fear always will be, whirlwinds and gusts that strike at the heights. And recall, if you please, to your memory the times that have passed since that wild Don Pelayo, in whom the royal order began, in whose shadow we live in this closer Spain, for before him the monarchy was longer and wider, and not so similar to the present one, and you will see clearly that calm has never lasted long when there was no war against enemies; because such is the animosity and spirit of Spain's nobility, that if it does not spend its strength on just war, it directs it instead toward those struggles that the Romans called "civil," because they responded to the state of the city's governance, although they later spread to other parts of the world; *and*

> *we, properly speaking, can call them "courtly," because they respond to the court's worth, although they spread to the realm's other provinces.*

Cartagena's initial question suggests that Santillana should persist in his studies, and particularly in his writing, in spite of Castile's ongoing "troubled times." His longer reflection on Castile's past and present, however, suggests that the cultural activities Santillana purports to view as an indulgent pastime may in fact constitute a remedy to endemic conflict. Spain's nobility, after all, is too "spirited" to remain peaceful in the absence of just war; yet Cartagena, despite a later allusion to the ongoing presence of Muslims on the peninsula (351), does not advocate a policy of perpetual just war. Rather, Cartagena's strong implication is that the *escripturas durables* of Santillana and like-minded nobles might represent a salutary response to Castile's plague of *contiendas cortesanas*, moulding the nobles' character through both their production and reception.

That Castile's political weakness stems from perceived cultural flaws is already suggested by Santillana in this first letter, when he condemns his compatriots for having forgotten Christ's lesson that "todo reyno en sí mesmo diviso será desolado e perdido" (349; "any kingdom divided against itself will be destroyed and lost"; cf. Mt 12:25). According to Santillana, this lesson had been corroborated in antiquity by Rome's civil wars (to which, as we have seen, Cartagena also refers), the Catilinarian conspiracies, and the Gallic wars, "las quales tanto nos son vezinas e de nuestro tienpo que todos días devrían ser ante nuestros ojos, de fecho ya olvidadas, ca lexos es de nos toda virtud, todo deseo de paz e todo amor de bien bevir" (349; "which are so near to us and our time that they should be before our eyes every day, [yet are] in fact already forgotten, for far from us is all virtue, all desire for peace, and all love of living well"). The consequences for such forgetfulness are harsh: "Ansí que denegados nos deven ser qualesquier galardones que fueron otorgados e prometidos a los virtuosos, pugnadores e deseadores del bien de la patria e propulsadores e debelladores de los enemigos de aquélla e defensores de la república" (349; "Thus any rewards should be denied to us that were granted and promised to the virtuous, who fought for and desired the good of their fatherland and drove out and conquered its enemies, and defended the republic").

It is precisely the spectre of the *galardón* cruelly withheld by the beloved that fascinates and haunts what Roger Boase termed Castile's "troubadour revival," the sudden, widespread flourishing of troubadour lyric in Castilian beginning in the last part of the fourteenth century and continuing, with an ever-increasing dominance of love poetry, into the early sixteenth.[6] Indeed, Santillana's second expression of reticence appears in a prefatory letter addressed to Pedro, Constable of Portugal (grandson of John I and son of the Infante Pedro, Duke of Coimbra, Portugal's regent from 1439 to 1448), who had requested a collection of Santillana's poetry.[7] The well-known *Prohemio e carta* (c. 1446–49) begins with a lengthy definition of poetry, but devotes an equal amount of attention, in its second half, to poetry's history, with significant passages on the Galician-Portuguese lyric and on Santillana's Catalan contemporaries, such as Jordi de Sant Jordi and Ausiàs March. It is this extensive history that Santillana fears will appear idle:

> E non vos maravilledes, señor, sy en este prohemio aya tan extensa e largamente enarrado estos tanto antiguos e después nuestros auctores e algunos dezires e cançiones dellos, commo paresca aver proçedido de una manera de occiosidat, lo qual de todo punto deniegan no menos ya la hedad mía que la turbaçión de los tienpos. Pero es asý que commo en la nueva edad me pluguiesen, fallélos agora quando me paresçió ser neçessarios. (Gómez Moreno, *El Prohemio e carta* 64; slightly modified)[8]

> And do not marvel, sir, if in this prologue I have so extensively and lengthily described these very ancient authors and, after, our own, and some of their *decires* and songs, although it may seem to come from a kind of idleness, thoroughly discouraged no less by my age than by the turbulence of the times. But it is thus that, if in my youth I enjoyed them, I found them now when they seem necessary to me.

This passage echoes the first in juxtaposing Santillana's historical and cultural curiosity to the *turbación de los tiempos*, adding the nuance that poetry, if it is an appropriate courtly pastime at all, is a young man's game (Santillana's love poems do date from his youth). It is nevertheless the present *necessity* of such *dezires e canciones* that Santillana stresses to the youthful Pedro, no more than twenty years old when he received the *Prohemio*.

A deflationary reading of these closing reflections from the *Prohemio* might understand Santillana's presentation of foregoing authors and their poems as "necessary" only as a preface to his own poetry. Taken together with the exchange between Santillana and Cartagena, however, this valedictory passage bespeaks a greater perceived necessity for the lyric in turbulent times. Thus, the fundamental questions raised by Santillana's letters are first, in what ways courtly poetry and, later, sentimental fiction respond to social conflict; and second, which elements of earlier courtly traditions are revived or renovated as part of this response and why.

The two letters also suggest that an exclusively or even primarily Castilian frame will lead to inadequate answers. On the one hand, each of the correspondents crossed Iberian frontiers at an early point in his intellectual and literary formation. Santillana accompanied Ferdinand of Antequera to his coronation in 1412 and remained at the Aragonese court for several years, becoming cupbearer to the prince Alfonso (the future Alfonso V of Aragon) in 1413. At this court, he is known to have met Jordi de Sant Jordi and is likely to have met Ausiàs March and Andreu Febrer (L. Cabré, "Notas sobre la memoria" 29); he would also have experienced directly Aragon's cultural engagement with Occitan literature and, through the latter, with Italian and French literature as well (Santillana, *Poesías completas* 10–11).

Cartagena's earliest works were translations of Cicero's *De officiis*, *De senectute*, and *De inventione*, the last of which was begun c. 1421–22 at the request of Portugal's prince Duarte (who would ascend to the throne in 1433) while Cartagena served as ambassador to the Portuguese court (*La Rethórica* 7). And finally, Duarte's nephew Pedro, the recipient of Santillana's *Prohemio*, met Santillana (and, possibly, Juan de Mena and Juan Rodríguez del Padrón) during a 1445 military expedition in aid of Álvaro de Luna against the *infantes* of Aragon, then lived in Castilian exile from 1449 to 1455 after his father's death in the Battle of Alfarrobeira. He was offered the throne of Aragon in 1464 by the Consell del Principat during the Catalan Civil War; he accepted, and after two inconclusive years of battle, died of tuberculosis in Granollers, near Barcelona, in 1466 (Gascón Vera 10–22).

On the other hand, one need not have recourse to the dense and sometimes bewildering realms of dynastic history and royal patronage to see the polyglot cultural relations at play in the development of medieval Iberian literature; they are plain in Santillana's letter, where the Marquis expresses his admiration for Catalan, Valencian, and Aragonese poets past and present as "grandes oftiçiales desta arte" (Gómez Moreno, *El Prohemio e carta* 58) and recalls that "non ha mucho tienpo qualesquier dezidores e trobadores destas partes, agora fuessen castellanos, andaluzes o de la Estremadura, todas sus obras conponían en lengua gallega o portuguesa" (60; "not long ago all poets and troubadours from these parts, whether Castilian, Andalusian, or from Extremadura, composed all their works in the Galician or Portuguese language"). Contact among courtly authors across Iberian territories and in multiple languages was, in short, the norm during this period. In this sense, Vicenç Beltran is undoubtedly correct to note that, for Santillana and his contemporaries, Alfonso X, who composed all of his poetry in Galician-Portuguese, was nevertheless to be considered a Castilian poet ("La encrucijada" X–XI) and to conclude elsewhere that "la identificación exclusiva de la literatura española con la literatura en castellano ha supuesto una grave mutilación de nuestro pasado histórico y cultural y ha dejado sin fondo ni basamento el rico florecer de la lírica en los cancioneros del siglo XV" (*La corte* 332; "the exclusive identification of Spanish literature with literature in Castilian has entailed a grave mutilation of our historical and cultural past and has left the rich flourishing of lyric in the songbooks of the fifteenth century without grounding or base").

Indeed, at a broader level, the courtly literature of late medieval Iberia constitutes one of the strongest cases for the emergent model of Iberian Studies, which holds that "the Iberian interliterary system is more than the sum of its parts and … no true representation of this system can emerge from the mere addition of these parts studied in isolation from each other" (Resina 12). Even a comparative approach will fail to capture what has always been an essentially relational system, in which, during the Middle Ages, writers travelled among multiple courts and consumed their cultural production while also drawing on past traditions whose writers had done much the same.[9] This process of exchange and influence is, of course, present always and everywhere to some extent, but the particular linguistic competencies and geographic mindsets of fifteenth-century Iberian writers deepened and accelerated the relationality of their texts, sentimental and otherwise. It is, after all, with a comprehensive peninsular invocation of "esta postrimera e occidental parte, que es la nuestra España" (Gómez Moreno, *El Prohemio e carta* 57; "this final western region, which is our Spain") that Santillana introduces his overview of Galician-Portuguese, Catalan, and Castilian poetry to his Portuguese correspondent.[10]

Reaction or Anticipation: The Obscure Semantics of Courtly Emotion

Santillana's reticence may have been elicited by persistent scepticism among the Castilian nobility toward the study of letters throughout and beyond the reign of John II (Round 214). As P.E. Russell has noted, Castile's *defensores* were devoted to a theory of social structure with rigid divisions between the warrior and the scholar, and given the ongoing presence of Muslim Granada to the south and the internecine conflicts to which Santillana alludes in his letters, they enjoyed a lasting cultural ascendancy that allowed them to impose this view broadly ("Las armas" 221). The *cancioneros* nevertheless bear witness to more than 400 named poets, of whom more than a third belonged to the upper nobility (Boase 3–4). One way to resolve the tension between cultural resistance to a genre such as troubadour lyric and its widespread production is to understand it as a form of reactionary conservatism in its particular context:

> The troubadour revival in late medieval Spain was a conservative reaction to social crisis by those who belonged, or were affiliated, to a powerful, expanding and belligerent aristocracy; the crisis was produced by a discrepancy between social theory and social reality which could never be resolved, because the theory was based on the belief in a divinely pre-ordained system of social stratification in which change was inconceivable. (7–8)

In contrast to Boase, Julian Weiss notes that much *cancionero* poetry was the product of a powerful and rapidly growing aristocracy whose hardly precarious social position gave rise to a literary perspective "firmly rooted in the here and now, constructed from a position of strength, and populated by fictions of aristocratic male power" ("Álvaro de Luna" 242–3). Such fictions, however, themselves drew on long-standing literary tradition, and Boase's account of a fundamentally nostalgic phenomenon has been reinforced in modern criticism by the very lateness, in the European context, of Castile's troubadour revival; after all, troubadour lyric had flourished in both Portugal and Aragon beginning as early as the end of the twelfth century, to say nothing of its emergence in the Romance vernacular in Occitania at the end of the eleventh and its possible ties to earlier poetry in Arabic and Hebrew.[11] The Castilian school of courtly poetry thus arrived so late as to be almost anachronistic even within a medieval context, and early critical appraisals of it by Spanish philologists were notoriously negative, dismissing almost the entire corpus as derivative, unimaginative, aesthetically sterile.[12]

While this point of view is most associated with the nineteenth-century critic Marcelino Menéndez Pelayo (Whinnom, "Towards" 118), it persisted into more recent and still-influential texts. Writing in 1976, for example, Ottavio di Camillo criticized the lack of "true intimacy" in the *cancioneros*' expressions of love: "Lejos de ser la causa de conflictos y contradicciones profundamente sentidos, con frecuencia se muestra como un sentimiento convencional en el cual la imagen de la persona amada aparece borrosa o truncada en su identidad humana" (96; "Far from being the cause of deeply felt conflicts and contradictions, it frequently presents itself as a conventional feeling in which the image of the beloved appears blurred or cut short in its human identity"). Di Camillo is doubtless correct in identifying the conventionality of emotional discourse in the *cancioneros* and their scarcity of references to material reality, the latter of which is shared by the earlier Galician-Portuguese *cancioneiros* (Hart, *En maneira* 22–3). In fact, at the lexical level, perhaps the most salient feature of *cancionero* poetry is the dominance of a restricted and abstract emotional vocabulary, one that is shared by Catalan poetry from the same period.[13] In one of the earliest calls to re-evaluate this corpus, Keith Whinnom argued that it was precisely this dense concentration of emotional abstraction that led to the early rejections of what is, after all, a voluminous and intricate body of verse:

> The constant repetition of a handful of words (for what is true of the nouns extends to the rest of the vocabulary also) diffuses their semantic content ... One might conclude – prematurely – that the poet has nothing to say, that these poems do not mean very much, that they are all alike, and that they are eminently forgettable ("tan pronto dichas como olvidadas"). But this is puzzling, since it is obvious that the *cancionero* poets have taken a great deal of trouble to polish their verses, as even the most hostile critics concede. ("Towards" 122)

If we wish to do justice to the trouble these poets have taken, then the most pressing methodological question is how to grapple semantically with their repetitive, conventional, abstract emotional discourse.[14] Yet the meanings of even apparently foundational terms such as "passion," "affect," "sentiment," "feeling," and "emotion" are notoriously hard to pin down. These terms resist definitional consensus and thus present a double instability: their medieval and modern usages are both inconsistent, so it becomes almost impossible to fix a critical starting point. In other words, neither modern critical discourse nor the historical discourse that constitutes its object of study is stable. "Emotion," which has been the dominant term since around 1800 (Rosenwein, *Emotional Communities* 3), suggests itself as an all-encompassing neutral term for analysis precisely because of its anachronism for the Middle Ages – but there is no contemporary agreement about what "emotion" describes. We might expect the field of psychology to have forged a technical definition, but as Theodore R. Sarbin writes, efforts in this direction have so far been unsuccessful:

> One outcome of the opacity of the term "emotion" is the failure to achieve a common definition. Some writers talk of "having" an emotion, others of the "experience" of emotion; some equate emotion with visceral activity, some with the perception of visceral activity; some use emotion and feelings as equivalents, others argue that feelings are constitutive of emotion; others treat emotions as patterned organismic responses. (85)[15]

The term is sometimes adopted openly as a convenience,[16] but its own resistance to definition – its "opacity" – means that it is as likely to hinder as to help a critical investigation. This opacity is compounded by the fact that terms such as "affect" and "feeling" are often found within definitions of "emotion," and not as pure synonyms. As such, adopting or asserting "emotion" as the broadest term is not necessarily a helpful heuristic strategy.

If modern usage turns out to be inconsistent, we might turn to a close examination of historical usage in an attempt to fix our object of study. Indeed, there is no doubt that research into historical usage and intellectual context narrows the interpretive field considerably. However, as I argue throughout this book, such an approach offers a beginning but cannot offer definitive answers about a field of disputation masquerading as a field of definition. What is true of modern authors is true of pre-modern ones: there was some consistency in their usage of terms such as "passion," "affection," and "sentiment" (Rosenwein, *Emotional Communities* 3), but there is enough variation among systematic treatments of the passions to give pause. The complexity only increases when we broaden our view to include pseudo-, non-, and anti-systematic treatments of the passions in lyric poetry and creative prose. Here, I wish to give a brief account of the modern terminological challenge before describing the ancient and medieval systems most relevant to my analysis of the Iberian context. Contemporary theorists often make lists of "primary" emotions, but "the number and type of emotions taken to be primary varies from one theorist to another" (Harré 3), and this inconsistency is present in ancient and medieval categorizations as well. Historically speaking, emotion words are like Fortune, constant only in their inconstancy:

> There has rarely been any consensus on the number of passions or of emotions that exist, nor on which of them are "basic" or "principal," nor on the way that they should be classified. This lack of consensus and the confusion that seemingly arbitrary differences between individual competing classifications has engendered is one of the

> invariant features of the history of theories of passions, affections, sentiments and emotions. (Dixon 43)

Attempting to delve even deeper into history through etymology turns out to be of limited use as well:

> No existe, en realidad, una raíz lexical indoeuropea de la que derive unívocamente un término equivalente a *pasión*, y la razón que alegan los especialistas para este hueco en el vocabulario originario es que a ese nivel de la historia no sólo no existía diferenciación entre emoción y pasión, sino ni siquiera las nociones abstractas de "pasión" o "emoción" tal como hoy las percibimos. (Bordelois 29)

> In reality, there is no Indo-European lexical root from which a term equivalent to *passion* can be unambiguously derived, and the reason alleged by specialists for this empty space in the originary vocabulary is that at that level of history there was not only no difference between emotion and passion, but the very abstract notions of "passion" or "emotion" did not exist as we perceive them today.[17]

This uncertain origin, along with the constantly varying usage that followed it, resists synthesis even if we limit our investigation to a particular time and place. In fact, even individual authors – perhaps especially poets – can be remarkably inconsistent in their emotional vocabulary. And to the extent that such vocabulary is inherently social in nature, how can we locate the varying usage of an individual author within broader, but unruly, social structures?

Social constructionists in the field of psychology have addressed this question, emphasizing rather than denying emotion's linguistic basis. They argue that varied usage (across time, space, and languages) does not obscure emotion as an object of study, but rather constitutes it:

> We can do only what our linguistic resources and repertoire of social practices permit or enable us to do. There has been a tendency among both philosophers and psychologists to abstract an entity – call it "anger," "love," "grief" or "anxiety" – and to try to study it. But what there is are angry people, upsetting scenes, sentimental episodes, grieving families and funerals, anxious parents pacing at midnight, and so on. There is a concrete world of contexts and activities. We reify and abstract from that concreteness at our peril. (Harré 4)

Eschewing reification is only the first methodological step, however. After all, we can no longer witness medieval anger, medieval love scenes, or medieval funerals: only their textual or visual representations.[18] Some grounding in the abstract, reified thought of these representations' time is essential for analysing them. And it is through studying ancient and medieval treatises on the passions that patterns start to emerge: categorizations of the passions varied widely, but a relatively constant and limited group of theoretical concerns central to those categorizations can be identified. These concerns, as articulated in the explorations of emotion carried out by Platonists, Peripatetics, Stoics, Church Fathers, Cartesians, early psychologists and evolutionary theorists, psychoanalysts, and social constructionists, are (at the risk of oversimplifying) the relationship of the soul or mind to the body; the participation of reason in the passions or the conflict between the two; passivity, activity, and the subject/object relation; and, most broadly, ethics or practical wisdom, which includes discussions of virtue and vice or sin and also of sociopolitical relations. These problems can be articulated separately but tend to be mutually implicated in historical discussions.

In his 1895 "Theory of Emotion," John Dewey attempts a synthesis of Charles Darwin's and William James's theories of emotion; the chief claim of this synthesis is that emotions do not precede and cause their physical manifestations (such as crying or laughing), but rather are attitudes we adopt toward those physical movements, which were originally purposive (see, for example, 1.6: 568–9). Thus, Dewey is mostly preoccupied with the mind/body relation, but he mobilizes the ethical understanding of emotion in justifying his focus on behavioural rather than "psychical" emotion: "We certainly do not deny nor overlook the 'feel' phase, but in ordinary speech the behavior side of emotion is, I think, always uppermost in consciousness. *The connotation of emotion is primarily ethical, only secondarily psychical*" (2.1: 17; emphasis added). Dewey's ultimately sociolinguistic observation that talk about emotion is talk about expressions of emotion (behaviour) dovetails with the teleological Darwinian argument that those physical expressions must have served some purpose in the early stages of humankind's development. Thus, when Dewey concludes that "the emotion is, *psychologically*, *the adjustment or tension of habit and ideal*, and the organic changes in the body are the literal working out, in concrete terms, of the struggle of adjustment" (2.1: 30; emphasis in original), his adherence to the historical and social (which accounts for the "ideal" held to be in tension with the evolutionarily useful "habit") demonstrates the ongoing theoretical link between questions of mind and body and questions of ethics.[19]

This persistence of ancient problematics in modern theorizing would have come as a surprise to René Descartes, who must have thought he was making a definitive break in opening his 1649 *Passions of the Soul* with a denunciation of all previous theories: "The defectiveness of the sciences we inherit from the ancients is nowhere more apparent than in what they wrote about the Passions" (18). In the treatise's preface, he has already made clear that he has not sought to explain the passions "as an Orator, or even as a moral Philosopher, but only as a Physicist" (17). Modern readers accustomed to considering emotion an empirical phenomenon might expect the first two of these disciplines to require more explanation than the last, but Descartes has identified here the two fields of inquiry, along with that of medicine, that had until the Renaissance provided the most extensive discussions and systematizations of emotion. In fact, the methodological division of Descartes's preface is anticipated in Aristotle's *De anima*:

> The natural philosopher and the dialectician would give a different definition of each of the affections, for instance in answer to the question "What is anger?" For the dialectician will say that it is a desire for revenge or something like that, while the natural philosopher will say that it is a boiling of the blood and hot stuff about the heart. And of these the one will be expounding the matter, the other the form and rationale. (403a).

Aristotle himself approached the problem both as a natural philosopher and a dialectician, but this approach was not the rule in the centuries that followed. Rather, the two traditions rejected by Descartes – rhetoric and moral philosophy – tended to remain apart from "Physics." Late antique and medieval rhetorical and moral treatments of the passions sometimes incorporate "naturalistic" humoral theory, but they are much likelier to focus, like Aristotle, on the soul and perception; early Christian accounts add the element of demonic persuasion or suggestion. It is these Stoic and patristic theories, with their ethical focus on reason and the will, that form the most direct basis for late medieval Iberian theories of emotion.

Cicero and Seneca were the most influential Stoics in medieval Iberian thought and two of the most important classical *auctoritates* in discussions of practical wisdom and politics. For the Stoics, and Cicero in particular, the fact that the cause of all emotion "is to be found entirely in belief" (*Tusculan Disputations* III.24) does not make emotions rational.[20] Cicero adhered to the four-fold Stoic classification of the emotions, in which pleasure and distress were reactions to present goods or evils, and appetite (or desire) and fear were reactions to future goods or evils (III.25).[21] More specifically, pleasure, distress, desire, and fear were judgments (IV.14) that came about through a loss of control (IV.22) and to which the mind assented voluntarily (III.61–6). Cicero himself summarizes these points with characteristic forcefulness: "As far as I am concerned, the entire theory of emotion[22] can be summed up in a single point: that they are all in our power, all experienced through judgment, all voluntary" (IV.65). In fact, knowledge of this "single point" also constitutes the "method of cure" for these "sicknesses of mind" (IV.83). For Cicero, then, the emotions constitute mistaken beliefs that can be purged through the exercise of reason.

The Greek name for this kind of self-control is *sōphrosunē*, which Cicero renders as "temperance," "self-control," or "moderation" (*temperantia*, *moderatio*, and *modestia*; III.16). Cicero suggests, however, that the best term for it might be "frugality" (*frugalitas*), since it refers not only to "restraint" and "harmlessness" but to "all the other virtues as well" (III.16). That is, frugality "implies the three virtues of courage, justice, and prudence," becoming in Cicero's system the fourth principal virtue, whose defining characteristic "is that it regulates and placates one's impulses to act, and so preserves that well-regulated consistency which on every occasion is opposed to desire" (III.17). The language of regulation, justice, and economy is key here because it is central to both Stoic social ethics and, as I discuss in part one, fifteenth-century Iberian political thought. Later in the *Tusculans*, Cicero argues that pity is not a useful emotion: "Why pity someone when you might assist him? Or are we incapable of being generous without pity [*misericordia*]? For our obligation is not to feel distress on account of others, but to relieve the distress of others if we can" (IV.56).[23] Here, frugality is not the opposite of generosity – clearly marked as a social virtue – but a reasoned commitment to helpful action whenever possible. In other words, an abstract, apparently "rational" duty replaces empathy as a spur to movement.[24] This is, in a condensed form, the tradition against which the authors I discuss throughout *Alone Together* will elaborate their own political and ethical systems of collective emotion.

Seneca grounds his analysis of emotion in questions of reason and speech and a fundamental contrast with the animals, because for him, reason and speech define emotion: "Wild animals are incapable of anger, as is everything, apart from man. Anger may be the enemy of reason. It cannot, all the same, come into being except where there is a place for reason … Without speech, animals are without human emotions, though they have certain impulses that are similar to them" (*On Anger* I.3.4–6). In *On Anger*, he goes further than Cicero in elaborating a model of assent in his picture of emotion:

> If you want to know how the emotions begin, grow or get carried away, the first movement is involuntary, a preparation, as it were, for emotion, a kind of threat. The next is voluntary but not insistent – I may, for example, think it right for me to wreak vengeance because I have been harmed or for him to be punished because he has committed a crime. The third really is out of control; wanting retribution not just "if it is right" but at all costs, it has completely overcome the reason. The first is a mental jolt which we cannot escape through reason … The other sort of movement, generated by decision, can be eliminated by decision. (II.4.1–2)[25]

Seneca's account is notable because it marries a classically rigid Stoic idealization of *apatheia* with an equally strident affirmation of reason's place in emotion. In his system, reason and the passions do not battle to gain control of the mind (or soul), but to *become* it: "It is not the case that the mind stands apart, spying out its affections from without, to prevent their going too far – the mind itself turns into affection [*in adfectum ipse mutatur*] … Reason and affection are the mind's transformations for better or for worse" (I.8.2–3).[26] Reason and affection are thus conceived of as ontologically contrary states of mind; their conflict was always an ethical one, but here it becomes the central fact of the soul's very existence.

The term "emotion" developed precisely as an "amoral" alternative to the earlier "passion" (Dixon 18). Yet, to the extent that emotion has been studied from the nineteenth century on with an eye toward regulation, it is subject to what Louis C. Charland calls "moral undertow," remaining "a *normative* enterprise" invariably tied to "values and morals" (84–5; emphasis in original). Medieval theorists, for their part, did sometimes seek to distinguish passions from "affections," and these distinctions were articulated in ethical terms on the basis of the kind of appetite to which they corresponded and the level of rational control to which they were subject. Augustine contrasted the "voluntary affections of the soul" with the "involuntary passions" and criticized the Stoics for considering all passions and affections to be vices (Dixon 46–7). Aquinas took up this distinction, locating the passions in the sensory appetite in contrast to "simple" affect, whose object is the good itself rather than sense objects and which is located in the intellectual appetite or will (Dixon 46).[27] This distinction allowed both Augustine and Aquinas to carve out a place for emotion in the rational mind:

> The rational mind had its own "emotions," namely those movements or acts of the will that were known as affects or affections. In other words, the reason-passion dichotomy was decidedly not a reason-emotion dichotomy. The higher part of the soul was properly moved in its voluntary acts – in the expression of its love. Its position above animal passion (sensory appetite) in the hierarchy did not exclude it from all the aspects of life that we would call "emotions," only from the wild, violent, unrestrained and unconsidered compulsions of passion that it would still seem reasonable advice to seek to avoid. (Dixon 53–4)

For Aquinas, these violent and sinful passions, although located in the soul, were distinguished by the transformations they effected in the body (*transmutationes corporales*), and they could be subdivided into the concupiscible, related to desire, and the irascible, related to anger (Rosenwein, *Generations* 147–50). Yet affections could also be sinful: they were sins of the soul turned away from the "incorporeal ideal" that was their proper object, rather than the passionate sins of the body (Dixon 56). In this account, a "perfected" human, free from the passions of the body, still expressed love of God, and had perhaps achieved this pious state through compunction or saving sorrow. Such affections were virtuous, however, only to the extent that they were governed by reason (Rosenwein, *Generations* 162). Thus, although this account specifies a positive and even indispensable role for certain forms of emotion, it remains in the end a rationalist account of emotional ethics. Undoubtedly one of the chief lenses through which later medieval authors took in the Aristotelian and Stoic theories of emotion as they related to the soul, it nevertheless stood alongside rhetorical accounts of the emotions, which had their own ethics and social applications. It is these latter accounts that suggest "passion" as the most productive term for the study of Iberia's sentimental literature.

Passion, Subjectivity, and Lyric Theory

The vocabulary of concupiscible and irascible passion arises with some frequency in the Iberian songbooks and sentimental prose studied here, but the distinction between "passion" and "affect" is largely effaced in lyric and even in theophilosophical texts. For example, Alfonso de Madrigal writes in his *Brevyloquyo de amor e amiçiçia* (discussed at length in chapter two) that it is "las fuerças *afectivas o passionales*" that can be divided generally into love and anger, the concupiscible and irascible (5v; emphasis added). The lack of a clear distinction persisted into the sixteenth century, as is evident in Juan Luis Vives's 1538 *De anima et vita*, where the Valencian humanist suggested one based on intensity rather than quality: "affections" should be considered "light disturbances" of the soul, whereas stronger disturbances should properly be called "'commotions,' 'agitations,' or as the Greeks would say 'passions' [*páthê*] because the soul is passively submitted to their blows and buffets" (5). I will return to the idea of passivity later, but what is revealing about Vives's approach is that it remains heuristic, not philological: he justifies the proposed distinction as a helpful way to think about the phenomena in question, not on the basis of historical usage or philosophical precedent, except to the extent that one authoritative culture, that of the Greeks, is selected as a model. In other words, he appeals to the Greeks' authority, but only as a way out of a pre-existing morass.

Faced with the dual confusions of historical and modern usage, pioneering historians of the emotions such as Barbara H. Rosenwein and William M. Reddy have sought, on the one hand, to mark out what consistency they can in historical usage and, on the other, to engage with psychology, anthropology, and philosophy to find the most widely acceptable definition of "emotion," not only across disciplines but across cultures.[28] In doing so, both authors have come to emphasize those aspects of emotion related to social regulation and governance. Rosenwein has proposed the concept of "emotional communities," that is, "groups in which people adhere to the same norms of emotional expression and value – or devalue – the same or related emotions" (*Emotional Communities* 2; she notes that multiple emotional communities may coexist in the same place and time). Rosenwein's concept draws, in turn, on Reddy's "emotional regimes," which "provide individuals with prescriptions and counsel concerning both *the best strategies* for pursuing emotional learning and *the proper end point or ideal* of emotional equilibrium" (55; emphasis in original). Although Rosenwein and Reddy derive these concepts from contemporary attempts to define emotions as real phenomena, their linguistic sensitivity and knowledge of cultural theory – along, perhaps, with the "moral undertow" internal to psychological theories – returns them to the realm of social ethics. Indeed, one need have no recourse to contemporary theory to see that emotional discourse is not "naturally" confused, but is rather, as Aristotle sees in his *Rhetoric*, a site for social and political contention.[29] Emotions, that is, are distributed unequally among and within communities, and this distribution is channelled and enforced through rhetorical acts. Emotional communities and regimes, in other words, manifest and indeed create hierarchies not only of virtue but of power. Thus, in the political economy of passion and *apatheia* described by Daniel M. Gross, "it makes a difference in the end not only what sort of passions are distributed to whom, but also how they are hoarded and monopolized and how their systematic denial helps produce political subjects of a certain kind" (49).[30] I add only that the subjectivity produced by these rhetorical economies of emotion need not be limited to the explicitly political.

Critical discussions of the emergence of literary and modern subjectivity have long dominated lyric theory – especially in analyses of medieval lyric – and it is here that passion, as opposed to emotion, affect, or sentiment, becomes a powerful heuristic. Broadly speaking, the concept of passion raises two highly productive paradoxes. There is, first of all, passion's combination of activity and passivity. The standard account of passion's etymology highlights the surprising shift from the passivity of *pathos* and *passio* to, in the words of Erich Auerbach, the "heated, stormy, and thereby active" connotations of "passion" today (289). As Auerbach has noted, however, already in Aristotle the association between suffering and potential makes possible a more active reading of passion, one that would develop into the concept of *motus animi*, movements of the soul (291). This notion of passion was important in Thomism (Rosenwein, *Generations* 150–1), but as Auerbach goes on to explain, it was the Stoic articulation of passion as incompatible with the wise man's apathy that came to dominate medieval thought. No longer opposed to action, passion was now opposed to reason (291), and it is this form of the opposition that dominates medieval ethics as manifested in medieval poetry. In this initial sense, insisting on passion emphasizes the particular ethical stakes of medieval lyric.

The Argentine linguist Ivonne Bordelois has noted a parallel case of historical transformation from passive to active: that of the subject (78). Robert Folger is no doubt correct that some scepticism is in order when pre-modern works are viewed through the lens of "subjectivity," both in the specific sense that one risks anachronism and in a broader sense that – like "emotion," I might add – philosophical and historical usage are not as coherent as one might wish (*Escape* 27–31). As in the case of passion, however, certain key problems arise persistently in debates about subjectivity. Étienne Balibar, Barbara Cassin, and Alain de Libera (to whose argument I return in chapter seven) delineate three "groups of meanings" that coalesce around the idea of the subject: "subjectness," a translation of the German neologism *Subjektheit* that "basically provides a link between the logical subject ('of which' there can be predicates) and the physical subject ('in which' there are accidents)"; "subjectivity," which "makes 'subject' the antonym of 'object' when a more specific distinction has to be made between the sphere of the psyche or the mental, as opposed to that of objectivity"; and finally, "subjection," which "implies the idea of dependency or subjugation, or any form of domination that subjugates, compels or obliges" (1069–70). These groups remained largely separate throughout the Middle Ages, allowing for a distinction between the active subject of thought and speech, on the one hand, and the passive subject of accidents, on the other.[31] Yet it is precisely this distinction between activity and passivity, inside and outside, through which passion, in its second productive paradox, penetrates. In the Stoic model of passions as mistaken judgments, passion constitutes, in the words of Michel Meyer, the "consciousness of the other in us which is both consciousness, thus reflection, and thoughtlessness as well, since its object is not itself but something outside" (64). On the one hand, rationalists have always denounced the passions as the enemies of reflexive consciousness, "this natural place wherein the empirical forces the door open illegally" (172); passion is exactly what needs to be mastered for the self-conscious subject to make progress toward what can be known with certainty. But on the other hand, passions have always been understood, even by Descartes, as *necessary* to a form of self-reflexivity: it is through the passions that consciousness becomes aware of otherness, and therefore, it is through the passions that consciousness becomes its own object of concern (78). "Passions," concludes Meyer, "constitute those rare moments of fusion between the consciousness of an object and the consciousness of the self, when the self refers back to itself by moods, and is itself immersed in the sensation as though all distance between these two types of perception is suddenly found to be effaced" (78). Passion, in other words, is both constitutive of the individual subject and what maintains that subject's permeability, the possibility of identification with other objects and other people.

Scholars of medieval lyric influenced by Paul Zumthor, who averred in *Toward a Medieval Poetics* that "the corpus of medieval poetry strikes us as almost entirely objectivized" (40), have long seen in troubadour poetry a resistance or alternative to the modern, self-conscious subject. Some of these scholars have nevertheless sought to qualify Zumthor's fundamental insight, identifying aspects of subjectivity that emerge in pre-modern literature and thought. As Judith Peraino explains in a recent overview of this critical tradition, through careful readings of the Occitan, French, and Italian troubadour traditions, critics such as Sarah Kay, Gerald Bond, and Peter Haidu propose that "subjectivity is identical to *self*-awareness," but that "the self is not identical to the subject" (Peraino 21); this idea allows them to give an account of troubadour subjectivity in which "the love song emerges in the interstices between the subject and the self as an artistic utterance that offers at least the representation of self-awareness (Kay), if not also its real possibility for ideological resistance (Bond, Haidu)" (21). Self-awareness becomes, in this reading, a tool poets can manipulate to poetic and intellectual effect.

There has long been resistance, then, to the oversimplified notion of an exclusively modern subjectivity. It was Hegel who identified lyric as the paradigmatically subjective genre (Culler, *Theory* 92), and it was post-Hegelian critics such as Jakob Burckhardt who articulated a vision of the Renaissance as "the *unprecedented birth* of the concept and possibility of the individual, subjective self, the private, self-determining, unique, autonomous ego" (Stone 1–2; emphasis in original).[32] Against Burckhardt's notion of the Renaissance "birth" of the individual, yet also in some tension with the readings of Kay, Bond, and Haidu, Gregory B. Stone has argued that certain medieval texts anticipate and consciously reject this possibility, defending an alternative, collective subjectivity:

> The late Middle Ages *does know*, that, though the revelation concerning the singularity of the ego has already taken place, the "truth" of this revelation has been rejected as an un-truth, as a philosophic loss to be resisted rather than a gain to be encouraged ... The Middle Ages consciously insists that *I* am *they*: that the individual subject is never singular, is always in some essential sense general, collective, objective. (4; emphasis in original)

For Stone, troubadour poetry enacts this resistance in two related ways. The first is the love poet's recourse to a shared, conventional language that is self-defeating in its assertions of individual identity:

> What makes the troubadour's task impossible is that there is absolutely no objective distinction between the true and the false languages of love: the troubadour's *I* always sounds just exactly like *them*, just exactly like his rivals ... Saying "I love you," that is, is always a convention, a *citation*; it does not so much distinguish an individual as it makes him resemble everyone else. The courtly love singer cannot appear as anything other than *they*, a subject without a name, a plural or collective rather than an individual ego. If the troubadour's love remains impossible, unfulfilled, it is because his impossible task has been to distinguish himself by using a language that does not allow individuals to distinguish themselves, to make a name for himself by using a language in which there are no names. (6–7; emphasis in original)

The second form of resistance is an aversion to historicizing or localizing the lyric "I"; troubadours refuse, Stone argues, to take the step from pronoun to noun (7).

If we do not read medieval lyric as the subjective expression of an interiority characterized by sincere (or dramatized, as in a dramatic monologue) emotion, how should we read a corpus in which first-person expressions of emotion predominate so thoroughly? And what creative or ethical resources might Iberian poets have sought to rescue in their late return to and revision of these traditions? It is here that the rhetorical approach to historical emotion reveals its greatest relevance to courtly lyric. Recent work on the theory of the lyric by scholars such as Jonathan Culler, for example, has emphasized epideictic, the rhetoric of praise or blame, as a central lyrical mode that is nevertheless frequently overlooked by modern critics (*Theory* 128). But already in 2000, John Dagenais had shown the centrality of epideictic to troubadour poetics (243, 247), and Ana M. Gómez-Bravo, through a detailed analysis of the Castilian poetic genres of the *decir* and the *canción* throughout the fifteenth century, has demonstrated the extraordinary responsiveness of

Castilian courtly poetics to contemporary developments in rhetorical culture ("*Decir canciones*" 174–5). The same can be said of poetry from Aragon. For example, the rhetorical awareness described by Gómez-Bravo, and awareness of epideictic in particular, is made manifest in Joan Ramon Ferrer's self-glossed *Sirventesch*, which includes the following gloss on "qui de bondats avia": "Car atribuesch a ell [that is, to Joan Valentí, the subject of the poem] virtuts e redundació de lahor, de la qual és compost lo present sirventesch, perquè, segons Rethòrica, és en lo linatge demonstratiu" (*Lírica trobadoresca del segle XV* 120; "For I attribute to him virtues and abundant praise, of which the present *sirventesch* is composed, because, according to Rhetoric, it is in the demonstrative genre").

Questions of subjectivity were not always treated in such definitive terms in Iberian lyric, yet certain conventional themes and stylistic devices played openly on the tension between activity and passivity and the distance between self and subject. A late but representative example can be found in a song by Garci Sánchez de Badajoz, who flourished around the turn of the sixteenth century: "En dos prisiones estoy/ que me atormentan aqui/ la una me tiene ami/ y la otra tengo yo" (lines 1–4; "I am in two prisons that torment me here: one of them holds me, and I hold the other").[33] The bilingual Catalan poet Pere Torroella (c. 1420–c. 1492), to whom I return frequently in this study, shows how enallage could be used to emphasize the alienation of the lyric from the living subject: "Ved que me vedes bivir:/ *non soy yo aquel que bivo,*/ que al triste de mí, captivo,/ Amor lo fizo morir" (XXXVI, lines 1–4; emphasis added; "See that you see how I live: *I am not the one I live*, for Love caused me, poor captive, to die").[34] Torroella was also exquisitely aware of the "impossible task" described by Stone, asking in another poem, "Per qual sguart no reserva serts mots/ ab què·ls devots/ seus degués tots, pregant, hoyhir?" (XVIII, lines 56–9; "For what reason does [Love] not reserve certain words with which to hear the pleas of all its devout?"). Yet Love set no such distinctive words aside; furthermore, the suffering poet's interiority was itself characterized by fragmentation, as in this well-known song by Lope de Estúñiga (1415–65):

> Llorad, mis llantos, llorad,
> llorad la passión de mí,
> llorad la mi libertad
> que por amores perdí;
> llorad el tiempo passado
> passado syn galardón,
> llorad la triste passión
> de mí, muerto et non finado. (6, lines 1–8)[35]

Cry, my tears, cry, cry for my suffering [*pasión*], cry for my liberty lost to love; cry for the time spent, spent without reward [*galardón*], cry for the sad suffering [*pasión*] of me, dead and not gone.

Later stanzas are addressed to the poet's moans (*gemidos*; lines 17–32), sighs (lines 33–48), and cares (*cuidados*; lines 49–56). As Culler notes, lyric apostrophe is related to epideictic in that it "evokes immediacy while adopting a temporality of deferral, as it repeats itself for readers in a future not even imagined, and articulates an attitude whose appropriateness future audiences of readers are to judge" ("Lyric, History, and Genre" 74). Here, however, the apostrophe is interiorized, opening a space between lyric expression and the inward and outward expression of emotional experience, a space of reflection in which the fragmentation of the scorned lover's living death becomes an ethical posture.

In the chapters that follow, I describe this ethical posture as one that, in making a display of self-alienation and inward fragmentation, seeks to vindicate collective invention, shared emotion, and intersubjective identification, especially through play on secular and sacred notions of passion as suffering and compassion, as in Estúñiga's stanza, just quoted. This vindication, as I have begun to demonstrate through my reading of Santillana's letters, responds to a perceived cultural crisis and draws on newly available vernacular translations that condition, but not determinatively, sentimental authors' revisions of troubadour convention. Love is these authors' emotional koine, but just as the lady was "an ideologeme male society used to think with [as] a free-floating signifier" (Haidu, *Subject Medieval/Modern* 93), amatory discourse became a space for the analysis of the other passions. Thus, the chapters of part one are devoted to concepts of friendship and pleasure as they relate to the theorization of community in political and theological treatises from across Iberia. I begin by describing the reception of classical and early Christian theories of social integration in treatises such as the anonymous *Tratado de la comunidad*, Diego de Valera's *Doctrinal de príncipes* and *Exortación de la pas*, and the Infante Pedro's *Livro da vertuosa benfeytoria*, this last an adaptation of Seneca's *De beneficiis*. I then examine the elaboration of friendship as a private and public virtue tied to notions of conversation and introspection in Alfonso de Madrigal's *Brevyloquyo de amor e amiçiçia*. I next turn to the ambiguous defence of ascetic rationalism in Duarte's *Leal Conselheiro*, which contains both a treatise on mind and will and an analysis of sadness drawing on Duarte's own experience of melancholy; I show that Duarte develops, against his own rather dogmatic rationalism, curative accounts of both compassion and pleasure. Finally, although these treatises carve out an important space for emotional regulation (rather than elimination) in private and public governance, I show that courtly writers continued to express a conventional pessimism toward emotion, opposing it to reason and doubting reason's ability to control it.

In part two, which traces notions of compassion and consolation in lyric poetry and sentimental fiction, I explore how courtly writers sought to model ways out of the stultifying opposition of reason and the passions by exploring modes of collective composition and identification through suffering. I begin by tracing notions of community and compassion in early Christian and later monastic writers, emphasizing the productive roles of intersubjective identification and emotions such as compunction in their practices of reading and prayer. I then discuss the role Christological identification played in the emergence of Castilian lyric in authors such as Pero López de Ayala. From there, I show how a large group of poets in Castilian and Catalan explored the inventive potential of passion, compassion, and quotation. The Galician poet Macías is a key figure in this practice of citational composition, for his own poetry and the concept of *comunaleza* that emerges from it, and also for his literary afterlife in lover's hells and other poems by Santillana, Juan Rodríguez del Padrón, Bernat Hug de Rocabertí, and others. Macías's status as a love martyr also gives rise to poetic play on compassion and Christ's Passion, but this play becomes increasingly orthodox as verse narratives of Christ's life (such as Diego de San Pedro's *Pasión trobada*) emerge in the final decades of the fifteenth century.

The poets who explored what I term "passionate quotation" frequently envisioned their own deaths; in the final two chapters of part two, I explore approaches to death and consolation in early sentimental fiction, especially Rodríguez del Padrón's *Siervo libre de amor* and Don Pedro, Constable of Portugal's *Sátira de infelice e felice vida* and *Tragédia de la insigne reina doña Isabel*, and in the poetry of Ausiàs March. I argue that the early authors of sentimental fiction were particularly adept at diagnosing what they saw as the mortal impasse at which courtly discourse on reason and the passions had arrived, and that March, in his lyrical analysis of grief and vision of a shared resurrection of lovers' bodies, proposed a radical break not only with ascetic rationalism but with the hylomorphic structures underlying troubadour love ethics. These explorations of compassion and consolation as poetic and ethical touchstones ultimately gave way before more orthodox notions of piety, implying a relationship between discrete subjects, although I illustrate in my concluding reading of Joan Roís de Corella's *Tragèdia de Caldesa* that this transition was not without grief.

Iberian authors were not merely the last wave of courtly defenders of pre-modern modes of intersubjectivity. On the contrary, in recuperating certain elements of Stoic, monastic, and troubadour thought on the emotions, they intervened creatively in a crisis of cultural discord that they themselves understood to be "courtly." That this intervention should ultimately have failed does not mark it as inherently nostalgic; rather, Iberian authors' effervescent and inventive exploration of passion at the end of the Middle Ages suggests new ways of understanding the tangled histories of emotion, subjectivity, and poetics.

PART ONE

Friendship and Pleasure

Del mismo porque salió vestido de negro yendo a unas fiestas

A las cosas del plazer
voy qual se que he de bolver

– Garci Sánchez de Badajoz

Chapter One

Classical Rhetoric and Vernacular Theories of Social Integration

Concepts of community in fifteenth-century thought from the crowns of Portugal, Castile, and Aragon drew on two principal intellectual traditions: Stoicism and Christian monasticism. Both of these traditions, drawing sometimes directly, sometimes indirectly on earlier Platonic and Aristotelian models, conceptualized moral deliberation as a conflict between reason and the passions. These models nevertheless recognized that the passions participated in some way in cognition; in fact, the passions were blameworthy to the precise extent that they involved judgment, rational assent. That the passions were at least partly cognitive, in turn, implied that their rhetorical manipulation could have a legitimate place in ethics and politics. Through rhetoric, the passions were linked to action and practical wisdom, such that an influential thinker such as Alfonso de Cartagena could define rhetoric as a moral science (see later discussion). Still, the rhetorical and ethical tradition that was most influential at the end of the Middle Ages in the Christian kingdoms of Iberia and beyond – the Ciceronian tradition – maintained Stoicism's stark affective asceticism. The passions were cognitive insofar as they constituted *mistaken* moral judgments.

The monastic tradition adopted a great deal of Stoic thought on the passions, but sought to cultivate certain forms of shared affect – charity and compassion – as approaches to moral purification and divine contemplation. This cultivation of affect involved the development of an epistemology of compassion in which compassion became a key tool of both rhetoric and hermeneutics. Monastic asceticism still involved a rejection of worldly passions as part of the commandment to love God, but the commandment to love one's neighbour, which had been key in the development of Benedictine monasticism in particular (Benedict xviii–xix), was progressively transformed into a set of discursive practices of community. These practices were sometimes organized under the rubric of friendship, but were more often a matter of *caritas*, a "communal ideal" that C. Stephen Jaeger explicitly opposes to the "intense personal attachments between exceptional men" that undergird classical thought on love and friendship, which Jaeger terms "charismatic," an "elitism of the emotions" (31). These communal ideals nevertheless involved the personal cultivation of strong emotions that constituted the basis of prayer and essential steps on the path to wisdom.

These, then, were the traditions upon which fifteenth-century courtly writers – understood both as writers who participated in one way or another in court life and writers who were conscious participants in a literary tradition in which "courtesy" was both an ethical and aesthetic ideal – could draw. As I began to describe in the introduction, these writers understood themselves to be confronting a violently divided political and cultural landscape in which communities of all kinds – political, social, religious – seemed frighteningly ephemeral, prone to internal strife and dissolution. This perception of crisis is implicit in a great deal of the vernacular political and social theory produced during the period, in which several largely complementary models and metaphors of social integration are articulated. However, this emerging body of vernacular thought remains more dogmatically bound to a rigid opposition of reason and the passions than do courtly poetry and sentimental fiction, and it thus constitutes a crucial background against which to read this paradoxical literary vanguard.

In this chapter, I will describe the principal notions of political community that emerge from fifteenth-century treatises such as the anonymous *Tratado de la comunidad*, Diego de Valera's *Doctrinal de príncipes* and *Exortación de la pas*, the Infante Pedro of Portugal's *Livro da vertuosa benfeytoria*, and Rodrigo Sánchez de Arévalo's *Suma de la política*. In particular, I will emphasize how these treatises clearly recognize that social cohesion depends on the management of emotion; how their authors theorize the ruler's emotional relationship to the community; and how certain emotional concepts, such as friendship and mercy, emerge as key virtues to be cultivated in ruler and subjects alike. Against this background, later chapters in part one will discuss authors who proposed more specific notions of friendship and pleasure on which to ground personal virtue and political community, along with the central place of language, as "communication" and "conversation," in these proposals. Finally, I will show how the underlying rationalist framework of the political, theological, rhetorical, and ethical treatises in question was in part shared by the poetic traditions of Castile and Aragon, but how courtly lyric and sentimental prose (which adopted many lyric conventions) nevertheless offered a way out of this framework through an alternate exploration of shared emotion and intersubjectivity.

As lay literacy spread in fifteenth-century Iberia, readers showed a marked preference for moral and didactic works. This preference may have been grounded in practical concerns; after all, "for the new lay readership of the fifteenth century, classical literature provided almost the only available texts for a study of statecraft, warfare and secular ethics based on empirical examples" (Lawrance, "Vernacular Humanism" 67). Cicero was one of the dominant objects of this new interest; his *De officiis*, for example, was widely translated throughout Iberia, into Aragonese, Catalan, and Portuguese, along with Alfonso de Cartagena's Castilian version (*Libros de Tulio* 12).[1]

Cartagena's translation differs from its counterparts, however, in that the bishop of Burgos considered Cicero's text a moral treatise, not a manual of good government (12–13). In his prologue to *De los ofiçios*, Cartagena explains that he chose this text not only for its moral doctrine, but for its rhetorical qualities: "tracta [Cicero] en él de las virtudes asaz fermosa e sçientíficamente so stilo dulçe e retórico" (207; "Cicero discusses the virtues in it with great knowledge and beauty, in a sweet and rhetorical style").[2] In fact, as he explains in the introduction to a partial translation of Cicero's *De inventione* carried out at the request of then prince Duarte, when he was a Castilian ambassador to Portugal, Cartagena considered rhetoric primarily a moral science, an idea he attributes to Aristotle: "Non entendió aquel philósopho que del todo acabava la obra moral, si después de las *Éthicas* e *Políticas* non diese doctrinas de lo que a la eloquençia pertenesce" (*La Rethórica* 30; "That philosopher did not understand that his moral works were completely finished, unless after the *Ethics* and *Politics* he offered doctrines belonging to eloquence"). In the same introduction, Cartagena insists that rhetorical training is necessary for the understanding of theology, law, and other "sciences and arts" (32), and that it is not just a matter of speaking with eloquence or writing in an orderly fashion, since classical rhetoricians "dieron sus generales doctrinas para argüir e responder, para culpar e defender e para mover los coraçones de los oyentes a saña o a misericordia o a las otras pasiones que en la voluntad humana cahen" (33; "gave their general doctrines for arguing and rebutting, for accusing and defending and for moving listeners' hearts to anger or mercy or the other passions that befall the human will"). Charles Faulhaber has shown that the classical rhetorics, especially *De inventione* and *Ad Herennium* (then attributed to Cicero), predominate in the Iberian manuscript record until the end of the thirteenth century, at which point the compositionally oriented *artes dictaminis* become more prominent (48–51). Here, Cartagena seems to militate for a return to a prior, more expansive understanding of rhetoric, encompassing both epideictic ("para culpar e defender") and the persuasive appeals to emotion that are central to Aristotle's theory. Along these lines, Cicero's thought on the emotions themselves was a further object of lay interest: nobleman Nuño de Guzmán commissioned an Italian translation of the *Tusculan Disputations*, whose manuscript dates to 1456 (Lawrance, "Nuño de Guzmán" 56).[3]

We should not be surprised to find Cicero's fingerprints on political texts produced during a time when the concept of the *bien público* or *bien común* was consistently exalted by the ruling Trastámara dynasty (Nieto Soria, *Iglesia y génesis* 205). But how exactly was the "common" understood in this literature? We may begin to answer this question by turning to the anonymous *Tratado de la comunidad*, a relatively conservative text (47) that represents the conventional wisdom of the period,[4] in which *comunidat* is defined as a

> cosa bien regida e governada por un rey o príncipe, o por pocos omnes buenos e virtuosos, o por todo el pueblo si tal es que lo pueda fazer. La cual comunidat es

> ayuntamiento de gente por consentimiento de derecho e conplimiento de provecho, e es fecha de personas mayores e medianas e menores. Las quales quando son de un coraçón e voluntat, la comunidat es bien regida e governada. (87)
>
> Community is something well governed by a king or prince, or by a few good and virtuous men, or by all the people if they are capable of it. This community is a union of people by rightful consent and for their benefit, and it is composed of people of great, average, and lesser stature. When these people are of one heart and will, the community is well governed.

In this definition, psychological unity (when the different social strata of a community are "of one heart and will") is both the goal and sign of good governance, through monarchy, oligarchy, or democracy. The image of the community's "one heart" recalls, furthermore, Title I, Law V of the second of Alfonso X's *Siete Partidas*, which states that just as the body's unity springs from its one heart, the members of a community should be loyal in service to their one king.[5] In this law, the king is compared not only to the heart, but also to the soul and head: as the soul resides in the heart and gives it life, justice resides in the king, giving life to his land; and as the body relies on the head's senses for guidance, so the people rely on their king. The *Tratado*'s definition of community, in turn, extends the metaphor of the body politic to encompass the interdependence of all members: "Que como el cuerpo natural, las partidas del qual sirva la una a la otra, e la una encubre el fallimiento de la otra, e la otra defiende a la otra, e la una endereça e basteçe la honrra de la otra, así las partidas de la comunidat se deven amar e querer e ayudar e defender las unas a las otras" (87; "Like the natural body, the parts of which serve each other, one making up for the other's failing, one defending another, one sorting out and shoring up the other's honour, thus the parts of the community should love and help and defend each other").[6] Communal life becomes here a kind of self-love whose intersubjective manifestation will, in turn, be conceptualized through a Stoic model of friendship based on identification. Indeed, as the *Tratado*'s anonymous author later explains, "amigo" means "ygual de mí" (127).[7]

The notion of equality in friendship would be taken up in surprising ways in fifteenth-century political thought throughout Iberia, where writers could draw on what was already quite a robust local tradition.[8] Indeed, the *Tratado* may also have been drawing on the *Siete Partidas* for its definition of friendship: many of the concepts central to the period's discussion of community, such as debt, concord, equality, and communication, are present in the section of Alfonso X's encyclopedic legal code devoted to friendship, which is largely Aristotelian in structure and substance. Friendship is initially conceptualized as a kind of loving debt: "Amistad es cosa que ayunta los corazones de los homes para amarse mucho; ca segunt dixieron los sabios antiguos, et es verdad, amor pasa todos los debdos"

(IV.xxvii; "Friendship is something that joins men's hearts so that they love each other greatly; for as the wise men of Antiquity said, and it is true, love surpasses all debts"). Friendship is not, however, the same as love, and it is also different from beneficence (*bienquerencia*) and concord, because it is necessarily mutual and symmetrical. Love and beneficence may not be reciprocated, and concord is possible without friendship (IV.xxvii.1). Cicero is named specifically as the authority for the claim that, when friends communicate, it is as if they were talking to themselves (IV.xxvii.3), and a reference to Augustine confirms the absolute equality among friends (IV.xxvii.5).

Mutual debt, love, and equality are all figures for empathetic participation, and they are all identified as important elements of broader forms of community. Parents and children feel natural love toward each other, as do spouses and fellow countrymen; this natural love is inferior, however, to that felt between (male) friends, which is founded on long-held, mutual recognition and admiration of goodness (*bondat*; IV.xxvii.4). Although the cited authority for this distinction is Aristotle, the *Siete Partidas* also echoes Cicero's discussion of human community in *On Obligations*.[9] Cicero's analysis moves from broad to narrow and back. He begins by seeking a natural basis for universal human unity:

> It seems necessary, however, to probe deeper into the fundamentals of community and human fellowship ordained by nature. First comes that which we see existing in the fellowship of the whole human race. The bond which unites them is the combination of reason and speech, which by teaching, learning, communicating, debating, and evaluating endears men to each other, and unites them in a kind of natural alliance. This more than anything separates us from the nature of the beasts. We often concede that animals such as horses and lions have courage, but lack justice, fairness, and goodness. This is because they lack reason and speech. (I.50)[10]

The communitarian potential of pedagogy and debate to "endear men to each other" thus gives speech, and especially oratory, definitional importance. Rhetoric is the point at which definitions of the human and human community converge.[11] From this broad base of universal human fellowship, Cicero traces a set of ever-narrower levels: from those united by "race, nation and tongue," to those from the same city-state, friends and business associates, and finally, family members (I.53). In analysing the inner workings of the family, however, Cicero broadens the picture once again. The universal urge to procreate leads to the primary bond of marriage and the secondary bond between parents and children. As these bonds expand (between brothers and sisters, first and second cousins, through marriage), they cannot be contained in a single household: "From such procreation and resultant offspring states have their beginnings" (I.54). The family structure appears to be both the end and beginning of human community.

Cicero does not, however, conclude with these family ties. As in the *Siete Partidas*, friendship, not family, is key: "Of all bonds of fellowship, however, none is more pre-eminent or enduring than the friendship forged between good men of like character" (I.55). "Likeness" here manifests itself as a kind of ethical attraction that, in the end, verges on participation:

> True, every virtue attracts us towards it, and causes us to feel affection towards those in whom we observe it, but justice and generosity induce this response most of all. Nothing inspires greater affection or intimacy than decency of character which is shared. When two people have the same ideals and aspirations, they take the same pleasure in each other as in themselves [*in quibus enim eadem studia sunt, eaedem voluntates, in iis fit ut aeque quisque altero delectetur ac se ipso*]. (I.56)[12]

On Obligations is a moral treatise in which Cicero sets out to establish a rational basis for human community; the virtues of wisdom, justice, generosity, and magnanimity, which constitute the sources of obligation, are analysed with particular regard to the role they play in "communal adherence" (I.20). Here, the mechanism by which justice and generosity effect such "communal adherence" becomes clear. When an ethical outlook is shared, it generates a kind of friendship, or affection that manifests itself as shared pleasure. Individual virtue and friendship represent processes that reinforce each other through speech – a case in point is *On Obligations* itself, dedicated, as it was, to Cicero's own son. Speech guides individual ethics and defines the broadest possibilities of human fellowship.

The Iberian treatises that spring, explicitly or not, from this aspect of the Ciceronian tradition arrive in sometimes surprising ways at a similar conclusion. The *Tratado*'s anonymous author places friendship under the heading of loyalty as but one of the qualities according to which a community should be governed; the others are justice, concord and unity, good advice, good customs, and "ordenada e derecha entinçión" (87; "orderly and right intention"). Without the last, the others are worthless: "Las cosas susodichas non son bastantes a buen regimiento de la comunidat si las partidas de aquélla non tienen una mesma entinción" (90; "The things said above are not enough for the good governance of the community if its parts do not share the same intention"). Intention is one of the key terms of Seneca's *De beneficiis*, indispensable for judging the virtue of a gift or favour.[13] If Cicero's political works were sometimes taken to be moral treatises, the opposite is true in the case of Seneca, or "nuestro Séneca," as Rodrigo Sánchez de Arévalo, John II's secretary, called the Cordovan philosopher in the dedicatory epistle of his *Suma de la política* (31), a text to which I will turn shortly. In the legendary versions of Seneca's life prominent in Iberia until the end of the Middle Ages, he is not a moralist – as he was generally considered to be in other parts of western Europe – but a political adviser (Blüher 82). Thus, *De clementia* was read as a mirror of princes, and *De beneficiis* as a "treatise on the *Liberalitas* of kings"

(Blüher 65; see also 102). In the early Middle Ages, Seneca's texts were not widely available in Iberia, but in the fifteenth century, Seneca becomes "an author whose production is widely read and easily accessible not only in its original Latin text, but also in numerous translations" (Blüher 113) – some of them, as in the case of Cicero, carried out by Cartagena.[14]

The *Tratado*'s invocation of intention seems to indicate, then, that the king's generosity is at issue, as it is, for example, throughout the *Secreto de los secretos*, a mirror of princes guided by a taxonomy of royal generosity (71–2).[15] It is royal mercy, however, that is most strongly recommended in the *Tratado*:

> El prínçipe deve ser misericordioso e begnino, que razonable cosa es quel padre de la tierra sea piadoso e begnino … Que el rey segunt umanidat non es mayor que aquél sobrel qual él quiere usar de poder absoluto o echar su saña; que los reyes e prínçipes son omnes e deven begninamente usar de su señorío sobre aquéllos que son de su natura. (91)
>
> The prince should be merciful and benign, for it is reasonable for the land's father to be pious and benign … For the king is not greater in humanity than him against whom [the king] wants to use absolute power and cast his anger; for kings and princes are men and should benignly use their lordship over those who are of the same nature.

The *Tratado*'s appeal to national fellow feeling as piety is Aristotelian in origin, and is also found, as we will see, in Madrigal's *Brevyloquyo de amor e amiçiçia*. Its appeal to shared humanity as a natural basis for mercy goes further, but is paired with a more traditional Stoic appeal to reason ("razonable cosa es"). The benignity that should exist between ruler and ruled is, in turn, paired with a loyalty that will also foster friendship ("amistad o bien querençia") among subjects (*Tratado* 89). The author mentions that this political virtue was highly esteemed by classical thinkers ("los antiguos"), but that it is also, sadly, hard to come by at court: "Que verdadero amor es en aquéllos que han verdadera caridat, que verdadera amistança apenas es fallada en aquéllos que están en grant onrra, e much[o] yerra el que busca amigo en la corte; porque cada uno de aquéllos siguen la corte más por provecho que por amor de otro, que cara cosa es amor" (115; "For true love is in those who possess true charity, and true friendship is hardly found among those who enjoy great honour, and he who seeks a friend in the court is in great error; for they all follow the court more for their own benefit than for the love of another, since love is a costly thing"). Cartagena's diagnosis thus finds its echo in this more conventional political treatise.

When the *Tratado*'s author referred to classical thinkers who held mercy in high esteem, he was likely thinking of Seneca, who, like Cicero, deemed certain "reasonable" affective phenomena to be virtues. Thus, in *On Mercy* (dedicated, ironically, to Nero), mercy represents both the central characteristic of good governance and also the most "humane" virtue of man, "a social animal born for the common good" (I.3.2). Pity, on the other hand, is a moral failing, irrational because it ignores causes: "Pity looks at the plight, not at the cause of it. Mercy joins in with reason" (*Misericordia non causam, sed fortunam spectat; clementia rationi accedit*; II.5.1). A wise man assists the community not out of pity, but out of the realization that he was born to "promote the common good" (II.6.3). Seneca illustrates the rationality of mercy (as clemency), especially in rulers, with a metaphor that we have already encountered in both the *Tratado de la comunidad* and the *Siete Partidas*, one that will be variably interpreted throughout medieval Iberia. The ruler is conceived of as part of a civic body, construed alternately as its mind or head. In the first case, the relationship is one of command:

> Compare the way in which the body is entirely at the service of the mind. It may be ever so much larger and more impressive. The mind may remain hidden and tiny, its very location uncertain. Yet hands, feet and eyes do its business … In the same way, this vast multitude of men surrounds one man as though he were its mind, ruled by his spirit, guided by his reason; it would crush and shatter itself by its own strength, without the support of his discernment. (I.3.5)

In the latter case, the relationship is one of mutual dependence: "He [the ruler] needs the strength, and the commonwealth needs a head" (I.4.3). The case for mercy is clear: cutting off a limb (that is, a subject) may sometimes be necessary, but it will (and should) always be painful. Or, in Seneca's words: "You are sparing yourself, when you appear to spare another" (I.5.1).[16] The metaphor of the ruler as mind or soul thus brings together two ethical controversies. The conflict between reason and the passions is resolved in favour of reason, and the politics of fellow feeling – whose potency was never denied by even the most rigid Stoic – is rescued through a figure of absolute psychological and physical unity.[17] It is a categorical error, then, to distinguish between private and public virtue. As Jaeger reminds us, private life was a matter of indifference to most medieval writers (18); the same cannot be said, however, for the question of personal virtue and public governance, which I explore in the next section.

Mirrors of Friendship

The fusion of private and public was worked out in Iberian texts in terms of the relationship between ruler and subject. For example, Diego de Valera (1412–88), a Castilian nobleman and tutor for the powerful Estúñiga family, wrote a series of texts intended for the moral instruction of princes.[18] His *Doctrinal de príncipes* (dedicated to Ferdinand II of Aragon and thus posterior to his assumption of Castile's throne in 1474) makes explicit reference to the *Siete Partidas* passage describing the king as head, soul, and heart of the kingdom (174), and both the

Doctrinal and the earlier *Exortación de la pas* (c. 1448; see Penna, *Prosistas* CXXII) make use of the argument that the king's subjects, as members of the king's own body, should be treated mercifully (Valera, *Doctrinal* 187 and *Exortación* 82–3). Citing Title 13 of the second *Partida*, Valera notes that subjects, in turn, owe their king both love and fear, specifying that the latter must be a "filial fear" (*temor filial*) accompanying "natural love," rather than a "servile fear" (*temor servil*) accompanied by hostility (*desamor*; *Doctrinal* 190, 200n15). As we have seen, this political *amor natural* was associated, in texts drawing on Aristotle, with both the love between parents and children and the love among inhabitants of the same land, all as forms of *piedad*. While this multifaceted *piedad* cannot be seamlessly identified with concurrent notions of mercy (themselves sometimes called *piedad*, but also, depending on context, *misericordia* or *clemencia*), the two sets of political passions often arise together in discussions of princely virtue. In the *Doctrinal*, for example, Alfonso I of Asturias (693–757 CE) is praised for his vigorous Reconquest activity, yet in Valera's account, it was the king's "merciful works" and "humanity" that earned him the epithet "el Católico" (176). In this way, Valera links mercy with political rebirth, just as Cartagena traces the roots of Castilian discord to Alfonso I's father-in-law, Pelayo. Mercy begins to emerge as an antidote to Castile's fractious political culture, and a notion of love that transcends cultural divisions is described as a religious and moral imperative: "Todo onbre, en quanto onbre, es de amar, que todo onbre es próximo, así el judío o moro como el christiano" (Valera, *Exortación* 84; "Every man, as a man, must be loved, for every man is our neighbour, Jews and Moors just as much as Christians").[19] Indeed, Valera explicitly analogizes royal to divine mercy, warning that kings who hope one day to face a "benign and merciful" God should treat their own subjects in just this manner (*Doctrinal* 188).

At this point in the *Doctrinal*, in a chapter describing forms of tyranny, Valera gives the example of Peter I of Castile who, despite his legitimate inheritance of the throne, lost his kingdom because of his own "cruesa e dura governación" (189; "cruelty and harsh government"). Meanwhile, although a usurper ("no le pertenesciendo de derecho"), Henry II – Ferdinand's great-great-grandfather and founder of the Trastámara dynasty – was able to establish his legitimacy (the pope approved his ascent to the throne) through virtuous governance (189). Here, Valera offers the "similar case" of the founder of Portugal's young Avis dynasty, John I (r. 1385–1433), whose own ascension came at the expense of another Trastámara, Henry II's son (and Ferdinand's great-grandfather) John I of Castile. Like Henry II, John I of Portugal made himself worthy of the throne through his "great virtues," and was thus able to pass it on to his descendants (189). This ethical history of recent Iberian succession is relevant here because one of John I's sons, Pedro, Duke of Coimbra, regent of Portugal from 1438 until 1448, when Alfonso V came of age, authored, along with his confessor, Frei João Verba, the *Livro da vertuosa benfeytoria* (*LVB*; c. 1429–30), perhaps the most granular examination of the relationship between rulers and subjects produced in fifteenth-century Iberia.[20]

The early generations of the Avis dynasty were exceptionally bookish, with (like many of their counterparts in Castile and Aragon) a particular interest in material related to ethics and princely education (Monteiro 93). Their writing is characterized, furthermore, by a vivid interest in applying classical thought to their own cultural context (Carvalho 57), an interest that could be turned toward both the preservation of traditional hierarchies and the "innovative" centralization of royal power (Monteiro 97–102). Pedro himself translated Cicero's *De officiis* (Dias 316), and the *LVB* draws heavily on both Seneca's *De beneficiis* and Giles of Rome's *De regimine principum* for inspiration in theme and structure.[21] Pedro's initial definition of *benefiçio* is largely psychological, emphasizing that a favour must be granted voluntarily, in the strict sense of having "sua nacença en o querer da voõtade" (Pedro and Verba 23; "its origin in the will's desire"), and in a disinterested manner, "nom sguardando o proveyto de si meesmo" (29; "without regard to one's own benefit")[22] Ultimately, these psychological considerations will be grouped under the heading of intention, since "entençom he aucto da voõtade e o beneffício procede della meesma" (32–3; "intention is an act of will, and favours proceed from it"). In its focus on the giver's mental state, Pedro's definition follows closely that of Seneca:

> What then is a favour? An act of benevolence bestowing joy and deriving joy from bestowing it, with an inclination and spontaneous readiness to do so. Thus what matters is not the deed or the gift but the mentality behind them: the kindness lies not in the deed or gift but in the mind itself of the person responsible for the deed or gift. (I.6.1)

For Seneca, these psychological requirements mean that favours are inherently personal: "favours should not be showered on the crowd, and it is not right to cast anything about – least of all, your favours. Take away the element of judgment and they cease to be favours" (I.2.1).[23]

In the case of the *LVB*, the element of judgment is more explicitly one of good governance geared toward stability and solidarity, what António José Saraiva calls a "subjective harmony" linking all social sectors (223). A favour can be defined as both an "affeyçom vertuosa de proveytar a outrem, mostrada per obra" (Pedro and Verba 26; "virtuous desire to benefit someone else, shown through deeds") and as a "ben feyto a outrem com entençom de lhe prestar" (26; "good done to someone else with the intention to help"). Although both definitions are accurate, it is the second, focused on the favour as deed, that will be the focus of the *LVB*; curiously, Pedro identifies this second definition as closer to the realm of feeling ("chegada ao sentimento"), "en que mais fazem exercicio as obras moraaes" (26; "in which moral works are most practised"). This distinction is terminologically revealing in that *affection* names a passive desire (a virtuous reaction to the predicament of another), whereas *sentiment* describes, less intuitively, the realm of action. We see here, again, the extent to which emotion was understood by political thinkers in ethical and practical terms as the decisive field defining the limits and play of social behaviour. In this context, Pedro emphasizes the necessary intersubjectivity of favours – "Nem chamaremos piedoso a quem se perdoa, nem misericordioso ao que sente e ha compayxom dos seus padecimentos" (31; "We will not call 'pious' one who pardons himself, nor 'merciful' one who feels compassion for his own suffering") – and, furthermore, identifies them as a crucial medium of communal adhesion, for which political leaders ("os senhores") are responsible. This special responsibility springs from the greater proximity of the nobility to God, not, Pedro clarifies, in terms of natural or spiritual quality, in which all are equal, but only with regard to moral stature, "que perteece aa governança do mundo" (78; "which pertains to the world's governance"). Thus, just as doctors err in treating acute pains without curing the general malady, rulers err in addressing the complaints of individual subjects without purging those of the "corpo da comũydade" (79–80; "the community's body").[24]

This generally communal outlook unfolds into an analysis of the feudal social structure as Pedro explores the exchange of favours between different estates.[25] According to Pedro, there are three links (*lianças*) that create mutual obligation. The first is spiritual, based on divine love or charity (95). The second is natural; it is felt between those who "share the same nature," and its strength is proportional to the degree of relation between two people (96). It is the third link, "political and moral," that is most relevant to governance:

> A iii[a] liança he politica e moral, e faz·se per concordavel e razoado desejo de muitos pera se manteerem bem en aqueste mundo, fazendo vida comũu. E en aquesto ha desvayramento porque, segundo que o senhor he mais universal, tanto deve seer mais desejado o seu proveito. Esto se entende se o proveyto he tal que faça melhoria en a comunidade. (96)

> The third link is political and moral. It is made through the concordant and reasoned desire of many, to live well in this world making a common life. And in this there is confusion, because the more universal the ruler, the more desirable his benefit. And this can be understood if the benefit is such that it improves the community.

In a community well governed through favours, reason cannot purge desire; Pedro has already cited approvingly the Augustinian sentence that "nunca se pode fazer obra razoavel se a voõtade nom tem em ella sua tençom" (32; "no reasonable deed can be done if the will's intention is not in it"). A "reasoned desire" is thus called for. There is also a fundamental but tenuous reciprocity to this *liança*: the ruler's greater cosmological weight ("mais universal") means that his profit is most to be sought and, by implication, most likely to benefit the entire community – although the final subjunctive construction makes it clear that this outcome is far from inevitable.

If the benefits of this *liança* are reciprocal, so are its obligations: "O principe e a comunydade teẽ antre sy special e stremada liança, per cujo aazo som tehudos de acorrerem aas neccessidades comuũes. E cada hũa persoa que vive en a comunydade a esto meesmo he obrigada" (103; "The prince and the community have between them a special and unparalleled link, through whose tie they are obliged to attend to common needs. And each person who lives in a community is obliged to this"). The mechanism that assures this sense of mutual obligation is *bemquerença* itself: "E porem deve a benquerença seer antre o princepe e o poboo tam firme que ambos ajam ygual sentimento de hũa desaventura e tomem hũu meesmo prazer pollo bem que ouverem" (104; "And therefore the good will between the prince and the people should be so strong that both suffer a misfortune equally and take the same pleasure in the good that comes to them"). Thus, the concept of *bemquerença* goes beyond "good will" or even "love"[26] into participatory or compassionate terrain, differing in this way from Alfonso X's earlier-cited notion of *bienquerencia*, which, unlike friendship for the Castilian king, is not necessarily mutual.[27] Here, the ruler, "sentindo a door da comũydade, avera compaixom dos membros que o soportam" (135; "feeling the community's pain, will have compassion for the members that support him"), and the subjects, "sentindo … per affeyçom leal, as neccessidades do princepe, desejaram de comprir a sua voontade" (139; "perceiving ... through loyal affection the needs of the prince, will desire to do his will").[28] Psychological unity – the compassion, affection, friendship, and shared intention, desire, or will between ruler and subjects, all of which are based on *bemquerença* – is here not the sign of a well-governed kingdom but the cause. Public *bemfeitoria* – the active outcome of the *bemquerença* at the heart of the third, political and moral *liança* – is the participatory manifestation of this unity.[29]

The characteristic that governs *bemfeitoria* is not compassion, however, but discretion: "Todos devemos seer principalmente fazedores das benfeyturias. E, porquanto pera esto avemos mester ajudoyro, he neccessario de seer nossa guyador a vertuosa discreçom" (89; "We should all be granters of favours above all. And to the extent that we need help in this, it is necessary that our guide be our virtuous discretion"). As I will discuss further in part two, discretion is key to early ascetic theories of emotion as the faculty that aids in discovering the origins of our potentially sinful "thoughts," and Pedro also identifies it as an instrument for acquiring self-knowledge. If for the Desert Fathers, however, this self-knowledge was oriented above all to the preservation of isolated contemplation, in Pedro it is yet another articulation between the individual and the collective, contributing to *bemfeitoria* principally by allowing us to understand our place in society: "E a discreçom … diz a cada hũu que dereitamente quiser dar beneffícios que primeyro conheça sy meesmo, sguardando quejando he o seu stado" (90; "And discretion … tells each person who wishes to do favours correctly that he must first know himself, considering the nature of his estate"). At the same time, discretion "beautifies" ("afremosenta") a favour by allowing its author to discern its potential benefit

(174). For Pedro, then, discretion is imagined as a guide that allows the unified, reasoned desires of a given society to be carried out.[30] It undergirds the favours that constitute the interface between ruler and subjects, favours that themselves arise from and generate the friendship and good will characteristic of the healthy body politic.

In discussing the obligations of subjects to their lord, Pedro, like Valera, describes not just the "loyal affection" inspired by royal mercy but also a rarefied notion of friendship grounded in the discrete expression of "true love":

> Lhe pode offerecer cada hũu seu sobjeyto verdadeyro amor de que elles sentem sobeja myngua, porque a ventura nunca fez alguem tam exalçado a que mais nom faleçam os amigos quando das outras cousas tem avondança … E, porque em os grandes stados elle [that is, this good] he dovidoso e nom pode ser conhecido, porem todos o cobiiçam con mayor afficamento, entendendo que os seus poderios som de pouco valor se nom teẽ em sua posse leal amizade, a qual nom he demostrada per os que muyto razoam com boas palavras nem per os que movem a cidade com saudaçóes, porque destes som as ruas cheas. E, quando alguem chega onde elles stam, sente o logar cheeo de homẽes e vazio de amigos, veendo seguir a cada hũu o seu proprio proveyto. Mas o discreto amador traucta com prudencia as cousas dovidosas do seu amigo e, soportando suas aversidades com forteleza, nom o desempara en sua tribulança. E, acompanhando sagesmente aquelle bem·aventurado de cuja benquerença he possuydor per conversaçom continuada falando ameude, mostra·sse ledo em sua presença. E quem souber offerecer ao seu princepe tal amorio sera com razom, antre muytos, specialmente stremado. (144)

> Each subject can offer them true love, of which they all [that is, rulers] feel a terrible lack, because fortune never exalted someone so much that he does not need friends even when he has all other things in abundance … And, because in great estates it is doubtful and hard to recognize, everyone desires it all the more, understanding that their dominion is of little value without loyal friendship, which is not demonstrated by those who speak many beautiful words, nor by those who move the city with their addresses, because the streets are full of ones such as these. And, when someone achieves this position, he feels the place to be full of people and empty of friends, seeing each seek only his own profit. But the discreet lover treats his friend's sensitive matters with prudence and, bearing his adversity with strength, does not abandon him in his tribulations. And, wisely accompanying that lucky one who possesses his good will with ongoing conversation, speaking often, he appears happy in his presence. Whoever is able to offer his prince such love will be, with reason, especially exalted among the many.

Many texts before and after the *LVB* stressed the great value and rarity of true friendship, especially for the rich and powerful. This passage is helpful, however, in condensing the ethical concepts that clustered around the question of friendship as a matter of language. The implicitness of the relationship is particularly revealing: it is simply the case that the quality of friendship is discerned through speech. Eloquence and mass persuasion are grounds for scepticism and even somewhat vulgar ("destes som as ruas cheas"), whereas prudence and moral fortitude constitute a form of love ("amorio"). If such a friendship has transactional aspects, as revealed by Pedro's talk of value and his conclusion that such a friend "merecerá qualquer galardom que lhe for outorgado" (144; "will be worthy of any reward he may be granted"), the ruler nevertheless remains fortunate to engage in ongoing, frequent conversation with a loyal counsellor bearing a happy countenance.[31]

Although many Iberian thinkers shared Pedro's emphasis on virtue ethics, not all conceived of the health of the community in terms of friendly exchange among ruler and subjects. In his *Suma de la política* (c. 1455), dedicated to Henry IV of Castile, Rodrigo Sánchez de Arévalo notes that many books have been written about politics, "en tal manera que fazen e constituyen una entera sciencia llamada política, aunque subalternada a la scientia moral" (32; "such that they make up and constitute an entire science called 'political,' although [it is] subordinated to moral science").[32] He thus follows Aristotle rather than Cicero in asserting that the primary goal of civil society is to allow citizens to live virtuously, not to protect their property (109). The pre-eminence of the moral is also reaffirmed when Sánchez de Arévalo identifies the management of public affect through mutual love as the prince's key task: "Primeramente, todo rey o príncipe deve amar sus súbditos, e, amándolos, fazer entre ellos gran unidad e paz e concordia, lo qual fará si procurare que entre ellos sea amicicia verdadera, lo qual el tirano no faze" (93; "First, all kings and princes should love their subjects and, loving them, foster among them great unity and peace and concord, which they will do if they promote true friendship among them, which a tyrant does not do"). The counterpart to the cultivation of friendship is the avoidance of conflict: "E por quanto el principal impedimento que corrompe toda çibdad o república es la división e intestina discordia de los çibdadanos e súbditos, por ende es muy cumplidero a todo príncipe e buen político escusar las tales discordias e divisiones, e travajar porque la çibdad o reyno sea mucho unida e concorde" (111; "And to the extent that the principal impediment that corrupts any city or republic is division and internal discord among the citizens and subjects, it is therefore very appropriate for all princes and good politicians to avoid such discord and division, and to work so that the city or kingdom will be very united and harmonious").

The principal cause of these divisions has already been identified as emotional strife: "Onde si los çibdadanos en su çibdad han mengua e angustia de cosas delectables e solazes, necessario es que injurien a los otros vezinos de quien temen aver tristezas e pesares" (57; "Where the citizens in their city suffer the lack and anxiety of delightful things and relaxation, it is necessary that they injure their other neighbours whom they fear as sources of sadness and sorrow"). Sánchez de

Arévalo proposes public entertainment as a solution to this problem: the prince should hire "maestros de prosas e famosos cantores para delectable armonía, e poetas e otros ministros, ordenando aun ciertas representaciones e juegos públicos en días sennalados para alegría e consolación de los abitantes en la tal çibdad" (58; "masters of stories and famous singers for delightful harmony, and poets and other ministers, ordering certain public performances and games on certain days for the joy and consolation of the city's inhabitants"). These public poets will be the emissaries of a hidden prince who loves his subjects from a safe distance:

> Todo rey e príncipe no ha de ser mucho familiar a las gentes, pero puesto que no se comunique a todas las gentes, deve fazer los fechos de todos, onde dize el nuestro Séneca en el primero De Clemencia al emperador Nerón, que el rey es assí como el ánima en el cuerpo umano, a la qual todos los miembros sirven e con gran lealtad la obedecen, puesto quel ánima esté encerrada, e en lo oculto no cessan de la servir e obedecer aunque la non vean ni la acaten ni sepan en dónde se asconde, e todos siempre, las manos e los pies, los ojos e los otros miembros, la sirven, e las cosas que ella manda en lo ascondido, ellos las cumplen en lo público. (94)

> Kings and princes should not be very familiar with their people, but although they should not communicate with all the people, they should do the tasks of all, whence our Seneca says in the first book of *On Mercy* to the emperor Nero, that the king is like the soul in the human body, served and obeyed by all the body's members with great loyalty, although the soul is enclosed, and while it is hidden they do not cease to serve and obey it although they neither see it nor observe it, nor do they know where it is hidden, and they all, the hands and feet, the eyes and other members, always serve it, and the things that it orders while hidden, they carry out in public.

Sánchez de Arévalo cites Seneca as the source for his metaphor of the prince as the city's soul. We have seen, however, that for Seneca, it was a metaphor of the city's obedience; here, the central political advice is about the prince's public (yet hidden) persona. Where other texts have stressed unity between ruler and subjects in matters of the soul – that is, in intention, will, sorrow, and joy, concepts whose psychological reality was often, although not always, located in the soul – the *Suma de la política* emphasizes the need for emotional distance ("Todo rey e príncipe no ha de ser mucho familiar a las gentes").[33] Royal authority is *clandestine* like that of the soul in the body, and this hiddenness is the basis for the virtues of loyalty and obedience. Public emotional interactions are crucial to political unity, but they are also the immediate task of poets, not princes.[34]

These examples from Valera, Pedro, and Sánchez de Arévalo illustrate the centrality of the management of public and private emotion in Iberian political thought as the Trastámara and Avis dynasties continued to consolidate their power, and they make it especially clear that Cartagena was not alone in his diagnosis of perceived crisis. Yet, even as these lettered nobles apply their substantial knowledge of Stoic rhetorical and political thought to the difficulties surrounding them, their treatises reveal, almost consciously, their own limited efficacy. Their virtue and their flaw, as instruments of political analysis, is to take as a given the social structures they inhabit; they ably restate the virtuous balance rulers must achieve between clemency and justice, love and discretion, and they even imagine, if implicitly, how this balance, once achieved, might be communicated throughout a harmonious city or kingdom. What is lacking in these texts is an account of interiority: it is not the same to efface, as many medieval texts do, the hard barrier between inside and outside, public and private, or to figure friendship as a form of intersubjective participation, as it is to empty the interior of content. Symptomatic of this tendency is Pedro's account of self-knowledge, which, as we have seen, is understood as a matter of discovering one's place in the social order: "Conheça cada hũu quem he e de que geeraçom" (Pedro and Verba 90: "May each discover who he is and of what origin"). Friendship is discerned through and manifested in speech, but speech itself is not a purely exterior phenomenon. The question of inner speech as it relates to friendship, self-knowledge, and governance was explored by Pedro's contemporary, Alfonso de Madrigal, in his *Brevyloquyo de amor e amiçiçia*, to which I now turn. Madrigal, who enjoyed great cultural prestige, went further than his contemporaries in describing a notion of civil friendship on which to ground political community, and he also theorized the relationship between this form of friendship, the self, and language in minute detail. His *Brevyloquyo* thus represents the period's most advanced articulation of the politics of friendship.

Chapter Two

Alfonso de Madrigal, el Tostado, on the Politics of Friendship

In the *LVB*, Pedro cites Macrobius's commentary on Cicero's *Somnium Scipionis* for the Delphic injunction "Conhece ty meesmo" (Pedro and Verba 90; "Know thyself"). The same injunction would be adapted by Baltasar Gracián in his 1647 *Oráculo manual y arte de prudencia* under the rubric of *Comprensión de sí*: "No puede uno ser señor de sí si primero no se comprende. Hay espejos del rostro, no los hay del ánimo: séalo la discreta reflexión sobre sí. Y cuando se olvidare de su imagen exterior, conserve la interior para enmendarla, para mejorarla" (171; "One cannot master oneself without first understanding oneself. There are mirrors for the face, not for the soul: let discreet self-reflection be [the mirror]. And when the exterior image may be forgotten, keep the inner one to emend, to improve it"). Without implying an entirely transcendental stance, Gracián's advice condenses certain key aspects of what has come to be seen, broadly speaking, as characteristic of modern subjectivity: self-mastery and self-reflection in the absence of an objective, overarching reflective structure; moral introspection that opposes the interior and exterior, privileging the former and treating the latter with broad scepticism.[1] Yet introspection in the Middle Ages from Augustine on had, for the most part, been practised precisely as a search for *un espejo del ánimo*, a mirror of the soul (a necessary complement, perhaps, to the mirrors of princes discussed earlier).[2] Belief in a divinely structured cosmos and in humanity as a microcosm thereof allowed forms of introspection that did not presuppose, morally or ontologically, the individual's discrete interiority.[3] Similarly, as mentioned in the introduction, even at the end of the Middle Ages it was possible for philosophers and theologians to conceive separately of the subjects of thought (for example, in their concept of *mens*), enunciation, and predication (the *subjectum*, to which affective phenomena pertain).[4] In this way, introspection and the sentiment provoked by it could be understood as essential elements of personal ethics leading not only to self-mastery and good citizenship but to a direct ontological relation with wider political and religious communities, and even with the divine.

As early as the mid-sixteenth century, the pronounced scrutiny of religious orthodoxy and ancestry in Spain had made the broader European concept of the "proprietary," and therefore individual, interior central to political subjection (Fernández 30, 34–5). By contrast, it is in view of the still permeable interiority outlined earlier that I wish to explore the cultural and political implications of two questions posed by the fifteenth-century theologian Alfonso Fernández de Madrigal, nicknamed El Tostado, in his *Brevyloquyo de amor e amiçiçia*: whether friendship with God is possible, and whether God talks to Himself. In both his *Brevyloquyo* and his 1436 *repetitio* at the University of Salamanca, *De optima politia*,[5] Madrigal develops a concept of civic friendship based on participatory communication. In exploring these intersecting notions of friendship and communication, Madrigal ultimately affirms the possibility of friendship with the divine, thus distancing himself significantly from Aristotle, the chief source of both the *Brevyloquyo* and *De optima politia*. However, Madrigal's non-Christocentric articulation of divine friendship, which includes important roles for passionate love and for *piedad* as both piety and pity, also distances him from the broad currents of medieval thought in this area, including those previously discussed. The communication underlying civic and divine friendship is figured as both individual introspection and intersubjective conversation, emphasizing the verbal aspects of Madrigal's political affectivity and thus casting a political light on Madrigal's long-recognized influence on fifteenth-century Iberian letters. Madrigal is known to have been a source of classical knowledge for later writers and would go on to teach poetics at Salamanca. Here, I explore his ideas about shared emotion and shared language, articulated under the concept of friendship although they also touch on love and compassion, as a key theoretical foil to the developments in lyric poetry and sentimental prose analysed in part two.

Madrigal was born around 1410 in Madrigal de las Altas Torres, near Ávila.[6] Legend has it that some Franciscans who came to the town of Madrigal to preach were impressed by the young boy's ability to understand their prayers and sermons, and decided to take him with them to their convent in Arévalo, where he first learned Latin. In the academic year of 1426–27, Madrigal began the course in Arts at the University of Salamanca, studying a slightly modified version of the *trivium* and *quadrivium* in which moral and natural philosophy played a larger role than usual. Madrigal became Master of Arts in 1431–32, immediately beginning to teach moral philosophy and work toward a master's in theology, which he would earn in 1441. At some later point in his academic career, he also earned a bachelor's in law. Madrigal was named *maestrescuela* (chancellor) of Salamanca in 1446, a position of importance in both the academic and ecclesiastical hierarchies. From 1446 to 1454, he held the evening chair in theology, teaching poetics in the morning. He would eventually become bishop of Ávila in 1454, dying only a year later.

The sporadic critical attention that Madrigal received in the twentieth century should not lead us to underestimate his intellectual and political influence in his own time.[7] Indeed, his learning and prolific writing soon became literally proverbial, expressed in the popular sayings "Sabe más que el Tostado" and "Escribe más que el Tostado" (Belloso Martín 35).[8] He was a trusted counsellor to John

II, and the first edition of his collected works was commissioned by Isabel of Castile. She died before the project was underway, but her husband Ferdinand set it in motion, and it was none other than Charles V who finally saw it through to completion in 1531 (Cuesta 325–6).[9] Madrigal's great project as a writer was to produce a commentary on the entire Bible; in the end, he finished commentaries on the five books of Moses, Joshua, Judges, Ruth, Kings, Chronicles, and in the New Testament, Matthew. Although his commentaries are based on the Vulgate, Madrigal is thought to have known Greek – a rarity in Iberia at the time – and enough Hebrew to cite both the Hebrew Bible and rabbinic sources.[10] In addition to these commentaries, he wrote texts devoted to Trinitarian doctrine, the question of Conciliarism in the Church, and the survival of the soul after death.[11] Finally, Madrigal's monumental commentary on Eusebius's *Historia ecclesiastica*, as well as his *Las catorze questiones del Tostado*, largely devoted to the exposition of Greek and Roman mythology, became invaluable references for courtly poets and writers of sentimental fiction, such as Juan Rodríguez del Padrón, author of *Siervo libre de amor*, and Pedro, Constable of Portugal, author of the *Sátira de infelice e felice vida* (and son of the Infante Pedro, author of the *LVB*).[12]

Madrigal's overarching project has been described as "un denodado esfuerzo de renovación moral, con una crítica, a veces implacable, de la sociedad corrompida de la época" (Castillo Vegas, "El humanismo" 11; "a daring effort of moral renovation, with a critique, sometimes implacable, of the corrupt society of his time"). In the *Brevyloquyo* and *De optima politia*, to the latter of which I will now turn, Aristotle's *Nicomachean Ethics* (henceforth *NE*) and *Politics* are the main foils for both renovation and critique – a fact that marks Madrigal as something of a cultural outlier. By the fifteenth century, most of Aristotle's known texts enjoyed long commentary traditions within the Iberian Peninsula. As Carlos Heusch has argued, however, the *NE* had returned to Iberia from Paris in the thirteenth and fourteenth centuries "tainted" by its association with Averroism and heterodoxy (94); in the absence of an Aristotelian ethical tradition, a distinctively Castilian moral tradition based on exemplarity and authority had arisen, leading to "una distribución de los saberes que encierra la filosofía (teología y lógica) en la escuela, y la moral en palacio" (96; "a distribution of knowledge that enclosed philosophy [theology and logic] in the schools, and moral wisdom in the palace").[13] In finding a philosophical and theological basis for the political deployment of friendship, however, Madrigal attempts to bridge this divide between school and palace in ethical reasoning and literary practice.

De optima politia: Language, Law, and Unity *Secundum quid*

It may be helpful to recall here that, around the time that Madrigal was writing, Alfonso de Cartagena had described how Rome's civil conflicts had become, in Castile, *contiendas cortesanas*. By contrast, Madrigal continued, at least in his formal political thought, to take the city as the paradigmatic space of governance. This stance is clearest in his *De optima politia*, initially composed in 1436 as a *repetitio*, an obligatory exercise for professors at Salamanca in which the material from the past year's course was recapitulated as a magisterial lecture for the entire faculty. The *repetitio* was not disputational and, in reality, seems to have been as much an occasion for the display of rhetorical ability as of doctrinal mastery or dialectical brilliance (Carreras y Artau, "Las 'repeticiones'" 214–15). We should not be surprised, then, when Madrigal opens *De optima politia* with an allegorical trip to Mount Parnassus and the Castalian Spring, and an invocation of the Muses.[14]

From this invocation, Madrigal proceeds abruptly to the declaration of his main purpose: the refutation of Plato's doctrine of the community of women, as articulated in book two, chapter two of Aristotle's *Politics*. The refutation begins with a restatement of, and commentary on, Aristotle's claim that

> it is necessary either that the citizens have all things in common, or that they have nothing in common, or that they have some things in common, and others not. It is clearly impossible that they should have nothing in common: the constitution of a city involves in itself some sort of association, and its members must in the first place share a common locality. Just as a single city [*polis*] must have a single locality, so citizens are those who share in a single city. (1260b)[15]

In Madrigal's *De optima politia*, the opening of this claim is rendered as "Necesse est autem omnes omnibus communicare cives, aut nullo, aut his quidem, his autem non" (28). Madrigal's Latin thus introduces the concept of *communicatio*, which refers to sharing or holding in common, but also to communication as verbal exchange. Madrigal uses the term in this more familiar sense explicitly in many of his writings, as when he writes about diplomatic communication between enemies in his commentary on Kings (Simó Santonja 75), but in fact this verbal sense is always present in Madrigal's use of the term and, indeed, constitutes the basis of his political thought. Thus, Madrigal goes on to declare: "Government is a form of communication [that is, participation]" (*De optima politia* 129),[16] adding that "if citizens shared nothing, there would be no reason not to call all people fellow countrymen [*concives*]. But only an insane person would accept that. Therefore, it is necessary that citizens share something [*necesse est cives aliquibus communicare*]" (130). Following Aristotle, Madrigal determines that, at the very least, citizens share a place, a city – and this leads him to discuss at length the history of the city as such.

If we accept Cartagena's claim that the court, not the city, is the correct structural analytic for fifteenth-century Castile's circumstances, then Madrigal's lengthy digression on the first cities seems hopelessly anachronistic. Whereas Cartagena has reduced the scope of politics from city to court, and from empire to kingdom, Madrigal returns the city to its place of honour and analyses it in the context of *universal* history. In the end, however, Madrigal, too, accepts the reduced scope of worldly politics, while recognizing the crucial place of affect therein. Nowhere is this point clearer than in his discussion of the Tower of Babel (built, after all, as part of a new city). For Madrigal, what is at stake in the famous episode is not the confusion of languages; in fact, he concludes that it was "most healthy" for the human race, an opinion consistent with his belief that sharing everything – that is, communicating everything – is a form of sharing nothing. Rather, Madrigal asks what the sin of Babel was, why God saw fit to punish the tower's builders. He frames the question, perhaps ironically, as a dispute between the Hebrew and Latin versions of the episode, beginning by discussing the tower's original purpose:

> The truest reason for this great tower consisted, according to the text of Genesis 11, in the fact that men, already multiplied, were planning on spreading out over the different parts of the world; so that something great and admirable made by the entire human genus would remain, they started to build that great tower and a greatly fortified city. And this intention seemed sufficiently honest, at least superficially, so that, supposing that later many works would be made by men, at least none of them would be as excellent as the one that the entire human genus had built together. (140–1)[17]

This "superficially honest" intention is, according to Madrigal, the one expressed in the Vulgate, but it is here that the Hebrew text differs: "The Hebrew text, however, presents this differently, that is, let us make a name for ourselves, that we not be separated among the lands. This certainly constitutes a very different claim, that is, that the men of that time wanted to live together, being relatives who loved each other because of their similarity of species" (141).[18] In the Hebrew version, then, the tower was not to be a mere monument to human unity, but an actual beacon allowing the peoples of the earth to reunite – a mechanism for literally achieving absolute human unity again at some future point. It is for this reason that Madrigal prefers the Hebrew text: God would have had no "reasonable" cause for punishing the tower's builders in the Vulgate's account, whereas the builders in the Hebrew version were justly punished (141). Nostalgia for human unity is divinely sanctioned; absolute human unity is divinely prohibited.

It is characteristic of Madrigal's thought to express admiration for absolute unity and perfection without trying to approach it. Thus, he follows Aristotle in asserting that rulers should not try to impose a perfect law, but rather a law adequate to the nature of their subjects. In doing so, he applies the scholastic distinction between approaching a problem *simpliciter*, that is, from an absolute and ahistorical perspective, and *secundum quid*, in which the problem is considered in a concrete historical context (Castillo Vegas, "Aristotelismo político" 45). Madrigal's preference for the *secundum quid* approach reflects two of his intellectual habits. First, as he explains in his commentary on Genesis 1 (*Commentaria*), he prefers literal (that is, historical) exegesis because "all of the books [of the Bible] are full of moral and allegorical considerations; by contrast, the literal sense is harder to penetrate."[19] This hermeneutic preference has ethical consequences: in the fourth of Madrigal's *Catorze questiones*, which asks whether practical or natural philosophy is more useful (*utile*), Madrigal explains that Scripture is similar to practical philosophy because Scripture "es pratica y no especulativa y assi es por obrar y no por entender y por ende saber mucho en la sancta escriptura y no obrar no es de loar alguno. Y obrar aunque hombre tenga poco entendimiento es loable" (75r; "is practical and not speculative, and so it is for acting and not for understanding, and therefore one should not be praised for knowing a great deal about Holy Scripture and not acting. And to act although one has little understanding is praiseworthy").[20] In his answer to the question, he applies the *simpliciter/secundum quid* distinction, concluding that natural philosophy is superior in an absolute sense, but "las virtudes y su bondad" may be superior "por respecto de algun fin" (75v; "with respect to some end").

Second, Madrigal is aware that eloquence is at the root of political community, having already summarized Cicero's account of the birth of the social: "When, in ancient times, men led a solitary life with no communication and no pact, someone to whom mother nature had granted profound genius invited, with the resources of eloquence, that harsh time and those very wild people to political life" (*De optima politia* 137–8).[21] As Rita Copeland has noted, epistemological and hermeneutic commitments to historical context are intimately tied to the rhetorical concept of *kairos*, "fitting persuasion to the right and appropriate circumstances of subject, audience, and moment" (19). In short, the need to tailor laws to historical circumstances may be a concession to our postlapsarian nature, but it is also a recognition of the role of language after Babel in grounding our no longer universal human communities.

From these intellectual underpinnings, we can see that Madrigal's approach to politics is above all practical, subject to history and human circumstances. In this vein, he considers and rejects the universal application of monastic rules:

> Given that the best form of government is that which distances us maximally from evil and incites and inspires virtue above all, and given that there is no law or constitution that does this better than monastic rules, in which each one makes a vow of obedience, chastity, and poverty, whoever wished to introduce the best laws into a political regime would impose the laws of monks. But who could imagine anything more foolish than such a policy? (*De optima politia* 145)[22]

Cities and their rulers, Madrigal concludes, should promote unity – concord – among their citizens without trying to achieve absolute unity. Thus, despite positing a kind of civic ontology in which "cities and any other thing, the more they are united, the more they *are* [*magis sunt ens*]" (142; emphasis added), and in contrast to Aristotle, Madrigal ends up endorsing democracy as the best form of government in practice, although monarchy is the best in principle (because sovereignty is united in one being). Cities, like men, simply cannot be reduced to absolute unity:

> Indeed, if we want to reduce man to the simplest unity, removing so much composition of parts and plurality of persons, he will no longer be a man; for his unity requires such enormous diversity. The same can be said of the city. A city is not a unit *per se*, but by association. In consequence, if we wish to reduce it to an exclusive unity such that it be a being *per se*, we are not taking into account the essential elements of the city's nature. (163)[23]

Madrigal thus endorses community – unity "by association" – not as the best social structure, but as the only *possible* social structure.[24] Community – communication – is the reality of political life; the question, therefore, is not how to achieve it, but *on what basis* to achieve and cultivate it.

The Divine Mirror: Passionate Love and Piety in the *Brevyloquyo*

To the extent that the *Brevyloquyo de amor e amiçiçia*, a sprawling *amplificatio* of books eight and nine of the *NE*, has a centre, it is this question of achieving human community through love (the subject of part one) and friendship (the subject of part two). In fact, however, the *Brevyloquyo*, which was drafted in Latin but translated by Madrigal himself and dedicated to John II,[25] takes as its starting point a teaching attributed to Plato: that we should befriend our friends' friends, but not our enemies' enemies.[26] Nevertheless, this question is deferred until the text's much briefer third part, in favour of an extended exploration of the definition and nature of love and friendship. A key thread in Madrigal's exploration – and one whose conclusions distance him most from his source texts – is the relationship between the human and the divine. This relationship constitutes, for Madrigal, the *espejo* in which ideal human relations can be reflected.

Madrigal begins exploring the relationship between the human and the divine in terms of resemblance:

> Non ay alguna propiedad segund la qual el onbre pueda segund semejança corresponder a dios. Sy non por amor & esto non fablando dela caridad la que es amor ordenado & formado segund la qual fazemos a dios que nos quyera bien mas fablaremos de solo el amor que es passional. Ca ansy como algunos aman a dios con caridad asy otros muchos lo aman con afiçion & pasional amor … Enpero sy dios nos amare responderle hemos con amor amando le por que nos ama & esto non solamente se faze con caridad mas aun con amor pasional. Pues bien aventurada pasion es aquella segun la qual el onbre corresponde en semejança a su criador. (6v–7r)[27]

> There is no property according to which man can correspond with God in similarity, except by love, and this not speaking of charity, which is an ordered and formed love according to which we dispose God well to ourselves, but we will speak only of passionate love. For just as some love God with charity, so many others love him

> with affection and passionate love … However, if God loves us we will respond with love, loving him because he loves us, and this is not just done with charity but with passionate love. For it is a blessed passion according to which man corresponds to his creator in similarity.

Madrigal's insistence on a passionate love for God seems to recall the mystical discourse so common in medieval monasteries, in which the rhetoric of not just passionate but erotic love abounds. Nonetheless, we would do well to recall here Madrigal's attachment to the literal. If humanity forges a similarity with God through passionate love, then this "correspondence" seems to imply the presence of passion in the divine. This implication would be less surprising if Madrigal were discussing here, for example, Christ's humanity, but the reference to the "creator" shows clearly that we are in the realm of God the Father, if not of Aristotle's unmoved mover. The passions, meanwhile, are firmly rooted in the corporeal, unlike the understanding (which Madrigal will cite elsewhere, and more typically for thinkers in the Augustinian tradition, as our most celestial faculty). The worldliness of the passions is further emphasized by the clear distinction drawn with charity, a theological virtue that Madrigal here associates with good will as *bienquerencia* ("segund la qual fazemos a dios que nos *quyera bien*"), a term that, as we have seen, is more often distinguished from friendship and love than assimilated into them in more traditional Iberian models of feudal emotion.[28] For Madrigal, by contrast, the exploration of the relationship between the human and the divine does not remove us from the exploration of purely human relations; rather, it represents an ideal *model* for human relations and for good governance:

> Conviene a los grandes señores & capitanes ganar para sy los coraçones delos suyos con dones … pues seer amado de todos aun segund pasional amor a cada uno delos onbres aprovecha ca ansy como dela caridad porque es ordenada & dela amyçiçia porque proçede por regimiento de razon asy del amor passional proçeden acçiones provechosas aun que non syenpre bien regidas. (7v)

> Great lords and captains should win the hearts of their subjects with gifts … for to be loved by all even according to passionate love benefits all, for just as beneficial acts arise from charity, because it is ordered, and from friendship, because it is governed by reason, so they arise from passionate love, although they are not always well governed.

Although this closing qualifier, "non syenpre bien regidas," indicates that Madrigal shared some of his contemporaries' scepticism toward the passions as moral phenomena, passionate love is seen here as an essential complement to the more rational friendship.[29] If this scepticism is a concession *secundum quid* to the contentious and violent circumstances of Castilian life during this period, we have seen that Madrigal does not consider it to be an unethical concession – indeed, to the extent that passionate love implies divine resemblance, he echoes the Sermon on the Mount in calling it "blessed" ("bien aventurada pasion es aquella segun la qual el onbre corresponde en semejança a su criador").

Furthermore, passionate love is not the only form of love whose political virtues Madrigal extols. In the very next chapter, he defines love of one's homeland as *piedad*, piety or pity: "Este es amor de la tierra natural al qual se llama piedad, ca piadosamente sea el que ha mysericordia de su tierra. & en esto mucho alabaron al amor dela tierra natural faziendo le llamarse tal nonbre como el amor & onrra de dios al amor en onrra de dios llamar piedad o religion" (8v; "This is the love of one's land of birth that is called piety, for pious be the one who has mercy for his land. And in this they praised the love of one's land of birth greatly, calling it by the name of the love and honour of God, 'piety' or 'religion'"). Here, the idea of passionate love takes on its more familiar guise, in Christian contexts, of compassion, bringing out explicitly the two senses of *piedad*.[30] Madrigal also makes explicit, then, the analogy between political and religious devotion. And to the love of country and love of God, Madrigal adds a third sense of *piedad* as love of family; what the three loves have in common is that they emerge in us naturally through participation, since from each of these sources we receive part of who we are (9r). This framing of piety as a kind of participation – a kind of compassion – situates Madrigal in a particularly fecund middle ground between ancient and modern thought. On the one hand, the analogy between governance of the city and the home is proposed by Aristotle in both book one of the *Politics* and book eight of the *NE* (the latter in the midst of a discussion of friendship), but neither piety nor pity is the basis of the comparison. On the other hand, as María Zambrano has written, piety now refers paradigmatically to our relationship to other "vital planes": "Cuando hablamos de piedad, siempre se refiere al trato de algo o alguien que no está en nuestro mismo plano vital; un dios, un animal, una planta, un ser humano enfermo o monstruoso, algo invisible o innominado, algo que es y no es" (*El hombre* 193–4: "When we speak of piety/pity, it always refers to the treatment of something or someone who is not on our same vital plane; a god, an animal, a plant, a sick or monstrous human being, something invisible or unnamed, something that is and is not"). In other words, for modernity, piety is no longer a matter of human relations (with the exception of care for the "sick or monstrous").

By contrast, Madrigal's interest in situated knowledge and shared emotion allows him to approach the divine, political, and family relation together through the conceptual frames of resemblance and participation rather than difference. This approach does not make piety purely a question of identity in the *Brevyloquyo* but, rather, reveals it to represent a manner of cultivating unity – "amor dela tierra natural" – without annihilating humanity's social and internal composition. As such, piety constitutes a key form of the imperfect ontological unity Madrigal had described in *De optima politia*.

"El que más conversa consigo es mayor": Communication and Introspection in the *Brevyloquyo*

The dominant conceptual frame for Madrigal's analysis of identity and diversity is friendship. Indeed, Madrigal follows Aristotle in positing friendship as a political force so powerful that it would, if it could be absolutely realized, obviate the need for laws, since "el amigo obrara aquel que es su amigo asy como a otro que es el mismo" (*Brevyloquyo* 36r; "the friend will act toward the one who is his friend as if toward another who is himself"). Madrigal's discussion of friendship proper begins on the familiar ground of common property (45v) and expands into the ground of common purpose, as he asserts that those who communicate attain a "perfecto grado de amar, ca son amygos & obran entre sy enteramente cosas de amygos" (53v; "perfect degree of love, for they are friends and carry out between them only friendly things"). To this sense of communication as participatory sharing or cooperation, Madrigal soon incorporates the explicitly verbal:

> Es comunicar lo que nos vulgarmente llamamos conversar. Comunicar o conversar non se dize de convite o convidado, ca convidar que es juntamente comer pertenesçe a las animalias bructas asy como a los onbres … Conversar es la cosa prinçipal que ay en la amyçiçia, segund que consiste en la cosa que es mas excelente en nos, nos seyendo razonable por naturaleza sobrepujamos a todas las cosas por el entendimiento. (54ra)

> Communicating is what we commonly call conversing. Communicating or conversing is not said of invitations or guests, for to invite is to eat together, which pertains to brute animals as well as to men … Conversing is the principal thing that there is in friendship, in that it consists in the most excellent thing in us, who being reasonable by nature surpass all other things because of our understanding.

Through this sense of communication as conversation, Madrigal has recourse to the traditional hierarchy of creation in which speech manifests humanity's capacity for reason ("nos seyendo razonable por naturaleza"). Once again, however, Madrigal moves from these universal considerations to the practical and circumscribed question of friendship's operation within established social hierarchies, recalling the *LVB* in emphasizing the importance of friendship-as-communication between lords and their subjects, despite the vast social distance that separates them.[31]

In Madrigal's analysis, the equality or identity implicit in friendship is not vitiated by social difference. Rather, in order to preserve the possibility of *verdadera amiçiçia* between lords and their subjects, Madrigal crafts a distinction between equality in quantity and equality in dignity. Pleasurable friendship (*amiçiçia delectable*) requires equality of quantity (that is, the two friends must love each other in equal amounts), but the friendship between fathers and sons, the old and the young, husbands and wives, and lords and servants must only be equal in proportion to the dignity of each friend (56v).[32] The question this distinction raises is what force the language of friendship retains once the principle of absolute identity is abandoned. In other words, why preserve the metaphor of friendship, with its implication of some sort of identity between subjects, to name social relations that imply difference, and for which other sentimental constructs (love, in the case of families, or *bienquerencia* between lords and vassals) exist?[33]

We can begin to answer this question by studying the next question posed by Madrigal: whether friendship with God is possible. Others who had taken up this question, such as Aristotle (*NE* 1159a) and Aelred of Rielvaux (*Spiritual Friendship* 1.51–3, 1.70), had denied the possibility; meanwhile, the trope of God as ideal friend in medieval devotional literature almost always invoked Christ's humanity.[34] Even Alfonso de Cartagena, Madrigal's closest contemporary analogue, who makes a similar argument about divine communication and friendship in his *Oracional* (c. 1454), grounds the possibility of divine friendship in God's mercy (*clemençia*) and calls this relationship a form of charity, never mentioning passionate love:

> Propia amistad … es quando el uno ama al otro e el otro a el; e este comun amor proçede de la comunicaçion que han los omnes en uno. E commo del onbre a Dios aya alguna comunicaçion segund que El por su infinida clemençia comunica con nos su bienaventurança, convenible cosa es que commo sobre la comunicaçion de los omnes unos con otros se funda la amistad humana. E asi sobre la comunicaçion que es de Dios a los omnes desçiende alguna amistad mas alta. E esta es la caridat que es aquel amor e amistad que es del omne a Dios e de Dios al omne. (58)

> Friendship proper … is when one loves the other and vice versa; and this common love comes from the communication men have together. And as there is some communication between man and God because He by his infinite mercy communicates his beatitude with us, it is desirable that human friendship should be founded on the communication among men. And in this way from the communication between God and men comes a higher friendship. And this is charity, which is the love and friendship between man and God, and God and man.

Madrigal, by contrast, affirms the possibility of divine friendship without reference to the Incarnation and not merely through the miracle of divine charity:

> La ynfinita bondad de dios causo esto que entre nos & el podiese ser verdadera & entera amyçiçia, ca aunque segun la naturaleza non tengamos alguna dignidad segun la qual podamos aver alguna egualdad con dios, enpero la infinita largueza del muy alto dios tiene por bien que la anima estoviere en caridad sea de tanta exçelençia que pueda ser fecha & dicha verdaderamente amyga de dios. E non solamente fizo esto en nos la infinita bondad de dios mas aun otra cosa mas lo qual al soberano grado del

bien muy alto pertenesçe. Ca la unidad que entre sy tienen los amygos es o ydentidad en amor, como ellos todos una cosa quieran & una cosa non quieran. Testigo çiçeron en el libro que fizo de la verdadera amyçiçia por virtud de la qual el amigo non se dize otro del todo apartado de su amigo, mas otro que es el mismo su amigo.[35] En tal manera que en la ydentidad este diversidad & en la diversidad este ydentidad. Esta ydentidad comunmente la pueden tener los onbres a dios. (*Brevyloquyo* 64r)

The infinite goodness of God caused this, that between us and Him there could be true and complete friendship, for although according to nature we have no dignity according to which we could have any equality with God, nonetheless the infinite generosity of God most high considers it good that the soul in charity be of such excellence that it can be truly made and said to be a friend of God. And not only did the infinite goodness of God make this in us, but also another thing that belongs to the sovereign degree of the highest good. For the unity that friends have with each other is identity in love, since they want one thing and do not want another. Witness to this is Cicero in the book he wrote on true friendship, by virtue of which a friend is not said to be another completely separate from his friend, but another who is the same as his friend, in such a way that there is diversity in identity and identity in diversity. This identity men can commonly have with God.

Like passionate love, friendship names a kind of identity between the human and the divine – one whose dependence on grace makes it no less real. In exploring this point in his divine mirror, Madrigal makes clear that differences in dignity do not rob friendship of its approximation of ontological identity. This capacity to achieve unity without eliminating diversity makes friendship the perfect – meaning most adequate – law for the city, which is itself a reflection of the nature of its human inhabitants.[36] But can friendship also encode the differences *internal* to each citizen, differences that make absolute unity impossible?

Madrigal again answers this question definitively in the affirmative, contradicting the objections of those who would claim that friendship and communication are necessarily interpersonal. Rather, it is perfectly possible to communicate with oneself:

Pues sy pudiere alguno comunicar consigo en coraçon diremos que puede verdaderamente con sy mismo comunicar. Enpero esto asaz paresçe que puede convenir a cada uno por respecto de sy. Ca el nuestro bevir es entender. Asy como en las otras animalias el bivyr es sentyr. Pues el que entiende bive … E quando para sy mysmo entiende o en sy mysmo con sy mysmo bive. E esto es comunicar o segun el vocablo latino convyvir. Dezimos que alguno entiende con otro o para otro quando las cosas que entiende para otro las entiende conviene saber para que ge las declare & esto syn dubda alguna llaman convevyr o comunicar. Ca esto es comunicar en coraçon & en palabra. Sy alguno para sy mismo entiende, pues asy mismo bive & consygo comunica. (93r)

For if someone can communicate with himself in his heart we will say that he can truly communicate with himself. But this certainly seems to be true of all with respect to themselves. For our living is understanding, just as in other animals living is feeling. Thus, he who understands lives … And when he understands for or in himself, he lives with himself. And this is communicating, or, according to the Latin word, coexisting. We say that someone understands with another or for another when he understands the things he understands for another, that is, in order to explain them [to another], and this is certainly called coexisting or communicating, for this is communicating in heart and in word. If someone understands for himself, in just the same way he lives and communicates with himself.

Madrigal assembles here an ingenious analogical chain that connects friendship, through life itself, to the understanding, which, as our highest faculty, encapsulates life itself, such that the effort to understand oneself becomes a kind of *convivencia* – and this "living together" is communication. Introspection as self-understanding is thus figured as both living and communicating with oneself.

Friendship-as-communication therefore links individuals seamlessly to their communities; just as the Ciceronian friend is a second self, living with others (as friends) mirrors virtuous solitude, living and communicating with oneself. It is important to note here, however, that the capacity for introspection is not productive of virtue; rather, it is made possible by virtuous action. Communicating with oneself, being with oneself, is not a method of purifying deeds or thoughts; rather, as for Aristotle, it is the sign of having *achieved* such an ethical purification:[37]

Assy diremos que esta con sy mismo quando apartadas todas las otras cosas asy solo consydera lo qual es verdadero & exçellente comunicar & es señal de bien non mediano. Ca non pertenesçe a cada uno estar con sy mismo & a sy solo acatar mas es de aquellos solamente que estan en mayor grado de virtud que los otros. Ca comunicar non puede onbre con el triste & con el non delectable segun la dotrina del nuestro aristotiles en el octavo de las ethicas. Conviene saber non puede algo comunicar con el triste syquier un dia … Pues sy alguno puede estar consigo necesario es que falle en sy alguna cosa muy deleytosa en lo qual syquiera detener … De lo qual se sigue que nos sienpre veamos que aquellos onbres que non son reçeptivos o capaçes de algun bien & del todo caresçientes de virtud non puedan estar con sy mismos. E sy contesçiere que ellos esten un poco solos han grande enojo & non podiendo esto sofrir grande tiempo buscan algunos con quien fablen. (93v)[38]

For it does not belong to everyone to be with himself and obey himself alone, but rather this belongs only to those in a higher degree of virtue than the others. For man cannot communicate with those who are sad and not delightful, according to the

> doctrine of our Aristotle in book eight of the *Ethics*. That is, one cannot communicate with the sad even one day ... Thus, if someone can be with himself it is necessary that he find in himself something delightful on which to fasten ... Whence it follows that we always see that those men who are not receptive or capable of some good, lacking in virtue, cannot be with themselves. And if it happens that they are momentarily alone, they get very angry, and unable to tolerate this for long, they seek out others with whom to talk.

If self-contemplation is not a method of achieving virtue, but rather a sign of moral perfection, it follows that God contemplates and communicates with Himself eternally; as Madrigal puts it, "es ynposible que dios algun tiempo çesando de considerar en sy consyderase en las otras cosas" (94r; "it is impossible that God ceases to consider Himself a moment when considering other things"). And it is here that our ultimate difference with the divine is found. Madrigal concludes this portion of the *Brevyloquyo* by admitting that someone who could spend all of her or his time alone would have to be either an animal or God: an animal, because animals are incapable of communication; God, because God has no need of communication outside of Himself (94r–v).[39]

Confession, Rhetoric, and the Literary

To the extent that the "emergence of the individual" in the Middle Ages has long been tied to the spread of individual confession after the Fourth Lateran Council in 1215,[40] we may expect to find a more hermetic individuality in Madrigal's account of confession than is found in his account of introspection.[41] Michel Foucault, for instance, considered the transition from the injunction to know oneself to the practice of confession (what he calls, alluding perhaps to Evagrius and Cassian, the "monastic precept" of confessing one's thoughts to a spiritual guide) to be important in the "genealogy of modern subjectivity" ("About the Beginning" 204). And yet, although they certainly presuppose some form of interiority, Madrigal's notions of introspection and confession find themselves somewhere outside of this genealogy. In his *Breve forma de confesión*, which, according to its editors, was intended more for penitents than for priests (21), Madrigal shows that, just as self-communication is made possible (and joyful) by ethical behaviour, confession is only effective for those who have already purged their sins:[42]

> Es de considerar que ante que el peccador se vaya a confessar se ha de tirar de todos los peccados de fecho y de voluntad proponiendo de nunqua tornar mas a ellos en otra manera non aprovechara la confession assi como si alguno tiene mal querencia de otro agora sea con razon agora sin razon primero deve perdonar al que mal quiere y perder toda la malanconia en otra manera non le aprovecha la confession nin lo pueden absolver. (5v–6r)

> It should be considered that before the sinner goes to confess, he must remove himself from all sins of commission and desire, proposing never to return to them, otherwise the confession will be useless; thus if someone bears ill will toward another, with or without justification, he must forgive that person and lose all melancholy, or else his confession will be useless and they will not be able to absolve him.

In Madrigal's discussion of confession as sacrament, then, effective signification, like communication, becomes possible as a *consequence* of virtuous action. In contrast to the opinions of both Aristotle and the Stoics, the ethical efficacy of Madrigal's notion of communication rests on neither moral deliberation nor the examination of conscience.[43] Rather, as a definitional component of friendship, it names a form of social relation to which human communities should aspire, *owing to its resemblance to humanity's relation to the divine and to the communicative nature of the divine being itself.* Communication, for Madrigal, places spiritual individuation in an explicitly intersubjective context and implies emotional concepts we might associate with *personality* (friendship, love, sorrow, anger), with no correlative distinction between the public and the private.[44] Madrigal's thought fuses Cicero's bipartite political principle of *ratio* and *oratio*,[45] elevating the emotional elements of communal life *qua* communication as both politically effective and personally reasonable.

Despite this ethical legitimation of the verbal, Madrigal's attitude toward literature was ambivalent at best. Echoing his preference for literal exegesis, he condemned the use of metaphor in poetry as mere ornament; indeed, his negative judgments regarding literature are largely found in his biblical commentaries, whereas more positive judgments are to be found in his commentary on Eusebius (Kohut, "Der Beitrag der Theologie" 205, 217).[46] Like Cartagena, Madrigal turned to classical literature for moral, rather than stylistic, instruction;[47] this form of erudition had the practical value of enabling one to know oneself, just as the Romans translated Greek works in an effort to discover their own weaknesses and limitations (Recio 146). Nevertheless, Madrigal was a professor of poetics, and toward the end of the *Brevyloquyo*, he recognizes that the writing of poetry is one way in which humans, to whose imperfect nature the imperfect law of communication corresponds, practice friendship: "Pues el comunicar es un bevyr. De lo qual se sigue que el que puso su vida en specular que con el amigo syenpre quiera specular & que el que en fazer obra poetica o qualquyera otra obra quiera comunicar con el amygo" (149r; "For communication is a form of living. Whence it follows that he who put his life in speculation will always wish to speculate with his friend, and the one who [puts his life] into making poetic work or any other work wishes to communicate with his friend"). As a form of communication, poetry enacts the reflection, *specular*, that traverses humanity's relation with itself (introspection) and with land, family, and the divine (*piedad*). It is perhaps for this reason that Madrigal, despite his own misgivings, became a touchstone for Castile's most creative literary developments in the years following his death.[48]

Madrigal's thought is both daring and supple in articulating an ethical and even pious vision of human society based on friendly communication. This vision is explicitly tied, furthermore, to literary and other acts of creation. At the same time, as we have seen, Madrigal's exaltation of friendship is not free from a certain rationalist undertow, and his endorsement of literature was contradictory and highly qualified. In chapter three, I will show how the conventional opposition of reason and the passions, more implicit in Madrigal than in his contemporaries, remained dominant in both ethical prose and love lyric, even as certain conceptions of pleasure were integrated into rationalist theories of emotional regulation.

Chapter Three

Reason and Its Discontents

Madrigal's ambivalence toward poetry mirrors a broad ambivalence toward sentiment itself in Iberian writers across multiple genres during this period. On the one hand, political thinkers, theologians, and poets alike were fascinated by the passions, dissecting them in minute detail; on the other, a conventional ethical discourse that can fairly be called "rationalist" remained present, although not always dominant, throughout the entire period in question. In this chapter, I will consider prose analyses of the passions by authors such as Duarte I of Portugal and Pere Torroella alongside numerous Castilian and Catalan poets (Torroella himself among them) to both illuminate the contours of this rationalist discourse and show how a sense of its limitations emerges in concessions to pleasure as an aid to reason or even an end in itself. The chafing against rationalism I present in this chapter lays the groundwork for my readings in part two of texts that explore compassion and consolation as alternate ethical ideals.

Theories of the Will in Duarte's *Leal Conselheiro*

A case in point of rationalist ambivalence is Duarte's *Leal Conselheiro* (hereafter *LC*), composed c. 1438, the year of the king's death. As Duarte explains in a dedicatory letter to his wife, Eleanor of Aragon, the *LC* is a compilation of various writings dedicated to "the good management [*regimento*] of our consciences and wills [*voontades*]" (1), an "ABC of loyalty" in which A refers to the "powers and passions" we all have, B to the good that follows from virtue and kindness, and C to the correction of "evils and sins" (3). The *LC*'s opening chapters comprise a treatise on the mind and soul, covering the understanding, memory, will, and the passions. To this foundation Duarte has attached a lengthy hodgepodge of other writings – some his own, such as three autobiographical chapters about his own struggle with melancholy, many translated or otherwise adapted from other sources – on topics ranging from the Immaculate Conception (chapter 35) to marital relations (chapter 55) and diet advice (chapter 100).[1] As I have noted elsewhere (Berlin, "Willing Reader" 206), ethical analysis is woven throughout most of the work, giving it a thematic coherence that it seems to lack with respect to subject matter.

Duarte describes the understanding as "our most principal virtue" (2), and in a brief consideration of methods of maintaining and increasing it, he insists "que nom sejamos vencidos desordenadamente em algũa paixom damor, temor e assi das outras que adiante se diram" (10; "that we not be overcome in a disorderly fashion by some passion of love, fear, or the others to be discussed subsequently"). We can see here how what is actually quite a detailed analysis of human feeling is apparently subjugated to the ethical order of the understanding; only the qualifier *desordenadamente* hints that some passions may have a role to play in the virtuous life. What Duarte may have in mind as an orderly role for the passions is revealed in the *LC*'s complex, four-part account of the nature of human will, drawn principally from the fourth of John Cassian's *Conferences* (c. 426–29).[2] Duarte first condemns the *carnal* will ("voontade carnal") because it leads to vicious desires and laziness. Yet he also condemns the *spiritual* will ("voontade espiritual") because it "quer seguir aquellas partes em que se mais inclinom as virtudes, e faz aos que se despõem a vida de religiom requerer que jejũem, vigiem, leam e rezem quanto mais poderem, *sem nenhũa descliçom*" (15; emphasis added; "wishes to follow those parts [of the will] most inclined toward the virtues, and it makes those who enter orders wish to fast, stay awake, read, and pray as much as possible, *without any discretion*"). Here, Duarte is following Cassian closely, since for the latter, discretion is "the begetter, guardian, and moderator of all virtues" (Cassian 87).[3] The risk of the spiritual will, then, is that it leads to disordered (because immoderate) fasting and praying. The constant conflict between these first two flawed wills gives rise to the third and most harmful will, the *tepid* will ("voontade tiba"), which seeks to satisfy each of the first two without offending the other (Duarte 15). All three of these wills are contrary to discretion in that he who obeys them will "vĩir a morte, sandice, ou enfermidade, perdimento de toda sua fazenda, pois nom guarda descliçom no que ha de fazer" (16; "come to death, foolishness, sickness, or loss of all his possessions, for he does not exercise discretion in what he must do"). But the tepid will is more dangerous than the others precisely because, in seeking "pleasant" moderation, it refuses to judge: "E a terceira por querer complazer a estas ambas e as de todo concordar, o que fazer nom pode por seer batalha que nosso senhor deos nos ordenou por nosso proveito, faz seguir as virtudes tam friamente que ja mais nunca trazerá aquel que per tal voontade se governar a nem hũu boo estado" (16; "And the third [will], because it wants to please the first two and maintain them in concord, which it cannot do because their battle was ordained by God for our benefit, makes one follow the virtues so coldly that it will never lead one governed by it to a good state").

The "perfect and virtuous" fourth will ("voontade perfeita e virtuosa") stands in stark contrast to the tepid will in that, in deferring to the understanding, it refuses to placate the carnal and spiritual wills:

> E a quarta todo per o contrayro, por que todallas cousas que sse apresentam ao coraçom de cada hũa destas tres as oferece ao entender *que julgue* se som de fazer ou leixar … assy esta quarta voontade todallas cousas faz ou leixa de fazer per exsame de entender e razom … E naquesto se desvaira esta quarta voontade muyto da terceira, por que aquella nom conssente em tal guisa contradizer as duas primeiras que algũu agravamento sentam, e aquesta de todo lho contradiz quando determina o entendimento e razom que he bem de o fazer assy. (16–17; emphasis added)

> And the fourth [will] is the complete opposite, because everything the first three offer to the heart, the fourth offers to the understanding *so that it can judge* if it should be done or abandoned … Thus, this fourth will does or abandons everything according to the analysis of the understanding and reason … And in this it differs greatly from the third, because the latter is not so willing to contradict the first two when they are aggrieved, and the former does contradict if the understanding and reason determine that something is good to do.

The role of discretion in Duarte's theory of the will thus echoes that of his brother Pedro in the *LVB*, where discretion is a guide for "reasoned desires." Here, discretion does not suppress emotional stimuli ("cousas que se apresentam ao coraçom"), but rather presents them to the understanding for judgment. Duarte's system reinforces the close relationship of discretion and judgment, adding, furthermore, *prudence* as a third related virtue, since "ssobr'esta quarta voontade faz fundamento a rreal prudencia per que scolhemos o bem do mal" (18; "royal prudence, through which we choose good over bad, is founded upon this fourth will"). And although Duarte's system seems to focus on individual virtue, its vocabulary of self-government – "que jamais nunca trazerá aquel que per tal voontade se governar a nem hũu boo estado" – suggests a broader application. The proximal concepts of "boo estado" and "se governar" indicate once again this period's constitutive analogy between the private and the public.

Duarte's enumeration of the specific errors caused by the tepid will in his next chapter further demonstrates how theories of mental and social structure could be mutually constitutive.[4] The chapter begins with a description of society's five estates: in addition to the familiar *oradores*, *defensores*, and *lavradores*, there are *oficiaes* ("consselheiros, juizes, regedores, veedores, scrivãaes e semelhantes") and a fifth unnamed category of artisans and professionals including doctors, musicians, and jewellers (20).[5] Duarte warns that "o mal que vem desta tiba voontade he que querem seguir as partes doces do mester ou oficio em que vivem, e leixar o amargoso sem o qual del bem nom podem husar" (22; "the evil that comes from this tepid will is that they want to follow the sweet parts of their vocation or office, and avoid the bitter without which they cannot carry out their tasks well"). For example, the *defensores*, who as such receive numerous social and economic benefits, may be led by tepid will to try to avoid the dangerous responsibilities of their estate by, on the one hand, taking religious orders or, on the other, entering the mercantile economy (21). Thus, the private failings of the tepid will – in this case, a kind of greedy cowardice – are seen primarily as a threat to the existing idealized sociopolitical structure. At the same time, the limits of that idealization are starting to show, in that even the nuance Duarte adds to it (the two new estates) is inadequate to preserve the rigidity of its categories. And crucially, if we take into account the way Duarte differentiates the tepid will from its "perfect" counterpart, the refusal of the king's subjects to adhere to his own structural idealization is presented as an unreasonable failure to exercise judgment.

In the subsequent chapters, Duarte describes a second four-fold taxonomy of the will, this one more in line with traditional philosophical psychology and with Aquinas's thought in particular. In this system, which complements the other one, the first three wills correspond to the vegetative, sensitive, and rational souls, and the fourth is free will. None of these wills is inherently good or bad; rather, they are divided according to the behaviours they regulate and the level of creation to which they belong. The vegetative will regulates activities, such as eating, drinking, and sleeping, that we share with plants and trees; the sensitive regulates that which we share with the animals; and the rational will, "in which men participate with the angels," regulates that which has to do with virtue, honour, discretion, and pleasure (25–7). Finally, the free will reigns "como senhor antre todas" (27; "as lord among them all") and "no conssentimento della esta o pecado e virtude" (28; "in its consent lie sin and virtue").[6] Despite this last statement, however, it is clear that vice and virtue are at stake throughout this taxonomy and emotion is at its centre: the sensitive will regulates the twelve passions,[7] and "por quanto em esto se resolve a mayor parte de todos nossos feitos, me parece bem conssiirarmos sempre como nos governamos em estas paixõoes" (26; "because the majority of our actions are resolved in this, it seems good to me always to consider how we govern ourselves in these passions").[8] The fact that Duarte attributes to the passions "the majority of our actions" demonstrates their centrality to moral (that is, practical) philosophy. And again, the free will's judgment (in the form of "consent") is the highest arbiter, which is why the cardinal virtue that corresponds to the free will is justice (28; the understanding requires prudence; desire, temperance; and irascibility, strength).

Rationalism, the Experience of Sadness, and the Absence of *eros*

These two models of will, in both of which virtue consists of submitting the passions to the scrutiny of reason or the intellect, reveal important points of contact between ascetic and scholastic theories of mind and emotion, but also demonstrate how these theories could run on parallel tracks when applied to practical philosophy. They furnished thinkers such as Duarte, but also the authors of courtly poetry and sentimental prose, with a set of abstract – but not, as Robert Folger notes (*Images* 77–8), truly allegorical – terms to be deployed in intricate and often playful ways. Yet the taste for abstraction is not general throughout Duarte's moral pedagogy. Or rather, at least in pedagogical terms, that taste is accompanied by a suspicion of imagination. Thus, despite the moral example's crucial place in Castilian wisdom literature (Heusch 96; Duarte himself owned a copy of Don Juan Manuel's *Conde Lucanor*[9]), Duarte announces in his introductory letter that the *LC* will not be a "livro destorias, em que o entendimento pouco trabalha por o entender ou se nembrar" (4; "book of stories, which the understanding hardly works to understand or remember"). Indeed, later in the *LC*, he associates storytelling, even in the context of "conselhos proveitosos," with the sin of idleness (104). The few narrative examples there are in the *LC* are overwhelmingly personal; along with the previously mentioned chapters on Duarte's melancholic episode, there is a long chapter (349–61) about his father's court and a mention of his cousin Henry V of England's exemplary determination during the Battle of Agincourt in 1415. In other words, experience is preferred to imagination, and in fact, Duarte claims that "experience and practice" (229) are crucial to the attainment of prudence, whereas emotion is an unreliable guide: "Sobre o que perteence aa virtude da prudencia, a mym parece que nom convem a perssoas que virtuosamente desejom vyver creersse per seus coraçõoes em qual quer estado, por as grandes mudanças de seus sentimentos" (213; "Regarding the virtue of prudence, it seems to me that those who wish to live virtuously should not follow their hearts in any state, because of the great changes in their feelings").

Duarte is thus remarkably interested in emotion, but shares the suspicion of it found throughout his period's moral literature; his own moral teaching combines systematic explorations of emotion and vice and virtue, with a strong emphasis on the related concepts of reason, judgment, discretion, and prudence. Among the methods of transmitting moral lessons on these concepts, Duarte emphasizes familial and personal exemplarity, recounting, for example, his own bout of melancholy "por tal que mynha speriencia a outros seja exempro" (68; "so that my experience may be an example to others").[10] In the foregoing chapter, Duarte has identified six sources of sadness, of which the fifth is a "desconcertada compreissom, que verdadeiramente doença de humor menencorico se chama" (67; "disordered complexion, which in truth is called the malady of melancholic humor").[11] This humoral etiology is nevertheless de-emphasized in the following autobiographical chapter, where Duarte returns to describing melancholy as the result of a disordered will (67).[12] At the age of twenty-two, having been left in charge of the court while his father laid siege to Ceuta, he found himself obliged to dedicate his entire day to his duties, abandoning almost completely his favoured pastimes of riding and hunting (68–9).[13] Then, there was such a severe outbreak of plague in

Lisbon that "poucos dias passavom que me nom fallassem em pessoas conhecidas que de tramas adoeciam e morriam" (69–70; "hardly a day went by in which I was not told of acquaintances contracting and dying from the plague"). Finally, he faced sickness himself:

> Hũu dia me deu grande sentymento em hũa perna, e me fez tal door com queentura, que me pos em grande alteraçom. E fuy logo remediado, que per graça de nosso senhor em breve spaço recobrei saude, mas filhei hũu tam rryjo penssamento com receo de morte, que nom soomente temy aquella, mes a que todos scusar nom podemos, penssando na breveza da vida presente. E aquel penssamento entrou em meu coraçom, que per seis meses hũu pequeno spaço nunca o del pude afastar, tirandome todo prazer e acrecentandome a mayor tristeza segundo meu juyzo que aver podia. (70)

> One day I felt a great pain in one leg, which hurt terribly and caused a fever, upsetting me greatly. And I was cured right away, for by the grace of our lord I regained my health in a short time, but I conceived such a strong thought and fear of death, that I not only feared that one [death from that sickness], but the one none can avoid, thinking about the brevity of this life. And that thought entered into my heart, so that for six months I could never push it away for even a moment, taking from me all pleasure and provoking in me, in my judgment, the greatest sadness that can be had.

The unexplained malady that Duarte describes – with its shades of a hysterical symptom – leads to a melancholic obsession with the "thought" of death. The language of a thought that enters the heart recalls Cassian, and indeed, it is here associated with fear ("receo") and, of course, sadness, itself the reflection of a lack of pleasure ("tirandome todo prazer"). Duarte sought the counsel of doctors, confessors, and friends – sources of physical, spiritual, and ethical or virtuous consolation – in vain; he remained in this state of suffering "compared to which any other malady would seem like good health" (70) until his mother, Philippa of Lancaster, fell ill with, and eventually died from, the plague.

As Duarte explains, he began to emerge from his melancholic state because Philippa's illness provoked in him such "sentimento" that he lost all fear of death, approaching and serving his mother without hesitation: "E aquesto foy começo da minha cura, por que sentindo ella, leixei de ssentir a mym" (71; "And this was the beginning of my cure, because as she suffered, I myself stopped suffering"). Duarte thus posits the compassion he felt for his mother as a form of palliative self-abnegation: the temporary interruption of his own suffering allowed him to believe that it might one day be completely cured. Duarte's newfound hope, in turn, allowed him to imagine – as he puts it, "filhey mais hũa maginaçom muy proveitosa" – that his melancholy might be an ordeal of divine origin, an opportunity to suffer "patiently and virtuously" in repentance rather than face worldly dishonour and eventual damnation (71–2). From this idea, Duarte derived a renewed vigour ("esforço"), buttressed by patience and good hope (72). Nevertheless, after his mother's decline and death, Duarte remained melancholic for three years, always improving but never experiencing true pleasure: "cadavez melhorando, nunca porem sentindo hũu soo plazer chegar ao coraçom" (72). At the end of the three years, "per special mercee de nosso senhor deos" (72; "by special mercy of our lord God"), Duarte returned to perfect health, happier, in fact, than ever before.

As an account of lived melancholy, these autobiographical chapters are unassuming in their idiosyncrasy. Like ancient and modern theories of melancholy, Duarte's account is libidinal, the limits of his experience clearly defined by an ability to feel pleasure. Yet his inability to feel pleasure is associated with neither sloth, the sinful *acedia*, *taedium vitae*, or *desidia* (idleness) that afflicted cloistered monks in the Middle Ages (Agamben 3), nor with erotic love, as is frequently the case in troubadour poetry from the twelfth century onward. As Giorgio Agamben has explained, the doctors of the Church described *acedia* as a kind of "anguished sadness and desperation," a shrinking away from the "particular spiritual dignity" God has granted humanity: "What afflicts the slothful is not, therefore, the awareness of an evil, but, on the contrary, the contemplation of the greatest of goods: *acedia* is precisely the vertiginous and frightened withdrawal (*recessus*) when faced with the task implied by the place of man before God" (5–6). *Acedia*, Agamben continues, is thus "*the perversion of a will that wants the object, but not the way that leads to it, and which simultaneously desires and bars the path to his or her own desire*" (6; emphasis in original). Furthermore, Agamben notes that parallel medical and astrological theories "associated the exercise of poetry, philosophy, and the arts with this most wretched of all humors … In this context, the elemental influence of the earth and the astral influence of Saturn were united to confer on the melancholic a natural propensity to interior withdrawal and contemplative knowledge" (12). The relevance of this definition to the troubadours' account of love and lovesickness, the *amor hereos* that is a perversion of the will through the obsessive contemplation of a mental image of the beloved (see, for example, Vilanova, *Tractat sobre l'amor heroic* 60), is evident.[14] Duarte's melancholy, by contrast, omits any reference to *eros* and results not from idleness but from an explosion of activity, an excess of duty to which Duarte abandoned himself despite his "nova hidade e pouco saber" (68; "young age and little knowledge"). This overwhelming occupation coincided with "the awareness of an evil," the inevitability of death, and these circumstances conspired to annihilate pleasure as a practical fact and psychic capacity. Only an experience of self-absence ("leixei de ssentir a mym") achieved, apparently involuntarily, through compassion allowed Duarte to conceive the spark of hope leading to a prolonged convalescence that would reach its ultimate success only through God's mercy.

In a chapter placed later in the *LC* but composed before (in 1418), Duarte offers advice to his brother Pedro on the occasion of the latter's departure for what would ultimately be ten years of travels. Duarte begins, knowing that his brother is somewhat upset about leaving (86), by advising Pedro to temper his emotions, *afeiçõoes*, in order to avoid any actions contrary to reason or justice (87). When he turns to the emotion of sadness in particular, however, Duarte's ascetic rationalism gives way to a recognition of the primacy of grace, implicitly echoing his earlier autobiographical narrative: "Da tristeza vos avisaae quanto com a graça de nosso senhor poderdes. E desto el soo he de todo meestre" (87; "Be as careful about sadness as you can, by God's grace. He alone is the master of this"). The virtuous, however, will seek to avoid sadness through a careful daily balance of exercise and rest (*folgança*) for what Duarte calls the three "powers" (*poderes*) we possess, that is, the vegetative, sensitive, and rational soul (87–8). Maintaining this balance is a matter of discretion:

> E assy nos entra a tristeza, posto que o nom conheçamos, [e] por teermos afeiçom a hũa das partes, nom sentymos o que da outra nos vem nacendo, assy como hũu devoto sem discreçom, sentyndo em sy grande folgança de vigilia ou de jejũu, cuidando muyto per aquelo prazer a deos, que perteence ao poder da rrazom, correndo per seu camynho muyto desordenadamente, nom proveendo ao que lhe demandam os outros poderes, se per sua special graça nom fosse guardado, de que se nom fazia cair em tristeza, e perder a folgança que penssava daver? (88–9)

> And in this way sadness enters us, although we may not recognize it, and because we favour one of the parts, we do not sense what is arising from the other, like a devout man without discretion, taking great pleasure in a vigil or fast, thinking in this way to please God greatly, which belongs to the power of reason, running along his way in great disorder, not providing what his other powers ask of him, how will he not fall into sadness, losing the pleasure he expected to have, if he is not protected by God's special grace?

Duarte's description of excessive fasting recalls the disordered spiritual will, although he does not here invoke his four-fold theory. Sadness, in this example, is the inevitable (barring divine intercession) result of an overindulgence of reason – no matter how devout the expectation of pleasing God – leading to the neglect of the soul's other powers. From an early point in the development of his thought, then, Duarte saw the monastic and Aristotelian (by way of Aquinas) theories of will as complementary, and discretion is the name most frequently applied to the virtue conjoining them. Furthermore, although Duarte advocates moderation in the care of the rational soul, it is affection (*afeiçom*) that leads his example's protagonist astray. As Josiah Blackmore explains, the term *afeiçom* was used frequently by late medieval Portuguese writers in both religious and secular texts; although it could describe an emotional bond, it generally referred, as in the passage just cited, to an inclination or predisposition ("*Afeiçom*" 16).[15] It was thus a key term in discussions of sin, sanctity, vice, and virtue, and Duarte typically opposed it – in the *Bem cavalgar* as well as the *LC* – to reason (17). In short, Duarte's advice to his brother considers sadness from a fundamentally ethical perspective, showing some flexibility in Duarte's characteristic rationalism but ultimately presenting this emotion as a question of self-governance against the threat of *afeiçom*.

This approach to sadness is brought into relief later in the same chapter when Duarte compares the foregoing description of sadness with one based on the humors:

> Do sobrepojamento dalgũus humores que desgovernam o corpo, que a este poder de ssua governança perteence, convem resguardar, por que algũas vezes vem por el a tristeza, mais nom sempre, porem errom muytos querendosse logo purgar ou sangrar como som tristes. E a tristeza nom he sempre dally, mas vem da myngua de nom dar a cada hũu destes poderes o que bem requere. (89)
>
> It is good to avoid the excess of some humors that disorder the body, which belongs to the governance of this power, because sadness sometimes comes through this, but not always, and therefore many err in wanting to purge or bleed themselves when they are sad. And sadness is not always from there, but is caused by failing to give each of these powers what it rightfully requires.

There is no doubt that the sentimental literature of Duarte's time is informed by humoral theory, but Duarte's assertion that "many err" by seeking to regulate their emotions medically rather than ethically is emblematic of courtly authors' deep and widespread preference for discourses of virtue. It is also characteristic of Duarte to reject, at key moments, certain authoritative sources; Duarte's assimilation of received wisdom is always conditioned by "a lived experience accumulated over the years and refined and sharpened through personal reflection" (Pacheco 430).[16] Indeed, the critical relationship between experience and intellect is central to Duarte's ethical outlook, since it is only through the will's activity that reason can be brought to bear on human experience (Pacheco 434). Purging and bloodletting may have a palliative effect on emotional phenomena (such as sadness) related to the will, but they foreclose the active application of the intellect and thus are of less interest to the author of an ethico-political treatise.[17]

It is thus no coincidence that Duarte's best-known disavowal of authority comes in his definition of *saudade* (in the chapter following his advice to Pedro), which is, as much as any single source, responsible for this emotion's traditional presentation as "the key feeling of the Portuguese soul" (Santoro 929). Duarte describes *saudade* as a feeling in the heart that comes from the senses and not reason, sometimes causing sadness or annoyance (*nojo*) and other times, pleasure (94). Information about this contradictory feeling cannot be found in other books: "E pera entender esto, nom compre leer per outros livros, ca poucos acharóm que dello fallem, mes cada hũu veendo o que screvo, conssiire seu coraçom no que ja per feitos desvairados tem sentido, e podera veer e julgar se fallo certo" (94–5; "And to understand this there is no need to read other books, for you will find few that speak of it, but each one, seeing what I write, should consider the feelings caused by diverse events in his own heart, and will thus be able to see and judge whether I speak the truth"). Duarte, through experience, has identified a feeling absent from the historical tradition but present in his own vernacular, and invites his audience to subject his own authority to personal experience, what each reader "ja per feitos desvairados tem sentido."[18] In fact, *saudade* is a feeling grounded in memory, a form of *afeiçom* or *deleitaçom* (pleasure, delight) caused by the relationship between a given memory and our present circumstances: it is only when we desire an impossible return to a past pleasure that *saudade* is accompanied by sadness (95–6). In this way, as Afonso Botelho has argued, Duarte's *saudade* privileges the emotions caused by real objects (encountered in the past), and thus stands in contrast to *désir*, the motto of his brother Pedro, a form of concupiscence that can be sublimated but never implies "a existência real de um ser ligado a outro ser, a convivência histórica e determinante, ora baseada na pura deleitação ora unida pela profunda afeição humana" (Botelho 35; "the real existence of one being linked to another historical and determinate coexistence, whether based in pure pleasure or united by profound human affection"). This contrast between abstract desire and experiential *saudade* underlies Botelho's alignment of Pedro's *LVB* with the medieval "separative" notion of fidelity and Duarte's *LC* with the "unifying" notion of loyalty, in which desire is subordinated to both memory (of lived experience) and the presence of pleasure, *prazer* (20–1).[19] In fact, when Duarte does refer to a feeling of *grande desejo*, it is the desire to return to a past happy state or *conversation* (95–6). Critically, although Duarte twice emphasizes that *saudade* comes from the heart rather than reason or good sense (*siso*), he here specifies that *saudade* provokes sadness when the desire to return to the past is *granted by reason*, "outorgado per toda mayor parte da rrazom" (96). However much Duarte's account of *saudade* may be characterized as "subjectivist" or "experientialist," it retains the ascetic rationalism of his more schematic theories of the will.

It is symptomatic of Duarte's scepticism toward literature that his descriptions of melancholy and *saudade* avoid the question of *eros* altogether.[20] His evocation of pleasure in past "states" and "conversation" studiously avoids the courtly commonplace, famously uttered by Francesca da Rimini in the *Inferno*'s fifth canto (that is, in the circle of lust): "Nessun maggior dolore/ che ricordarsi del tempo felice/ ne la miseria" (Dante V.121–3); as I will discuss later, Santillana voices this lament through the poet Macías in his *Infierno de los enamorados.*[21] In short, the closest analogue to the bitter side of Duarte's *saudade* is rooted in the erotic pessimism of the troubadours, and *eros* is thus notable in its absence from Duarte's analysis. When Duarte does turn to the sin of lust directly, his advice is largely practical, involving the love of chastity and the avoidance of occasions to sin (120–1). Yet it is in this chapter that Duarte articulates a general rule about virtuous forbearance and pleasure: "Sobr'esto he hũa regra geeral de todallas virtudes: que as nom possue como deve quem em ellas nom sente mais prazer e folgança, que pena em contradizer aos pecados seus contrairos" (121; "About this I have a general rule about all the virtues: that those who do not feel more pleasure and comfort than pain in contradicting their opposing vices [that is, of the virtues] do not possess them as they should"). This rule, though applying generally to all the virtues, is personal ("*I have* a general rule"), grounded in lived experience, and subject to its own need for moderation:

> Ca em quanto se guarda com mayor trabalho e tristeza que prazer, posto que dos malles se afaste, nom os fazendo, ainda vyve na parte da continencia, a qual porem he bem de louvar, mas nom possue tal virtude como graças a nosso senhor bem vy esta praticar a pessoas em ella muy acabadas, com que ouve grande afeiçom, que vallentemente o pecado seu contrairo sempre contradisserom e vencerom, os quaaes nom sollamente som delle guardados sem tristeza, mes trazem boo avysamento de temperar o prazer que syntem na guarda da virtude, temendosse cayr por ello em pecado de vaam gloria. (121–2)

> For to the extent that a virtue is held with greater effort and sadness than pleasure, although the evils are avoided and not carried out, he still lives in the realm of containment, which is certainly worthy of praise, but he does not possess virtue in the way that God allowed me to see it practised in people who had perfected it, which affected me greatly, for they always valiantly contradicted and vanquished its opposing vice, not merely avoiding the sin without sadness, but being careful to temper the pleasure they feel in practising virtue, fearing it might cause them to fall into the sin of vainglory.

Erotic pleasure is as absent from Duarte's discussion of lust as it is from those of melancholy and *saudade*, but it seems to lurk here behind the king's consideration of pleasure as both essential to virtue and a temptation in and of itself. The virtuous must resist temptation with a moderate pleasure that avoids ostentation, yet it was precisely in witnessing this delicate balance that Duarte felt himself greatly affected, *afeiçom* here connoting the inclination toward virtue gleaned from direct experience ("bem vy") of exemplary behaviour.[22] Implicit, thus, in Duarte's normative and biographical account of pleasure is a model of temperate *afeiçom* that greases the wheels, so to speak, of the ethical application of reason to the interface between will and the world. Excessive pleasure, like excessive sadness, is sinful, but the exercise of the will in courtly pastimes or in edifying conversation aligns *afeiçom* with reason and the understanding. As Duarte shows in his description of *saudade*, even this virtuous *afeiçom* could become a temptation to sin as an object of reminiscence, but this risk is unavoidable since the management of sadness requires the active care of all three powers of the soul. *Afeiçom* and pleasure thus form part of a difficult ethical balance that must – and can, from the *LC*'s overarching perspective – be maintained. As I will now show, the courtly poetry of Duarte's time also develops a curative notion of pleasure, but it is less sanguine about the possibility of incorporating that decidedly erotic pleasure into a rationalist ethical system.

Pleasure and Pessimism at Court

At the end of the prologue to his *cancionero*, Juan Alfonso de Baena famously states that, to be successful, poets must either be lovers or feign love, "que siempre se preçie e se finja de ser enamorado" (15). As Robert Folger has argued, the poet's feigning "demonstrates his superior rationality" because it is achieved through the moderation of the powerful passion of love; furthermore, this effort at "self-mastery" implies "a reflective stance, a self-surveillance which would become a defining feature of modern subjectivity" (*Escape* 67). Yet the mere practice of tempering or otherwise controlling the passions cannot be understood as modern unless, like Foucault, one locates the deep roots of "modern" subjectivity in Stoic and other early ascetic "technologies of the self."[23] The hint of modernity in the courtier poet's act of self-mastery springs from its artifice, its teleology of feigning rather than self-knowledge.

The Iberian poets compiled by Baena and others throughout the fifteenth century, in feigning love, rarely feign moderation and mastery; rather, they alternately lament and celebrate their own subjugation at the hands of the beloved and of love itself. According to its internal logic, then, their lyric discourse on the passions is not *rational* in the sense described by Folger, but *rationalist*, identifying passion with suffering and disorder much as Duarte and other contemporary prose moralists had. In fact, as María Rosa Menocal has argued, the very illogic of the poets' suffering brings into relief the reflectivity of their pose:

> It is the disappointment itself, *too often without logical reason*, that is the subject of this poetry. The obstacles, when and if they are specified, are rarely if ever as significant as the simple fact of unfulfillment, which is clearly at the center of the poetry's concerns … It is hard to escape the tentative conclusion that this is poetry very much for itself and conscious of itself as its own principal pleasure and subject, and that the recurring theme of unsatisfactory love is a thematic vehicle particularly well suited to this sort of poetic narcissism. (107; emphasis added)

Menocal is here describing the troubadour tradition writ large, but the point is even truer of its several Iberian currents. Here, the "real" obstacles found so frequently in Occitan poetry – the beloved's husband, her guards, and the court's ill-intentioned flatterers and gossipers – fall away almost entirely, leaving only the beloved's virtuous recalcitrance or cruelty to safeguard the poet's unfulfillment.

That this rejection is rational when viewed from the perspective of the beloved's social circumstances is a fact left largely implicit in most *cancionero* poetry but explored in excruciating detail in sentimental fiction, and it also figures heavily into the *cancionero* poets' self-portrayal as *sandios* or *locos*, that is, irrational actors. They have surrendered themselves into the grip of the passions without a reasonable hope of reward.

The ethical conflict at the heart of the rationalist pose could, from the earliest courtly poetry in Castilian and Catalan, be stated very directly or be the subject of punning and other lyric play. In a relatively small subset of poems, such as Juan Rodríguez del Padrón's "Siete gozos de Amor," poets adopt technical Stoic vocabulary:

> El primero movimiento
> al segundo
> nunca pudo contrastar,
> avido conoscimiento
> en el mundo
> tú ser la más singular (lines 116–21)[24]

> The first movement could never contradict the second, once the world knew that you were the most singular [of women].

The broader framework of the passions as subject to reason's consent is found much more frequently throughout the tradition, as in the following anonymous song compiled in the *Cancionero general*:

> Es victoria conoscida
> quien de vos queda vencido
> que en perder por vos la vida
> es ganado lo perdido
> Pues lo consiente razón
> consiento mi perdimiento
> pues vuestro merescimiento
> satisfizo mi passion (69, lines 6–13)[25]

> It is a recognized victory to be conquered by you, for in losing one's life for you, what is lost is won. Since reason consents to it, I consent to my loss, for your worth satisfied my passion.

Here, the poet justifies as reasonable his suffering owing to his beloved's great virtue; reason's judgment (the second movement) was not mistaken despite the passion to which it gave rise. It is appropriate that this song should be anonymous, because this rhetorical move is very common throughout the Iberian songbooks, although, as we will see, poets also frequently decry the beloved's *merecimiento* as insufficient reward for their amatory service.

The opposition between reason and will remains whether reason is portrayed as a giver of consent or a victim of force, as in Jorge Manrique's paradigmatic formulation: "Es amor fuerça tan fuerte/ que fuerça toda razon" (4, lines 1–2; "Love is such a strong force that it forces all reason").[26] Similarly, in a poem offering advice to Henry IV of Castile, the satirical poet Antón de Montoro warns that "muchas vezes voluntad/ puede mas que la Razon" (lines 327–8; "the will is often stronger than Reason").[27] And, as Carvajal states plainly in a short poem from the *Cancionero de Estúñiga*, when the will dominates, it is not just reason but goodness itself that suffers: "Do rige la voluntad,/ sujeta razón et bondad" (150, lines 3–4; "Where the will reigns, it subjects reason and goodness").[28] In a song attributed to Francisco de Villalpando in the *Cancionero de Herberay* – one of the rarer poems that allude directly to the lover's obstacles – the unfortunate lover implicitly analogizes his position to that of reason, scorned by the will:

Aunque se qu'eres amada
de quien de ti me departe
no ay remedio sino amarte.

Es contraria la razon
a la firme voluntat
y la poca lealtat
triste faz mi coraçon.
Mas la voluntat firmada
pone la razon aparte
no ay remedio sino amarte. (CXXXIX)[29]

Although I know you are loved by the one who separates me from you, there is no remedy but to love you.

Reason is contrary to the firm will, and lack of loyalty saddens my heart. But the confirmed will puts reason aside; there is no remedy but to love you.

Despite the categorical phrasing of lines 4–5, the song describes the individual (if archetypical) circumstances of a conflict between the poet's reason and will: given that the beloved's lover ("quien de ti me departe") is no mere flatterer, reason calls on the poet to stifle or redirect his desire. The will remains firm, however, so that, just as the poet is kept apart from the beloved, reason is set aside by the will. The repetitive rhyme, *departe*/*aparte*, draws attention to the paradoxical analogy in which the poet is identified with reason (occupying a parallel position in the poem's implied narrative) through its own negation. The song thus reveals how the opposition between reason and the will is as constitutive of poetic unfulfillment as the genre's narrative conventions.

Reason was associated with a series of other virtues, which broadened the ethical palette of this fundamental opposition. For example, after Santillana describes the loss of his free will ("franco alvedrío") at the hands of Fortune in the opening stanza of his *Infierno de los enamorados* (lines 7–8), he groups reason with *mesura* among the faculties powerless before Fortune's rapture: "e yo, commo non sabía/ de mí, sinon que ventura,/ contra razón e mesura,/ me levó do non quería" (lines 53–6; "and I, knowing nothing of myself but that fortune, against reason and moderation, carried me where I did not wish to go").[30] Santillana's pairing recalls, in turn, one of the earliest poems compiled by Baena in his *cancionero*, Macías's "Provē de buscar mesura":

> Prove de buscar mesura
> o mesura non fallesçe,
> e por menguada ventura
> ovyeronmelo a sandeçe;
> por ende dyrey de sy
> con cuidado que me creçe
> un trebello, e dyse asy:
>
> "Anda meu coraçon
> Muy triste e con rason." (310, lines 1–9)[31]

I tried to seek moderation where moderation is not lacking, and to my misfortune they considered it foolish; therefore I will tell of myself, with growing unease, a joke, as follows: "My heart feels very sad, and with [good] reason."

Like Santillana's *Infierno*, the opening of Macías's poem – whose quoted refrains will be discussed in part two – groups together *mesura*, *ventura*, and *razón*, adding the public judgment that Macías's striving amounted to *sandez*, nonsense. Thus the stated opposition here is between moderation and nonsense, wisdom and foolishness. The "rason" of the poem's first refrain does not refer (as in Santillana's poem) to the mental faculty, but rather to the related sense of "a reason," a legitimate cause for the poet's sadness. Yet an audience primed by the foregoing stanza's discussion of sense and nonsense will perceive in the refrain not just that the poetic voice "is right" to be sad, but that it is on the side of reason.

This kind of play on the different senses of *razón* – along with the mental faculty and the idea of cause or justification, the sense of speech itself, as in *razonar* – is fundamental to Iberian courtly discourse on the emotions, as its presence in

Macías's oeuvre indicates. We find similar punning, for example, in a *villancico* by the much later Sánchez de Badajoz:

> Al principio de mi mal
> llorava mi perdimiento
> mas agora ya esto tal
> que de muerto no lo siento
> para tener sentimiento
> tanta tengo de razon
> que no puedo llorar non (35, lines 18–24)[32]

At the beginning of my suffering I mourned my loss, but now I am in such a state that, dead, I do not feel it. I am so right to feel sorry that I cannot cry, no.

This stanza concludes the poem, in which Sánchez de Badajoz has explained that suffering (his *pesares*) has dried his eyes and heart (lines 1–2), leaving him "muerto en vida" (line 8; "dead in life"). Here, the poet engages the two senses of *razón* active in Macías's poem as well, playfully juxtaposing reason and sentiment while literally claiming that his sentiment is justified. At the same time, Sánchez de Badajoz puns paradoxically on *sentimiento* itself as both sensation or perception ("que de muerto no lo siento") and suffering: his suffering is so justified, and therefore so great, that it has exhausted his very ability to feel. These narrative facts are set out plainly in the poem's *cabeza*, but it is their psychic and ethical background that provides a subject for Sánchez de Badajoz's lyrical ingenuity.

A *decir* attributed to Gonzalo de Torquemada in the *Cancionero de Palacio* playing on the same pairing of reason and sentiment introduces the concept of consent as well:

> Como quier que me non dexo
> nin por esto [the lack of a reward] deservir
> al Amor, de quien me quexo
> con razón de me sentir,
> que non quiere consentir
> quitarme de sujebción
> de quien ya mi corazón
> es cierto de non partir
> fasta morir. (CXXI, lines 28–36)[33]

Although I do not allow myself, even for this, to cease serving Love, about whom I justifiably complain for my suffering, because He will not consent to free me from subjection to the one from whom my heart is now certain never to take leave, until death.

This poem's relatively dense syntax serves initially to obscure the attribution of blame for the poet's inevitable and thankless death. Although the literal meaning of line 31 is simply that the poet's resentment is justified, the impression of an implied antithesis of reason and sentiment is only strengthened by the invocation of consent – normally the responsibility of reason – in the following line. Yet Torquemada's implication is deceptive because, in fact, it is Love and not reason whose consent is withheld: only Love could free the poet from his otherwise fatal amatory subjection. In short, the god Love stands in godlike Reason's customary place: an ethical spin on the troubadours' *religio amoris*.

A similar role reversal can be found when poets play on the relationship between reason and speech. Santillana, in remembering and versifying the rapturous visions of his *Infierno* (*Poesías completas* 263–4), feels threatened with a loss of sense:

> ¿Quién es que, metrificando
> en coplas nin distinçiones,
> en prosas nin consonando,
> tales diformes visiones,
> sin multitud de renglones,
> el su fecho decir puede?
> *Ya mi seso retroçede*
> *pensando tantas razones.* (lines 97–104, emphasis added)

Who could, versifying or in distinctions, in prose or rhyming, describe such deformed visions without a multitude of lines? *My sense retreats, considering such reasons.*

Here, the poet's mind recoils before the task of giving his "deformed visions" form in language; that such language would take the form of *razones* epitomizes its inadequacy to the task. More often, however, *razón* as speech is opposed to the will or passions, as in the following example from Pedro de Santa Fe in the *Cancionero de Palacio*:

> *Mi passión fable por mí*
> *e no razone mi lengua,*
> que ya de ti es grant mengua
> lo fablado fast'aquí;
> d'oy más, plazer, non dolor;
> al que yaze ya por tierra
> conpassión, paç et no guerra,
> blandeza et no terror. (CCLXXIX, lines 21–8, emphasis added)

May my passion speak for me and my tongue be silent, for what has been spoken of you until now is already very lacking; from today on, pleasure, not pain; compassion for the one stretched out on the ground, peace and not war, gentleness and not terror.

The antithesis of passion and reason – again, introduced obliquely through the verb *razonar* – prefigures the antitheses of pleasure and pain, war and peace, gentleness and terror with which the poem concludes. The order is reversed in one of Pere Torroella's Castilian songs:[34]

> Mira qué casos tan feos
> comete tu crueldat:
> dar muerte por gualardón
> de mis tan buenos servicios
> y que tengan por tal son
> virtudes lugar de viçios
> *e voluntat de razón.* (XXV, lines 57–63, emphasis added)

> Look what ugly deeds your cruelty commits: to give death as a reward for my outstanding services, and that in this way virtues are in the place of vices, *and the will in that of reason.*

It is cruelty that turns the world upside down, setting the will in reason's rightful place. Yet we may ask whether Santa Fe's *plazer* or Torroella's *galardón* are themselves perceived as reasonable in Iberian troubadour discourse.

Beginning in the late fourteenth century, the Catalan lyric tradition developed a highly intellectualized amatory vocabulary, which would later be taken up with gusto in Catalan and Valencian epistolary and sentimental literature. This tradition emphasized the role of pleasure, denominated as *alt*, *grat*, or *delit*, in the process of falling in love. The theory is laid out with substantial complexity in a poem by Jaume March (1334/35–1410), "Dos són los alts, segons lo meu parer." March (the uncle of Ausiàs March) was involved in the founding of the Barcelona Consistori in 1393, and was confirmed alongside Lluís d'Averçó as its *mantenidor* by Martin I of Aragon in 1399 (*Obra poètica* 24); that he was held in high esteem as a poet is evident not only from his position at the Consistori but also from the wide diffusion of his poetry (29). March's two *alts* fuse medieval theories of love grounded in sight (such as that of Vilanova) with the Stoic vocabulary of first and second movements. The first, essential movement is a glimpse of the beloved: "Aquest aytal mou dels hulls, he primer/ de dar al cor que l'altre moviment;/ per qué tal alt, si no·s primerament,/ no pot depuys esser tan vertader" (I, lines 21–4; "This way of the eyes strikes the heart before the other movement; for if this *alt* does not come first, it cannot later be so true"). This first movement is complemented by a second, intellectual pleasure:

> Enaprés ve l'altre que us dich darrer,
> qu·en l'espirit fa son bon fonament,
> car vol bondat, gràci·e sentiment,

> ab gentil cor, seny, virtut e saber.
> *De cosas tals e semblants se contenta*
> *l'enteniment hi s'i va delitant.* (I, lines 25–30; emphasis added)

> Then the other one I describe comes after, whose good grounding is in the spirit, for it wants goodness, grace, and sentiment, with a courteous heart, sense, virtue, and knowledge. *The understanding is pleased by these and similar things and takes delight in them.*

This second *alt* derives from an Aristotelian tradition – what Pedro M. Cátedra calls, in the Iberian context, "naturalismo amoroso universitario" (*Amor y pedagogía* 62) – that appears in Madrigal's *Brevyloquyo* and in short prose works in Catalan such as Torroella's *Resposta de Pere Torroella a una demanda de Francesc Ferrer sobre el grat* and, from the next generation, Francesc Alegre's *Sermó d'amor* (Cátedra, *Amor y pedagogía* 54, 62). If we turn to the objects of this second, intellectualized pleasure, we may be surprised to find *sentiment* included among more plainly spiritual concepts such as goodness, gentility, good sense (*seny*), virtue, and wisdom. As Francisco Rodríguez Risquete notes (Torroella, *Obres completa* 1: 242n9), "sentiment" could refer to both "internal senses" and love itself, and in the former sense, the Catalan tradition tends to group it with the intellectual virtues. Thus Rodrigo Dies, a contemporary of Ausiàs March (Torró, *Sis poetes* 24), could advise that "*seny ni rehó ni sentiment*/ no pot bestar ha fer egual/ l'amor de una dona tal,/ sinó·l voler ab moviment" (I, lines 13–16, emphasis added; "*neither sense nor reason nor sentiment* is enough to make equal the love of such a woman, but only the will with movement").[35] *Moviment* here recalls the Stoic term but also refers to the activated will necessary for amorous reciprocation.[36] As in the case of *sentiment/sentimiento*, this coincidence of the internal and external was exploited with considerable ingenuity by writers such as Torroella, Alegre, and Romeu Llull (c. 1439–96), in the last of whom's *Despropriament d'amor* an exasperated woman complains of the protagonist and men like him: "Si bé de vosaltres los primers moviments solen sempre ésser tals per fer-nos de leuger e fàcilment creure lo que sperimentat no tenim; fent-vos cert que ans que de mi promesa alguna hajau, que lo temps ensemps ab la speriència ne sia mestre delliberat tinch" (Llull 216; "If your first movements tend always to make us lightly and easily believe what we have not experienced, I assure you that before you have any promise from me, I have decided to make time along with experience the master").[37] Here, "primers moviments" can be understood to mean both the courtly lover's attempts at seduction and the impression they incite – thus mirroring Llull's account of his own falling in love, which immediately precedes the lady's sceptical remark: "Per la qual [that is, the lady] vist, per los [senys] incitat, acompanyant aquells lo grat, e consentint-y la voluntat, executant aquella dels tres lo tal delliber, a la dama que sola passajava, humilment e reverent saludada, presa-la per lo bras, a ella me acostí" (215; "Seen by her, sparked by the senses accompanied by *grat*, and with the will's consent, this last executing the intention of all three, I humbly and reverently greeted the lady, who was strolling by herself, taking her by the arm and sidling up to her"). The lady thus presents herself as executing the reasonable judgment (the rejection of treacherous first movements) that the male protagonist, overcome by *grat*, has failed to carry out.

Francesc Alegre (c. 1450–c. 1508–11), author of five sentimental works, translator of Leonardo Bruni's *First Punic War* and Ovid's *Metamorphoses*, and participant – alongside Torroella and Romeu Llull – in the epistolary *Debat sobre la figura d'honor* (*Obres de ficció sentimental* 7–9),[38] puns on *moviments* in his *Requesta d'amor recitant una altercació entre la Voluntat i la Raó* (1472–86), which, as its title indicates, stages a debate between reason and the will.[39] When Reason asks the Will, "Quin desorde assenyalen los vostres no acostumats moviments?" (39; "What disorder do your unusual movements indicate?"), the Will asks in return, "Què us ha mogude en voler-me blasmar, stimant mos moviments y desigs pendra sment e[n] desonesta part, d'on tan lunyats se troben quant mereix son valor? Y vull primer dar-vos rehó com en res de ma honor no falte" (40; "What has moved you to wish to denounce me, believing my movements and desires to be fixed on some dishonest part, from which they are as distant as their worth deserves? And I want to first account for you how nothing is lacking in my honour"). Reason's accusation of disorderly movement in the Will maintains the soul's traditional ethical hierarchy, but the Will seeks to provoke disorder through the rhetoric of its interrogation, attributing to Reason its own passive susceptibility to movement and its own (bad) will ("Què us *ha mogude* en *voler-me* blasmar"). The traditional hierarchy is also threatened by the Will's ability to give reasons, "vull primer dar-vos rehó com." In short, the Will attributes desire to Reason and rationality (as both the ability to reason and to speak persuasively) to itself, frustrating the framework that divides reason from the will and subjects the will to reason's dispassionate judgment.

Thus, Romeu Llull's *Despropriament* separates the experience of *grat* from the consent of the will to the passion of love, and Alegre's *Requesta* complicates the inherited narrative of reason's ideal mastery. The picture is even more complicated in Torroella's response to a *demanda* from the poet Francesc Ferrer on the nature of *grat*.[40] In his poetry, Ferrer portrays *grat*, similarly to Llull, as a force that overpowers the soul's diverse faculties:

> Lo grat, sens pus, és lo qui·m fa l'engan,
> que·en mi rahó no·m pot fer ni desfer,
> que tots ensemps, poder, voler, saber,
> sobrats del grat, tot ço que vol, ells fan.
> E jo, catiu, sostench ma passió
> tant asprament que m'acost a morir. (III, lines 9–14)

> *Grat* and nothing else is what fools me, and reason can do nothing about it, for all together, power, will, knowledge, overcome by *grat*, do all that it wants. And I, captive, bear my passion so harshly that I approach death.

Ferrer's closing declaration of the passionate extremity in which he finds himself emphasizes his total subjection to *grat*, and especially reason's suspension as a cause of, or protection against, mistaken judgments. Yet even this small space between *grat* and the higher powers of the soul is closed in Torroella's analysis:

> Si yo no m'engan, grat és aprobació d'enteniment en aquelles coses que als sentiments se demòstran amables, y és pròpiament lo mitgà per lo qual amor pren forma. Y en aquesta manera, la voluntat és naturalment criada per amar, e aquesta és la proprietat sua. És ver que jamàs se mou per si matexa, mas con als corporals senys algunes coses plazibles se presenten, reportades per aquells al seny comú e fantasia e a l'estimativa e pensament, mira l'enteniment aquelles qu·estima bones, algunes voltes ab consell de l'appetit sensitiu, altres de l'intel·lectiu, qu·és la rahó. E açò és en quant la calitat de les coses e la inclinació del recebent. E segons són dispostes les coses amables al mostrar e los sentiments a compendre, se fa major lo grat d'entre·bdues les parts procehint. Del qual escassament ha vist lo juý, l'enteniment, que la voluntat va presta en amar aquell. E com aquest grat és tan gran per si, nodrit per si matex, los altres sentiments lo seguexen. (2: 227)

> Unless I am mistaken, *grat* is the understanding's approval in those things that show themselves pleasing to the sentiments, and it is properly the medium through which love takes form. And in this way, the will is naturally shaped by loving, and this is its property. It is true that it never moves itself, but rather when some pleasant things present themselves to the bodily senses, reported by these to the common sense and fantasy and to the estimative and thought, the understanding looks at those it considers good, sometimes advised by the sensitive appetite, other times the intellective, which is reason. And that is according to the quality of the things and the inclination of the receiver. And according to how the pleasant things are disposed to show themselves and the sentiments to comprehend them, *grat* increases, proceeding from both parts. Of which the judgment, the understanding have seen little, when the will is ready to love. And as this *grat* is so great in itself, nourished by itself, the other sentiments follow it.

Torroella elevates *grat* by identifying it with the affirmative judgment of the understanding in matters of love. As love's medium, it engages the will through different faculties of perception (the *sensus communis*, *phantasia*/*imaginatio*, *virtus aestimativa*, and *virtus cogitativa*) and through both the sensitive and intellectual appetites.[41] Crucially, *grat* itself originates neither in the perceived object nor in the perceiving (and judging) subject; rather, it "proceeds" from objective qualities and subjective inclinations, and thus allows the will, "naturally called to love," to realize its purpose. Torroella emphasizes above all *grat*'s independence: it is great in and of itself, nourishes itself, and thus it is only natural that the other *sentiments* should follow it. Judgment, although identified in its outcome with *grat*, is in the end scarcely involved.

Torroella goes on to delineate three forms of *grat*. The first, carnal form enters through the eyes and causes "stremes passions," but vanishes once its goal is achieved; carnal *grat* is not properly a form of love, but rather a "furor" (2: 228). The second form occurs when two people with highly compatible natural qualities meet; this *grat* does cause submission to love – "força las castas voluntats a la obediència de Venus y als savis empenyorar lo seny" (2: 228; "it forces chaste wills into obedience to Venus, and the wise to pawn their good sense") – but its highly impulsive movements often cause it to unravel. Finally, there is the *grat* that occurs "migançant rahonabla cognexença entre persones en saber hi en virtuts conformes" (2: 228; "through reasonable recognition between people alike in wisdom and virtue"). This third *grat* begins slowly, because the understanding is engaged before the will, but is ultimately the most furious and forceful of all (2: 228). It is also the form most closely related to friendship: "ha certament gran participació ab amistat" (2: 228). In fact, it only differs from friendship in provoking erotic desire, but even this desire is not an end in itself, only another of the many delights toward which love is naturally inclined (2: 228).

Friendship was itself, of course, a "passion," as Ferrer makes clear in a letter offering advice to the governor of Valencia, Joan Roís de Corella:[42] "Passió de gran amistat no us encegue, ni lige los braços a la rahó" (270; "May the passion of great friendship not blind you, nor bind reason's arms"). The governor should, however, be "friendly" toward pleasing pastimes, especially music: "Hajau per amigablles e familiars tots los migans dels delits e tota art de música, perquè ajuden a comportar mils los treballs a vostra persona e sentiment" (271; "May all forms of delight and all musical art be friendly and familiar to you, for they aid you and your sentiment in better bearing labours"). This reference to the governor's *sentiment* echoes a similar shade of meaning the term takes on in panegyrics associated with the court of Alfonso the Magnanimous. For example, in the *Cancionero de Palacio*, Pedro de Santa Fe praises Isabel de Foxá for her "graçia, sentir et beldat" (CCLXI, line 1; "grace, feeling, and beauty") and her "sentimiento que trahe/ assí la razón perfecta" (CCLXI, lines 7–8; "sentiment that thus bears perfect reason"). Santa Fe's *sentimiento* names an intellectual refinement close to *seny* and thus to reason itself. In a poem to Alfonso himself on the occasion of the king's departure for Naples, Santa Fe offers similar praise: "Non faç tal començamiento/ por sola naturaleza,/ mas su propïa nobleza/ mesclada con sentimiento" (CCLXXI, lines 13–16; "He does not begin such an undertaking by nature alone, but by his own nobility, mixed with sentiment"). In Ferrer's letter, a refined *sentiment* is related to the administration of justice and, in particular, the defence of the innocent, as the musical metaphor in the following passage makes clear: "A l'indefès defeneu-lo, que no solament sou per castigar lo colpablle, mas per defenre e rahonar lo procés de l'ignocent. Altrament, auríem a dir que vostres instruments sonarien més a la part de dolor que de consolació" (271; "Defend the defenceless, for you are not only there to punish the guilty, but to defend and articulate the innocent's case. Otherwise, we would have to say that your instruments sound the painful part louder than the consolation"). Along with music, Ferrer recommends attending recitals of "fictions" and poetry, further "friendly" arts: "Hoïu parenceries e fichcions, perquè és art amigablle la de poesia, e aprofita molt a enbelir los rahonaments; mas vostre repòs sia en filosoffia, que és ben hobrar" (272; "Listen to stories and fictions, for poetry is a friendly art, and helps greatly in beautifying speech; but take repose in philosophy, which is doing good"). Yet this recommendation betrays Ferrer's commitment to a rationalist frame, distinguishing between the ultimately ornamental "rahonaments" of poetry and the practical reason of philosophy, which is not a *delit* but rather a *repòs* similar to Duarte's self-regulatory *folganças*.

Ferrer's letter to Roís de Corella is thus not entirely consonant with the advice he himself received from Torroella, who, after his initial definition of *grat*, offers Ferrer some commonplace remedies for love's passion but concludes that they are unlikely to be effective, going so far as to imply that they are in fact anti-natural:

> Si una de les principals potències de l'ànima, qu·és la voluntat, és apropriada a l'amor, e la principal part del cors, qu·és la concupiscible, tant neguna altra cosa desiga, ab qual part de nosaltres contrastarem a l'Amor? Lo voler l'abrassa, l'enteniment la·n-sercha, la memoria la conserva, lo pensament la nodrex, lo desig la demana, la rahó restant sola entre sí e no, dubtosa calla, e si murmura no troba part ny ajuda que a parlar l'esforce, e si parla neguna cosa demana que contrast a l'amor. (Torroella 2: 230)
>
> If one of the principal faculties of the soul, which is the will, is proper to love, and the principal part of the body, which is the concupiscible, desires no other thing more, with what part will we resist Love? The will embraces it, the understanding pursues it, memory conserves it, thought nourishes it, desire demands it, [and] reason, left alone between "yes" and "no," keeps a doubtful silence, and if it murmurs, it finds no part or help that encourages it to speak, and if it speaks, it asks for nothing that resists love.

Nowhere is courtly scepticism toward the dominant ethos of ascetic rationalism clearer than in Torroella's short letter. Reason is baffled before Love, either silent or abandoned by even thought and the understanding itself, dragooned into Love's service alongside the will and memory. Only the religious, "qui ... de vida d'òmens són transpostats en àngels" (2: 230; "who ... from their life as men are transposed into angels"), can defend themselves.[43] This scepticism is woven thoroughly into Torroella's poetry, as in the exemplary exclamation, "O Passió, que sens poder has fforça,/ la voluntat ffent senyora, sirvente!" (1: V, lines 1–2; "O Passion, without power you have force, making of the servile will a lady").[44] The military puns here on *poder* as "troops" and *força* as *fortí*, "fortress" (1: 233n1) are accompanied by the wry, abstract observation that passion is a more effective cause than the so-called powers of the soul.

In a lengthy epistolary debate with Pedro de Urrea preserved in the same manuscript as the foregoing letter to Ferrer,[45] Torroella criticizes his interlocutor's excessively abstract and generalizing analysis, reiterating the inadequacy of scholastic language, reason, and any kind of ordered naturalism to the understanding of love:

> Mas si la manera de mi razonar a la vuestra non sigue, non vos maravilléys, como yo haya tomado opinión que las generales reglas, los scientes argumentos e los latinados vocablos por a tractar los fechos d'amor non ser assás convenibles, ca muncho han de sí las generales reglas por encerrar en ellas los movimientos d'amor tanto ligieros, delegados e variables quanto en el rayo del sol los átomos aparescen; ni los scientes argumentos podemos buenamente aprovar, que una cosa tanto en sí variable, guiada por voluntad y de la razón enemiga, ¿cómo por ordenada creencia puede ser drechamente seguida? (2: 279–80)

> But if my way of speaking does not follow yours, do not be surprised, for it is my opinion that general rules, knowledgeable arguments, and Latinized words are not appropriate for discussing matters of love, for it is a lot for general rules to themselves enclose the swift movements of love, as delicate and varied as atoms appear in a ray of sun; nor can we rightly approve of knowledgeable arguments, for something so variable in itself, guided by the will and an enemy of reason, how can it be rightly followed by orderly belief?

Torroella here once again draws attention to the fact that the genre of discourse known as "reasoning" ("mi razonar") is not apt for a passion so capricious in its movements as to defy the "general rules" of natural order. Love becomes, like Fortune and *grat*, a self-causing phenomenon that cannot be described, let alone tamed, by reason. The suffering caused by unrequited love leaves reason at an impasse, torn between "yes" and "no," unable to make a judgment and thus to speak or be heard: *dubtosa calla*.

Torroella's debate with Urrea revolves around a hypothetical comparison, posed by Torroella, of two women, identical in virtue, beauty, wisdom, and graciousness, who love and are loved by two worthy young men. One of the women is prevented from acting on her love by jealous guardians, but the other is at war with herself owing to "some opinions," wasting away as she resists her own desire (2: 261). The question, then, is which of the two suffers more, the one battling opportunity (*avinentesa*) or the one battling herself. Torroella takes the latter's side, suggesting that, in the case of the guarded woman, who gives herself over to love but cannot act on it, reason is dominating love ("rige Amor la razón"), and because reason seeks the good, eventually love's goal will be achieved (2: 281–2). The woman at war with herself, however, can be compared to the protagonist of the following passage from Rodríguez del Padrón's "Siete gozos de Amor":

> Como el qui es puesto a tormiento
> por fuerça
> su mal viene a confessar,
> e tornado al sentimiento
> más s'esfuerça
> de lo encobrir e negar. (Torroella 2: 282)[46]

> Like the one who is tortured and forced to confess his evil, and returning to his senses, tries even harder to hide and deny it.

None should dare call any other suffering equal to that agony: "No sea, por Dios, pues, ninguna passión aquesta igualada, por la piadat de la qual ruego Aquel que solo cuentra Amor puede que, con algún medio a ella plaziente e no al amante enojoso, ponga a sus males determinado fin" (2: 282; "Let no suffering be compared to this, for the pity of which I ask Him who alone can triumph over Love to, in some way pleasing to her and not obnoxious to the lover, bring her ills to a determined end"). The woman's resolution to resist love in silence represents not reason's victory but its defeat; like reason, she is paralyzed between "yes" and "no," and the pity of the situation is such that only through divine intervention might a happy resolution be achieved.

This letter is the first in the exchange to conclude with a quotation, but it will not be the last: Urrea, in his reply, concludes with lines 45–8 from Ausiàs March LXXXVIII, "Malament viu qui delit pert de viure," a poem in which March suggests that reason does – for better or for worse – have power over the passions.[47] Torroella, in his reply, lists a genealogy of love poets – Petrarch, Ausiàs March, Santillana, Arnaut Daniel, and Jean de Meun, among others – whose verse reveals love's fundamentally paradoxical nature.[48] In a passage that recalls both Cartagena's advice to Santillana and Madrigal's thought on self-communication, Torroella reiterates that inner conflict is the greatest passion:

> Quanto de cosas más conjuntes, semejantes e más allegadas al contracte proceye, tanto mayor, más fuerte e más continua es la pasión; conoscida la fuerça que los semejantes torna contrarios, dexa en mayor grado el danyo de la contradición, que entre los vecinos es más que en otra parte danyosa. Quien consigo non ha paç, de ninguna cosa es seguro, e quien ha a sí mesmo guerra de todos es offendido. Roma, de muchos grandes e foranos enemigos contrastada, victoriosa pasó; mas la guerra, dentro sus muros venida, de su presta desolación fue causa. (2: 293)

> The more it proceeds from things that are united, similar, and given to conflict, the greater, stronger, and more continual is passion; when the force that turns similar things into opposites is known, it raises to a greater degree the harm of contradiction, which is more harmful in neighbours than anywhere else. He who does not have peace with himself is safe from nothing, and he who makes war on himself is offended by all. Rome, attacked by many great and foreign enemies, emerged victorious; but war within its walls caused its swift destruction.

Torroella concludes the paragraph with his own citation, lines 2–3 from Ausiàs March LXX, "Per què m'és tolt poder delliberar?": "La mort no·ns fa tant mal, a mon parer,/ com gran contrast dins si matex haver" ("Death does not do us such harm, it seems to me, as having great conflict within us").[49] He thus transposes very directly the "courtly conflicts" defining, in Cartagena's view, the military and political crisis in Castile and beyond into the language of courtly verse. The "living death" of the courtly lover – Torroella in his *demanda* to Urrea says that the conflicted lady "vive no vida, mas una manera de muerte que moriendo le consiente bevir" (2: 261; "does not live life, but rather a kind of death that permits her to live dying") – mirrors civil conflict precisely because it is a question of "contrary sameness" rather than essential difference. And, as paradoxical inner conflict – self-contradiction – it is beyond the reach of reason.

In fact, Ausiàs March himself, in poem LXXXVII, "Tot entenent amador mi entengua" – the most extensive exposition of March's theory of love and the roles of body and soul therein – confirms his belief that this conflicted form of inner desire, the very one of which the troubadours write, is situated outside of the rational soul:[50]

> D'aquest voler los trobadors escriuen,
> e, per aquest, dolor mortal los toca;
> la racional part de l'arma no·ls broca;
> del sensual aquests apetits viuen.
> Ésser bé pot que l'om simplament ame:
> d'arma sens cors e ab lo cors sens arma;
> amant virtut, hom de tal amor s'arma,[51]
> y el cors és cert que d'un brut voler brame. (*Poesies*, lines 41–8)

> It is this will that poets talk of, and through it mortal pain afflicts them. It is not the rational part of the soul which spurs them on: such appetites thrive on the sensual will. It is quite possible for man to love simply, with the spirit and without the body, and with the body but without the soul. If a man loves virtue, then it is with such love that he arms himself, while there is no doubt that the body, for its part, groans with a brutish desire. (Trans. Robert Archer)[52]

The mixed will of troubadour love is thus distinctly human yet resolutely irrational. Indeed, although a peaceful truce between carnal and spiritual desire produces marvels (lines 55–7), it is best for these wills to remain conflicted, precisely because their agreement draws the soul away from reason and leads the body toward death (lines 58–60).[53] Furthermore, the pleasure (*delit*) achieved through this mixed desire when it is in harmony is brief (lines 301–2). By contrast, purely spiritual love, attained through the understanding, produces entirely harmonious desires (lines 141–8), and March asserts that it is strong enough to defeat other forms of love (lines 181–4). Yet the long autobiographical reflection that brings the poem to a close (lines 201–34) describes the poet's apocalyptic, boastful, yet unfinished struggle to achieve this happy form of love, freeing himself from mixed desire and its attendant delights. As I will show in chapter seven, even the doctrinal rationalist certainty of this poem is shaken in the face of the beloved's death.

Who may speak while reason keeps a doubtful silence? Torroella's letters to Urrea invoke Juan Rodríguez del Padrón, whose denied but versified confession moves its audience to pity, and Ausiàs March, whose self-contradictory approach to reason and love lays bare the depths of courtly suffering. This, suggests Torroella, is the way out of rationalism's impasse: a collective externalization of inner conflict and contradiction, a creative method based on citation and repetition. The entire exchange between Torroella and Urrea is highly instructive in this sense. They communicate in Castilian, but quote freely in Castilian or Catalan, constructing the Iberian courtly tradition as a resource for thought that, for Torroella in particular, avoids the misguided idealism of scholastic, medical, and ethical discourse.[54] The point is not only that lyric better captures the problem in its taste for antithesis and paradox, but that lyric's mode of composition complements its conceptual substance such that it allows for creative speech, whereas doctrinaire rationalism leads to a verbal paralysis preliminary to, and perhaps worse than, death. In part two, I will explore two areas of emotional discourse, compassion and consolation, that, initially in poetry and then, increasingly, in sentimental prose, sought ways out of reason's impasse without bracketing the erotic in favour of friendship. Rather, as in the case of Torroella's ideal *grat*, which participates in but is not circumscribed by friendship, they seek to outline a path in which the creativity of conflicting passions can be shared across and among subjects.

PART TWO

Compassion and Consolation

¿Éstas son sus congoxas? ¡Como si solamente el amor contra él asestara sus tiros!

– Fernando de Rojas, *La Celestina*

Chapter Four

Impassibility, Pity, Community

Facing the impasse, internal and external, of ascetic rationalism, Iberian authors developed an alternative discourse of both the passions and the common that was nonetheless composed largely of the same key concepts: reason, the will, desire, discretion and prudence, love, sadness. As troubadours had always done, they sought to use the same language to say something different. This difference was rhetorical in two ways. First, in the compositional sense: they drew on the formal resources of troubadour lyric and developed a novel genre of sentimental prose to reshape the meaning and ethical valence of feelings of all kinds. Second, in the demonstrative sense: their poetry and prose models an ethics of fellow feeling through a highly conceptualized, analytical display of suffering. This display can be described as "passionate," not only in connoting at once suffering and hyperbolic emotion but also, in the authors to be discussed in this chapter, in frequent allusions, alternately sly and overt, to Christ's Passion and the metaphysics behind it.[1] Such allusions were not just sublimating or parodic instances of the *religio amoris* (see the discussion later in this chapter and in chapter five); rather, they offered authors a language and conceptual framework for exploring at once their own compositional methods and the relationship between Christian Passion and worldly compassion, so frequently invoked in the many traditions of troubadour verse.

In this chapter, I explore the early Christian and monastic roots of the notions of passion and compassion that emerge at the turn of the fifteenth century in Castilian and Catalan verse. I then show, through readings of Pero López de Ayala's *Libro rimado de Palacio* and Santillana's *Gozos de Santa María,* how ideas about lyric poetry in particular were associated with compassion and consolation. I conclude by exploring how modes of lyric composition that proceed through the incorporation of verse quotations relate to the metaphysics of the Passion along both Mariological and Christological lines. The relationship I outline lays the groundwork for my discussion, in the remaining chapters of part two, of intersubjective ethics in the Iberian songbooks and sentimental fiction of the fifteenth century.

Compassion and suffering were not, of course, the only emotions of troubadour discourse, but rather were woven into a broader network including friendship, pleasure, pity, anger, fear, and love itself. As the fifteenth century advanced, literary approaches to these emotions became increasingly dense and abstract in both poetry and prose, with later texts making explicit relationships that were explored elliptically and allusively by earlier Iberian poets. Yet even these apparently more systematizing texts raise difficult questions about the sentiments they describe. The first stanza of a song by Diego de San Pedro, to whose concluding stanza I will return later, makes manifest the tangle of emotional concepts in which explorations of passion and compassion were articulated:

Pues no sufre lo que siento
que biva con tal passión,
sufra vuestra compassión
que se salve el sentimiento
en la fe del coraçón.
Y si pïedad ninguna
no tenéis con vos aquí,
yo's podré prestar alguna
de la que tengo de mí. (9, lines 1–9)[2]

Since what I feel does not permit me to live with such passion, may your compassion allow this feeling to be saved in the heart's faith. And if you have no pity with you here, I can offer you some from the pity I have for myself.

These nine short lines deploy the concepts of suffering (in both *sufrir* and *pasión*), feeling, compassion, faith, and pity; the only apparently concrete noun, *corazón*, is of course metonymous for another host of emotional concepts. Just as *piedad* encompasses both religious and secular notions of fellow feeling, *fe* is a courtly synonym for amorous passion, as in the first words – a repeated lament – spoken by Leriano in San Pedro's best-known work, *Cárcel de amor*: "En mi fe, se sufre todo" (*Obras completas, II* 81).[3] Yet the religious notion of faith, even before San Pedro refers to Christ's Passion in the second stanza, is undoubtedly activated not only by proximity to the polysemic *piedad* but also by the notion of salvation that arises in the previous line. This dense tangle of abstract emotion raises questions that are potentially intractable: Do "compassion" and "pity" name two separate concepts here, or is this merely a case of inelegant variation? Does the notion of "passion" always and everywhere activate the religious connotations of suffering and faith? And if so, is this just a late and meaningless instance of the archi-conventional sacred hyperbole found from the very beginnings of courtly verse in Castilian, subject to the "semantic diffusion" that led to the aesthetic rejection of *cancionero* verse by early philologists (Whinnom, "Towards" 122)?

San Pedro is asking here, after all, for the highly conventional *galardón* (reward), most often figured in *cancionero* verse as *merced*, *compasión*, or *piedad*. If we turn to early lexicographical sources, such as Covarrubias's *Tesoro*, to try to get to the bottom of these terms as they were used in this particular time and place, we find that *merced*, for example, signified *galardón* both in the sense of a reward owed for prior service and of something given freely; but already, the sense of "mercy" appears in the expression *darse a merced*, that is, to place oneself at the mercy of one's enemy (546–7). *Piedad*, meanwhile, denotes the quality of *mercy* above all (*misericordioso*; 588), and yet one cannot help but detect the notion of *piety*, as devout, but also simply officious or courteous, behaviour in the descriptions of feminine virtue found throughout *cancionero* verse and sentimental fiction. At times, all three of these notions appear to function interchangeably; at other times, to emphasize different qualities. And in addition to these "sincere" senses, there is also the vast potential of the *galardón*, like its occasional antithesis, *la muerte*, to function as a sexual euphemism (Whinnom, *Spanish Literary Historiography* 105–6; "Towards" 123–7).

Beyond the polysemous nature of these key terms of courtly discourse on the emotions, there is also the spectre of inconsistent usage on the part of individual authors. As such, the question of the *galardón* as mercy, compassion, or pity functions as a microcosm of the difficulties presented by purely philological approaches to the analysis of historical discourses on emotion. A way out of this conundrum is suggested by two other features of San Pedro's poem: the commonplace notion of the lyric voice's impending death from lovesickness and the notion of a pity that transcends interiority arising from the ironic loan proposed by the lyric voice in the stanza's closing lines. As we have seen, writers interested in the emotions in fifteenth-century Iberia inherited from the Stoics and early Christian ascetics a rationalist system whose constraints they sought to loosen. This system was not, of course, the only discourse on the emotions available to them, although it was certainly the one they cited the most directly. Even as other Christian authorities – and sometimes, in fact, the same ones – remained broadly sceptical of the will and of literary pursuits, they articulated a role for emotions other than charity, such as sorrow and compunction, in prayer and in the pursuit of spiritual knowledge. In the exegesis of figures such as Bernard of Clairvaux, desire and experience became central to the pursuit of spiritual knowledge (Leclercq 5). Such an application of emotional experience, although highly relevant to individual prayer and contemplation, was bound up with communal forms of life and worship, and therefore with Christian conceptions of social relations as such. These conceptions drew their ultimate justification from Christ's experience of suffering, which had been voluntary but was necessary from the perspective of a properly human redemption. Yet writers looking to the Passion as a literary and ethical resource also had to confront orthodox scepticism toward classical accounts of literary compassion and toward the appetitive will as such.

Augustine, in the *Confessions*, describes passion as the "consequence of a distorted will" (VIII.v.10), and he famously expresses sardonic scepticism toward the pity inspired by literature: "What is more pitiable than a wretch without pity for himself who weeps over the death of Dido dying for love of Aeneas, but not weeping over himself dying for his lack of love for you, my God?" (I.xiii.21). Even more famous is his condemnation of the apparently pleasurable suffering provoked by tragic theatre (III.ii.2–3), which he contrasts with "authentic compassion," which is free of pleasure:

> Today I have more pity for a person who rejoices in wickedness than for a person who has the feeling of having suffered hard knocks by being deprived of a pernicious pleasure or having lost a source of miserable felicity. This is surely a more authentic compassion; for the sorrow contains no element of pleasure [*haec certe verior misericordia, sed non in ea delectat dolor*][4] … Even if we approve of a person who, from a sense of duty in charity, is sorry for a wretch, yet he who manifests fraternal compassion would prefer that there be no cause for sorrow. It is only if there could be a malicious good will (which is impossible) that someone who truly and sincerely felt compassion would wish wretches to exist so as to be objects of compassion. Therefore some kind of suffering is commendable, but none is lovable. You, Lord God, lover of souls, show a compassion far purer and freer of mixed motives than ours; for no suffering injures you. (III.ii.3)

The duplicitous (because ill-intentioned) mercy inspired by "fictitious and theatrical inventions" (III.ii.2) is thus to be distinguished from the "commendable" pity one feels for an unrepentant sinner – but even the latter pales before the perfection of divine compassion, a perfection resting paradoxically on divine impassibility (in effect, a compassion without passion). It is also key here that tragic pity is purely passive: "A member of the audience is not excited to offer help, but invited only to grieve" (III.ii.2).[5] Augustine, despite his abiding interest in rhetoric and signification, thus shows himself to be sceptical of secular art's edifying role in inspiring fellow feeling. Nevertheless, an alternative relationship between compassion and composition grounds his *Confessions*, which opens with repeated invocations of divine mercy: "Have mercy so that I may find words" (I.v.5); "Nevertheless allow me to speak before your mercy, though I am but dust and ashes (Gen. 18:27). Allow me to speak: for I am addressing your mercy, not a man who would laugh at me. Perhaps even you deride me (cf. Ps. 2:4), but you will turn and have mercy on me (Jer. 12:15)" (I.vi.7). Divine mercy is both the origin and audience of the work.

A similar tension between, on the one hand, scepticism toward the human will and secular literature and, on the other, a productive role for sorrow and mercy in prayer and contemplation is repeated in varying ways by monastic writers. Evagrius of Pontus defined the practical life of the monk as "the spiritual method for purifying the passionate part of the soul" (Sinkewicz 110), and his disciple, John

Cassian, asserts that only the prayers of a mind "cleansed of all the dregs of the passions" may reach God (331–2). The initiate reading the *Rule of Benedict* (c. 540) is instructed: "Hate your own will" (Benedict 18). Early Christian monastics thus undoubtedly sought impassibility, their own form of *apatheia*, but at the same time, their commitment to *caritas* and compassion as elements of Christian dogma changed their ethical approach to questions of emotion. This delicate balance has been described by Thomas Dixon as a "Christian desire to say both – against the Stoics – that some human feeling or affection is proper and necessary to this life, but also that God, the angels and perfected humans are free from the turmoil and perturbations of sin and the passions" (61). The emotion of pity was one of the key pivots of these changes, as these thinkers revised Stoic ideas about pity in order "to avoid a disastrous scenario in which pity's moral intelligence degenerated into a fallacious logic of justice unbecoming of the gospel's injunctions of undiscriminating love of neighbor" (Blowers 8). In this revision, "the higher goal was the christocentric reconstruction of pity and empathetic mercy as *theologically virtuous* emotions, deifying emotions" (27; emphasis in original). In other words, Christ himself and Christ's Passion became the models for the rehabilitation of pity as compassion. As the Middle Ages progressed, the ascent implied by this "deification" took on increasingly epistemological tones, as compassion became not just an ethical obligation but a tool for exegesis and the rhetorical composition of prayer in monastic settings.

We should not lose sight of the fact that the monastic pursuit of impassibility was undertaken in community. It was through the codification of the emotions, or "thoughts," as deadly sins in this communal context that compassion and empathy became central concerns of hermeneutics, which itself took on increasingly rhetorical characteristics as the Middle Ages progressed. The designation of what came to be called passions and, later, emotions as "thoughts" is telling in this regard. Ultimately, the Desert Fathers and their medieval followers bent the cognitive elements of emotion toward the pursuit of divine knowledge through affective prayer and contemplation. It should be remembered, of course, that as this transformation took place, emotion never lost its pre-eminent role in theories of vice and virtue. Furthermore, although these modes of prayer could be undertaken in isolation, they remained permeated by a sense of collective invention.[6]

It was Evagrius of Pontus (c. 345–99 CE), an early Desert Father from the town of Ibora in Helenopontus, who first identified "eight thoughts" that troubled monks: gluttony, fornication, avarice, sadness, anger, acedia, vainglory, and pride.[7] The model of how these thoughts overcome a monk in his "Treatise on the Practical Life" owed much to Stoic theories that emphasized assent or decision: "Whether or not all these thoughts trouble the soul is not within our power; but it is for us to decide if they are to linger within us or not and whether or not they stir up the passions" (97–8).[8] Evagrius also accepted Plato's tripartite division of the soul, arguing that the practical life purified its two passionate parts (110). Thus, in its early forms, monastic thought internalized both Platonic and Stoic models of soul and emotion, seeking, through a shared holy life, an "impassible" tranquility from which to practice divine contemplation.[9]

At the same time, certain emotions played an increasingly important role in monastic prayer. In his *Conferences*, Cassian adopts Evagrius's model of the "thoughts" and assent (1.17.1), but he also consistently associates prayer with the tears provoked by a feeling of compunction, saving sorrow. Forced tears are discouraged because, like Evagrius's demonic thoughts, they "drag down the mind of the person praying, to lower it, submerge it in human concerns, and displace it from that heavenly height whereon the awed mind of the one praying should be irremovably stationed" (9.30.1–2). The sources of compunction are many and varied, but the power of compunction to move the heart to prayer (and thereby to contemplation) is not condemned as necessarily contaminated with sinful passions or carnal desires.

Cassian goes farther in carving out a productive role for affective participation in his recommendation of contemplating and memorizing the Psalms. Repetition of the Psalms leads to identification with the prophet and an initial feeling that the repeated words are "daily borne out and fulfilled in [the monk]" (10.11.4). This phenomenon is developed into a broader paradigm of empathetic hermeneutics: "Thriving on the pasturage that [the Psalms] always offer and taking into himself all the dispositions of the psalms, [the monk] will begin to repeat them and to treat them in his profound compunction of heart not as if they were composed by the prophet but as if they were his own utterances and his own prayer (10.11.4)." Interpretation and composition are melded here in a process parallel to the empathetic melding of prophet and monk through compunction.[10] Eventually, "experience" becomes the monk's guide to the meaning of the biblical text: "When we have the same disposition in our heart with which each psalm was sung or written down, then we shall become like its author, grasping its significance beforehand rather than afterward" (10.11.5). This passage's move from audience and interpreter to author suggests the close relationship that will develop between rhetoric and hermeneutics in the later Middle Ages, and it is no coincidence that emotion serves as their articulation, allowing for the temporal jump to the moment before meaning is enunciated. This method is crucial not only for scriptural interpretation but, as Cassian suggests, for the broader project of communal pedagogy represented by the monastic movement. The experience of shared emotion is the best hermeneutic for grasping "the very nature of things" – worldly and divine.

Two important phenomena are forming here. The first involves the status of praxis in the "hermeneutic spiral," in which, as Douglas Burton-Christie has argued, "interpretation both derived from and led toward praxis" (165). In the desert, "Scripture was seen as the source of praxis; praxis acted as an organizing principle which sent one to search for particular texts; these texts in turn deepened and purified praxis and clarified its purpose and meaning" (171–2). This belief led to a kind of experiential hermeneutics of personification: "The ultimate expression of the desert hermeneutic was a *person*, one who embodied the sacred texts and who drew others out of themselves into a world of infinite possibilities" (300; emphasis in original). This hermeneutics, in turn, leads Cassian to emphasize judgment and community in discussing discretion, which is achieved through humility, submission to the elders' exemplarity. Those who lack discretion trust disastrously in their own judgment: "Whoever lives not by his own judgment but by the example of our forebears shall never be deceived, nor shall the crafty foe be able to take advantage of the ignorance of a person who does not know how to hide all the thoughts coming to birth in his heart" (2.10.2). Those seeking to avoid temptation consulted exemplary figures in hopes of receiving a "word," such that "the words of elders and of Scripture constituted a double tradition of authority for those living in the desert" (Burton-Christie 110). This practice lays bare how at least one form of "authority" implied the necessity of community for interpretation; communal experience and example are the best hermeneutic for the sinful temptation of the emotional thoughts whose source, more often than not, is demonic.[11] The outcome of willful individual emotion is misinterpretation.[12] Courtly poets in fifteenth-century Iberia will become conscious of themselves as members of such an emotional interpretive community, and the ethical outlook of their amorous and pseudo-religious songs will, in turn, reflect this consciousness.

The emotional rhetoric of this courtly literature reflects a second important phenomenon involving the *productivity* of emotion (compunction) for both interpretation and what Mary Carruthers has called the "craft of thought." Carruthers takes as her starting point the Desert Fathers' concept of *mneme theou*, "memory of God" (2), noting further, however, that for the Desert Fathers, "memory" means something closer to "cognition," "the construction of thinking," such that "monastic meditation is the craft of making thoughts about God" (2). It was for this reason that monastic rhetoric emphasized "invention" and was thus "practiced primarily as a craft of composition" (3) whose main material was *phantasiai*, mental images that were "emotionally laden" (14). Contemplation based on these images is thus tied, through emotion, to rhetoric's productive *inventio* and to its central place in practical wisdom: "The matters memory presents are used to persuade and motivate, to create emotion and stir the will ... Though it is certainly a form of knowing, recollecting is also a matter of will, of being *moved*, pre-eminently a moral activity rather than what we think of as intellectual or rational" (67–8). As Carruthers later notes, the compunction provoked by this process was both "the beginning of prayer" (96) – as a process of rhetorical invention – and an essential element of monastic reading practices (100).[13] The productive space carved out for compunction by the Desert Fathers thus brought rhetoric and hermeneutics into very close contact, and this space of contact was morally charged through the concepts of praxis, example, and sin.[14]

Even the sceptical Augustine began to develop an epistemology of compassion. In the final and most directly rhetorical book of *On Christian Doctrine*, Augustine takes a scriptural approach, adopting Cicero's doctrine of teaching, giving pleasure, and moving audiences (4.17.34) and illustrating it through examples from the gospels.[15] When used by a teacher, this last method leads to a collapse, similar to the one described by Cassian for monks reading the Psalms, of speaker and audience, teacher and learner: "For so great is the power of sympathy, that when people are affected by us as we speak and we by them as they learn, we dwell each in the other and thus both they, as it were, speak in us what they hear, while we, after a fashion, learn in them what we teach" (Augustine, *First Catechetical Instruction* 12.17).[16] These models of reading and preaching illustrate how, as Rita Copeland has written, "medieval exegesis replicates rhetoric's productive application to discourse" (64). Compassion, a step in the individual ascent toward divine knowledge through correct interpretation, becomes a pedagogical tool for preachers, who are also, through the practice of charity, purifying their own will.

Christ's example is pivotal in this pedagogical approach because exegetical mysteries can be explained as the result of concessions to our human condition, concessions that were also reflected in the Incarnation (Brown 24). In later monastic thought, then, Christ-like purification through compassion becomes an explicit epistemological model. This is especially true in Bernard of Clairvaux's "On the Steps of Humility and Pride" (c. 1124), which takes as its starting point Benedict's chapter on humility. Here, Bernard elaborates a three-step approach to Truth through humility: "For we seek truth in ourselves, in our neighbors, and for its own sake … We seek it in ourselves in judging ourselves (1 Cor 11:31), in our neighbors by suffering with them (1 Cor 12:26), and in itself by contemplating it with a pure heart (Mt 5:8)" (III.6). Bernard echoes Augustine when he writes that the merciful will have "hearts purified by brotherly love" (III.6). Experience again plays a crucial role in this compassionate ascent, with Christ's Passion as a key example:

> But to have a heart which is sad because of someone else's wretchedness you must first recognize your neighbor's mind in your own and understand from your own experience how you can help him. We have an example in our Savior. He wanted to suffer so that he should know how to suffer with us (Heb 2:17), to become wretched so that he could learn mercy, as it is written, "He learned obedience from the things he suffered" (Heb 5:8). He learned mercy in the same way. It is not that he did not know how to be merciful before. His mercy is from everlasting to everlasting (Ps 102:17). But what he knew by nature from eternity he learned from experience in time. (III.6)[17]

If Christ's entrance into time was the scandal of early Christianity (Cullmann 24), Bernard makes here the potentially scandalous claim that Christ learned something – mercy – during his time as a man. Conversely, mercy becomes here an explicitly deifying emotion, as contemplatives make spiritual progress by emulating Christ's example. Christ's suffering also raises the question, alluded to by Blowers earlier, of divine impassibility:

> I do not doubt that [God] was impassible before he emptied himself and took the form of a servant (Phil 2:7), for just as he had not experienced wretchedness and subjection, so he had not known mercy or obedience by experience. He knew by nature, but not by experience … He lowered himself to that form in which he could suffer and be in subjection, for, as it is said, what he could not suffer in his divine nature he learned by the experience of suffering: mercy, and to be obedient in subjection … Yet by that experience there grew, as I have said, not his knowledge but our faith, when by this wretched mode of knowledge he who had gone far astray brought himself near to us (Eph 2:13). When should we have dared to approach him if he had remained impassible? … But now, with the Apostle's encouragement, we are urged to come in faith to the throne of his grace (Heb 4:16), for, as it is written elsewhere, we know that he bore our weariness and grief (Is 53:4), and we can be sure he will have compassion on us because he has suffered himself (Heb 2:18, 4:15). (Bernard, "On the Steps" III.9)

Bernard answers the objection that the impassible divine cannot truly suffer by attributing to the incarnate Christ a similar rhetorical motive to the one that accounts for mysterious scriptural passages:

> He did not intend to remain wretched among them, but to free those who were wretched as one made merciful. "Made merciful" (Heb 2:17), I say, not with that mercy which he who remained happy had had from eternity (Ps 102:17), but with that mercy which he discovered as a mediator who was one of us. The work of his holiness, which began at the prompting of the first mercy, was completed in the second; not because the first mercy was not enough, but because only the second kind could fully satisfy us. Both were needed, but the second kind fitted our condition better. (III.12)

The Incarnation becomes here a kind of divine *kairos*: Christ's suffering is fitted to our condition, not God's, and therefore it is our faith, not Christ's knowledge, that it feeds. Not just our faith, however – our knowledge, as well. Bernard admonishes his audience that if they are not merciful, neither will they be good teachers (IV.13). Mercy is a pedagogical and pastoral necessity.

At the same time, mercy remains key to spiritual ascent. Bernard analyses the three steps of the ascent (humility, compassion, and contemplation) to the Persons of the Trinity, and explains that the first step is achieved through reason, the second through affection, and the third through purity (VI.19). Through this epistemological model based on compassion, Bernard resolves the conflict of reason and the passions. The Son empowers our reason, whose judgment makes us humble; the Holy Spirit empowers our compassion, which purifies the will. The Father then gathers this soul purified in reason and will to himself, allowing for divine contemplation (VII.21). Affective participation, possible everywhere but fostered in monastic communities as a devotional practice, imparts both individual virtue and divine wisdom.

Similarity and participation arise repeatedly in the sayings attributed to Bernard in the *Floresta de philósophos*, traditionally attributed to Fernán Pérez de Guzmán (c. 1377–1460), Santillana's uncle and himself a key Castilian cultural figure, as both poet and historian, in the first half of the fifteenth century.[18] Among the first of Bernard's sayings compiled by Pérez de Guzmán are the following two, which are consecutive and seem to form an enthymematic ethical argument:[19]

> 2071. Entre el fijo de Dios e nos grand parentesco ay, ca el es fecho a la ymagen de Dios, e nos a la suya.
> 2072. El que es fecho a la ymagen de otro conviene que concuerde con su ymagen e non trayga consigo en vano el nombre de la ymagen. (96)
>
> 2071. There is a close relationship between the son of God and us, for he is made in the image of God, and we in his.
> 2072. He who is made in the image of another should match that image and not bear the name of the image in vain.

A series of later sentences clarify the stakes of concordance (or vain discordance) with the divine image:

> 2100. Quien ama a si non deve amar a Dios, e quien ama a Dios ama al proximo. (98)
> 2106. Honrra grande es a Dios semejarle nos e darle reverencia.
> 2107. A Dios semeja quien es piadoso, e a Dios semeja quien es misericordioso. (99)
> 2112. Quien non es ayuntado con Dios es partido de si mesmo. (99)
>
> 2100. He who loves himself should not love God, and he who loves God should love his neighbour.
> 2106. It is a great honour to resemble God and give him reverence.
> 2107. The pious resemble God, and the merciful resemble God.
> 2112. He who is not united with God is separated from himself.

Taken together, these sentences delineate a spiritual ethics in which self-love is, paradoxically, a form of self-estrangement. Concordance with the divine image consists in following the double commandment to love God and neighbour. Union with the divine, meanwhile, is not figured as a loss of self (as sometimes occurs in mystical discourse), but rather as union with the truest self. Pity and compassion are thus a matter of divine resemblance, not only as a matter of moral exemplarity but ontologically, as the only guarantee of one's own unity. When this form of love is directed toward the self, it is comparable to alms as a sign of charity: "2331. La limosna que el hombre a su anima debe es caridad e misericordia" (112; "The alms one owes to one's soul are charity and mercy").[20] Completing the circle, just as love of God implies love of neighbour, love of neighbour is a necessary condition for divine love: "2186. El que non ama a su proximo que ve, como amara a Dios que non vee?" (104; "How will the one who does not love the neighbour he sees love God, whom he does not see?"). Finally, the sayings about consolation compiled by Pérez de Guzmán follow the same trajectory as those about divine love and participation:

> 2151. Aquellos que de aqueste mundo son consolados non son dignos de la consolacion de Dios.
> 2152. Muy justa cosa es que quien participa con Dios en la tribulacion participe con el en la consolacion. (102)
>
> 2151. Those who are consoled by this world are not worthy of God's consolation.
> 2152. It is very just that the one who shares in God's tribulation share also in God's consolation.

Self-love and other worldly pleasures are a distraction from divine contemplation, contrasted explicitly with the love of God without which reading and prayer are themselves vain.[21] Compassion – "participation with God in tribulation" – is itself a form of consolation. This Christian ethics of compassion, although doubtless an important context for the "proto-humanist" interest in Stoic thought on mercy and clemency discussed in part one, is directly cited much less frequently than the classical virtue ethics of Seneca and Cicero (authors on whom Pérez de Guzmán also drew liberally in compiling the *Floresta*). I seek to demonstrate in what follows that it nevertheless underlies the courtly discourse of mercy, compassion, and consolation so urgently explored across fifteenth-century Iberia in songbooks and, later, in sentimental fiction. That courtly discourse is sometimes modelled on, and parodic of, religious discourse is of course well known, in the Iberian context and beyond; my specific argument is that the Iberian sentimental literature of this period explores this ambivalent relationship as an answer to the impasse of ascetic ethics – as, in other words, a renewed ethical resource in which certain emotions are rehabilitated for the purposes of civic concord.

Piety and the Emergence of Castilian Lyric

The various monastic orders were, of course, deeply entwined with temporal power centres throughout Portugal, Castile, and Aragon. We have seen, from the examples of Pedro's *LVB* and Duarte's *LC*, the crucial role that royal confessors played in the intellectual life of the Avis dynasty. Although the well-known concept of sacred monarchy was not dominant in Iberia – in Teófilo F. Ruiz's pithy phrase, "those who ruled and those who wanted to rule had, more often than not, one body instead of two" ("Unsacred Monarchy" 131) – the Trastámaran dynasty was deeply involved in ecclesiastical politics, and its kings did not shy away from promoting themselves through religious imagery.[22] The most common form of royal portrait during the Trastámaran reign was the "rey orante," and liturgical ceremonies played a much wider role in Trastámaran propaganda than they had in previous dynasties (Nieto Soria, "Del rey oculto" 18, 22). Private devotion was also a political matter; thus, the royal confessor played an increasingly important role in the Castilian court and was often a key liaison between the crown and the confessor's monastic order (Nieto Soria, *Iglesia y genesis* 141). The Franciscans were particularly involved in both Portuguese and Castilian political culture (Gomes 149–50; Nieto Soria, *Iglesia y génesis* 245), and although it initially faced resistance from the Galician pactual monastic tradition, broadly speaking, from the thirteenth century onward, Benedictine monasticism in its various forms was dominant in Iberia (Bishko 41; cf. Álvarez Palenzuela 163–5). The Cistercians, meanwhile, received important support from the crowns of Castile and Aragon, with the bulk of foundations taking place in the second half of the twelfth century; Bernard's order also inspired the military orders of Calatrava and Alcántara (Álvarez Palenzuela 170–1).

Santillana is himself portrayed as an *orante* in his well-known portrait from Jorge Inglés's *Retablo de los Gozos de Santa María* (1455; *Altarpiece of the Joys of Holy Mary*), commissioned by the Marquis himself. The altarpiece, which also features a portrait of Augustine, derives its name from Santillana's eponymous poem, whose verses are incorporated in scrolls displayed by angels in the altarpiece's upper panels.[23] Santillana's poem, in turn, belongs to the long Iberian literary tradition of Marian devotion, which, in Castile, most famously includes Alfonso X's *Cantigas de Santa María* (1270–82) and Gonzalo de Berceo's *Milagros de Nuestra Señora* (c. 1246–52).[24] More specifically, these *Gozos* belong to the lyric genre that celebrates the Joys of the Virgin, of which Alfonso X's first *Cantiga de Santa Maria* is one example; Juan Ruiz's *Libro de buen amor* (*LBA*; 1330–43) includes four more (stanzas 20–32, 33–43, 1635–41, and 1642–8).[25] Ruiz presents his first versification of the Joys as a way of seeking consolation from Christ: "Gáname gracia e bendiçión/ e de Jhesú consolaçión/ que pueda con devoçión/ cantar de tu alegría" (21; "Win for me grace and blessing, and consolation from Jesus, so that I may sing of your joy with devotion"). Indeed, although Ruiz's lines are in one way a conventional plea for the Virgin's intercession, they also reveal an emergent association between lyric (song) itself and consolation.

This association manifests itself in another late work of the so-called *mester de clerecía*,[26] the *Libro rimado de Palacio* of Santillana's onetime tutor, Pero López de Ayala (1332–1407).[27] The work, composed in stages over several years (if not decades) and left in a form that likely diverges significantly from its chronology of composition, has traditionally been divided by critics into three parts:[28] an opening confession, containing wide-ranging criticism of contemporary society, in the *mester de clerecía*'s traditional *cuaderna vía*; a "lyric parenthesis" that is largely devotional, including several poems to the Virgin; and a lengthy adaptation, again in *cuaderna vía*, of Gregory the Great's *Moralia in Job*. Ayala was deeply involved in Iberian politics for several decades, carrying out numerous embassies and intervening in the Schism of 1378 before being named *canciller mayor* in 1398; he was present as royal counsellor at the Battle of Aljubarrota (1385), falling prisoner for a period that may have been as long as two years. In the *Rimado*, it is in seeking consolation during this imprisonment that Ayala turns to lyric:

> Non puedo alongar ya más el mi sermón,
> ca estó tribulado en cuerpo e coraçón,
> e muy mucho enojado con esta mi prisión
> e querría tornar a Dios mi coraçón.
>
> Quando aquí escrivía, estava muy quexado
> de muchas grandes penas e de mucho cuidado;
> con muy grandes gemidos a Dios era tornado,
> rogando l' que quisiese acorrer al cuitado.
>
> E fize estonçe así, por me más consolar,
> pidiendo a Dios merçed, que m' quisiese librar,
> e quisiese valer me, sin me más olvidar,
> deziendo yo así aqueste mi cantar. (729–31)[29]

> I cannot further extend my sermon, for I am troubled in body and heart, and very angry about my imprisonment, and I would like to turn my heart toward God.
>
> When I was writing here, I was very upset about many great pains and many cares; with great sighs I was turned to God, praying that he come to aid me in my troubles.
>
> And then I did this, to console myself more, asking God for mercy and that he free me, and help me, no longer forgetting me, reciting in this way my song.

The *mester de clerecía* is primarily a narrative genre, although, like later *arte mayor* verse, it could be put to doctrinal purposes, as in the *Rimado*'s long opening confession, here referred to revealingly as a "sermon." Although the first-person voice was not foreign to the *mester* – it dominates Ruiz's *LBA* and the *Rimado* itself until the adaptation of Gregory's *Moralia in Job* – Ayala pivots to lyric ("mi cantar") when seeking consolation for his *cuita*, the emotional cornerstone of Galician-Portuguese love lyric.[30] From the autobiographical standpoint of the *Rimado*, Ayala's *cuidado* is not a form of lovesickness, but rather the unsurprising result of his imprisonment; yet imprisonment was such a common metaphor for love and lovesickness that its juxtaposition with emotional suffering and the resulting need for consolation evokes an unspoken association of the lyric mode with love. This connection is balanced by the parallel notion of prayer as a form of song, and indeed, the *Rimado*'s lyrics oscillate between devotion, including two prayers to the Virgin offering pilgrimages, and confession, the first-person voicing of emotional suffering.

In an earlier section of the *Rimado*'s confession dedicated to prayer ("Rogaría"), having invoked the Virgin as his advocate (402a), Ayala advises continual prayer in the face of suffering:

> Por ende quien nos faze grant enojo e tristura,
> devemos perdonarle e no 'l tener rencura,
> con buena paçïencia sin ninguna falsura,
> sofrir la penitençia aunque sea muy dura.
>
> E nuestra oraçión sienpre la continuemos;
> aunque él acorra tarde nunca desesperemos,
> ca Dios acorrerá en lo que l' rogaremos,
> e nos dará mejor de lo que nos pidremos. (409–10)

> Therefore we should forgive those who cause us great anger and sadness, bearing no grudge, with good patience and no deception, bearing the penitence even if it is very hard.
>
> And let us continue always our prayer, never despairing although he delay in coming to our aid, for God will help in what we pray for from him, and he will give us more than we ask.

The notion of continual prayer is found in Cassian's *Conferences* in the context of emotional ascesis: "This, I say, is the end of all perfection – that the mind purged of every carnal desire may daily be elevated to spiritual things, until one's whole way of life and all the yearnings of one's heart become a single and continuous prayer" (376).[31] Furthermore, as implied in the *Rimado*'s repetition of *acorrer* (López de Ayala 410bc), this single prayer in Cassian's *Conferences* is one of aid:

> This, then, is the devotional formula proposed to you as absolutely necessary for possessing the perpetual awareness of God: 'O God, incline unto my aid; O Lord, make haste to help me' … Not without reason has this verse been selected from out of the whole body of Scripture. For it takes up all the emotions that can be applied to human nature and with great correctness and accuracy it adjusts itself to every condition and every attack. (379)

Ayala's invocation of "enojo e tristura" (*Rimado* 409a) as the emotions to be purged through forgiveness (409b) and endured as penitence (409d) anticipates themes that run through both the lyrics composed explicitly as prayers and songs of Marian devotion and those that hew closer to the inherited language of secular song later in the *Rimado*. The first lyric, a prayer for forgiveness, frames Ayala's confession in juridical terms: "Señor, si Tú tienes dada/ tu sentençia contra mí,/ por merçed te pido aquí/ que me sea revocada" (732; "Lord, if You have given your sentence against me, I ask you here to revoke it out of mercy"). Ayala pleads with the divine judge for mercy rather than cruelty: "e con crüeza non ande/ en juizio la tu espada/ e sea me otorgada/ pïedat, si fallesçí" (737e–h; "and may your sword not proceed with cruel judgment, and may I be granted pity, if I failed"). This plea recalls earlier lines from a section of the *Rimado* on the need for royal counsellors to advocate for mercy:

Sienpre deve el consejo dezir al rey verdat,
e sienpre lo inclinan a fazer pïedat;
todo el tienpo lo guarde non faga crüeldat,
ca clemençia es en reyes muy loada bondat. (276)

The council should always tell the king the truth, and urge him to show pity; prevent him always from being cruel, for clemency is a highly praised virtue in kings.

Such an exhortation to mercy would typically be balanced by an inverse warning that excessive clemency is itself a form of cruelty; in Ayala's confession, however, the focus remains on mercy. The avoidance of cruelty, for example, is central to the section of the *Rimado* devoted to justice:

Muchos ha que por crüeza cuidan justiçia fazer,
mas pecan en la manera, ca justiçia deve ser
con toda su pïedat e la verdat bien saber;
al fazer la execuçión sienpre se deve doler. (346)[32]

There are many who intend to do justice through cruelty, but they sin in this way, for justice should be done with all their pity and the truth fully known; one should always feel pain in carrying out the execution.

Piedad and compassion ("se deve doler") thus characterize the just and virtuous ruler whether the sentence is carried out or commuted. In this example, the revelation of the truth parallels confession, and the king's merciful attitude, no matter the outcome, approaches the perfection of the divine mercy sought by Ayala in his opening lyric. Ayala's later advice to the condemned complements his promotion of royal mercy, since they are to confess, ask God for forgiveness, and understand their punishment as "penitençia que aquí ha de pasar" (612c; "penitence to be undertaken here").

In the *Rimado*'s second lyric, composed in *arte mayor* and identified as a *deitado* (739c), Ayala adopts a more passive rhetoric in recognizing that the contrition necessary for an effective confession is itself a gift from God: "De todas mis maldades fago mi confisión,/ Tú, por la tu merçed, da me la contriçión" (743ab; the idea is repeated in 821d; "I confess all of my evils, You, by your mercy, give me contrition").[33] From this passive positioning, Ayala turns to a description of his own suffering, drawing together several of the foregoing discursive threads:

> Grant tienpo ha que como mi pan con amargura:
> nunca de mí se parten enojos e tristura;
> Señor, Tú me ayuda e toma de mí cura,
> e sea en penitençia el mal que padesçí,
> e me libra de cuitas e cárçel e tristura
> e entienda que me vales, después que a Ti gemí. (750)

I have long eaten my bread with bitterness: vexation and sadness never part from me. Lord, You help me and take care of me, and may the evil I suffered be in penitence, and free me from worries and prison and sadness, and may I understand that you aid me, since I moaned to You.

The lexicon marshalled to describe Ayala's suffering – *cuitas, cárçel, tristura, el mal que padesçí* – is indistinguishable from that of the secular amorous lyric on which Ayala was clearly drawing. It is only the material context of composition – the literalness of Ayala's imprisonment – that allows the poet to make something new from this necessarily shared vocabulary.[34] Indeed, the introduction to a subsequent lyric (following a section dedicated to the Virgin) concedes the worldliness of this vocabulary: "Pero que non podié el mundo así del todo olvidar … fize luego deste fecho aqueste breve cantar" (782a, d; "Although I could not entirely forget the world … I composed after this event this brief song").[35] Ayala's song develops the lightly paradoxical trope in which emotions associated with loneliness and isolation are figured as "company":

> Me dexaron olvidado
> en una prisión escura,
> do Cuidado e Tristura
> me fallaron muy penado,
> pues me vieron apartado
> nunca se parten de mí;
> desde entonçe fasta aquí,
> dellos ando aconpañado. (786)[36]

They left me forgotten in a dark prison, where Care and Sadness found me very pained; since they saw me so alone they never leave me alone; from then until now, I am always accompanied by them.

The polyptoton *apartado/se parten* would be taken up by many later *cancionero* poets, reaching hyperbolic heights in the *Cancionero general* in poems such as the Comendador Pirro Luis Escrivá's "Yo me parto sin partirme."[37] Ayala, however, retreats from this lyric self-indulgence, immediately forswearing such worldly thoughts: "Después desto acordé dexar así de pensar/ en el mundo, e torné a otra razón cuidar,/ de lo que el santo Job dizié por nos conortar" (790a–c; "After this I decided to stop thinking about the world in this way, and I turned my attention to another subject, what holy Job said to comfort us"). Although Ayala's adaptation of Gregory's *Moralia in Job* does not begin here, this lyric is in fact the last apparently secular one of the *Rimado*. What follows is a series of octosyllabic songs devoted to the Virgin: promises of pilgrimage (813–19, 884–90, and 901–5); reflections on the Virgin's metaphorical names (867–73 and 875–81); and a final song in praise of the Virgin's "sweet hope," guarantor of the singer's joy (910–19).

The sequencing of the lyrics and their *cuaderna vía* frame thus narrativize the abandonment of secular lyric as a mode of consolation in favour of a relatively orthodox piety, albeit one that manifests local (Castilian) customs: despite scattered references to the Passion (for example, 803cd), the *Rimado*'s prayers are addressed primarily to God and the Virgin, largely omitting Christological themes and language. This absence, in a text dissecting at length the experience and expression of personal suffering, thus reflects, as Cynthia Robinson points out, the "striking scarcity in Castile of devotional literature to which Christ's humanity and Passion are central, literature that is by contrast plentiful in most European contexts" (10).[38] While most Christians were exhorted to contemplate, and weep over, texts and images exhibiting the tremendous physical suffering of the Passion, Castilians "would … have been hard-pressed to find images that either suggested or facilitated intimacy of any sort with Christ's tortured and suffering human body" (111); the texts that were available to them, such as excerpts from Eiximenis's *Llibre del Crestià*, which were translated by the Hieronymite Fray Gonzalo de Ocaña and circulated as early as the 1430s, describe a Christ who is "who is almost exclusively divine and all-powerful" (11–13). A further group of imported texts that circulated alongside that of Eiximenis "demonstrate a marked preference for lyrical, poetic, and often Psalms- or Song of Songs–based allusions to or evocations of the Passion as salvific theological concept over the narrative, graphic evocations of the Passion as historical event that had begun to characterize Franciscan thought in particular as early as the mid-thirteenth century" (112–13). In short, to the extent that Castilians of the generations of Ayala and Santillana meditated on the Passion, it was less as an episode of extraordinary sacrifice and human suffering than as a sign of God's redemptive power, one that was, furthermore, associated in formal terms with scriptural song.

It has long been noted that the Castilian songbooks are distinguished by the absence of the female body in favour of a particularly detailed portrayal of the (male) lover's psychic experience (Lapesa, "Poesía de cancionero" 150). Keith

Whinnom has expressed scepticism toward the view that Spanish love poetry represents "some rarefied, high-minded, 'pure,' strictly non-physical passion" (*Spanish Literary Historiography* 21), and he is doubtless correct that the Castilian songbook tradition is as replete with innuendoes and double entendres as any other. In fact, to the obscene verse adduced by Whinnom, one might add the *Cancionero de Baena*'s invective, which includes frequent accusations of transgressive intercourse, themselves related to accusations of judaizing and other forms of apostasy.[39] Yet, as David Nirenberg has shown, "in the world of Baena's *Cancionero* the discourse of Judaism, like that of sexuality and animality, was as much a language of literary criticism as that of meter and form … We could interpret the critical accusation of Judaism developed by the poets of Baena's circle in the years following the mass conversions [of 1391] as being about language, not lineage" ("Figures" 416). To criticize a poet's verse as "Jewish" was to question it as a vehicle for the communication of spiritual truth, to suggest that it lacked the "infused grace of God" described by Baena's prologue as the distinguishing characteristic of good poetry.[40] *Cancionero* poetry of both insult and praise thus takes up the problematic relationship between spirit and flesh through expressions of disgust and awe, contempt and adoration. The absence of Christ's body parallels the absence of the beloved's body, not as a matter of prudishness or even of intellectualized devotion but rather as a strategy for thinking about literary composition as it relates to the passions and, in certain cases, to broader questions about matter and spirit, body and soul.

In this context, what is notable about Santillana's *Gozos* is their frequent recourse to the direct quotation of verses from Latin poems to the Virgin; the first stanza, for example, incorporates lines from the poem that begins *Gaude, Virgo, Mater Christi/ quae per aurem concepisti,/ Gabrielle nuncio* (*Poesías completas* 574n1743; italics in original). These quoted verses are, for the most part, incorporated into the Castilian rhyme scheme as well, such that the overall effect is not one of estrangement but rather of sophisticated but seamless transposition. Sarah Kay, guided by medieval usage, has described inserted verse quotations of this kind as "grafts" in trees of communal knowledge, such as the *albre d'amor* in the Franciscan troubadour Matfre Ermengaud's *Breviari d'amor*, a verse encyclopedia composed in Occitan c. 1288–92 ("Grafting" 361–2). Such grafts do not so much introduce new knowledge as "graciously" articulate knowledge already circulating within a discursive and moral community (368), and Kay goes on to note that the matter of love in particular is "the means to a decentred and yet interconnected, spoken yet read, community of knowledge in which the laity can be united with the divine" (372).[41] From the point of view of Christian theology, intersubjective identification with the divine was facilitated when, as Santillana puts it in addressing the Virgin, whom he has just described as "vaso de nuestro Mexías" ("our Messiah's vessel"), "pariste/ Dios y homne por misterio" (575, lines 15, 17–18; "you bore God and man as a mystery"). In the life of Christ, this form of identification is associated not with his miraculous birth but with the Passion, in which the compassion the devout feel for Christ is at once direct and mediated through that of the Virgin.[42]

In what follows, I will explore how the verbal and sentimental identification of the Passion with the poet-lover's *pasión* or *passió* gave rise, from the late fourteenth century onward, to concatenating lyric play linking poets within and across the Castilian and Catalan songbook traditions. A foundational link in this chain was the fourteenth-century Galician troubadour Macías, a legendary love martyr whose lyric identification with Christ gives rise to a rich compositional practice exploring verse as a medium for, and expression of, intersubjective feeling. For, as Simon Gaunt has argued in a brilliant reading of an earlier troubadour love martyr, Bernart de Ventadorn, "sacrifice is at the heart of the Christian religious experience. A troubadour's claim to be a martyr to love needs to be considered in this light for it is perhaps this, *rather than the apparent elevation of his lady to the status of a divinity*, that gives the impression that a troubadour seeks to imbricate love and religion" ("A Martyr to Love" 488; emphasis added). For Gaunt, "it is the insistence on sacrifice … that enables the love lyric to elaborate an ethics of its own and to become a forum for ethical debate" (488). The intersubjective lyrical ethics developed, with the Gloria Passionis as its master metaphor, across the traditions of the fifteenth-century Iberian songbook, moreover, responds inevitably to the debates about the passions and political community discussed in part one, broadening their emotional palette and introducing new poetic forms of intellectual discourse.

Chapter Five

Passionate Quotation

"Es me dios comunaleza"

Readers sensitive to paronomasia – as medieval troubadours of all stripes most certainly were – may already have noticed that a thin line divides "Macías" from "Mexías." Although only five poems can be attributed to him with any certainty, Macías became, almost immediately after his death, the archetype of the tragically loyal courtly lover for generations of Portuguese, Castilian, and Catalan authors.[1] One of the five poems attributed to him in Baena's *cancionero*, "Amor cruel e bryoso," is an invective against Love, personified as a king who mistreats his vassals. Among the litany of charges against this cruel king, one, "non fazes comunaleza," is particularly helpful in establishing the foundational notion of the common that would be developed by later generations of Iberian poets:

> Rey eres sobre los rreyes
> coronado enperador,
> do te plase van tus leyes,
> todos an de ty pavor;
> e pues eres tal sseñor,
> non fases comunalesa;
> sy entyendes que es proesa
> non soy ende judgador. (308, lines 13–20)[2]

> You are king of kings, crowned emperor, your laws go where you wish, all fear you; being such a lord, you do not do what you should [*non fases comunalesa*];[3] if you believe this to be a great deed, I cannot judge.

In what follows, I seek to understand with precision the substance of this attack, "non fases comunalesa," and to examine the deployment of such an attack, with its juridical, political, and theological undertones, in *lyric* discourse in particular.

I then trace notions of the common, compassion, composition through quotation, and identification through suffering that later Castilian and Catalan poets developed through imagined encounters with Macías – in dreams, in the underworld, in the grave – in poems that allude to the earlier poet or, more often, quote him directly. From Pere Torroella and Jordi de Sant Jordi, who undermine the notion of the self in citational songs, to Diego de Valera, who does the same through religious parody, to Santillana and Rodríguez del Padrón, who explore the link between Macías's emotional themes and approach to lyric composition, the poets of the early Castilian and Catalan songbooks develop an ethics of shared suffering and shared language that would only fade, I conclude, when the Passion narrative emerged more directly in Iberian vernacular literature in the final decades of the fifteenth century.

To begin with this poet and this poem situates us liminally in at least two ways. First, Macías – as his work appears in the fifteenth-century Iberian songbook tradition[4] – is an essential representative of the so-called Galician-Castilian poetic school, which occupies the transitional phase between the dominance of Galician-Portuguese lyric in the thirteenth and early fourteenth centuries, on the one hand, and fifteenth-century Castilian *cancionero* poetry, on the other. Viewed from the perspective of the medieval Galician-Portuguese and early modern Portuguese poetic traditions, this Galician-Castilian period, whose relative high point stretches from about 1350 to 1400, has been figured as "the largest gap in the history of peninsular lyric,"[5] the "Silent Century of Portuguese Court Poetry,"[6] and, in the subtitle of Ricardo Polín's critical edition, a decadence: "*Corpus* lírico da decadencia." In the early twentieth century, scholars such as Hugo Rennert[7] and Henry Lang[8] sought to fill this gap by "reconstructing" Galician versions of poems such as "Amor cruel e bryoso" – efforts that would come to be viewed quite critically by later philologists.[9] The poetry of the Galician-Castilian school thus manifests, in the history of Iberian lyric, a transition in linguistic dominance only fully realized in Santillana's generation, and then for motives that reflect "el resultado de una opción cultural y poética … pero no de una disposición política explícita, ni de la presión del poder establecido para uniformizar a sus vasallos, que fue mucho más tardío" (Beltran, *La corte de Babel* 335; "the result of a cultural and poetic choice … and not an explicit political disposition, nor the pressure of establishment power to bring vassals into line, a much later development"). Yet the embrace of Castilian as a privileged mode of lyric expression cannot be understood as a rejection of Macías and other transitional poets. Rather, Castilian (and Catalan) poets returned incessantly to Macías's legend and – more important – verse as a foundation for their own creative expression. Such a return is especially evident in their practice of verse quotation, a technique found in the Occitan troubadours and likely incorporated into the western Iberian tradition by Macías himself (Lida de Malkiel, "Juan Rodríguez del Padrón" 326; cf. Casas Rigall, *Agudeza* 174).

Before turning to this practice of quotation in later Iberian troubadours, let us address the second limit at which "Amor cruel e bryoso" situates us. The poem's rubric in the *Cancionero de Baena* (the earliest manuscript witness) reads: "Esta cantyga fiso Maçias contra el amor; enpero algunos trobadores disen que la fiso contral el rrey Don Pedro" (II: 675; "Macías wrote this song against love; however, some troubadours say that he wrote it against King Peter") – that is, Peter I of Castile (r. 1350–66, 1367–69), known by his partisans as "the Just" but by his triumphant detractors as "the Cruel." As a matter of chronology, it is unlikely that Macías's poem was an attack on the king; however, to the extent that this reading was plausible in the years immediately following Peter's death, Baena's rubric places us somewhere between moral and political allegory, with the term *comunalesa* signifying the point where these two allegories meet and fuse together as, furthermore, a principle of poetic composition.[10]

Yet it must be recognized that the abstract noun itself, *comunalesa*, or, with the suffix found more commonly for other abstract nouns, *comunaleza*, is exceedingly rare in the Castilian *cancioneros* – it appears in only one other poem, which I discuss next – and it is entirely absent from the earlier Galician-Portuguese *corpus*. In the Genre/Historical section of Mark Davies and Michael Ferreira's *Corpus do Português*, it appears only once, in a translation of the *Siete Partidas* c. 1300.[11] This single appearance, from a manuscript containing Alfonso X's first *Partida*, is suggestive, since it refers to the exorcism of the blessed salt in the rite of baptism, in which the devil is admonished to retreat, trembling and whimpering, from the newly baptized servant of God, "não avendo comunaleza nenhuma com ele" ("having no *comunaleza* with him"). The word appears again in the Castilian version of the same *Partida* when excommunication is defined as "*descomunaleza* that separates and excommunicates Christians from the spiritual goods performed in the Holy Church" (I.ix.1). Finally, in the second *Partida* (also translated into Portuguese by about 1325), it is stated that the king should have *comunaleza* "toward all those of his dominion, in order to love, honour, and protect each one according to who he is, or to the service received from him" (II.x).[12] In reading that this portion of the code will explain how the king should be "commonly [*comunalmente*] toward his entire people," we encounter an interesting clarification of this last term:

> Cuidan algunos homes que pueblo es llamado la gente menuda, así como menestrales et labradores, mas esto non es asi, ca antiguamente en Babilonia, et en Troya et en Roma, que fueron logares muy señalados, et ordenaron todas las cosas con razon, et posieron nombre á cada una segunt que convenia, pueblo llamaron el ayuntamiento de todos los homes comunalmente de los mayores, et de los menores et de los medianos. (II.x.1)

> Some men think that the "people" means the little people, such as artisans and labourers, but this is not so, for a long time ago in Babylon, and in Troy, and in Rome, which were very distinguished places, where everything was organized according to

> reason, and everything was named appropriately, they called the "people" the assembly of all men commonly, the great, the small, and those in between.

This secular sense of *comunaleza* and its more common adjectival form, *comunal*, is expanded in the *Diccionario de autoridades*, in which three definitions of *comunaleza*, all marked as antiquated, appear: *medianía*, or ethical moderation;[13] *comunicación, trato y comercio*, communication, negotiation and commerce; and *comunidad de pastos y aprovechamientos*, the shared property that would still be called "the commons" today.[14]

Such a range of meanings can certainly be detected in the other poem in which *comunaleza* appears, a praise poem dedicated to Alfonso V of Aragon attributed to Fernán Mújica. Here, Mújica, interpreting the king's emblem of the sheaf of wheat, praises the king's generosity:

> E tan bien es franqueza
> Que senbrades proveyendo
> E quando mas yo entiendo
> Es me dios comunaleza
> Que prueve en vuestros fechos
> E consejos muy derechos
> Con estos tenes estrechos
> Los que vos muestran braveza (lines 273–80)[15]

> And it is also generosity that you, providing, sow, and when I further understand, *es me dios comunaleza*, which may be proved in your deeds and good counsel; with these, you rein in those who challenge you.

"Es me dios comunaleza" is likely a copyist's error (reproduced in both surviving witnesses) for lines praising the king's judicious and fair treatment of his subjects, who are thereby kept in line ("estrechos") despite occasional rebellious displays. *Comunaleza* in Mújica's poem describes, therefore, the way in which Alfonso V's subjects are bound to him, as the sheafs in the king's emblem are bound together. The appearance of the divine in the copyist's error, meanwhile, recalls the binding or unbinding of Christian community in Alfonso X's definition of excommunication as *descomunaleza*. We can perhaps glimpse, underlying the copyist's misunderstanding (or distraction), the etymological sense of "religion" as binding, *religare*, an etymology found in Cartagena's *Oracional* (84).[16] This admittedly speculative reading presents a microcosm of all of the senses of *comunaleza* that have arisen so far: the economic, of property held in common and property given as a generous gift; the social, in the sense of a royal bearing and equanimity that is owed to all subjects and sows unity rather than discord among them; and, in the misreading "Es me dios comunaleza," that particular blend of spiritual and material sharing signified sacramentally in communion and embodied by the Church. In view of this semantic proliferation, Macías's "non fases comunalesa" cannot be seen as a mere accusation of tyranny, defined traditionally as seeking one's own rather than the common good; rather, especially when we hear the Christological allusion in "Rey eres sobre los rreyes," a deeper, multifaceted commonality is at stake in the troubadour's invective.

"Non te posso dizer al"

But perhaps, in drawing on Alfonso X's legal code and Mújica's royal panegyric, I have focused too much on kingship and not enough on love (after all, those who saw an allusion to Peter the Cruel in Macías's poem were likely mistaken). Turning to love also places us more firmly in the realm of the lyric, which, as Jonathan Culler has noted, is too often read in post-Romantic criticism as dramatic monologue – and thus, the expression of a real, or realist, subject – rather than as epideictic discourse ("Lyric, History, and Genre" 74–5). This tendency represents a particular problem in the case of later troubadour lyric, in which "rhetorical concepts of praise and blame played a key role in shaping fourteenth-century poets' conceptions of how troubadour lyric should be written and in forming audiences' ideas of how it should be read or listened to" (Dagenais 243). Indeed, as Culler reminds us, epideixis in lyric is not exclusively a matter of praise and blame, but rather includes a wide variety of statements of value (*Theory of the Lyric* 128). Yet praise and blame were, of course, central to the Galician-Portuguese *cantigas de amor* and *de escárnio e maldizer*, and in this sense, Macías's invective against Love – which, unlike God and Christ themselves, is never the direct target of a *cantiga de escárnio* (Casas Rigall, "El enigma" 33) – is generically and rhetorically circumscribed by the Galician-Portuguese tradition, but thematically liminal.

Thinking in epideictic terms allows further inroads into the Galician-Portuguese *cancioneiros* on which Macías drew, where we do not find *comunaleza*, but do find the adjective *comunal* as a frequent term of praise, and its opposite, *descomunal*, as a frequent criticism. We are also thereby pulled back into the royal orbit, as no Galician-Portuguese troubadour uses these terms more often than King Dinis (r. 1279–1325).[17] A particularly relevant case is Dinis's praise of his beloved as *comunal* in "Quer'eu em maneira de proençal":

> Ca mia senhor quiso Deus fazer tal,
> quando a fez, que a fez sabedor
> de todo bem e de mui gram valor,
> e com tod'est[o] é mui comunal
> ali u deve (43, lines 8–12)[18]

For when he made her, God made my lady thus, knowing all good things and of very great worth, and despite all this she is very humble where she should be.

Dinis's praise is the mirror-image of Macías's blame; whereas Macías's Love is *descomunal* despite the power it wields, Dinis's beloved is *comunal* despite her great worth, *gram valor*. Dinis also shares with Macías the habit of foregrounding his literary borrowings, identifying this poem's form of praise as the "Provençal style," in much the same way that, in the *Siete Partidas*, the authority for the *comunaleza* owed by the king to his entire people is transcultural and transhistorical, at once Babylonian, Greek, and Roman. Dinis's opening declaration of his poetic debt is not a straightforward appeal to authority, however. Rather, it exemplifies one way that the common is figured in medieval literature, what Peter Haidu has called "conventionality," a dominant phenomenon in which "even when an element is newly introduced into the domain of literature, it is immediately 'conventionalized,' fictitiously treated as a pre-existing convention" ("Making" 4). Dinis, owing especially to *cantigas de amor* such as this one, has himself been the subject of a vigorous debate regarding the aesthetic and ideological implications of lyric convention.[19] Julian Weiss in particular, with evidence from the *cantigas de amor*, has criticized Haidu's "idealist" notion of conventionality for flattening readings of what is actually a complex and often contradictory deployment of tropes in a way that masks "the ideological force that fiction exerts … in shaping the social world" ("On the Conventionality" 230). By the same token, however, the self-consciousness (or even irony) of lyric conventionality – "lyric *about* lyric," lyric as "grammar," as *langue* rather than *parole*, or as "essentially style" (Haidu, "Making" 5) – does not empty medieval poetry of ideological content or disqualify it as exemplary of an ethical ideal. Rather, we can read in conventional consciousness and its praise of the common what Gregory B. Stone has called "resistance to the Renaissance," the idea that, in at least some late medieval literature, "though the revelation concerning the singularity of the ego has already taken place, the 'truth' of this revelation has been rejected as an un-truth, as a philosophic loss to be resisted rather than a gain to be encouraged" (4).

Dinis was himself clearly aware of the problematic interface between convention and sincerity since, in another poem, "Proençaes soem mui bem trobar," he denounces the artificiality of singing of love only in the springtime. In this sense, we might read the qualification that his lady is *comunal* "ali u deve," where and when she should be, as a subtle echo of Dinis's own choice to draw on the Provençal tradition for the purposes of this specific poem. Like Alfonso V (in Mújica's account), Dinis and his beloved are judicious in administrating the space of the common. It is in this context that we should read the closing claim of Dinis's poem, that, in the case of his *senhor*, "nom sei hoj'eu quem/ possa compridamente no seu bem/ falar, ca nom há, tra'lo seu bem, al" (lines 19–21; "I know of no one today who could speak comprehensively of her goodness, for there is no goodness beyond hers"). The impossibility of speaking in troubadour lyric is always, as I discussed in the introduction, the impossibility of speaking with distinct sincerity; Dinis's gesture is to recognize this impossibility and reshape it as praise. The impossibility of fully articulating the worth of Dinis's beloved is not one of subjective expression or of the inherent inadequacy of the medium of language, he asserts, but rather of objective excess. In other words, when Dinis concludes that there is "nothing beyond her goodness," he means that she is not merely beyond compare (a conventional conclusion in amorous poetry found, for example, in Torroella's "Maldezir de mugeres"), but infinitely good. To describe her worth completely ("compridamente") would be to speak forever, without limit.

Those who raged against the limits of courtly praise rather than working creatively within them were likely to fall prey to *coita descomunal*, extraordinary suffering.[20] The point can be illustrated with a poem by Alfonso Álvarez de Villasandino, another leading light of the Galician-Castilian school, praised by Santillana in his *Prohemio* (62–3) and by far the best-represented poet in the *Cancionero de Baena*. The protagonist of "Entre Doiro e Minno estando," one of Villasandino's poems written at the behest of Henry II of Castile for his lover Juana de Sousa, is travelling sorrowfully, worried that his departure has left his beloved sad, when he encounters a nightingale who seeks to assuage his sorrow by explaining that lovers often boast of their fear of parting, but that if he only remains loyal while away, he will reap a reward:

"Heu sey ben ssyn falimiento
tu morte e tu ssoedade;
andas por ssaber verdade
de teu alto penssamento,
e trages maginamiento,
cuidado que tu ffesiste
una grant dona ser triste
por teu fol departymento.

"D'esto non aias pavor,
que que den amor se çinge
por moytas veces se fynge
qu'ello fas faser temor;
et tu ssey sabidor
que avras d'ela bon grado,
ssy fores leal provado
en loar seu grant valor." (11, lines 17–32)[21]

"I know well, without doubt, your death and solitude; you seek the truth of your high thought, anxiously imagining that you made a great lady sad in foolishly parting.

"Have no fear of this, for the one bound by love often feigns this [sadness] in order to cause fear; know that you will greatly please her if you prove to be loyal in praising her great worth."

The first cited stanza both recalls the Galician-Portuguese tradition in its diagnosis of the lover's suffering as both a kind of death and *ssoedade* (*saudade*) and exemplifies the close relationship between amorous suffering and intellectual constructs such as thought, imagination, and even *cuidado*, which is in apposition to *maginamiento* and could be rendered as "care" or "worry" but also, in its verbal form, often denoted belief or judgment.[22] The entire passage is grounded in the nightingale's claimed familiarity with the travelling lover's predicament ("Heu sey ben"), and although the nightingale only claims that the lady's fear of parting – not, that is, her love itself – is feigned, its advice infuriates the protagonist:

Respondile con grant saña:
"Rruyseñor, sy Deus te ajude,
vayte ora con ssaude
parlar por essa montaña;
que aquesta cuyta tamaña
es mi placer e folgura,
membrandome a fermosura
de miña señor estraña.

"Amor sempre ove mal,
e de ty, seu menssajero,
sempre te ache parlero,
mentidor descomunal:
non te posso diser al,
mas conven de obedeçer
a de noble padeçer
que no mundo muyto val." (lines 33–48)

I replied with great anger: "Nightingale, God help you, go talk on that mountain, farewell; for this great care is my pleasure and rest, remembering the exceptional beauty of my lady.

"I was always harmed by love, and by you, its messenger; I have always found you to be a big talker, an extraordinary liar: I can say nothing else to you, but must obey the noble sufferer who is worth much in this world."

I have quoted this poem at some length in order to demonstrate that what is framed as a furious rejection ("Respondile con grant saña") is in fact an intricate repetition. First, that the traveller takes pleasure in recalling his beloved's beauty merely confirms, to the letter, the nightingale's knowing perception of his *ssoedade*. Thus, while it may be tempting to understand the valedictory "non te posso diser al" as a dismissive "I have nothing more to say to you," we must first examine the "talk" that gives rise to the insult "mentidor descomunal." For the nightingale's "extraordinary lie" is to suggest that, if his interlocutor remains loyal, praising his beloved's great worth, he can expect her gratitude (in whatever form it may take) upon returning. But this is just what our traveller has promised at the end of the poem: to obey his nobly suffering beloved, whose "great worth in the world" he praises. The true sense of the dismissal is literal: above all, "non te posso diser al" means "I can say nothing else to you but *what you have said to me*." Speech that is *descomunal* cannot actually be represented in the amorous discourse of troubadour lyric: at a minimum, it is equally possible for the flattering *mentidor descomunal* to be identified with, or confused for, the loyal and laudatory lover.

Lyric Quotation and the Loss of Self

It would be tendentious to conclude that Villasandino stages this exchange between king and nightingale to show that all troubadour verse is quotation. What the poem does exemplify is a foundational tendency in the Castilian tradition to explore the expressive capacity of quoted or otherwise repetitive speech as such. In particular, poets return to the idea that the anguish – feigned or not – long at the heart of troubadour practice found its most engaging expression through a compositional foregrounding of the common. In doing so, these poets could draw on earlier romance works such as Petrarch's "Lasso me, ch'i' no so in qual parte pieghi" and the *Perilhos tractat d'amor de donas*, the lengthy lyric anthology that concludes Ermengaud's *Breviari*.[23] In Catalan, poems incorporating lyric quotations such as Jordi de Sant Jordi's *Passio amoris secundum Ovidium*, Francesc Ferrer's *Lo conhort*, and Torroella's *Tant mon voler*, all of which I discuss later in this chapter, drew directly but dialogically on Ermengaud.[24] Juan Casas Rigall distinguishes between two types of verbatim quotation in the Castilian tradition of this subgenre, *cita* and *acomodación*. *Cita* describes the insertion of a quotation, generally maintaining its original meaning, in a way subordinated to the main level of discourse (for example, by attributing it to a discrete character in a narrative poem), whereas in the case of *acomodación*, the quotation is inserted at the same discursive level as its context, and its meaning has often been manipulated through this recontextualization (*Agudeza* 171).[25] A further helpful taxonomic distinction has been made by Isabella Tomassetti, between what she calls *decires con citas*, which quote other lyric texts, and *decires con refranes*, which quote popular sayings.[26] Tomassetti also echoes Casas Rigall in contrasting the "dramatic" strategy of lover's hells with the "interpretive" or amplificatory strategy of incorporating quotations into unbroken first-person discourse; this latter technique is taken up by later poets in the genre of the *glosa* ("Sobre la tradición" 1720–1).

In her recent study of troubadour quotation, Sarah Kay has argued that, unlike verse insertions in narrative texts, which emphasize emotion, lyric quotations "tend to home in on the moral, reflective, or other sententious aspects of troubadour poetry, inscribing it less in the field of affect than of knowledge" (*Parrots and Nightingales* 14). Kay marshals compelling evidence to support this broad distinction between insertion and quotation for the French context, but the practices of quotation in Macías and his Iberian followers do not conform to Kay's second distinction, between affect and knowledge. Neither – despite a marked tendency toward sacro-profane *contrafacta* and other forms of religious parody, discussed at length later in this chapter – are their poems the devotional "scripts" devised to instil compassion through "iterative affective performance" that have recently been described by Sarah McNamer (1–2). Rather, in these authors, collective emotion and intersubjective identification become paths to both spiritual and ethical knowledge. Thus, by the middle of the fifteenth century, a poet such as Torroella – drawing simultaneously on the Castilian and Catalan traditions, as well as on Occitan and French sources – would come to articulate expicitly his verbal identification with his poetic forebears as a matter of emotional intensity and truth:

Tant mon voler s'és dat a·mors[27]
que tots quants dits de trobadors
 lig ne recort
és mon parer façen report
de ço qu·enemorat soport,
 no gens content.
Ho Amor nos féu d'un sentiment
ho en profetar ço que jo sent
 fforen spirats.
Lurs rahons tròban actoritats
en refermar les veritats
 de mon esser,
e no dupteu quin strany pler[28]
trobe com trob no sol esser
 en mas dolors.
De companyia prench repòs:
aquest sol bé tinch, amadors,
 per ser dels vostres. (XXII, lines 1–18)

My will is so given to love that all the sayings of the troubadours I read or recall seem to express what I, most unhappy, suffer in love. Either Love made us of the same feeling, or they were inspired prophets of what I feel. Their words are authorities in intensifying the truths of my being, and do not doubt what a strange pleasure I find, when I find that I am not alone in my pain. I take comfort in company: this is the only good I have, lovers, from being one of yours.

Torroella's is far from the earliest of the so-called citation songs in Catalan or Castilian, but I open my discussion with it because of Torroella's characteristically systematic approach in addressing the link between quotation and sentiment.[29] The poets Torroella reads and recalls seem to report his own feelings; either love had an identical effect on them, or they were merely prophesizing what he now feels. The company of these earlier poet-lovers is not only a source of relief (*repòs*), as this opening stanza concludes; rather, their words (*rahons*) confirm or intensify (*refermar*) what Torroella feels, producing a "strange pleasure." In describing this consolation that transforms, rather than diminishing, suffering, Torroella plays on the senses of *trobar* as an act of both composition ("Lurs rahons tròban actoritats") and discovery ("quin strany pler/ trobe com trob no sol esser").[30]

Gemma Avenoza has suggested that the invocation of the troubadours' authority in Torroella's opening stanza recalls the introductory verses of Ermengaud's *Perilhos tractat*: "D'aquest'amor vos hai tractat/ leialmen seguon veritat;/ empero mais en tractarai, e·l tractat examinarai/ seguon los digz dels trobadors" (*Breviari d'amor*, lines 27771–5, quoted in Avenoza 33; "I have explained this love to you loyally and truthfully; but I will explain it further, examining it through the sayings of the troubadours"). Furthermore, Ermengaud's tratadistic polyptoton (*tractat/tractarai*) emphasizes, as Kay suggested, the sententious plan of his anthology, in which both troubadours who praised and cursed love will be quoted in order to better convey the truth ("per mielhs la veritat trobar," line 27806), that is, the rewards awaiting those who love loyally ("los bes que d'amor pren/ qui domnas ama leialmen," lines 27809–10). Yet even Ermengaud cautions that "perfect knowledge" of passionate love comes only with experience: "Pero qui d'amar no pensa/ no pot haver conoichensa/ bem perfiecha d'auqest'amor,/ ni apenre d'esenhador,/ quar aquest'amors mais s'apren/ e plus fermamen s'escompren/ per vezer, no fai per auzir/ quan plazers la vol retenir" (lines 27811–18; "But he who has no thought of love can have no perfect knowledge of this kind of love, nor learn it from a teacher, for this love is better learned, and lovers more enflamed, by sight, it does not proceed by hearing when pleasure wishes to embrace it"). The lyric voice of Torroella's *Tant mon voler* sidesteps the question of *conoichensa bem perfiecha*, presenting the quoted material as confirmation of personal experience, "the truths of my being" rather than the truth as such. Even the pleasure afforded by belonging to the company of lovers is "strange," a term whose straightforward meaning in this context is "unusual," but that here plays on its other sense, of foreignness, belonging to another.[31] Indeed, what the beloved finds amidst the complex of quotations introduced by this stanza is a ghostly remnant of self-abnegation:

Què us diré, trist? Yo só negú,
e so que veu
és un cors fantàstich que féu

tot de novell l'amorós déu
de passions,
ab los membres d'opinions
e·ls spirits d'envensions. (XXII, lines 202–8).

What can I, full of sorrow, say to you? I am no one, and what you see is a fantastic body made anew by the god of love out of passions, with members of opinions and spirits of inventions.

It is no accident here that alienation ("Yo só negú") is presented as a problem of speech: "Què us diré?" What is confirmed by the poetic voice's identification with the verse of others, the "truths of my being" described earlier (lines 11–12), is not the subjective "I" but the passions themselves that compose the "fantastic body" perceived by the beloved, and not just love (I: 380nn202–8) but sadness ("Què us diré, *trist*?"). The "spirits" in question are, as Rodríguez Risquete notes (Torroella I: 330nn153–6, 380n208), the vital spirits, whose role in communicating between body and soul is disrupted by the passionate lover's overheated heart. Yet there is a certain strangeness in attributing medical spirits to an immaterial ("fantàstich") body, a strangeness at least partly explained by the "inventions" of which these spirits are made. Such inventions, especially in parallel, as they are, with "opinions," would typically be understood as fictions or lies.[32] To the extent, however, that the body of *Tant mon voler* is constructed from verse borrowings, Torroella may also be pointing to *inventio* in its rhetorical sense, whose basis in discovery is also latent in the *trobar* associated with the truth of the lyric voice's experience in the poem's first stanza. The question of truth and opinion, in turn, arises later in the poem when the aphasia of a body made of, or filled with, passions makes its return:

De les altres són oppinions,
mas de vós totas las rahons
referan bé.
Què·s la rahó, yo no u diré,
pus és de més dir lo per què
hon sentir basta.
Per ço desig fon e desguasta
e de passions abasta
esta persona
vostra tota … (XXII, lines 473–82)

What is said of other women is [mere] opinion, but all speak well of you. What is the reason, I will not say, for there is no need to explain why where feeling is enough. This is why desire melts and dissipates and fills with passions this person [who is] entirely yours.

Here, reason as speech ("totas las rahons"), cause ("lo per què"), and mental faculty collapse into silence in the face of sentiment. The poet's confusion is subtly indicated by the juxtaposition of an assertion that it is superfluous to enumerate causes (lines 477–8) with a causal explanation ("*Per ço* desig"). This confusion, in turn, is figured as a conventional loss of self-possession ("esta persona/ vostra tota"), which paradoxically introduces a stanza from Francesc Ferrer's "Enamorats, doleu-vos de ma vida," whose opening lines constitute a firm assertion of identity and effective worth (precisely, that is, what is omitted and erased in Torroella's foregoing verses): "Si dona·l món s'ateny per ben servir,/ *yo son* aquell qui·n done tall *rahó*" (lines 488–9, emphasis added; "If any woman in this world can be attained through good service, *I am* the one who gives good *reason* for it").[33]

In Torroella's poem, what is ultimately silenced is the cry for mercy:

Al temps que deig clamar merçè
me possa un tan aspre fre
a mon lenguatge,
qu·abans acordàs lo passatge
dintre·ls inferns e tot ultratge
de mort cometre
que rahó de mon propòssit retre. (XXII, lines 594–600)

When I should cry for mercy, my language is so harshly restrained that I would sooner visit the underworld or commit any mortal outrage than reveal my true desire.

The silent suffering incumbent upon the lover is here opposed to the indiscretion of crying out and, in so doing, revealing the suffering's cause, *retre raó* – a phrase that recalls the *donar raó* of the lines quoted from Ferrer. In contrast to Ferrer's assertion of merit, however, Torroella's phrasing draws attention to the polysemy of *raó* as speech and cause, the question of what *reason* demands in such a situation hanging all the while over the lover's mortal self-restraint, which is after all opposed to what he *should* do ("Al temps que *deig* clamar merçè").

Such a promise to face death rather than reveal a secret love is, of course, conventional, and poets before and after Torroella would imagine a passage through hell or through other allegorical spaces of suffering in their explorations of love's effects and aftermath. One of *Tant mon voler*'s sources, for example, is Jordi de Sant Jordi's *Passio amoris secundum Ovidium*, a citation song narrating its protagonist's unhappy passage through the castle of the God of Love. The *Passio amoris* is one of two Sant Jordi poems praised by Santillana in the *Prohemio*, and the two poets had in fact met at the court of Alfonso V, where Sant Jordi was a valet of the king's chamber (*cambrer*).[34] Sant Jordi's *Passio amoris* draws inspiration from the *Perilhos tractat*, but its opening lines anticipate Torroella's *Tant mon voler* more clearly than they allude to Ermengaud's treatise:

> *Cant vey li temps camgar e·nbrunusir,*
> *que non aug chant d'auzelh, voltes ne lay,*
> me sent al cor un tal smay
> quant mi recort
> que per amor Jesús pres mort
> e tuig li san,
> e pens d'amor lo bell afan
> que·m fa passar … (XVIII, lines 1–8)

> When I see the season change and darken, no longer hearing birdsong, trill or lai, I feel in my heart such dismay, when I recall that Jesus died for love, and all the saints, and I think of the beautiful struggle to which love subjects me.

The poem begins by citing the first two verses of the Catalan troubadour Guillem de Berguedà's "Qan vei lo temps camjar e refrezir," a song asserting the lover's sincerity by excoriating those troubadours who only sing in spring.[35] Yet here, the singer does not proclaim his own persistence in love and song, but rather his dismayed recollection of the deaths of Christ and all the saints "for love" – that is, as a consequence of the love they felt, which he compares to the "beautiful struggle" (*bell afan*) to which love is subjecting him. In this way, as the poem's title implies, the lover's suffering becomes a martyrdom comparable to those of the saints and to Christ's Passion itself, thus blurring the traditional distinction between *eros* and *agape* (a blurring that, in the foregoing centuries, had been frequent in devotional texts by Bernard of Clairvaux and others[36]).

Indeed, Sant Jordi's poem stands out in the Christological tradition I trace later precisely because the lyric voice identifies not only with Christ's suffering but with his love as well. Following an invocation of Ovid (line 9), the poet defines love in terms that clearly align with the troubadour tradition, yet also characterize divine love: constant and unchanging (lines 11–14), a "power/ grounded in wisdom" (lines 21–2), a form of friendship (line 29).[37] In the case of this last quality, an inserted quotation from Guiraut Riquier's "Fis e verays" clarifies that this friendship is an obligation among all lovers, including those whose love is unrequited ("*celh qui ama e no·s amatz*"; lines 30–2). This quotation forms the bridge between the poem's definition of love and its properly allegorical section, which, as the poem's editor, Aniello Fratta, explains (Sant Jordi 200), constitutes an allegorical *via crucis* in which the protagonist enters the castle of the *Dieu d'Amor* through the door of Joy (Joya) and leaves through the door of Pain (Dolor).[38] The quotation is also a bridge between first- and third-person perspectives, the first person only returning from this point in the *Passio* in quoted verses. Thus, at the castle's entrance, Valor inspires the lover to cry out, citing Bernart de Ventadorn's "Non es meravelha," "*No·s meravelha si yeu xant/ mils de nulh autre xantador*" (lines 41–2; "It is no marvel if I sing better than any other singer"); this quoted assertion of singularity is revealed by Sant Jordi's allegory to be the motto of the troubadours' koine, the shared password that opens the door to the castle of Love. Once inside, the lover is abandoned by Joy (line 63) and, although welcomed by the God of Love (lines 82–3), he is immediately set upon by Pain's minions, Envy and Libeler (Malalengua; lines 93–5). Forsaken by Love and Will (Voler; lines 104–9), the lover quotes an anonymous song lamenting that his joy has turned to sadness: "*que·l gaug m'és a tristor cangats/ e·l plaser mi va dexandén*" (lines 112–13). The poem closes with a quoted cry of betrayal, taken from Catalan troubadour Ponç d'Ortafà's "Si ai perdut":

> E clou les portes de l'hostal
> e roman lay,
> cridan ab gran votz d'esmay:
> *"Sí n'ay perdut mon sauber,*
> *qu·a penes say on m'estau*
> *ne d'on vench ne vas on vau,*
> *ne què·m fau lo jorn ne·l ser,*
> *car trasit suy en cresensa."* (lines 147–54)

> And I close the house's door and remain there, crying with a great, dismayed voice: "So I have lost my senses, for I barely know where I am, nor whence I come nor where I am going, nor what to do day or night, for I am betrayed in my belief."

Ortafà's lost mind recalls the *Passio*'s identification of wisdom (*saviesa*) as love's foundation, but this decisive loss, figured spatially and practically (lines 151–3), is not just of love but of self. The speaker's profound disorientation is the result of a betrayal of belief – not merely, therefore, of rejection by an intransigent beloved – and thus, in the context of Sant Jordi's allegory, alludes subtly to a key turning point in the Passion narrative. Yet the traitor here appears to be the God of Love himself, since that is where the lover's belief was deposited. The poem's rather abrupt ending – Fratta suggests that the one surviving witness may not represent a fully polished version (Sant Jordi 201) – does not make explicit the target of this final accusation, but Macías, whom we have already seen criticizing love as an unjust king, would also go further than Sant Jordi in extending his Christological identification to another cry of betrayal from a later point in the Passion.

"Chamaré, ora, por mí"

Later Castilian and Catalan love allegories – visions of lovers in the afterlife, whether infernal, such as Santillana's *Infierno de los enamorados*, or bucolic, such as Rocabertí's *Glòria d'Amor* (c. 1453–61) – often included encounters with Macías, whose poetic vow of lover's silence, "Cativo de miña tristura," was, like Torroella's vow, composed through the incorporation of citations (in Macías's case, as we will see later, of popular refrains). In contrast to Torroella's analytic approach and to Sant Jordi's direct allusion to Christ, the matrix of composition, quotation, and passion remains largely implicit in the poetry of Macías, but is ingeniously thematized in a poem attributed to him in the *Cancionero de Palacio* in which he quotes perhaps the best-known cry for mercy in the Christian tradition:

Pues me falleçió ventura
en el tiempo de plazer,
non spero aver folgura
mas por siempre entristecer;
turmentado et con tristura,
chamaré, ora, por mí:
~~*Deus meus, Elly, Ely*~~
~~*e lama zabatany.*~~

Quien supiese mi tristura
e mi dolor et quebranto
et de mí s'adoleçiese,
comigo fará planto;
quánto más si bien supiesse
el gran ben qu'eu perdí:
~~*Deus meus, Elli, Ely*~~
~~*e lama zabatany.*~~ (CCL)[39]

Since fortune failed me in the time of pleasure, I expect no rest, but to be sad forever; tormented and with sadness, I will cry out, now, for me: *My God, Eli, Eli, lema sabachthani?*

Whoever hears of my sadness, and my pain and affliction, and feels compassion for me, will weep with me; and even more, if he knows the great good that I lost: *My God, Eli, Eli, lema sabachthani?*

This poem manifests two courtly commonplaces: the loss of love as lyric theme and the hypothetical empathy of a community of readers, listeners, and fellow poets. Macías puts these two familiar elements in dialogue with a third, the use of quoted refrains, common to his well-known *Baena* poems "Cativo de miña tristura" and "Provémde buscar mesura," to which I will turn shortly. But here, he does so in a surprising way, ventriloquizing Christ's final anguished cry on the cross, "My God, my God, why have you forsaken me?" (which Matthew [27:46], like Macías, quotes in Aramaic).

At first glance, readers familiar with any tradition of troubadour lyric might find this variation on the so-called *religio amoris*, Macías's conflation of erotic loss with Christ's Passion, too common to shock and too frivolous to offend. We have already seen the conflation of spiritual and carnal love in Sant Jordi's *Passio*, a poetic gesture that gives credence to Auerbach's insight that the "tormenting love" of God found in Passion devotion was a key source of the "antithetical paradoxes" so common in late medieval European love poetry (307n14). Further examples from the Iberian context in particular have been traced and analysed by Lida de Malkiel,[40] E. Michael Gerli,[41] and Casas Rigall.[42] While the best-known aspect of the *religio amoris* is the divinization of the beloved, often through a comparison to the Virgin Mary (although sometimes more directly, as in Calisto's provocative "Melibeo soy" in the *Celestina*), occasional, varied comparisons to Christ arise as well: in the *Laberinto de Fortuna*, for example, Juan de Mena compares John II, hearing the complaints of the nobles in Medina del Campo, to Christ during his arrest (Lida de Malkiel, "La hipérbole" 125). Nevertheless, there is reason to believe that this particular example retained its power to shock: as I have indicated, the biblical quotation is crossed out both times in the *Cancionero de Palacio* by a hand that does not appear to be much later than that of the copyist (Gerli, "La 'Religión'" 73n20). Furthermore, Macías is singled out for condemnation as the source of this blasphemous trend in Fray Íñigo de Mendoza's 1482 *Coplas de vita Christi*, in which the Franciscan (and descendant, on his father's side, of Santillana) criticizes courtiers for

> su morir noche y días
> para ser dellas [their ladies] bien quistos;
> si lo vieses, jurarías
> que por el dios de Macías
> venderán mil Ihesus Christos. (lines 353–7)[43]

> their dying night and day to be loved by [their ladies]; if you saw it, you would swear that they would sell one thousand Jesus Christs for the god of Macías.

Yet as I have alluded to earlier, Macías himself had a rich tradition to draw from, one that contained harsh and direct invectives against both Christ and God.[44] By contrast, in "Pues me falleçió ventura," Macías identifies his suffering with that of Christ by claiming, like Torroella in *Tant mon voler*, that it can be expressed through the same words: "chamaré, ora, por mí: *Deus meus, Elly, Ely/ e lama zabatany.*" Through these words, the poet convokes an empathetic audience, who, upon hearing his cry, might feel his suffering ("de mí s'adoleçiese") and collaborate in purging it ("comigo fará planto"). The lyric voice thus becomes a bridge uniting two instances of intersubjective expression. On the one hand, Macías communicates the depths of his most personal anguish through the words of another; on the other hand, he reacts to that anguish through a process of collective, poetic grief.

One historical attempt to sanitize the religious daring of this poem – a more creative attempt than merely crossing out the offending verses – is particularly telling in this regard. In three of the six surviving witnesses, in place of "chamaré, ora, por mí," we find "llamare orad por mi" ("I will cry out, 'Pray for me'").[45] Although this emendation does not fully negate the charge of the biblical quotation, it attenuates the otherwise direct identification between the poet and Christ, all the while making explicit, and explicitly pious, the convocation of an empathetic community. At this point it is important to recall that Christ's own cry places him within a community of believers, for the cry is itself a quotation, and a quotation of a song, Psalm 22: "My God, my God, why have you forsaken me?/ Why are you so far from helping me, from the words of my groaning?/ O my God, I cry by day, but you do not answer;/ and by night, but find no rest" (Ps 22:1–2).[46] This buried intertext, likely familiar to many listeners,[47] discloses the poetic voice's anguished fear that his cry will go unanswered. Thus, in Macías's song, the lyric voice's self-identification with Christ goes beyond the content of any given quotation to the compositional and impassioned practice of quotation as such. Far from blasphemous, the poem in fact "cites" Christ as at once a poetic authority and a member of a textual community, making a citational argument for the potential of lyric dialogue and quotation to express deep sentiment and to deliver from suffering.

Religious Parody and the Betrayal of Love's Doctrine in Diego de Valera

In both Castile and Aragon, the generations of poets writing after Macías explored the nexus of quotation, composition, and religious feeling through a variety of strategies. Two examples from the poetry of Diego de Valera (whose doctrinal texts were discussed in part one), for example, develop formal and thematic features found in "Pues me falleçió ventura." First, Macías's "chamaré, ora, por mí" is an early example of what Tomassetti has called the "enunciative formulas" that, in the Castilian songbook tradition, precede quotations, identifying them as such and frequently specifying the form of their source (*cantiga*, *canción*, *exemplo*, *letra*, and so on; "Sobre la tradición" 1709). These formulas, Tomassetti goes on to argue, constitute a "making explicit of the text's process of composition" (1709), and they bear extensive repetition in some songs. Such is the case in Valera's "Despedimiento," almost half of which consists of quotations from Santillana, Macías ("Cativo de miña tristura"), other poems by Valera himself, or unidentified sources. The first introductory formula emphasizes both the song's borrowed nature and its emotional reframing: "Pues por bien servir yo peno/ cresçiendo vuestra porfia/ *aqueste refran ageno/ cantare syn alegria*" (Torre y Franco-Romero

275, lines 1–4; emphasis added; ID2124). Further stanzas repeat this gesture, sometimes combining *decir* with other forms:

> E dire mas con pesar/ como quien ya desespera/ tal cançion que bien cantar/ devo yo fasta que muera: (lines 9–12)
> Cantare con grant razon/ quanto biva triste yo: (lines 18–19)
> Endechando asy dire/ por mi fortuna menguada: (lines 26–7)
> Cantare con grant tristeza/ de mi mesmo aborresçido: (lines 34–5)
> … dire syn ser culpado/ por mi grant desaventura: (lines 42–3)

> And I will recite with sorrow, like one already hopeless, such a song as I must sing until I die:
> I will rightfully sing for as long as I live in sadness:
> Singing sadly I will say, because of my lost fortune:
> I will sing with great sadness, detesting myself:
> I will say guiltlessly, because of my great misfortune:

The formulas described by Tomassetti thus specify not just a form but also a situation, the latter most frequently an emotional attitude ("con grant tristeza/ de mi mesmo aborresçido"), complaint against fate ("por mi fortuna menguada"), or ethical judgment ("dire syn ser culpado"). Valera's poem concludes with a formula introducing the coming silence as an absence of song: "Con doloroso quebranto/ por vuestra grant desmesura/ fenesçe mi triste canto/ syn dar fiyn a mi rencura" (lines 48–51; "With painful affliction caused by your great immoderation, my sad song ends without ending my rancor"). The song's end is framed, in turn, by the emotions of *quebranto* and *rencura*. Although *quebranto* initially calls to mind a break, it was also a synonym of "lástima, commiseración, piedad o compassión" (*Diccionario de autoridades* 1737). The time of song, which is here closely identified with the repetitive weaving of lyric quotations, lasts as long as compassion holds out; it gives way to the silence of *rencura*, which is not just anger but "enemistad antigua, ira envejecida" (*Autoridades* 1737). Valera, albeit in defeat, opposes compassion to long-standing anger, the traditional amorous and courtly dissensions he attacked in his didactic prose.

Valera was also the author of a long amorous parody of the seven penitential psalms, and this development of *contrafacta* from religious sources is the second compositional strategy rooted in (what was perceived to be) Macías's work.[48] Like Tomassetti, I consider the seven *contrafacta*, linked by a repeated refrain under the rubric of "Gloria," to constitute a single *decir* ("Los *Salmos*" 266). In a corrective gesture of piety similar to those undergone by "Pues me falleçió ventura," the poem's original rubric, "Salmos penitençiales que hizo diego de valera diligidos al amor" ("Penitential psalms written by Diego de Valera to love"), has been modified by another hand with the addition of "de Dios" ("attributing to it a pious content it evidently did not have"; 271).[49] The poem is indeed quite direct in transposing Love for God, making the former the object of prayers for mercy and salvation. Direct translations from the parodied psalms are few (268), but the theme of penitence is preserved and explored from multiple angles. Taken together, the seven parodic psalms constitute a kind of *summa* of the psychology of courtly love in a confessional (penitential) framework.

The poem's first section, corresponding to Psalm 6, *Domine, ne in furore tuo arguas me neque ira tua corripias me*, establishes the stakes of the lover's penitence. Valera's adaptation follows the reasoning of the original psalm's prayer for mercy before a looming death. The lover, driven to mortal despair by Love's cruelty, is no longer able to remember Love (XV, lines 23–6) and is therefore himself beyond redemption: "Que en el ynfierno esperar/ No podemos redençión/ Ni basta la contriçión/ Para del nos delibrar" (lines 33–6; "For in hell we cannot await redemption, nor is contrition enough to free us from there"). In invoking both redemption and contrition, Valera expands here on the Vulgate's concise rhetoric of confession: "In inferno autem quis confitebur tibi?" (Ps 6:6).[50] The lover thus declares his intention to purge his sins in life, through the tears of saving sorrow: "Con gemidos lloraré/ Todas mis culpas agora/ E ningund tienpo nin ora/ De plañir no cesaré;/ E mi lecho regaré/ De lágrimas con dolor,/ E jamás con gran temor/ De ti siempre biviré" (lines 41–8; "With moans I will mourn all my faults now, and I will never cease weeping, and I will water my bed with tears of pain, and I will always live in great fear of you").[51] The poem's next section, based on Psalm 31, *Beati, quorum remissae sunt iniquitates et quorum tecta sunt peccata*, fleshes out the nature of the lover's punishment, establishing a distinction between love's inevitable suffering (*cuytas*) and the mortal condition of the lover who sins by refusing to undergo that suffering. Those who suffer the travails of love are rightly rewarded: "Y Señor con que rrazon/ Aquellos que a ti se ofreçen/ E por ti cuytas padeçen/ Bien meresçen galardón" (lines 57–60; "And Lord, how rightly those who offer themselves to you and suffer cares for you deserve a reward"). The poet, by contrast, admits to having sought to avoid Love's commandments and recognizes that he is currently facing the consequences: "Agora soy castigado/ Y de tu mano tañido,/ Tanto, que soy aborrido/ Amador no bien amado" (lines 73–6; "Now I am punished and struck by your hand, so much, that I am abhorred, an unloved lover"). This is the paradigmatic situation of the unhappy poet-lover, which will be painstakingly explored through narrative by Rodríguez del Padrón and later authors of sentimental fiction (see later discussion). Here, Valera affirms that mercy should be the reward of contrite sinners who practise confession, love, and song: "Pues confieso mis errores/ Merezco ser perdonado/ Y de ti galardón dado/ Pues amé bien por amores./ ¡Ó Señor de los Señores!/ En tu gloria cantaré/ Y en todo tiempo daré/ A tu santidat loores" (lines 77–84; "Since I confess my errors, I deserve to be forgiven and given a reward by you, since I loved well. Oh Lord of Lords! I will sing in your glory, and always give praise to your holiness"). At this point, Valera takes up the original psalm's image of wasted bones that cry out (lines 85–6; cf. Ps 31:3), concluding that a truly compassionate Love would be patient and understanding when faced with human sin: "Que, Señor, si tú sintieses/ La pena del desamado/ Amador desconsolado/ Y de aquella padesçieses,/ Pienso bien que conosçieses/ No ser de maravillar/ A nosotros el errar/ Des que tal cuyta sufrieses" (lines 93–100; "For, Lord, if you felt the pain of the disconsolate, unloved lover, and took pity on it, I think you would recognize that it is no marvel for us to err, if you suffered such a care"). This experience of human suffering is, as we have seen in authors such as Bernard of Clairvaux, what made Christ's mercy perfectly suited to the human condition; it is the withholding of this recognition ("Pienso bien que conosçieses"), in turn, that makes Love's cruelty worthy of condemnation.

This contrast in experiences of suffering is thematized in the next section of the *Salmos*, based on Psalm 37, *Domine, ne in furore tuo arguas me neque in ira tua corripias me*:[52] "Nin te plega ya *sufrir*/ Ser desamado quien ama/ Nin tanpoco quien desama/ Ser amado con sentir" (lines 109–12; emphasis added; "Let it no longer please you to *suffer* lovers to remain unloved, nor that the one who denies love be loved with feeling"). There is thus an implicit contrast between the lover's intolerable suffering and Love's tolerance (*sufrir*) thereof, a tolerance that is unjust because Love's arrow robbed the lover of his free will in youth (lines 113–20).[53] The overwhelming wound wrought by God's anger in the original psalm (Ps 37:6–9) is figured in primarily psychological terms by Valera:

Ya soy fecho miserable
Tanta pena padesciendo,
E por ti siempre seyendo
En cuydado ynumerable.
Tu saña muy espantable
Me pena de tal manera
Que mi seso desespera
Con dolor inestimable.

E turbado es mi sentido
En tu yra maginando
E yo cativo clamando
Con cuytas envegecido… (lines 129–40)

I am now made miserable, suffering so much pain, and because of you always having care beyond measure. Your terrifying anger pains me so much that my mind becomes desperate with inestimable pain.

And my sense is disturbed, imagining your anger, and I, a captive, crying out with cares and grown old.

The lover's *padecer* is juxtaposed with Love's *sufrir*, the latter of which constitutes a form of anger that interferes with the lover's inner and outer senses (*seso*, *sentido*), provoking only an anguished cry. This cry is given form in the poem's next section, which adapts the well-known Psalm 50, *Miserere mei, Deus, secundum misericordiam tuam*, as "Miserere mey Cupido" (line 157).[54] Valera describes Cupid as "hijo de la madre santa" (line 158), thus conflating Venus and the Virgin in an ambiguous mesh of parentage and divine authority. The *Miserere* is a prayer for absolution whose singer recognizes his sin; as the Vulgate's rubric makes clear, the song is occasioned by David's confrontation with the prophet Nathan after the king's transgression with Bathsheba. In taking up the original psalm's themes of sin and absolution, Valera opens key stanzas with direct quotations: "Lávame de todo error" (line 165; cf. Ps 50:4; "Cleanse me from my sin"); "Ante ti sólo pequé" (line 173; cf. Ps 50:6; "Against you alone have I sinned"). Nevertheless, the sin to which Valera confesses inverts that of David:

Agora ya maldiré
Con rrazón á la fortuna,
Pues amando sólo una
Bien sirviendo te enojé.

Aquesta sola serví
No pensando que te erraba
Ni cuydando que pasava
Tu santa ley [que] aprendí. (lines 177–84, slightly modified)

Now I will justly condemn fortune, since loving only one and serving well, I angered you.

I served this one alone, not thinking that I offended you, nor considering that I transgressed your holy law, which I had learned.

To the extent that the *religio amoris* was perceived as blasphemous by early readers such as Fray Íñigo de Mendoza, the particular sin was idolatry, the worship of worldly figures in place of the divine (a beloved lady in place of the Virgin or, as in Mendoza's example, Macías in place of Christ). Valera's excessive fidelity in "bien servir" – "Aquesta sola serví" – is here ironically figured as its own kind of idolatry: he worshipped a single lady rather than Cupid and his mother themselves (the "monotheism" of his love service thus becoming another implied sin). In this courtly psalm, then, Valera crafts a surprising frame for the lover's impossible predicament, revealing a central contradiction in the purported system ("ley") of true love: adherence to love's laws requires a singularity of worldly devotion displeasing to transcendent beings, orthodox and unorthodox alike.

It is in this context that Valera, in the poem's next section (based on Psalm 101, *Domine, exaudi orationem meam et clamor meus ad te veniat*), refers to "the doctrine of Macías," adherence to which has led to his current tragic circumstances: "Que sólo por yo seguir/ La dotrina de Maçías,/ Bien como sombra mis días/ Pasaron sin reçebir/ Galardón, ante sofrir/ Muchas cuytas me feziste/ E tantas penas me diste/ Quantas no puedo dezir" (lines 217–24; "For only because I followed the doctrine of Macías, my days passed like a shadow, without reward; rather, you made me suffer many cares and gave me more pains than I can say"). The apparently commonplace hyperbole of this stanza's concluding line takes on new meaning when we recall that Valera will go on to describe this very poem as a *dezir* (line 316). This invocation of a suffering beyond articulation or versification, in turn, lays the groundwork for the agonizing cry of the poem's subsequent adaptation of Psalm 129, *De profundis clamavi ad te, Domine.*[55] What in the Vulgate is an exhortation to hope becomes, in Valera, a recriminatory cry of despair: "De lo más baxo del suelo/ A grandes voces yamé/ A ti, Señor, y alçé/ Mi gemido fasta el cielo;/ E jamás mi grave duelo/ Nunca te plogo entender/ Nin tu cabeza volver/ A mí, triste, sin consuelo" (lines 261–8; "From the greatest depths I cried out loudly to you, Lord, and raised my cry to heaven; and you never deigned to understand my deep pain, nor turn your head toward me, sad, inconsolate"). Confession and devotion were rewarded with worry and sadness (lines 269–72); consolation (*conorte*) was therefore to be sought elsewhere: "Quen verdad munchos ley/ Que en grandes yerros cayeron/ Y de ti bien rreçibieron/ De los quales munchos vi;/ Y el conorte que sentí/ En el punto que estos leo/ E saver mi buen deseo/ Con que sienpre te seguí" (lines 285–92, slightly modified; "For in truth I read of many who fell into great error, and received good from you, of whom I saw many; and the comfort I felt at the moment of reading of these is to know the good desire with which I always followed you"). Reading is portrayed here as a double consolation: first, it is a source of hope, providing examples of redeemed sinners against love; and second, it confirms for the poet his own pure intentions and fidelity as a follower of Love. Having established this, he can pray to achieve "aquella vitoria/ Que tus santos de la gloria/ Ganaron con discriçión" (lines 306–8; "that victory that your saints in glory won with discretion"). Discretion is thus identified as the virtue through which Love's iniquity can be overcome.

The relationship between discretion and rhetoric arises in the poem's final section, based on Psalm 142, *Domine, exaudi orationem meam, auribus percipe obsecrationem meam in veritate tua.* If discretion aids us in discerning the source of our thoughts, those who lack discretion often err in both speaking and keeping silent: "Que muchas veces fablando/ De tu merced blasfemamos,/ Con la vyda que pasamos/ Nuestras cuytas remenbrando;/ Y tanvien, Señor, callando/ El tu nombre maltratamos/ Con la pena que esperamos,/ De ti mucho nos quexando" (lines 329–36; "For we often blaspheme in speaking of your mercy, with the life we lead, remembering our cares; and also, Lord, in silence we mistreat your name, with the punishment we await, complaining of you so"). The lover, recalling his suffering and giving voice to his complaints, blasphemes divine mercy; yet dwelling on those complaints in bitter silence is an insult to the divine name. One may find in this last sin an allusion to the secrecy to which courtly lovers are sworn, a secrecy often betrayed not through words but through other outward signs of emotional torment (such is the case, for example, of the lover in Macías's "Cativo de miña tristura," to which I will turn shortly).[56] Valera here begins to enumerate some of love's torments (lines 337–52), but ultimately opts for a silent appeal to Love's mercy: "Aquestos [males] quyero callar/ My dezyr abreviando/ A tu merced suplicando,/ Que quyeras, Señor, dexar/ Nuestros yerros y pensar/ Las cuytas que sostenemos" (lines 353–8; "I wish to shorten my poem, no longer speaking of these ills, and begging of your mercy that you might, Lord, look past our errors and consider the cares that we bear"). The poem concludes with a final repetition of the *Gloria* refrain: "A ty, Señor, soberano/ Den gloria todas las gentes,/ Pues señores y sirvientes/ Goviernas con la tu mano" (lines 361–4; "May all peoples give glory to you, sovereign Lord, for you govern masters and servants with your hand"). This recognition of Love's omnipotence, woven through a prayer for just, merciful treatment, echoes Macías's demand for Love as king to be *comunal*, but it is characteristic of Valera to describe the divine power of Love in terms of governance. Valera's substantial engagement with the penitential psalms, occasionally hewing closely to their themes or citing specific verses, more often adapting them freely with an unexpected development of ideas, makes it impossible to view his *contrafacta* as the product of lighthearted parodic play. Tomassetti views them as an attempt to renew courtly discourse through the adaptation of religious imagery and language ("Los *Salmos*" 268); yet their repeated invocation of governance also connects them to Valera's ethical treatises, showing that the problem of mercy in the courtly paradigm could also propel ethical thought in new directions. *Cancionero* lyric of this kind thus becomes a vehicle for synthetic approaches to the multiple discourses of mercy, compassion, confession, and redemption to which fifteenth-century writers had access.

Envisioning Macías

The salvific logic underlying poems in this vein helps explain Macías's lyric afterlife as a ghostly voice in dream visions or a damned soul in lover's hell. An early example is Santillana's "Querella de Amor," which narrates a dream in which the lyric voice's sleep is interrupted by the plaintive singing of an unknown sufferer. Each stanza of the narration concludes with that singer's words, drawn principally from poems attributed to Macías.[57] The third and fourth stanzas present the initial exchange between lyric voice and ghostly singer:

> Pregunté: "¿Por qué fazedes,
> señor, tan esquivo duelo,
> o si puede aver consuelo
> la cuita que padesçedes?"

Respondióme: "Non curedes,
señor, de me consolar,
ca mi vida es querellar,
cantando así como vedes:
Pues me fallesçió ventura
en el tiempo de plazer,
non espero aver folgura,
mas por siempre entristeçer."

Díxele: "Segund paresçe,
el dolor que vos aquexa
es alguna que vos dexa
e de vos non s'adolesçe."
Respondióme: "Quien padesçe
cruel plaga por amar
tal cançión deve cantar
jamás, pues le pertenesçe:
Cativo de miña tristura,
ya todos prenden espanto
e preguntan qué ventura
es que m'atormenta tanto." (3, lines 25–48)

I asked: "Why are you mourning in such isolation; can the care you suffer find consolation?" He responded: "Do not try to console me, for my life is lamentation, singing, as you see: *Since fortune failed me in the time of pleasure, I expect no rest, but to be sad forever.*"

I said to him: "It seems that the pain that afflicts you is from a woman who abandons you without pity." He responded to me: "He who suffers a cruel wound for love should always sing such a song, since it belongs to him: *Captive, my sadness now frightens all, and they ask what misfortune it is that torments me so.*"

Santillana's recontextualization of the opening lines of "Pues me falleçió ventura," insisting, as it does, on the impossibility of consolation, appears in some ways to distort the cited poem in omitting the latter's invocation of a community of fellow sufferers in its final stanza. In fact, however, the following lines of the "Querella" allude to this omitted verse in both their reference to abandonment ("alguna que vos dexa") and, in a near quotation, to the abandoner's lack of compassion ("e de vos non s'adolesçe"). The poetic voice's speculative interpretation poises him to offer compassion in place of the cruel beloved. The suffering singer's reply, however, emphasizes that passionate suffering ("Quien *padesçe*/ cruel plaga por amar") both *enjoins* and *entitles* the sufferer to sing Macías's words, which have become his own ("tal cançión *deve cantar*/ jamás, *pues le pertenesçe*").[58] The mysterious interlocutor sings *as* Macías, and Santillana subtly *redoubles* this quotation through his own reworking of lines and themes from the quoted song. Finally, as was frequently the case in *decires con citas* (Tomassetti, "Sobre la tradición" 1709), the lines quoted here as refrains are in fact the opening lines of their respective poems, creating a form of backward enchainment that emphasizes the creative compositional potential of quotation. The quoted lines belong to later poets as a matter of both identification (a shared emotional experience authorizes the direct appropriation of earlier verse) and composition (earlier verse is matter for adaptation, recontextualization, and thematic reinvention).

If martyrdom is what links Macías to the discourse of passion in later troubadours, his compositional habits associated him with conscious reflection on poetics and the troubadour tradition. These two aspects of Macías's legacy are joined in the lover's hell, a poetic genre "very characteristic of fifteenth-century poetry," grounded in Dante and established in the Castilian tradition by Santillana's *Infierno de los enamorados* (Pérez Priego 66–7). The *Infierno* opens when Fortune, robbing the protagonist of his free will, transports him to a wooded mountain where he eventually encounters a monstrous, barking pig (lines 95–6). Here (in a stanza quoted in a different context in part one), the poet admits that his vision was not merely beyond description, but specifically beyond poetic, rhetorical, and scientific language:

> ¿Quién es que, metrificando
> en coplas nin distinçiones,
> en prosas nin consonando,
> tales diformes visiones,
> sin multitud de renglones,
> el su fecho dezir puede?
> Ya mi seso retroçede
> pensando tantas razones. (lines 97–104)

> Who could, versifying or in distinctions, in prose or rhyming, describe such deformed visions without a multitude of lines? My sense retreats, considering such reasons.

I argued in part one that this stanza's closing lines play on the dual senses of *razón* as enunciation and reason, as the protagonist's sense is overwhelmed in its attempt to formulate language descriptive of its experience. This poetic paralysis also reflects the protagonist's alarm before the monster, from which he is rescued by Hippolytus, a guide immune to love's temptations: "'Amigo,' dixo, 'non curo/ de amar nin ser amado,/ e por Dïana vos juro/ que nunca fue enamorado'" (lines 217–20; "'Friend,' he said, 'I care neither to love or be loved, and I swear by Diana that I have never experienced love'"). Hippolytus leads the protagonist through a lover's hell populated exclusively by classical figures until he finally encounters Macías, to whom he is drawn because the troubadour is overheard speaking Castilian.[59] Macías, before revealing his identity, declares:

La mayor cuita que haver
puede ningún amador
es membrarse del plazer
en el tienpo del dolor (lines 489–92)

The greatest care a lover can suffer is to remember pleasure during the time of pain.

Recall that the sentiment here attributed to Macías is a translation of a line spoken by the tragic lover Francesca da Rimini in Canto V of Dante's *Inferno*.[60] This translated, imagined quotation emphasizes, again, the status of allusive, speculative, alien language as especially suited to convey the deepest sorrow. Dante, upon hearing Francesca's lament, promptly faints: "for pity/ I swooned as if in death./ And down I fell as a dead body falls" (V.140–2; trans. Robert and Jean Hollander). The lines Santillana attributes to Macías not only recall Macías's own quotational practices, but allude, furthermore, to an exemplary case of empathetic identification embodied by an authoritative poet.[61]

The association between love martyrdom, composition, and quotation is further dramatized in Bernat Hug de Rocabertí's *Glòria d'amor*, a vision of the afterlife that combines the lover's hell and the lover's paradise (*Història de la literatura catalana* 412). Rocabertí (c. 1416–85) was born to a powerful family and belonged to Pere Torroella's literary circle (410); he seems to have composed a first version of the *Glòria* before 1457, which he then extended after the death of Violant Lluïsa de Mur, viscountess of Luna in 1467 (414). The *Glòria* shows the clear influence of Dante's *Commedia*; Boccaccio's *Amorosa visione*, *Ameto*, and *Fiammetta*; Petrarch's *Trionfi*; and of French poetry as well, especially Chartier's *Belle dame sans merci* (413). Along with these foreign influences, the poetry of Ausiàs March emerges recurrently throughout Rocabertí's text (413).

Like Santillana's *Infierno*, the less-studied *Glòria* "sentimentalizes" Dante (Cañigueral Batllosera); like Torroella's *Tant mon voler*, it includes lyric quotations in French, Castilian, and Catalan. The 1544-line poem opens with a prose prologue addressed to the young from the perspective of a long-suffering lover, warning them about Love's garden that "qui mes hi entr' e de sos delits vol mes sentir, cau en major dolor" (Rocabertí 49; "the farther one enters and the more one wishes to feel [Love's] delights, the greater the pain into which one falls").[62] The protagonist then recounts the vision he has had, guided by the beautiful Conaxença, of Love's castle and its garden, home to the famous lovers of the past, happy and unhappy.[63] This vision is framed by the protagonist's hyperbolic suffering, which moves the avatars of historical cruelty to pity: "Flames d'amor

Citarea lançava/ D'un estrany foch qui dins amor se creha,/ Cremant tan fort que remey no trobava./ Pirrus, Nero e los altres cruels,/ Vent mon turment, dolor gran los venia;/ De pietat se obrien los cels" (lines 13–18; "Aphrodite launched flames of love, of a strange fire created in love, burning so fiercely that I could find no remedy. Pyrrhus, Nero, and all of the cruel, seeing my torment, felt great pain; the heavens opened with pity"). Medieval thinking about cruelty, drawing on Seneca, had long been characterized by an opposition between cruelty and justice (Peter I of Castile is, of course, an emblematic figure of this binary; see Baraz 13, 132); this opposition in turn informed a notion of tyranny according to which "kings are cruel out of necessity, whereas tyrants do so for their own pleasure" (Baraz 15n5). As Daniel Baraz has noted, however, in the late Middle Ages descriptions of cruelty become "more explicit, more detailed, and more affective" (142). This characterization is yet another form of sentimentalization carried out by Rocabertí: Pyrrhus and Nero were famous as cruel killers, but the latter was also emblematic of a cruel indifference to death, and the compassion they are here said to feel thus sets in relief the absolute cruelty of the *belle dame sans merci*.[64] In the face of such suffering, Hope flees (lines 19–21), and the Understanding, in pain and deserted by Reason, is gripped by a new desire: "L'enteniment qui tal dolor sentia,/ Novell desig lo prengue d'altra forma,/ Pusque raho, fugint d'ell, se partia" (lines 22–4). Like other poets in his milieu, Rocabertí gives an account of passionate love that is broadly coherent with the image of a disordered soul whose cogitative faculties are misdirected by desire. The particularity of Rocabertí's portrayal is that – to the extent that a linear narrative can be discerned from these skeletal lines – it is pain, rather than desire, that appears to have provoked Reason's flight.

That the *Glòria*'s protagonist should have arrived at Love's castle impelled by pain complicates his wish to enter. When he knocks on the door, a sweet feminine voice (the as yet unidentified Conaxença) explains that it is not Love's will to receive him: "Lo pensament qui es sens mi,/ Amor james no·l reculli" (lines 164–5; "Love never admitted the thought that lacks me"). This affirmation recalls the protagonist's own observation in the prologue that many men seek to enter the garden of Love, "companyia sercant a llur pensament conforma" (Rocabertí 50; "seeking company in conformity with their thought"). *Pensament* here refers both to a form of melancholy care (similar to *cuidado*) and to the experience of love that provokes it;[65] it names the activity of the desiring, and suffering, intellect. This scene thus dramatically recreates a central paradox of the courtly love paradigm: only fortunate lovers may enter the castle, but it is the frustrated quest for this "conformity" that leads sufferers to the door. It is in this context that the protagonist successfully pleads for entry into the castle: "Ab tant cridi, lo seny cansat/ Per lo turment: 'De pietat!'" (lines 172–3; "I cried out, my sense exhausted by the torment: 'For pity's sake!'"). "Pity" is itself, of course, a synonym of gratitude/*conaxença* in courtly discourse, and these are in turn associated with the *grat* discussed by Torroella and Ferrer (see part one): "Amor es grat nudrit de fantesia;/ Mor per desdeny de bruta companyia" (lines 232–3; "Love is pleasure nourished by fantasy; it dies from the disdain of discourteous company"). The protagonist's definition mixes *grat*, an element of happy (requited) love, with fantasy or imagination, more often associated with the obsessive fixation of lovesickness, a fixation that typically would be morbidly resistant to rejection by *bruta companyia*. When Conaxença agrees to accompany the protagonist, thus allowing him to enter the castle and its garden, her gesture of *pietat* thus fuses the literal (pity) and euphemistic (erotic) senses of the term.

Notions of company, conformity, and reciprocation are also key in Rocabertí's idiosyncratic treatment of the figure of Macías. The troubadour appears in a "portico of entwined jasmines" (33) where, to the protagonist's delight, many lovers are found happily engaged in a variety of games and other pastimes (lines 1030–9). While some of these revellers are reading (line 1035) or reciting (line 1039), Macías sits in isolation ("Apart de tot"), reading and sighing (line 1040). Conaxença advises the protagonist, whose firm desire is to speak with Macías, to ask in the name of *fin' amor* that Macías reveal to him what lovers normally conceal ("ço que amant denegue," line 1045). The protagonist approaches Macías and asks for consideration as a newcomer ("per ser novell," line 1048), but the perturbed troubadour merely looks up from his reading and then takes his leave, sadly reciting the following lines: "Pues veho que mi dolor/ Por amar siempre recresse,/ Dire como quien padesse:/ A pesar de ti, amor,/ Soy leyal tu servidor" (lines 1052–6; "Since I see that loving only increases my pain, I will say, like one who suffers: in spite of you, love, I am your loyal servant"). Macías is thus portrayed first and foremost as a reader, and his first speech is a song framed as a quotation in the *Glòria*, which may itself be a quotation as recited by Macías.[66] This song, moreover, follows the poetic structure of the *decir con citas*, including the introductory enunciative formula "Dire como quien padesse," which strongly suggests that the song's concluding couplet is a quotation. At the same time, this introductory formula suggests that the language of love's suffering is impersonal or shared, a discursive ambivalence mirrored by the singer's account of his own emotional experience: he both suffers ("veho que mi dolor/ Por amar siempre recresse") and speaks *like* a sufferer.

Taken aback by Macías's apparent distress, the protagonist must be encouraged to persist by Conaxença, who explains that the troubadour is only angry to have been distracted from his thoughts and their pleasure, but will surely now answer (lines 1063–5). When Macías does invite a question, the protagonist first composes himself, then his thoughts:

Jo, vent en ell son gracios respondre,
Prengui esforç del primer moviment;
A·l satisfer forçat me fon compondre:
"Ta gran dolor a mi grant turment dona
Qui·m fa pensar en retraure·m d'amor,
Sabent los fets que fama de tu sona.

Tu sol servist amor per lo contrari
Tant leyalment com los altres amants
Amen la fi per lo pler voluntari.
Donchs, sabent jo esser tu singular
Sol de servir amor per sa semblança,
De semblant dol me vull maravellar." (lines 1069–80)

I, seeing his gracious reply, took strength from the first movement; to satisfy him, I was forced to compose: "Your great pain torments me greatly, making me think of retreating from love, knowing the events reported by your fame. You alone served love through adversity, as loyally as other lovers love for its end of desired pleasure. Therefore, knowing you to be singular, alone in serving love in its image, I am amazed by such suffering."

The protagonist's question is remarkable in several ways. First, if his familiarity with the concept of first and second movements is in line with that of other poets such as Rodríguez del Padrón, it is rare indeed that such knowledge should be put to use in analysing his emotional struggle when faced with another poet-lover. The poet seems aware of this peculiarity, playing on the link between emotional and discursive composition ("Prengui esforç … forçat me fon compondre"). The question also returns to the problem of singularity and similarity: Macías has managed to stand out from other lovers for remaining loyal through adversity (lines 1075–7), yet this singularity consists in a form of divine resemblance ("Sol de servir amor per sa semblança"). Heaton translates the closing line's "semblant dol" plausibly as "seeming affliction" in his paraphrase of the poem (Rocabertí 34), but it is also an emphatic echo of the preceding line's "semblança," implying that, if Macías's fidelity distinguished him, his suffering, however extreme, ties him to other troubadours. As if emphasizing this connective emotional tissue, the protagonist's "dol" recalls the "dolor" in the first line of Macías's song, making his interrogative "composition" citational in its own way.

Macías answers, in a Castilian dotted with Catalanisms (as Heaton notes in his comments on lines 1040–93 [Rocabertí 126]), that the same love that made him worthy turned against him, condemning him to the eternal reading of his own lost pleasure: "É mi plaser que de leyer no·m lexa,/ Por onde jo padesco atal vida" (lines 1089–90). Ultimately, then, Macías's appearance in Rocabertí's *Glòria* echoes that of Santillana's *Infierno*: his martyrdom consists in the forced recollection, through reading, of the pleasures of the past. In this sense, Rocabertí's portrayal of Macías's afterlife lays bare how "reading, memory, and composition are part of a creative continuum" for medieval writers (Weiss, "Memory in Creation" 151). Together, the visions of Santillana and Rocabertí round out this general principle by setting in relief the further association of memory and emotion, which is in turn associated with a particular, citational form of composition. With respect to passionate love, this web of associations produces – as it had in earlier troubadour traditions – conventional warnings such as that of the *Glòria*'s narrator, who interprets Macías's example to mean that no good can come from loyalty in love ("Sobres leyal d'amor be no alcança," line 1093).[67] The continued lyric exploration of passionate love and love martyrdom in the face of this inescapable conclusion reflects a desire to suss out the other ethical possibilities implicit in this mode of haunted creativity. It is perhaps for this reason that allusions to Macías, whether as quotations or as fictive encounters, often involved visions not just of the troubadour's tortured soul, but of the poet's own death.

With Macías in the Grave

It is in the second poem quoted by Santillana in the *Querella*, "Cativo de miña tristura," that Macías most famously used quoted refrains, and later poets returned to this poem perhaps more than to any other. Macías's poem ends with the poet's resolution not to divulge his romantic suffering, all the while knowing that his silence is powerless to prevent tongues from wagging:

Pero mays non saberan
de miña coyta lasdrada
e por en asy diran:

"Can rravioso e cosa brava
de su señor se que trava." (306, lines 32–6)[68]

But they will learn no more about my unhappy suffering, and thus they will say: "Rabid dog and fierce thing, I know it tears into its master."

Poets citing this song tended to reflect on both its form (the incorporation of quoted, in this case popular, refrains) and the closing theme of courtly secrecy. Gonzalo de Torquemada's "Maldita sea tal vida,"[69] for example, functions as a sprawling gloss on the song's first stanza. After an initial refrain ending in "cativo de minya tristura," each stanza proceeds from the subsequent line of Macías's song (that is, the first full stanza begins "Ya todos prenden espanto," the second "Et preguntan qué ventura," and so on). Each stanza then concludes with a repetition of the refrain, ending, again, in "cativo de minya tristura." The final stanzas thematize silence and repetition:

Quien bien see nunca devría
moverse como yo fize,
porque mi corazón dize
que callar nunca podría. (lines 60–3)

He who is well should never move as I did, because my heart says that it could never keep silent.

Al pensar que faz follía
dé lugar por que padeçco
tan gran mal que bien mereçco
repetir según solía:
¡O, maldita sea tal vida
pues no me basta cordura!
Que jamás no se m'olvida
de dezir por mi ventura:
cativo de minya tristura. (CXIX, lines 69–77; punctuation lightly modified)

Thinking that it is folly, cause me to suffer such a great evil that I deserve to repeat, as I used to: Oh, damn that life, since I lack good sense! For I never forget to recite for my misfortune: *cativo de minya tristura.*

What for Macías is the folly of thinking or planning something new when one is already well situated[70] becomes, in Torquemada's gloss, the error of having been moved, which makes silence impossible (lines 61–3). The substance of this speech, as revealed in the final stanza, is the dolorous repetition of the poem's refrain (that is, the poem itself). The gloss, while of course pointing readers to the earlier song, is in its conclusion self-referential to the point of circularity, achieving through *amplificatio* its own form of captivity.[71]

Macías's most devoted fifteenth-century follower was undoubtedly the Galician troubadour Juan Rodríguez del Padrón, who inverts the citational strategies of Santillana and Torquemada in "¡Ham, ham, huíd que ravio!" which expands in a playfully paradoxical way on the tension between silence and communication present in the closing stanza of "Cativo de miña tristura." Rodríguez del Padrón's poem takes up the closing image of the lover whose inarticulate raving betrays his suffering – a betrayal made manifest by the popular saying Macías appropriates – giving voice, in effect, to the lover's ravings:

Si yo ravio por amar,
esto no sabrán de mí,
que del todo enmudescí,
que no sé si no ladrar.
¡Ham, ham, huíd que ravio!
¡O quien pudiese travar,
de quien me haze el agravio
y tantos males passar!
Ladrando con mis cuidados,

mil vezes me viene a mientes
de lançar en mí los dientes
y me comer a bocados. (III, lines 5–16)[72]

If love makes me rave, they will not learn this from me, for I am totally mute, knowing only how to bark. Woof, woof! Flee, I am rabid! Oh, to be able to bite the one who offends me and causes me so many ills! Barking from my cares, I think a thousand times of tearing into myself with my teeth, devouring myself bite by bite.

This poem demands that readers or listeners understand its articulate verses to be distinct from the "barking" to which the lyric voice declares itself reduced; Rodríguez del Padrón in effect scripts an alternate interior monologue for Macías's lyric voice. Like the gossiping crowds alluded to in Macías's final quoted refrain, he interprets the original poet's anguished silence, but he does so lyrically in a kind of imagined quotation, which complicates the image of self-destruction in lines 13–16. The lyric voice, frustrated that it cannot tear into the source of its suffering, contemplates cannibalizing itself – but the "self" alluded to is in fact, at least in part, that of another. Indeed, "Ladrando con mis cuidados" is a punning *amplificatio* of Macías's possibly already punning "coyta lasdrada." Thus, both speaking and feeling inhabit a liminal, permeable space between the two poems and the two poets, making plain the lyric resistance to an easy identification of the subject of enunciation with the subject of predication and, more generally, the subject of thought with the subject of feeling. The impossibility of absolute silence and secrecy, whose narrative implications will be explored by writers of sentimental fiction (see chapter six), is here revealed as the other side of the impossibility of distinctive troubadour speech. In these circumstances, it may be that, as the poem concludes, "el remedio es callar" (line 28; "the remedy is to be silent"), but the likelier outcome, as Rodríguez del Padrón makes clear, is pathological inward violence.[73]

Given that the conventional outcome of this inward violence was death, many Iberian poets eschewed the narrative frame of visions such as Santillana's *Infierno* and Rocabertí's *Glòria* in favour of a direct lyric reckoning with their own deaths, in the form of an imagined burial. Rodríguez del Padrón's "Siete gozos del amor," for example, concludes with the following wish, addressed to his beloved:

Si te plaze que mis días
yo fenezca mal logrado
tan en breve
plégate que con Macías
ser meresca sepultado;
y dezir debe

do la sepultura sea:
Una tierra los crió,
una muerte los levó,
una gloria los possea. (I, lines 227–36)

If it please you that I end my days so soon, ill-fated, may it also please you that I be entombed with Macías; and wherever the tomb may be, it should say: *One land raised them, one death took them, may one glory possess them.*

If the insuperable contradictions of courtly love make union with the beloved impossible – reason inevitably overcome by passion, cruelty and disdain immovable – what can be hoped for is unity in death with an exemplary lover and poet, a spiritual union that courtly lovers insist is the only reward they sought in life. The reference to a shared birthplace ("Una tierra los crió") is consonant with notions of *piedad* as love between countrymen. Meanwhile, the reference to an afterlife of glory, in a poem parodying a genre of Marian devotion, implies that the conventional feminine cruelty of troubadour poetry is in effect a form of intercession allowing male poets to achieve literary consecration. Underscoring this point is what Dorothy Sherman Severin calls the "gentle irony" of Rodríguez del Padrón's poem: the joys he describes are really sorrows, given that "the lady ignores him" throughout ("Juan Rodríguez del Padrón" 81).[74]

This last point takes on particular significance when we recall that the poem as a whole plays on the "double-entendre of joy-*gozo* as a sexual euphemism" (Severin, "Juan Rodríguez del Padrón" 76). The seventh joy, anticipating the opening section of *Siervo libre de amor*, is to love and be loved, but this joy has already been denied to the poet when he reveals, in the lines immediately preceding those cited earlier, that he feels death approaching:

La muerte siento venir;
del cuerpo no sé que fagas;
muévante las cinco plagas
(celos, amar e partir,
bien amar sin atender,
amar siendo desamado,
y desamar no poder),
pues no te pueden mover
los goços que te he cantado. (lines 218–26)

I feel death approaching; I don't know what you should do with my body; may the five wounds (jealousy, loving and parting, loving hopelessly, loving but not being loved, and being unable to stop loving) move you, since the joys I have sung to you cannot.

The five wounds here enumerated allude not only to Christ but also to St. Francis (Severin, "Juan Rodríguez del Padrón" 81); Rodríguez del Padrón became a Franciscan late in life, contributing to the founding of the Franciscan convent in Herbón (Lida de Malkiel, "Juan Rodríguez del Padrón" 315). At this point in the poem, the status of the *muerte* awaited by the poet, sexual euphemism or mortal outcome of lovesickness, remains unresolved, an ambiguity redoubled in the following line, whose *cuerpo* may be a cadaver or, if the beloved is moved by the wounds of the unfortunate lover, may be restored to life by joy. It is only when this hope fails that identification with a suffering but still living Christ is supplanted by one with the martyred Macías, whose ultimate fate, as revealed by the optative "Una gloria los possea," remains uncertain.

At stake in these transsubjective identifications, whose potential is perceived and realized through shared language, is the possibility of worldly (courtly) redemption. As such, poets despairing of receiving compassion in this life at times imagined a belated redemption in the postmortem tears of the ladies who had rejected them. Yet these speculative tears were a poignant but imperfect solution to the lover's dilemma; their redemptive power remained doubtful. In another religious parody invoking Macías from the beginning, Rodríguez del Padrón throws into relief the uncertainty of this view beyond the grave:

Sólo por ver a Macías
e de amor me partir,
yo me querría morir,
con tanto que resurgir
pudiese dende a tres días.
Mas luego que resurgiese
¿quién me podría tener
que en mi mortaja non fuese,
linda señora, a te ver,
por ver qué planto farías,
señora, o qué reir?
Yo me querría morir,
Con tanto que resurgir
Pudiese dende a tres días. (V)[75]

Only to see Macías and to take my leave of love, I would like to die, as long as I could revive three days later. But once revived, who could stop me from going in my shroud to see you, beautiful lady, to see how you would cry, my lady, or laugh? I would like to die, as long as I could revive three days later.

Rodríguez del Padrón's identification with the wounded Christ in "Los siete gozos" and with the resurrected Christ in this poem thus frame Macías's identification with the agonizing Christ in "Pues me falleçió ventura." Unlike Macías, Rodríguez del Padrón couches this moment of identification in an openly ironic attitude, more even than in "Los siete gozos." This irony notwithstanding, the poem remains a declaration of love beyond death, as the resurrected poet imagines himself investigating, in his shroud, his beloved's emotional response to his demise. Might grief effect the redemption denied in life by the withholding of compassion? What, in turn, would be the effect of laughter? And if it is the intention of this very poem to provoke laughter, which is the preferred outcome in the postmortem scenario? Only the guarantee of resurrection – along with the pleasure of Macías's company – makes the gamble worthwhile. Although Macías's poetry goes uncited here, he is, from a compositional perspective, at the origin of the speculative identification explored by Rodríguez del Padrón. Passion, then, in this poem and others, stands for the power to move others (to tears, to laughter) while also opening a possibility of intersubjective identification through which the lyric voice demonstrates poetic mastery, rooted, in this particular case, in the glorification of a personal and personified literary heritage. At the same time, the uncertain or even pessimistic framing of this gesture of mastery is true to Michel Meyer's notion of passion as the "illegal" and unpredictable invasion of alterity that nevertheless constitutes us (172).

Rodríguez del Padrón was not alone in incorporating Macías into a vision of his own burial. Alfonso Enríquez, for example, composed a verse will (*Testamento*), sworn before the God of Love (*Cancionero de Palacio* CCCXIV, line 1; ID0135), that plays on the trope of living death by itemizing bequests to be granted both before and after the poet's death.[76] To his beloved are given his body and soul, to be treated as she pleases until his death (lines 9–20); the archbishop of Lisbon is to be his executor (*curador*; lines 21–4).[77] At this point in the poem, Enríquez describes his desired tomb and also the ceremony he foresees at his burial, a series of songs (quoted in the poem) performed by courtly ladies arrayed around the tomb. At the head of the tomb will be "Clara la muy especial" ("the very special Clara"), who will sing "con grito muy cordïal" ("with a very cordial cry") the first four verses of "Amor cruel e bryoso" (lines 65–72). It may very well be the case, as Beltran suggests, that, despite its macabre subject matter, this poem was a "courtly diversion," one of many such poems praising ladies at court for their beauty and artistic skill ("El *Testamento*" 71–2). Nevertheless, the *Testamento* is further evidence of a particular association, however lighthearted in this case, of Macías with troubadour quotation and the envisioning of death and burial. Thus, a poem attributed to Montoro in *Cancionero de Palacio* quotes Villasandino ("Loado seas, amor"; ID0663), an anonymous song ("Adeus miña boa senyor"; ID2505), Garci Fernández de Jerena ("Ruyseñor veo te quexoso"; ID1680), and Macías's "Amor cruel e bryoso" in explaining his torment and, echoing Enríquez's satirical will, his desire to set his life in order ("Hordenar quiero mi vida"; CXXXV, line 13).[78] Montoro goes beyond Enríquez, however, in concluding with a wish to be buried alive:

> Ya non puedo más durar
> esta vida padesçiendo
> et pues muero así biviendo
> bivo me quiero'ntenrar;
> ...
> *cativo de minya tristura*
> *pues me fallesçió ventura*
> cobrirá mi monimiento. (lines 21–8)

> I can no longer endure this life of suffering, and since I die living this way, I want to be buried alive ... *Cativo de minya tristura/ pues me fallesçió ventura* will adorn my tomb.

Montoro's song makes explicit the analogy between suffering as passion and living death, *vivir padeciendo* and *morir viviendo* (lines 22–3). The epitaph envisioned by Montoro rhymes the first lines of two poems by Macías, and the poem's earlier paired quotations (lines 10–11 and 18–19) rhyme first lines by different authors.[79] Through these rhymes, Montoro draws attention to the troubadours' shared language of suffering and collective form of composition, but rather than seek compassion, he renders the grave itself a space of sad captivity through his citational epitaph, eschewing any hint of redemption.

Passionate Identification and the Passion Narrative

Poets in subsequent generations would explore the relationship between compassion-as-reward and the Passion without the intercession of Macías. Perhaps the best example is Diego de San Pedro, who took a particularly dense, analytical approach to questions of courtly sentiment and whose *Pasión trobada* (composed in the 1470s) versified the life of Christ.[80] What is revealed by San Pedro's approach to the pairing of Passion and compassion is that, even as the comparison became more explicit in Castilian verse, the possibility of lyric identification through passion that we have been tracing in earlier poets was in fact in the process of disappearing as verse narratives such as the *Pasión trobada* became popular in late medieval Castile.[81] In short – and here we return to the song "Pues no sufre lo que siento," whose first stanza was discussed in chapter four – citational identification has been supplanted by a more literalizing and pious form of comparison:

> Ved lo que devo sentir,
> cuando no puedo hallar

remedio para bevir,
ni fuerça para sufrir,
ni poder para olvidar.
Havedme ya compassión;
no muera con falta d'ella,
por amor de la Passión
de Quien quiso padescella
como yo, sin merescella. (*Poesías* 9, lines 10–19)

See what I should feel, when I can find no remedy to live, nor strength to suffer, nor power to forget. Have compassion for me; let me not die for its lack, for love of the Passion of the One who chose to suffer it, as I do, without deserving it.

The similitude asserted by San Pedro resembles Macías's appropriation of Christ's anguish in "Pues me falleçió ventura" superficially, but the two are actually at a significant rhetorical and conceptual remove: "como yo" marks a distinction between subjects across which compassion is extended, similar to the way in which pity is loaned and returned in the poem's first stanza. In other words, compassion no longer erases the distance between subjects; it merely crosses it. In other places in San Pedro's love poetry, an older notion comes through, as when, in "Dama que mi muerte guía," he writes that his own verses "van apartando/ a mí de vos y de mí" (*Poesías* 1, lines 16–17; "are separating me from you and from myself") – they occupy, that is, a space of enunciation somewhere between himself and his lady. It is thus not surprising when, later in the same poem, we find a more direct and yet unspoken Christological identification: "Y sufro este trago fuerte/ donde hay dolores tan fuertes,/ por ver si podrá mi suerte/ despedir con una muerte/ la muerte de tantas muertes" (lines 26–30; "I suffer this harsh blow [literally: draught] in which there are such strong pains in order to see whether my fate will be able to dismiss with one death the death of so many deaths"). Here, the redemptive potential of this form of lyric identification is fully present, underscored by San Pedro's stylistic recourse to verbal repetition in which semantic variation (a definitional component, for example, of Occitan *rims equivocs*) is minimal. Redemption in this context is, in short, more a matter of sameness than of similarity.

At other times, the pairing of passion and Passion is a matter of memory and forgetting. Thus, San Pedro opens a poem set on Palm Sunday with the following reflection: "Cuando, señora, entre nós/ hoy la Passión se dezía,/ bien podés creerme vos,/ que lembrando la de Dios/ nasció el dolor de la mía" (*Poesías* 5, lines 1–5; "When, my lady, the Passion was recited today between us, you can well believe me, that in remembering that of God, the pain of my own was reborn"). Again, the comparison at the root of San Pedro's suffering is a matter of resemblance and remains the case when, in the *Pasión trobada*'s prefatory verses,

San Pedro invokes a desire to forget through devotion: "Pues no es pequeña razón/ que deva yo desear/ tener tanta devotión/ que llorando la Passión/ pueda la mía olvidar" (stanza XII, lines 1–5; "For it is no small reason for me to desire to have such devotion that, mourning the Passion, I might forget my own [suffering]"). The point is further emphasized in San Pedro's invocation of the Virgin: "ella me quiera alcançar/ del immenso Dios tal don,/ que pueda yo bien trobar,/ y trobando bien llorar,/ el dolor de su Passión" (stanza 5, lines 1–5; "may she help me attain from God such a gift, that I be able to compose well, and, composing, mourn well the pain of his Passion") In these lines, inspired compositional memory produces compassion and saving sorrow, which had of course long been considered productive for prayer, but is here tied to poetic practice, *trobar*. What this comparison suggests is that, in the rise of a more Christological Passion devotion in Castilian culture, compassion-as-identification has lost its poetic independence. Even an early call in San Pedro's text for the contemplative reader to feel what Christ felt – "Siente agora, peccador,/ lo que su alma sentía" – is immediately tied to contrition: "¡O quién contrición toviesse,/ que pensándolo pudiesse/ quebrantar el coraçón!" (stanza 32, lines 1–2 and 8–10; "Oh, to have the contrition whose contemplation would cause the heart to break!"). Indeed, contemplation is frequently figured as spectatorship, as in Mary's understated lament: "Mirad si mi mal es fuerte;/ mirad qué dicha es la mía;/ mirad mi captiva suerte,/ que le están dando la muerte/ a un hijo que yo tenía" (stanza 189, lines 6–10; "See if my pain is strong, see how fortunate I am, see my captive fate, for they are putting a son I had to death"). The discourse of sight, even if tied to the production of mental images, marks the distance between subjects in setting the scene of compassion.

The manuscript version of the *Pasión trobada*, which differs from all subsequent printed editions, ends with a final pairing of compassion and Passion in a prayer to Christ: "Y Él, que padeció pasión/ por nuestra culpa salvar,/ por la su resureción,/ haya de nós conpasión,/ y nos quiera perdonar" (264A; "And may He, who suffered passion to redeem our sins, by his resurrection, have compassion for us, and wish to forgive us"). As in Fray Íñigo de Mendoza's roughly contemporary *Coplas de vita Christi*,[82] the pairing of passion and compassion is no longer one of identification; compassion has its own, very distinct identity as pity taken by one on another. This form of compassion was always, of course, implicit in the courtly notion of compassion-as-*galardón*, but it coexisted with a notion of shared passion as the basis for poetic invention, just as the exaltation of reason coincided in ethical texts with clearly delineated, positive notions of love, friendship, sorrow, and compassion. San Pedro and his contemporaries inherited these tropes from earlier generations and deployed them with great frequency, complexity, and tonal variation; but one already detects in their passionate and compassionate play the emergence of a subjective atomism that was not unknown to Macías, Rodríguez del Padrón, Santillana, and others, but was rather actively resisted by them. As I will discuss in the conclusion, this atomism, also emergent in San Pedro's masterpiece of sentimental fiction, *Cárcel de amor*, would come to be seen as the way out of the paradoxes of courtly love and its attendant ethics. It was not, however, the first remedy explored by earlier authors of sentimental fiction such as Rodríguez del Padrón and Pedro, Constable of Portugal, whose diagnosis of the courtly impasse was nevertheless substantially the same as San Pedro's. As I argue in the next chapter, these authors sought to retain a lyrical ethics of compassionate identification while fully exposing the implications of the courtly lover's predicament through narrative.

Chapter Six

The Impasse of the Courtly Reward

Among the tragic lovers surveyed in Rocabertí's *Glòria* alongside Macías are Ardanlier and Liessa (see lines 777–812), the doomed protagonists of the *Estoria de dos amadores* in Rodríguez del Padrón's *Siervo libre de amor*, generally held to be the first Castilian work of sentimental fiction. The external boundaries and internal cohesion of this notoriously hybrid genre have been the subject of a vigorous scholarly debate that cannot be rehearsed here in comprehensive detail. Rather, in what follows, I will focus on two related aspects of the genre that are not in dispute: structural hybridity and the predominance of psychological action.[1] In this vein, Alan D. Deyermond summarizes the genre's main characteristics thus: "brevity, the predominance of psychological interest over external action, a tragic vision of love, autobiographism (first-person narration or a narrator who is also a character), and the inclusion of letters or poetry (or, often, both) in the narrative" (*Tradiciones* 47).[2] Deyermond's apt description is typical in setting formal factors (such as brevity and the inclusion of letters or poetry) alongside psychological ones ("a tragic vision of love"), but the relationship between form and content in the genre has been understood in different ways. For example, Gerli relates sentimental fiction's foregrounding of emotion and the psychological faculties to the genre's roots in *cancionero* poetry:

> The sentimental romance seeks to be lyrical through narrative. Like the courtly lyric from which in large part it doubtless developed, the sentimental romance sets out to express intimate experience, to create mood and sympathy before explaining or justifying the origins of those feelings … Through the exploitation of verse, epistles, and allegory, the romancers sought to create the aesthetic effect of poetry in order to represent and investigate in detail the hidden world of emotion and motivation. ("Toward a Poetics" 476)

Gerli goes further, arguing that sentimental fiction's focus on emotion to the detriment of "battles and thrilling adventure" was a crucial step in the development of the novel (480).[3] On the other hand, the representation of emotion in sentimental fiction, while painstakingly intricate, is not necessarily recognizable from a modern point of view as psychological realism (Varela 11), and a focus on emotion may not be an end in itself, but rather a polemical gesture: "a vociferous reaffirmation of sentiment as a faculty and noble, trustworthy form of human perception" (Varela 32). As such, the critical debate around sentimental fiction reproduces, in its own way, the tensions already present in the works themselves: emotion can be an escape from fantasy or from reality; it can transfer "poetry's function as a timeless and spaceless medium of self-analysis" (Gerli, "Toward a Poetics" 477) to the realm of prose or make an epistemological claim valid for both the interior and exterior world; poetry, letters, and glosses can be present as vestiges of a medieval past or harbingers of a modern future. In the end, what the critical debate highlights is the need to move away from panoramic or synchronic views (while not ignoring the relationships among individual texts) – that is, away from what Jauss calls the "rule-and-instance" conception of genre (80) – and toward a hermeneutic that considers individual authors' recontextualizations and structural juxtapositions from a wider, but fluid, perspective.

There are several relationships to untangle here: that of the structural elements of the text (prose, poetry, gloss) among themselves; that of private and public virtue; and, from the broadest perspective, that of interiority and exteriority, of narrativized sentiment and historical example. We may begin by noting the different names that have been proposed for the genre, both of which have already arisen previously: sentimental romance or novel (*novela sentimental*) and, the term I have preferred, sentimental fiction. All three foreground emotion: as Folger observes, "virtually all scholars" of the genre agree that "the primary focus of the texts grouped under this generic headline lies on the exploration of the emotional processes underlying and caused by 'amorous captivity'" (*Images in Mind* 63). *Novela sentimental* was coined by Menéndez Pelayo, and as Marina Brownlee notes, the Castilian term *novela* denotes both "romance" and "novel" in English (4), thus synthesizing (or leaving unresolved) backward- and forward-looking critical perspectives. The term is therefore most suggestive for the diachronic unfolding of these texts' sources and legacy.

Ficción sentimental is not just a broader and less generically fraught alternative to *novela*, however. Rather, as I employ the term, it serves to emphasize the process highlighted by both Gerli and Folger, that is, the transposition of the emotional conventions and preoccupations of courtly lyric into prose narrative. I take as my starting point a distinction between "fiction" and "action" found in a section of Cartagena's *Oracional* devoted to the five intellectual virtues: intelligence, knowledge, wisdom, art, and prudence or discretion ("*prudençia* que comunmente llamamos *discreçion*"; 64). Here, Cartagena defines art (*arte*) as "la recta e derecha rrazon que dispone las cosas fictibles que son fuera del omne" (65; "right reason that arranges those things that can be fashioned that are outside of man"), explaining further:

> Ca aquello propiamente sse llama *fiçion* que faze su acto fuera del omne, commo hedificar e otros actos, quier sean sotiles quier groseros. *Acçion* propiamente se llama aquella que exerçe sus actos de dentro del omne commo disponer sus pasiones e quitar e paçificar su coraçon conformándole con las virtudes. (65)
>
> For *fiction* refers properly to what acts outside of man, such as building and other acts, whether subtle or crude. *Action* properly refers to what acts inside man, such as disposing his passions and quieting and calming his heart, bringing him into conformity with the virtues.

Although sentimental fiction portrays the inner landscape of emotional experience in great detail, in allegorical debates corresponding to Cartagena's virtue-oriented "action," it sets itself apart from the equally intricate (indeed, often identical) portrayal of emotion and emotional conflict in earlier lyric precisely by contextualizing that conflict in external, narrative action. The question is whether, on the one hand, the authors of sentimental fiction seek to recreate, express, and explain the emotional predicaments of courtly lyric in their prose – "be lyrical through narrative," in Gerli's terms – or, on the other hand, whether the shift to narrative prose was meant to develop or challenge lyric convention.

Complicating this interpretive binary is the extensive inclusion of lyric poems in the earliest works of sentimental fiction. Louise M. Haywood perceives inserted lyrics as essentially complementary to the narrative portrayal of erotic suffering: "Together with first-person expressive devices like letters, monologue, apostrophe, and dialogue, lyric is especially apt for conveying the romances' emphasis on the effects of an idealistic concept of love on an individual" (197). For Brownlee, however, these inserted lyrics serve "to represent and to problematize the referentiality of language per se" (7). In other words, to the extent that sentimental narrative seeks to innovate by moving beyond lyric, lyric persists and resists this "fictional" (in Cartagena's terms) gesture, highlighting the distance between words and things just as it highlights the distance between pronoun and noun, resisting, that is, "the naming of names that determines the subject as someone with a certain *historia*, with a singular, limited, and individual 'life story'" (Stone 7). From this point of view, although most early works of sentimental fiction are pseudo-autobiographical, they retain the inherently collective subject position of courtly lyric.[4]

In this chapter, I analyse three of the earliest works of sentimental fiction: Rodríguez del Padrón's *Siervo libre de amor* (c. 1440), and Pedro, Constable of Portugal's *Sátira de infelice e felice vida* (c. 1448–53) and *Tragédia de la insigne reina doña Isabel* (1457). The key ethical terms and fundamental emotional circumstances explored in these works are taken directly from the paradoxes of courtly lyric, but their adaptation into narrative produces two important changes. First, the ethical stakes of the conflict between compassion, desire, prudence, and reason are rendered in exquisite detail through the juxtaposition of prosopopoeic debate and narrative action. Second, narrative allows for a more direct encounter with death, which in turn manifests a more direct sense of ethical urgency and raises the notion of consolation alongside that of compassion as a moral, social, and literary imperative.

The degree to which the narrative frames of early sentimental fiction are individualizing varies considerably; there is no doubt, however, that the translation to narrative of the constitutive antitheses of courtly lyric subjects them to considerable strain.[5] The frustrated love of the poems I have studied thus far is fundamentally static, with death an imagined or even expected, but resolutely future event; narrative in sentimental fiction sets the stage for the possibility of death's presence. If Iberian courtly lyric already sought a way out of these contradictions through the rhetorical and artistic valoration of compassion and other forms of shared emotion, sentimental fiction dramatizes the fatal consequences of failure to escape. Such dramatization remains a problem, however, for first-person narratives such as Rodríguez del Padrón's *Siervo libre de amor* and Pedro's *Sátira.* Rodríguez del Padrón's *Siervo* addresses this problem through the insertion of a secondary narrative, the *Estoria de dos amadores,* through which the author (and readers) can contemplate and learn from the deaths of others. At the same time, *Siervo* maintains considerable continuity with the thematic and compositional concerns of Rodríguez del Padrón's poetry and, in particular, with his exploration of citational composition. Indeed, the ethical implications of creative quotation are decisively exemplified in the fates of Ardanlier and Liessa: if lyric has shown that collective composition favours the merciful virtues, the *Estoria* narrates the tragic and self-destructive consequences of a cruel refusal to quote in good faith.

Siervo libre de amor: Compassion and the Ethics of Quotation

Siervo libre de amor, which survives in one manuscript (Biblioteca Nacional de España, ms. 6052), opens with a short preface explaining the work's allegorical structure: it is divided into three parts representing three "times" ("tres diversos tiempos"), each of which is symbolized by a path and a tree that also stand for three parts of man, that is, the heart, free will, and understanding.[6] The first time, of loving and being loved, is represented by the green myrtle and the path followed by the heart; the second, of loving and not being loved, by the white poplar and the "descending path of despair" followed by the free will; and the third, of neither loving nor being loved, by the green olive and the path followed by the understanding, "por donde siguió [el siervo], después de libre, en compañía de la discreçión" (10; "taken by the Siervo, once freed, in discretion's company"). The first part of the text is presented as a letter from Rodríguez del Padrón to Gonzalo de Medina providing a key to interpreting the text as a whole and describing the psychological havoc wreaked by an unhappy love affair, ruined when the author revealed his secret to a friend he had mistakenly judged to be "discreet" (16). This description includes an early intervention by the author's Discretion, seeking to convince him to abandon his love service. In the second part of the text, described as a "solitary and grievous contemplation" (18), the author wanders through the "dark wood of his thoughts" (18), coming upon the three paths described in the preface and, at the instigation of his Free Will, opting for the "desçendiente vía que es la desperaçión" (19; "descending path of despair"). Here, the author is confronted by his Understanding, which pleads with him to turn back and take the third path of neither loving nor being loved, "however harsh it may be" (22). Free Will rejects the Understanding's entreaty, and the author is eventually abandoned by his heart, Free Will, and Understanding, leaving him to plead for a death similar to that of Ardanlier, whose story is recounted in the third part of *Siervo*, the aforementioned *Estoria de dos amadores*. Finally, at the conclusion of this rather lengthy tale, the author, reciting songs of desperation to the fleeing birds, is visited by "an aged lady dressed in black," later identified as Synderesis (40), the "spark of conscience" identified by Aquinas and Bonaventure as "the faculty of the human soul that is a remnant of prelapsarian perfection, allowing the immediate, unmediated, and infallible apprehension of good and evil" (Francomano 143n2). It is to this feminine personification of wisdom that the author recounts his "aventuras," giving the work as a whole a circular structure.[7]

The preceding summary gives only a sense of the structural complexity of *Siervo* and, in particular, largely omits the many interspersed lyrics that will figure in my analysis of the text. Furthermore, there is significant disagreement about whether Rodríguez del Padrón is the author of the initial preface and other paratexts.[8] It is not my intention to carry out a comprehensive interpretation of the text, but rather to trace how several of the conceptual and ethical approaches to passion arising in the lyrics by Rodríguez del Padrón and others discussed in the previous section are adapted and altered in *Siervo*'s allegorized narrative and, in particular, in the *Estoria de dos amadores*. Although Brownlee associates allegory and lyric in sentimental fiction by showing that allegory is undermined, as is lyric, in a way that calls attention to the imperfect referentiality of language (7), Folger argues convincingly that debates between first-person narrators and mental faculties such as Discretion or Understanding would not have been read as properly allegorical: "for a contemporary [that is, medieval] reader the faculties of the soul, their activity and struggle, are signified, not symbolized. They do not require interpretation because they are directly understood" (*Images in Mind* 77–8).[9] It is nevertheless the case that, in such debates, personification is a strategy for formalizing the expression of what are otherwise disturbingly ineffable emotional phenomena (think, for example, of Macías's howling dog, driven to vocalize despite the courtly prohibition of indiscreet speech). Along these lines, Óscar Martín has argued that the prominent shift to allegorical discourse in sentimental fiction represents an attempt "to mask, by means of deflecting what is unexpressible, the perception of social displacement suffered by the nobility" (134). Allegory in this reading would constitute a second reactionary wave, following what Boase described as the Castilian aristocracy's nostalgic return to courtly lyric at the end of the fourteenth century (7–8; see introduction). As Martín explains, this displacement was felt not merely in material terms, but as "linked to the emergence in Castile of an incipient, but rapidly formed, modern and economic subjectivity, one that shifts away from aristocratic subjectivity" (134). However, I seek to show here that, just as rhetorical explorations of passion and compassion in Iberian lyric constitute both a recognition of sociopolitical crisis and an attempt to address the crisis through a revision of the tools of troubadour subjectivity rather than a turn to the individual ego (as I argue in previous chapters), the early works of sentimental fiction constitute a continuation of this approach. Through allegory and the juxtaposition of prose narrative and lyric, they reveal and exemplify the untenability of the contradictions of courtly love, all the while offering revised notions of discretion and pity as paths out of the "dark wood."

Mirroring Rodríguez del Padrón's presentation of *Siervo* as an allegory of paths leading to wildly divergent outcomes, the criticism to which it has given rise has followed divergent paths to sometimes diametrically opposed conclusions. Thus, critics disagree about whether *Siervo* is complete, or missing a third part; about what that third part might have contained; about the function of allegory in the text; about the relationship of the intercalated lyrics and *Estoria de dos amadores* to the text as a whole. Of particular relevance where questions of emotion are concerned is the debate surrounding the text's ultimate view of good love, *bien amar*. Several critics view *Siervo*, in the end, as a rejection of courtly love in favour of spiritual love understood as divine devotion and contemplation. Eukene Lacarra's encapsulation of the text's central aim is in this respect paradigmatic: "It seems evident to me that one of Rodríguez del Padrón's objectives was to write a *reprobatio amoris*. However, his true aim is more ambitious, given that it is not limited to condemning love but rather shows us a model of conduct to follow, the arduous and demanding path of indifference to the world [*desamor al mundo*] and love of God" (165).[10] Dissenting from this view are Olga Todurică Impey, for whom the text is an "anti-code" recommending human love (*amor mixtus*) over frustrated desire (183), and Patricia Grieve, who has written that "Siervo may find a higher plane for his need to love, in his pursuit of God, but this realization of what we might call a hierarchy of love service does not, of necessity, require a condemnation of other kinds of love service" (24). More recently, drawing on Aquinas's understanding of synderesis and the potential of the emotions to be morally good when voluntary and arguing convincingly for the identification of Synderesis and Discretion in the text, Folger has explained that Synderesis "advises the lover to accept Love's reign and embrace his feelings with good will" (*Images in Mind* 114; on Synderesis and Discretion, 109). Indeed, Cátedra has argued that the most truly unifying element of the sentimental fiction genre as a whole is the attempt to elaborate a "properly courtly and poetic" conception of love (*Amor y pedagogía* 144). The question this argument raises is why these authors would seek to elaborate, through an experimental, generically hybrid, and highly allegorical literary mode, this courtly conception of love if, on the one hand, it was already susceptible to definition in lyric and other forms of verse (Ermengaud's *Breviari*, for example) and, on the other, Christian charity was already available as a model of good love.

The answer begins with the realization that, even beyond the frequently satirical *religio amoris*, these writers did not understand charity as the only form of spiritual love. In *Siervo*'s opening dedication to Gonzalo de Medina, Rodríguez del Padrón describes himself as "el menor de los dos amigos eguales en bien amar" (10; "the lesser of two friends equal in loving well"). The descriptor *menor* has been read as a sly allusion to the author's Franciscan vows, but we should also note that this allusion to friends who are "equal in loving well" frames the work within the onto-ethical discourse of Madrigal's *Brevyloquyo*. What Rodríguez del Padrón offers his friend is indeed a lesson in loving well, in the form of "fiçiones segund los gentiles nobles de dioses dañados e deessas, no por que yo sea honrrador de aquéllos, mas pregonero del su grand error y siervo indigno del alto Jhesús" (11; "fictions in the style of the noble gentiles, of aggrieved gods and goddesses, not because I am their worshipper, but rather proclaimer of their great error and unworthy servant of Jesus most high"). These "fictions" constitute, when correctly understood, a *reprobatio amoris*:

> Ficçiones, digo, al poético fin de aprovechar y venir a ti en plazer con las fablas que quieren seguir lo que naturaleza no puede sufrir; aprovechar con el seso alegórico que trahe consigo la ruda letra, aunque pareçe del todo fallir, la qual si requieres de sano entender, armas te dizen contra el amor. (11–12)

> Fictions, I say, for the poetic purpose of benefitting and pleasing you with fables that seek to follow what nature cannot allow; benefitting through the allegorical sense borne by the rude letter, although it may seem entirely lacking, which if approached with a healthy understanding, arms you against love.

As the text's editor clarifies, what "nature cannot allow" is a fiction that lures readers away from the truth (11n17). In this case, however, it is the fiction of the *Estoria de dos amadores* that returns the author to the truth by manifesting "the real contradictions of the individual and of the social group in which both the 'auctor' and Rodríguez del Padrón himself are inscribed" (Dolz 123, 127–8). The "external" story, neither feigned autobiography nor prosopopoeic inner struggle, suggests a resolution to the otherwise fatal contradictions of courtly love – contradictions that even the Understanding fails to overcome. In this sense, it is significant that, despite framing his work as a *reprobatio amoris*, Rodríguez del Padrón insists that "en señal de amistad te escrivo de amor" (12; "as a sign of friendship I write to you of love"), suggesting a kind of continuity between the two emotions to the extent that the analysis of erotic and spiritual love might serve the purposes of friendship as, respectively, an alternative and complement.

This dedicatory phrase also suggests the emotionally complex modes of social cohesion explored by and effected through the lyric dissections of love discussed in the previous chapter, where quotation might be seen as itself a form of friendship providing refuge from the vicissitudes of love's contradictions. *Siervo*, in its simultaneous incorporation of allegory and lyric, subsumes this mode of invention into the lover's inner struggle. Thus, after the prefatory remarks addressed to Medina, the newly unhappy lover is confronted by his own Discretion, who rebukes him by quoting his invective against love back to him: "¿Y qué merced esperas del contra ti airado amor, que así maltrataste por tu odiosa cançión?" (13; "And what favour do you expect from love, which is furious at you, who mistreated it so in your hateful song?"). The song's familiar complaint is that love withholds just rewards for loyal service: "¿Qué hombre puede sofrir/ más sin razón,/ que del señor reçebir/ mal galardón?" (14, lines 18–21; "What man can tolerate such injustice, to receive a bad reward from his lord?"). The invocations of both *merced* and *galardón* return us to the terrain of *piedad*, and indeed, from this point on, *Siervo* (and many subsequent works of sentimental fiction) will precisely explore the mortal consequences of loving without receiving this compassionate reward. But here again, it is important to note that *piedad* was tied to public as well as private virtue, as Cartagena, echoing Madrigal's *Brevyloquyo*, makes clear in his *Oracional*:

> La virtud que se llama *piedad* estrechamente tomada consiste en fazer honrra e ayuda razonable a los padres e a otros asçendientes e parientes segund su grado e proporçion e a la tierra de su naturaleza e a los çibdadanos [e amigos] della. E aun podemos esto considerar acatando el vocablo que lo paresçe mostrar. Ca dezimos *piedat* commo sy dixiesemos *patriedat* que es por respecto a los padres e patria e non enbarga a esto que comunmente dezimos *piedad* a la *conpasion*. (86)
>
> The virtue called *piety* consists, strictly speaking, in honouring and helping one's parents and other relatives according to their degree and proportion, and also one's birthplace and its citizens and friends. And we can also consider this referring to the word itself, which seems to show it. For we say *piety* as if we said *paternity*, which refers to parents and fatherland, and this is so although we commonly refer to *compassion* as *pity*.[11]

Cartagena goes on to distinguish this familial and national fellow feeling from charity, which is inherently universal and thus cannot be applied to smaller forms of human community (86). From this point of view, then, what is at stake in *Siervo*'s exploration of *amor* and *piedad* is not just the psychological and mortal fate of its protagonist, but the role of these passions in the broader web of human relations.

The author's heart answers the invective quoted by Discretion with a *decir con citas* whose first stanza concludes with a popular saying: "Quien no segura, no prende" (*Siervo* 14, line 3; "One who offers no guarantees in love cannot retain it"). The second stanza quotes lines composed by an unidentified king: "El señor rey lo dizía/ por su gentil invençión:/ bien amar, aunqu'es follía,/ quiere arte y disçreçión" (14–15, lines 5–8; "The king used to say it in his elegant invention: loving well, although it is foolish, requires art and discretion"). Discretion sees itself as apart from, and resistant to, the passions, but the heart's quoted verses reinscribe discretion as a courtly virtue, a technique of good love rather than a form of resistance thereto. Finally, the heart quotes Juan de Padilla: "El gentil Juan de Padilla,/ quando de amor se partía,/ dixo con pura manzilla:/ 'no só ya quien ser solía'" (15, lines 13–16; "The gracious Juan de Padilla, taking leave of love, said with pure compassion: 'I am no longer who I once was'").[12] Although the abandonment of love is figured here as a loss of self, the value of self-identity is already thrown into doubt through the multiple layers of quotation, as personal suffering is expressed through alien, and alienated, language. The heart, through the multiple quotations of its song, does not merely defy Discretion's ability to control the passions; rather, it subtly undermines the very allegorical frame of an interior struggle between Discretion and the passions. Reason and passion are not, the heart suggests, discrete categories, and the struggle between them, such as it is, is neither wholly individual nor wholly internal.

At this point in the text, the author is deserted by his warring faculties, finally giving voice to his own song, an invective against love that synthesizes the author's parallel loss of self and community: "Malquisto de vos y quanto/ paso la desierta vía,/ amadores, con espanto,/ fuyen de mi compañía" (22, lines 6–9; "Detested by you and going along my lonely way, lovers, frightened, flee my company"). Todurică Impey considers this the first of *Siervo*'s lyrics to diverge from its prose introduction and notes that the other lovers' flight is not typical of the troubadour tradition, suggesting that they are reacting to his status as "malquisto" or simply to the overwhelming excess of his suffering (Impey 174). In either case, she concludes, these fleeing friends must be Castilian rather than Provençal (174). I believe that the author's poem does indeed allude to the roots of the Castilian troubadour tradition, and specifically to the sad lyric voice of Macías's "Cativo de miña tristura," from whom "ya todos prenden espanto" (line 2). This lyric allusion anticipates *Siervo*'s conclusion, which, as we will soon see, situates the author in a lineage of exceptional lovers descended from Macías. On the path to this conclusion, but now in the depths of utter despair, the author is visited by a dream vision in the form of a short romance, the *Estoria de dos amadores*, which tells the story of the doomed lovers Ardanlier and Liessa. Unlike earlier and subsequent allegorical passages in *Siervo*, the *Estoria* is both removed from the author's first-person perspective[13] and free of lyric insertions; yet it still narrativizes a paradigmatic failure of quotation and of mercy, thus approaching shared thematic and compositional concerns through formal difference. In the *Estoria*, Ardanlier, prince of Mondoya, defies his father, king Croes, and abandons the kingdom after a series of chivalrous exploits – including an ambiguous dalliance with the French princess Irena, who secretly commissions a golden lock symbolizing her chaste fidelity to Ardanlier, giving him the key – to live in hiding with his lover, Liessa.[14] Tragically, seven years later, Croes finds the lovers' hideout while Ardanlier is hunting, leaving the vengeful king alone with Liessa and a servant, Lamidoras. Liessa pleads for mercy, but Croes refuses: "Demandas merçed: rey soy, no te la puedo negar. Mas dize el verbo antigo: 'merçed es al rey vengar de su enemigo'" (26; "You ask for mercy: I am a king, I cannot deny it to you. But as the old saying goes, 'it is a mercy to the king to take vengeance on his enemy'"). Croes then slays the pregnant Liessa, condemning himself unknowingly to political disaster in the future. Croes's cruelly mistaken political choice, then, is portrayed as a rhetorical mistake; in effect, the misinterpreted and inapt maxim through which he rejects the counsel of mercy dooms him.[15]

This link between citational and political error is emphasized when Ardanlier returns home to find Liessa's cadaver and accuses his loyal servant, Lamidoras, of her murder. For, in making this false accusation, Ardanlier unknowingly echoes the recently departed Croes: "Salvaçión es del señor matar al siervo traidor" (27; "It is the lord's salvation to kill the traitorous servant"). Unlike Croes, however, Ardanlier can be talked out of his murderous intent, precisely through the relation of his own father's inhuman cruelty: "Con mucha mesura pidía merçed, mas el furioso rey Croes, cruel más que las fieras animalias brutas que no han sentido de piedat, no lo quiso padeçer" (27–8; "She asked for mercy with great courtesy, but the furious king Croes, crueler than the brute, wild animals who have no sense of pity, refused to suffer it"). Lamidoras's portrayal of Croes's refusal to hear Liessa's composed pleas, "no lo quiso *padeçer*," locates his cruelty at the crux of his insensitivity to language and lack of compassion. Ardanlier, by contrast, can be returned to his senses precisely because he is exquisitely sensitive to the problem of compassion and does not wish to be perceived as cruel. Indeed, before taking his own life, he writes to Irena that this perception is his only fear:

> E ya sólo pavor he, de mí predicarse de mi tan grand crueldat e cómmo es de consentir yo ser amado y no amador de tal presionera de mí. ¡O desseada Irena!, no quieras dar el nombre cruel al piadoso amador ni más affligir al aflitto. Piensa lo que creo pensaras si tú fueras madama Liesa según que Irena e vieras a mí, requestado de nueva señora, amar en despreçio y olvidança de ti. (28)

> And I now fear only that my great cruelty will be proclaimed, and that it will be asked how it could be permitted that I be loved by, yet not love, a captive such as you. Oh

> desired Irena! Do not bestow the name "cruel" upon the pious lover, nor further afflict the afflicted. Think of what I believe you would think if you were madam Liessa and not Irena, and you saw me, summoned by a new lady, love again, disdaining and forgetting you.

The *Estoria* thus inverts the gender dynamic of courtly love lyric, in which the demands of feminine virtue appear cruel to the frustrated male lover.[16] Here it is Ardanlier who, in seeking to avoid this perception, must invoke Irena's own empathetic imagination. Although he will perish, he will be remembered as merciful rather than cruel. Meanwhile, his father Croes, whose violent vengeance has earned him the unending enmity of the Emperor, will be condemned by his cruelty to a cycle of violence, as the Emperor makes clear to him in a letter declaring him anathema: "Por ende tú, que eres vitorioso contra las flacas mugeres más dignas de piedat, cumple que de aquí adelante aperçibas ser vençido o vençedor de los hombres; que más vale con destreza ser vençido de los vençedores que sin denuedo ser vençedor de los vençidos" (31; "Therefore it is fitting that you, who are victorious against weak women more deserving of pity, from now on prepare to be conqueror or victim of men, for it is better to be skillfully vanquished by the victorious than to be effortlessly victorious over the vanquished"). While the main thrust of the Emperor's condemnation rests on Croes's act of violence against a woman, his language – "cumple que de aquí adelante aperçibas ser vençido o vençedor de los hombres" – also makes clear that the king's lack of mercy makes violence, in victory or defeat, the only possible mode of relation in his future.

The *Estoria* comes to an end as Irena converts the secret home Ardanlier and Liessa had made for themselves into a magically sealed tomb into which only the purest of lovers could penetrate. All attempts to enter would end in failure until the success of Macías, of whom, in a subtle nod to *Siervo*'s dedicatory address, the author declares himself to be the lowest descendant, "el menor" (35). Here, the author awakes from his dream, determined to turn back from his own previously suicidal intent. As he makes his way back, however, he sings two consecutive songs, both paraphrases of Macías. *Siervo*'s editor writes of these songs that "the lyric ending acts as a propaedeutic for the restoration of [the author's] faculties and the imminent reinstatement of grace" (39n213). And it is certainly true that the first song describes the author's amorous suffering as a problem of alienation and psychic integrity: "Cativo, libre naçí,/ y después, como sandío,/ perdí mi libre alvedrío,/ que no soy señor de mí./ Sin cobrar lo que perdí/ nin fallar mi poderío,/ ¿cómo diré que soy mío?" (36, lines 3–10; "Captive, I was born free, and after, like a fool, I lost my free will, for I am not my own master. Without recuperating what I lost or finding my authority, how can I say that I am mine?").

Later in the same song, the author asks an apparently similar rhetorical question: "Tantos males he passado/ que, pardiós, aunque me vía,/ ¿pensáis que me conoçía?" (37, lines 49–51; "I have suffered so many ills that, by God, if I saw myself, do you think I would recognize myself?"). And yet the address to a sympathetic crowd in the question "¿pensáis que me conoçía?" alludes to the palliative effects of compassion central to the foregoing plot. *Siervo*'s final poem thematizes this need, as the author articulates the pain of singing of love without receiving a response from his audience of birds. After a failed initial attempt, he redoubles his efforts: "E por los más atraher/ a me querer responder/ en señal de alegría,/ cantava con grande afán/ la antigua canción mía:/ Pues que Dios y mi ventura/ m'a traído a tal estado,/ cantaré con grand cuidado,/ cativo de mi tristura" (39, lines 28–36; "And to better entice them to respond to me, in a sign of joy, I sang with great zeal my old song: Since God and my fortune have brought me to such a state, I will sing with great sorrow *cativo de mi tristura*"). The irony, of course, is that "Cativo de mi tristura" is not *his* old song, but rather Macías's well-known composition, one that, as we have seen, thematizes through the use of quoted refrains the futility of courtly discretion. To the extent that the author's unhappiness stems from the betrayal of his lover's secret, this closing lyric quotation seems to undermine all that has gone before, inscribing a lyric circularity within the circularity of *Siervo*'s narrative frame. This circularity is why the rejection of worldly love that some perceive the author to achieve upon the arrival of Synderesis fails to encapsulate the work's overarching ethical thrust. It is not, in the end, that worldly passion must be rejected. For synderesis, in Franciscan ethics, belongs to the will, not the understanding (Cátedra, *Amor y pedagogía* 147), and the will closed to compassion will fail to transcend courtliness's fatal contradictions.[17] Or, as another refrain in "Cativo de miña tristura" has it, "Quien en carçel suele vivir/ en carçel deseja morrer" (lines 19–20; "The one accustomed to living in captivity desires to die in captivity").

Sátira de infelice e felice vida: The Rhetoric of Cruelty

Rodríguez del Padrón's most immediate literary disciple is Pedro, Constable of Portugal (1429–66), the son of the Infante Pedro, Duke of Coimbra. The Constable's *Sátira de infelice e felice vida* (c. 1448–53), a text that exemplifies the structural and discursive complexity of the nascent genre of sentimental fiction, has been shown to draw heavily on *Siervo* for its sentimental narrative (Serés, "Ficción" 38).[18] Yet sentimental narrative is but one of the three literary modes the *Sátira* comprises. The second, shared (as we have seen) by *Siervo*, is courtly poetry. The *Sátira* diverges from its sources, however, in its inclusion of a third literary mode, numerous encyclopedic glosses (composed by Don Pedro himself), which draw on diverse cultural traditions, especially classical literature and the Stoic and ascetic moralism deeply rooted, as we have seen, in the Portuguese court of the Constable's father and of his uncle, Duarte. The resulting juxtaposition of these modes, however, is hardly syncretic. Rather, the text is characterized by both open and clandestine polemic: the author debates allegories of his own Discretion and of his cruel lady's virtues, and the dispassionate glosses are a stark counterpoint to the hyperbolic sentiment of the almost eventless narrative. The one constant feature of this fractured text, I argue, is a rejection of cruelty in favour of compassion, an insistence on the moral possibility and necessity of the *galardón*. In the *Sátira*, the Constable rejects the traditional links between the passions and sin, on the one hand, and the passions and suffering, on the other, stripping away the tropic stylization of the compassionate *galardón*. The *Sátira*'s staged confrontation between emotionally ascetic moralism and courtly sentimentality is an attempt to make a central space for compassion in ongoing debates about princely education and good governance. To the binary of reason and will, common to moral philosophy and courtly literature, the Constable seeks to add an axis of compassion and cruelty.[19]

The Castilian version of the *Sátira*, based on an earlier Portuguese version, now lost, was produced by the Constable in Castilian exile. His father served as regent from 1439 to 1448, after Duarte's death and during the minority of Alfonso V, repeatedly clashing with a group of proverbially unruly nobles throughout this period; ironically, the origin of the conflict appears to have been the very act of naming his son Constable, sometime before 1444.[20] The conflict came to a head in 1447, when Pedro was forced by the young king to retire to his lands in Coimbra, even though, by this time, Alfonso was married to Pedro's daughter, Isabel. Finally, in 1449, Alfonso declared Pedro a rebel, and the two entered into direct, armed conflict. On 20 May, Pedro was killed at the Battle of Alfarrobeira, forcing all of his children but Isabel into exile; most fled to Burgundy, where their aunt was duchess, but the Constable went to Castile, where he would remain for the next six years. This exile was not the Constable's first time in Castile; in 1445, he had taken part in an expedition supporting Álvaro de Luna in his struggle against his own unruly nobles, the *infantes* of Aragon. Although the Constable arrived after the battle had already been won, he was received with great pomp at the court of John II, where he made the acquaintance of the greatest literary lights of the day, chief among them Santillana.[21] The Constable's later Castilian exile both cemented his political impotence and returned him to the scene of his literary awakening, and it constitutes his main period of activity as a writer. Although he wrote mainly in Castilian, he is from a biographical perspective a truly pan-Iberian figure: upon returning to Portugal in 1456, he participated in domestic politics and in several expeditions to northern Africa. It was during one such expedition, to Morocco in 1463, that he received an invitation to become count of Barcelona and king of Aragon from the Consell del Principat, which had risen up against John II of Aragon. Don Pedro's claim to the throne rested on the fact that his mother was the daughter of the last Count of Urgel, whose own royal aspirations were dashed in the Compromise of Caspe (1412). The Constable proved to be an ineffectual ruler (he is remembered as the "Intruder King"), and he died of natural causes in 1466.[22]

The *Sátira* opens with a dedicatory letter to the Constable's sister Isabel, wife of Alfonso V. The sentimental narrative then begins in the prison of love, where the lovesick author, recalling the lyric antithesis of solitude and company with which Ayala described his literal imprisonment (see chapter four), finds himself "retraydo de humana compañía, mas non de cuydados, anxias, congoxas e ravias" (18; "distanced from human company, but not from cares, fears, sorrows, and rages"). Immersed in his suffering, he imagines a conversation with cruelty and lodges a complaint against fortune before being scolded by his own Discretion, to whom he responds silently, with tears and sighs (43).[23] The author then leaves the prison, only to be confronted by the seven virtues; Prudence and Pity engage him in debate, praising his lady and defending her from his accusations. The author eventually wins the debate, and there follows a poem exhorting the lady to pity and warning her of the risks of her cruelty. The sentimental narrative closes as the desperate author tries to decide whether to kill himself or live on, suffering, in the dubious hope that his beloved will eventually grant him the *galardón* of her pity (174).[24] Accompanying this narrative are 102 glosses, comprising mainly explanations of the Constable's numerous classical allusions, but also a number of miniature treatises on crucial concepts of moral philosophy, such as the will. Thus, in its courtly setting, staging of the conflict between reason and love, preoccupation with feminine virtue, and ostentatious display of erudition in the service of moral exemplarity, the *Sátira* embodies many of the cultural complexities typical of a period widely recognized, even at the time, as one of crisis and flux.

It was perhaps that feeling of crisis that led Castilian humanism to have a "dominant concern for the education of the statesman" (Weiss, *The Poet's Art* 12). As J.N.H. Lawrance has shown, in the fifteenth century "reading became not merely a means to an end for a professional minority, but an end in itself for a whole privileged section of society" ("The Spread" 80). As we saw in part one, this new readership sought out vernacular translations of classical authors, eschewing the lyric poetry, satire, and drama that would become popular later in favour of didactic and moral works. The understanding of classical allusion as a primarily didactic mode suggests the contexts of princely education and theory of statecraft for the *Sátira*, and indeed, Luís Adão da Fonseca, in his introduction to the text, characterizes Don Pedro as a resolute patriot who "valorizes the necessity of a link between the subject and society, in which the love of the '*pátria*,' the citizen's responsibility, and the urgency of an attitude oriented toward serving the community are constant references" (Pedro, *Sátira* XI). On the other hand, this point of view stems from an almost exclusive emphasis on the *Sátira*'s glosses, whose relation to the rest of the text is in fact a contentious point, whereas the sentimental narrative, while still overwhelmingly concerned with virtue, is focused almost entirely on the author's inner life, leading Elena Gascón Vera to claim that, for Don Pedro, "man's duty is to himself, dedicating his activity to the pursuit of individual virtue" (55).

This dual tension, between, on the one hand, interiority and exteriority, and on the other, the disparate structural elements of the *Sátira* – what might be called the inner experience of the narrative and the historical exemplarity of the glosses – reflects the diversity of Don Pedro's sources but is not explained by it. Guillermo Serés, having identified Alfonso de Madrigal's *Las diez qüestiones vulgares* as the main source for the *Sátira*'s glosses ("Ficción" 39), elsewhere dismisses the Constable as a typical noblemen – and a young one at that – eager to show off his second-hand erudition:

> The *Sátira* is thus a product typical of the mode of composition employed by most of the "*caballeros*" interested in approaching the *auctores* and demonstrating a certain degree of erudition; in both cases, however, they do not manage to escape from encyclopedic culture, which, in this case, is represented by the bishop of Ávila [that is, Alfonso de Madrigal]. ("Don Pedro" 982)

Few now contend, however, that the *Sátira*'s encyclopedic glosses – which also describe key figures of courtly culture, including, in succession, *Siervo*'s Ardanlier and Macías himself (38–40) – are ornamental to, or in any way separable from, the sentimental narrative. Rather, narrative and glosses are typically held to be in some form of dialogue, be it complementary or subversive. The latter view is argued most forcefully by Brownlee, who holds that the *Sátira* subverts both "the amorous discourse that it purports to valorize" (106) and allegory and gloss themselves as heuristic modes (111–16).[25] For Brownlee, this subversion is a reaction to the "semantic exhaustion" of the courtly aesthetic, so that "by consistently juxtaposing the subjective states of the individual with historicity, the tension of self and other … Don Pedro is replacing the anticipated lyric structure with novelistic discourse" (116). Gerli, by contrast, sees the *Sátira*'s contribution to the "development of European imaginative prose" as its "subversion of the medieval narrative esthetic," in which it adopts lyric poetry's focus on the speaker's subjective state to produce "action conceived for the sole purpose of producing and sustaining emotion" ("Toward a Revaluation" 115). It will be noted that both of these compelling readings presuppose an understanding of lyric as the paradigmatically subjective poetic mode, which clashes here with two different conceptions of narrative (historical exemplarity and chivalric adventure) as objective. Once again, however, our reading of the *Sátira* may shift if we perceive the lyric tradition on which it draws in epideictic terms. Such a reading is suggested by Don Pedro's introductory letter to his sister, wherein he explains the aims of "satire" and the role the glosses play in furthering them.

Reprehensión

Toward the beginning of the letter, Don Pedro offers a definition of "sátira," one that holds none of the comedic connotations now associated with satire: "quiere dezir reprehension con animo amigable de corregir; e aun este nombre satira viene de satura, que es loor, e yo a ella primero loando, el femineo linage propuse loar, a ella amonestando como siervo a señora, a mi reprehendiendo de mi loca thema e desigual tristeza" (*Sátira* 5; "it means scolding [*reprehensión*] in a friendly, corrective spirit; and this name 'satire' comes from 'satura,' which is praise, and I, praising her first of all, set out to praise the entire feminine lineage, admonishing her as a servant does his lady, and scolding myself for my mad theme and unequalled sadness"). This definition is not original to Don Pedro: similar ones are found in Santillana's *Comedieta de Ponça*, Mena's *Coronación*, Diego de Valera's *Defensa de las virtuosas mugeres*, and Enrique de Villena's *Los doze trabajos de Hércules* and *Eneyda*, and it originates in Saint Isidore (Serés, "Ficción" 36).[26] As it happens, Don Pedro fails to carry out this "satirical" program, triumphing in his debate with the personified virtues and thus making his lady, and not himself, the ultimate object of moral critique. This forensic exemplarity reflects Don Pedro's definition of satire as *reprehensión*, a key rhetorical technique within the contemporary understanding of rhetoric as a moral science. As we saw in part one, Alfonso de Cartagena, in the translation of *De inventione* carried out at the behest of Don Pedro's uncle Duarte, included Aristotle's *Rhetoric* in a moral trilogy alongside the *Ethics* and *Politics* (*Rhetórica* 30); thus, in his *Cinco libros de Séneca*, Cartagena writes that "la rhetorica se trabaja en loar lo honesto & *reprehender* lo torpe, segund que por los libros della asi de aristotiles com(m)o de tulio paresçe" (cited in Kohut, "Der Beitrag" 194n37; emphasis added; "rhetoric is exercised in praising the honest and *admonishing* the misguided, as can be seen in the books of Aristotle and Cicero dedicated to it"). In the Constable's cultural milieu, then, rhetoric was understood as an instrument and constitutive element of moral philosophy. Cartagena's translation of *De inventione* includes another, slightly different definition of *reprehensión*: "Reprehensión es aquella por la qual argumentando omne o destruye o aflaca o adelgaza la confirmaçión de los adversarios" (*Rethórica* 92; "*Reprehensión* is that through which the debater either destroys, weakens, or narrows the claim [*confirmación*] of his adversaries"). This understanding of *reprehensión* as rebuttal reveals the extent to which the structure of debate characterizes the entire *Sátira*: beyond its prosopopoeic debates, *reprehensión* underlies its entire complex structure, making it an extended moral refutation. And as in *Siervo*, it is not ultimately passionate love but cruelty, personal and public, that is condemned.

The *Sátira*'s dedicatory letter also explains the presence of the glosses, comparing them to the 100 eyes of Argus, himself said to represent prudence (12). As eyes take in light and guide the body, the glosses will guide the reader, clarifying the text's obscure points. However, as Brownlee points out, Argus – who failed to protect Io when Hermes lulled all of his 100 eyes to sleep – is an astoundingly bad choice as prudence's representative (111–12). For Brownlee, this inapt allusion is part of the text's subversive program. But Argus's death at the hands of Hermes is not the end of the myth, nor of Don Pedro's retelling thereof: "porque en la narraçion preçedente dize la piadosa Juno, *de conpasion movida*, la cabeça de Argos muerto trasmutar en la fermosa cola de pavon, la qual muchos ojos grandes e pequeños possee" (13; emphasis added; "because as the foregoing narrative relates, the pious Juno, *moved by compassion*, transformed the dead Argus's head into the peacock's beautiful tail, which has many eyes, large and small"). Thus, compassion itself is placed at the mythic origin of the glosses, and it is also, therefore, placed in an epistemologically primary position, an originary element of the clarity (and adornment) that the glosses provide. If Argus's eyes are a figure for perspectival instability, the multiple perspectives they represent are nonetheless rooted in Juno's compassionate gesture. Don Pedro offers compassion, not prudence's failure, as the hermeneutic key to the *Sátira*. And it is the moral and epistemological privileging of dispassionate prudence – along with discretion and reason – that is the target of Don Pedro's *reprehensión*.

A further question is to whom the *confirmaçión* of prudence, discretion, and reason should be attributed. In addition to the convention of opposing reason and the passions or will in troubadour lyric, examined in part one, there was a broader tradition of literary debates between these two forces; one prose example, in which the will emerges as the eventual victor, can be found in the next (chronological) work of sentimental fiction, the *Triste deleytaçión* (3–18).[27] One of the chief features of *Triste deleytaçión*'s debate is Reason's wariness of the Will's rhetorical ability. Thus, Reason says of the Will: "Vuestras fengidas razones con alguna color de verdat reçitadas no dan a mí causa de alguna neçesidat uviese de dar fe en ellas" (4; "Your deceitful arguments, recited with a certain colour of truth, give me no necessary reason to believe them"). "Colour" here recalls the rhetorical "colours" or techniques found in medieval rhetorics.[28] In this and other sentimental texts, rhetoric is conventionally but pointedly aligned with the passions against the truth. Cartagena, by contrast, also draws attention to the link between rhetoric and the passions, but without condemning the latter as false, when he writes (as cited earlier) that the "princes of eloquence" did not just write composition guides, "mas dieron sus generales doctrinas para argüir e responder, para culpar e defender *e para mover los coraçones de los oyentes a saña o a misericordia o a las otras pasiones que en la voluntad humana cahen*" (*Rethórica* 33; emphasis added; "rather, they gave general doctrines for arguing and responding, accusing and defending, *and for moving the audience's hearts to anger or mercy or the other passions of the human will*"). This last rhetorical operation is, of course, the subject of the second book of Aristotle's *Rhetoric* and thus is also held to be morally charged. And in Iberia's fifteenth-century discussion of moral philosophy, all three rhetorical modes – deliberation ("argüir e responder"), forensics ("culpar e defender"), and epideixis – revolve around the value of discretion.

Discreçión

As an essential element of judgment, discretion was central to princely education; according to the *Tratado de la comunidad*, for example, the king who lacks discretion is incapable of judging (94). But in the fifteenth century there was no real distinction between public and private discretion, understood as discriminating prudence:

> Aristotle differentiates between prudence as the power of discrimination, and the virtues as the forces necessary to act honorably. However, this is not reflected in the medieval system of virtues: in the Middle Ages prudence is in fact one of the virtues. This accounts for the reticence to describe politics as a domain of the practical world as opposed to a system of moral values. Medieval authors deal only with the moral system, which accounts for every human action … The king's role is seen only from the perspective of his function as ruler, and the moral system only from the perspective of free will, vice, and responsibility. There is no distinction between the ethical character and the social condition of the king or the duties that concern him. (Rohland de Langbehn, "Power and Justice" 202)

In fact, prudence's role in medieval moral theory can be usefully analogized to the king's role in feudalism: just as the king was the most powerful, but not the only lord, prudence is pre-eminent among the virtues, both of them and prior to them. As Santillana writes in his *Proverbios o Centiloquio* (written at the request of John II for the instruction of the future Henry IV):

> Çiertamente bien mereșçe
> Preminençia
> quien de doctrina e *prudençia*
> se guarnesçe.
> El comienço de salud
> es el saber
> *destinguir* e conosçer
> quál es virtud. (383, lines 117–24; emphasis added)

> He certainly deserves pre-eminence who furnishes himself with doctrine and *prudence*. The foundation of health is knowing how to *distinguish* and recognize what is virtuous.

The ability to resolve internal moral dilemmas is perfectly analogous to the ability to judge difficult cases – the latter an ability Santillana considers essential for winning the affection of one's subjects (Rohland de Langbehn, "Power and Justice" 210). Furthermore, prudence is superior to eloquence: "Si fueres gran eloquente,/ bien será;/ pero más te converná/ ser prudente,/ que el prudente es obediente/ toda vía/ a moral filosofía/ e sirviente" (Santillana 383–4, lines 137–44; "It is good to be very eloquent, but better to be prudent, for the prudent are always obedient servants to moral philosophy"). There is a strangely unresolved tension here between eloquence and moral philosophy encapsulated in the words "toda vía." If they are taken to mean "in all ways," it points to the moral neutrality of eloquence, showing prudence to be the decisive factor in eloquence's moral possibilities. However, they also seem to imply, through their homophony with "todavía," that the prudent retain a moral obedience that the eloquent transgress. The rhetoric of judgment is thus subtly distinguished from eloquence as such.

Already in Cartagena's *Rethórica*, eloquence is posited as a morally neutral source of social cohesion. In a speculative passage on the origins of civilization, Cicero argues that a great, eloquent man must have arisen from the savage masses to persuade them to organize themselves. This man met first with resistance, but soon was able to persuade the others: "E luego a comienço reclamavan con la sobervia que tenían, e después por la razón e por la eloquençia oían más voluntariosamente e de fieros e crueles que eran, tornó-los mansos e paçíficos" (Cartagena, *Rethórica* 36; "And in the beginning they complained because of their arrogance, and after, through reason and eloquence, they listened more willingly, and he made them, cruel beasts that they were, meek and peaceful"). The key here is not the meek state to which the audience was reduced, but the fact that they were persuaded to listen willingly. The sentence re-enacts in miniature the conflict between reason and the will, and eloquence's target is shown to be the passions. But Cicero is also speculating about a supposed neglect of rhetoric in ancient times, and he posits that it came into disrepute because of some eloquent but ill-intentioned men who brought great destruction to the cities they came to rule through their very eloquence (38). Eloquence is therefore placed at the origin of both political community and corruption; it is no wonder that medieval authors sought to avoid destructive eloquence by advocating prior discretion.

In this way, the private virtue of discretion becomes the key to both virtuous eloquence and good governance. The king protects and foments communal morality through a two-fold exercise of discretion that, again, traverses the public and private. The explicitly public element of the king's moral leadership is the administration of justice, but the king whose superior discretion leads to virtuous private behaviour also serves his subjects as an exemplar of morality. For Santillana, these two roles (judge and exemplar) are inextricably linked: "Pues devémonos forçar/ a bien fazer,/ si queremos reprehender/ o castigar" (388, lines 213–16; "We should oblige ourselves to do good if we want to admonish or punish"). The concept of *reprehensión* has made its return here, corresponding to the exemplary role of kingly virtue. The *Proverbios* are an important precursor to the *Sátira*, since in them Santillana anticipates Don Pedro's self-glossing. Even erudition should serve the goal of *reprehensión*: "Non cobdiçies ser letrado/ por loor,/ mas sçiente *reprehensor*/ de pecado" (382, lines 101–4; emphasis added; "Do not desire to be a man of letters for praise, but an informed admonisher [*reprehensor*] of sin").[29] Discretion, knowledge, and eloquence enable the king to watch over public morality.

In the *Sátira*, Don Pedro affects to be exercising his erudition and eloquence in the service of *reprehensión*. It should alarm us, then, that his author defeats personifications of his own Discretion and his lady's Prudence in debate, only to end up in a moment of supreme indecision (incapacity to judge), able neither to take his own life nor to willingly endure his ongoing suffering. If we take the author to be merely a negative example whose bad end is a lesson to others, then his emotions become rhetorical instruments of Don Pedro's overarching moralism, and his eloquence in relating and defending them would simply lay bare rhetoric's moral vacuity. If that were the case, however, the author's full-throated condemnation of cruelty would also be fatally undermined. In effect, to ask readers simply to take the author's bad end at face value as a warning of love's risks is to leave unresolved the conflict between reason and will: reason's triumph is also cruelty's, and as the author himself says early on while inveighing against fortune, no two things are more opposed than cruelty and virtue: "Et quales son o a do se fallaran mayores contrarios que crueldat e virtud? Tu los ayuntaste en la mas perfecta señora que bive, tu fesiste que su virtud e beldat engañassen mi coraçon, que de libre fuesse cativo e subjecto, e que su crueldat amenguasse e destruyesse en mi juvenil edat muy apressuradamente la mi vida" (33; "And what are, or where could one find, greater opposites than cruelty and virtue? You joined them in the most perfect lady alive, you caused her virtue and beauty to fool my heart, caused me to go from freedom to captivity and subjection, and caused her cruelty to diminish and destroy, very quickly and at a young age, my life"). In other words, to understand the *Sátira* as a *reprobatio amoris* is to ignore its central tension. On the other hand, to take the author at his word that compassion, the *galardón* he seeks from his virtuous but cruel beloved, is his only salvation is to reject the model of virtue as subjugation of the will to reason – and it is through discretion that this subjugation takes place. Thus, Don Pedro dramatizes in the *Sátira* two moral conflicts: alongside the traditional one between reason and the will is another between compassion and discretion.

Discretion's Plea

In the *Sátira*'s introductory letter, Don Pedro twice emphasizes his work's novelty: he translated it into Castilian because "everything new is pleasing," and his self-glossing is also a novel feature (9). He asserts self-glossing's novelty by constrasting it with ancient practice: "Ffize glosas al testo, aunque no sea acostumbrado por los antiguos auctores glosar sus obras" (9; "I made glosses for the text, although it was not usual for ancient authorities to gloss their own works"). The daring of these novel practices should not be confused with arrogance, however; Don Pedro has already clarified that he wrote in Castilian "mas costreñido de la neçessidat que de la voluntad" (9; this is a reference to his exile; "more out of necessity than desire"), and he added glosses out of the fear that his text would raise more questions than it answered (9–10).[30] This letter's content may, in broad outline, contain all of the elements of medieval *accessus ad auctores* (Serés, "Ficción"

48), but its discussion of novelty and fortune also introduces the theme of the will overcome. Don Pedro's will was not, however, overcome by his reason or discretion; rather, circumstances led to his adoption of Castilian, which is only retrospectively justified as an aesthetic choice. The *Sátira*'s glosses follow the opposite path: the text's classical allusions were first the product of his increasing pleasure ("gozo") in writing about the "worthwhile lives of Antiquity" as he discovered them, and only later did he realize that they would require explanation (10). In narrating the production of his novel work of moral instruction, then, Don Pedro emphasizes aesthetic choices based on circumstance and pleasure, to a certain extent undermining any universalizing or encyclopedic pretensions that might be imputed to him. At the same time, the ultimate motive of his writing is his amorous suffering, which led him to try to "declarar mi apassionada vida" (4; "describe my life of suffering"). Even the didactic goal of *reprehensión* is retrofitted into these emotional circumstances, so that the *Sátira* is ultimately presented as a work in which the moralistic impulse occasioned by emotional suffering is successively hijacked by historical circumstance, the pure pleasure of study, and finally, the alternative moral response of compassion, exemplified by Juno's transformation of the eyes of her imprudent, murdered sentinel into those of the peacock's tail.

The rhetorical nature of the *Sátira*'s opening (both its dedication and introductory chapter) is not exhausted by its reference to *reprehensión* or its structural similarity to the *accessus ad auctores*. The first chapter opens in the prison of love, where the author is a captive; he gives the day, month, and hour in which the narrative begins and also tells readers of his young age (15–20). In his gloss on "En el comienço de la terçera edat de mis años" (23; "At the beginning of my life's third age"), he explains that the inclusion of this information is evidence of the author's emotional state, since those who are suffering mark time more closely. Furthermore, he specifies his age in order to provoke the compassion of "aquella persona a quien se quexava" (23; "the person to whom he was complaining"), since he was too young for such suffering. In this way, novelty, youth, and suffering are linked, given that "toda nueva dolor al humano coraçon mas llaga e fiera que otra alguna" (23; "each new pain wounds the human heart more fiercely than any other"); this gloss is thus the mirror-image of the introductory letter's association of novelty with pleasure. The formulation "aquella persona a quien se quexava" refers ambiguously to the author's beloved or to Don Pedro's sister; at the same time, the author has not yet begun to speak (or complain), and in the very sentence in which he reveals his age, he explains that even now he lacks the daring to speak of or write about "tan desiguales penas e desmesuradas cruezas" (20–3; "such unequalled pains and excessive cruelties"). In other words, in the sentimental narrative, the author tells us that to this day he lacks the daring to complain, whereas in the gloss, we are introduced to an *auctor* who is already complaining in an effort to provoke compassion. To the extent that the authors of the narrative and glosses are identified with one another, the sentimental narrative must itself constitute the complaint, whose diegetic target (the author's beloved) is not party to the glosses. Readers can therefore imagine themselves taking in the plaintive narrative alongside the beloved, but with the exegetical advantage of the glosses, which foster the compassion the beloved lacks.

There is a further rhetorical basis for phrasing this appeal to the audience's compassion in terms of the author's novel and unique suffering. Cartagena's translation of *De inventione* ends with a discussion of the *conquistión* or *quexamiento*, "aquella fabla que procura mover a los oyentes a misericordia e compasión: e en esta conquestión e quexamiento conviene primeramente fazer el coraçón del oyente misericordioso, porque más ligeramente se mueva a la misericordia que le piden" (*Rethórica* 109–10; "that speech that seeks to move the audience to mercy and compassion: and in this *conquestión* and complaint one should first make the listener's heart merciful, so that it can be more easily moved to the mercy asked of it"). The gloss on the author's age, which closely associates complaint ("se quexava") and compassion, carries out this operation in the indicated place and through one of Cicero's recommended methods: "declarar los tiempos e dezir por quien e en quales males fueron e son e serán" (Cartagena, *Rethórica* 110; "declare the times and explain who is responsible and in which bad circumstances [the speaker] finds and will find himself"). The gloss makes this operation explicit but specifies a misleading target, so that the rhetorical seeking of compassion from the beloved becomes itself a technique for arousing the compassion of the reader. Such rhetorical doubling recurs throughout the *Sátira*.

As the first chapter comes to a close, the author imagines how cruelty might respond to his complaint (by arguing that the examples of historical suffering he has adduced far outstrip his own) and then, as we have seen, condemns fortune for having united cruelty and virtue, which should be the greatest opposites, in his beloved (33). The figures of cruelty and fortune are not allegorized, however; this dialogue is consciously imagined, taking place in the realm of *pensamiento*, and the author's interlocutors never speak directly for themselves. After condemning the conflation of cruelty and virtue in his beloved, the author experiences a crucial mental break: "Assy estando, a oras fablava, a oras callava ... Ya mis sentidos enmortesçidos, ya mi seso, ya mi entendimiento, cansados de tan continuos males, me reprehender mi libre voluntad en contra de quantos biven, desseava mi mal e mi final perdimiento" (33–4; "In this state, I sometimes spoke, sometimes kept silent ... My senses had swooned, my brain, my understanding, were tired of such continuous suffering, my free will admonished me that I alone among the living desired my own ill and my final loss"). The allegorical debates that follow this break are thus set beyond the reach of the understanding, after its failure to cope with erotic cruelty, and the author's Discretion steps in as reason's last champion.[31] The battle has probably already been lost, however, since it takes place definitively on the terrain of the passions, and Discretion's very personification shows that the ground has shifted. Furthermore, Discretion is represented as having been blindfolded for the last five years (34), when compassion is elsewhere in the *Sátira* associated with sight. Finally, Discretion speaks "mas por faser lo que devia que por contrastar mi infinito querer" (34; "more to do what it should than to resist my infinite desire") and is thus associated, as it is in Duarte's *LC* and Pedro's *LVB*, with duty, which turns out to be an inadequate moral motive – as Discretion's failure in the ensuing debate makes clear.

Discretion quickly identifies the free will as the central variable in the author's moral equation: "O çiego ombre, conosçe lo que fases! Piensa lo que faras! Que te puedo dezir, salvo el mas malaventurado de los nasçidos, *pues tu pena quieres, e tu pena seguiendo desseas?*" (35; emphasis added; "Oh blind man, recognize what you are doing! Think about what you are going to do! What can I call you but the most unfortunate of the living, *since you want your pain, and pursue it in your desire*?"). Predictably, then, Discretion tries to draw the debate into the familiar moral territory of action ("Piensa lo que faras") and decision; if the author's actions can be ascribed to his free will, he becomes the only responsible moral actor. Discretion's short speech ends with a plea for the author to free himself from the prison of love by fighting against his will: "O ombre cativo, desencarçela tu libertad de la tenebrosa e muy amarga carçel! Pelea, pelea con tu voluntad e, otra ves te digo, pelea, e non con otro, synon contigo mesmo, e non seas contento nin seas deseoso de tantas penas sofrir, syn aver piedat de ty e de la triste vida tuya" (41; "Oh captive man, release your freedom from its dark and most bitter prison! Struggle, struggle against your will and, I say again, struggle, and not with another, but with yourself, and do not be content to suffer such pain and even desire it, without pity for yourself and your sad life"). This final plea is emblematic of the moral tradition that stresses the achievement of individual virtue through the purging of the passions (which, after all, is what it would mean to free oneself from the prison of love). Morality is thus reduced to a battle between the appetitive and free will; the inward isolation of this battle is stressed by the emphatically repetitive call to have pity on himself and on his sad life.[32] The Constable's goal in the rest of the *Sátira* will be to reassert intersubjective compassion (through the figure of the beloved who takes pity on her servant) as a vital factor in moral calculation, in essence highlighting the mortal stakes of mutual obligation.

Discretion deploys the example of Macías as a warning to the author. Although the explanatory gloss is dedicated to the poet's legend rather than his verse, it is worthwhile to recall here that "Amor cruel e bryoso" concludes with a bitter complaint about love's unjust rewards: "quien te sirve en gentylesa/ por galardon le das morte" (lines 35–6; "you give the one who serves you graciously death as a reward"). This complaint raises the question of what a truly appropriate *galardón* would be. Pity, rather than amorous acquiescence, was the traditional reward – but admitting to seek more than mere pity was itself a courtly trope (Green 60–4). In a similar vein, while debates between reason and will were a courtly commonplace, these lyric debates actually included a wide variety of allegorical participants; for example, *sensualidad* or *amor* could replace *voluntad*. Don Pedro's dogged insistence on compassion or pity for his *galardón* and his choices of Discretion and Prudence as his principal opponents cannot therefore be dismissed as "mere" tropes or borrowings. Furthermore, like all authors of sentimental poetry or prose, Don Pedro adapts courtly tropes to his own purposes. For example, when Discretion finishes admonishing the author for voluntarily abandoning his free will, his wordless response – "Gemir, sospirar e plañir le di por respuesta ... Por ende, dexe el fablar, e recogime al pensoso silencio" (43; "Moaning, sighing, and wailing I gave her in reply ... Finally, I stopped speaking, and retired into pensive silence") – recalls the courtly poet's embarrassed silence before his lady, but recontextualizes it as an element of interior moral strife. Having left behind the realm of the understanding and admitted the defeat of his Discretion, the author compares himself to those who, "pasando los Alpes, el terrible frio de la nieve e agudo viento dan fin a sus dolorosas vidas; et, assy pegados en las sillas, elados del frior, siguen su viaje, fasta que de aquellas, non con querer o desquerer suyo, son apartados, e dados a la fria tierra" (44; "while crossing the Alps, the cold snow and sharp wind bring their painful lives to an end; and stuck to their seats, frozen solid, they continue their journey, until they are separated from their seats, neither willingly nor unwillingly, and fall to the cold ground"). This image of death in life – the frozen riders remain on their horses for a way before falling to the ground – again recalls a courtly trope, but here it emphasizes a deprivation of will that leads beyond captivity to death, thus anticipating the mortal dilemma of the *Sátira*'s closing scene.

Cruelty

Before that closing scene, the author engages in a lengthy debate with Prudence – not his own now, but that of his beloved. When Prudence first appears (accompanied by the other six virtues), she is described in her gloss as "sovereign" among the cardinal virtues; charity is the highest theological virtue, but the present work "mas fabla de moral doctrina que de theologico documento, e a cosas mundanas se dirige et no a divinas" (51; "speaks more of moral doctrine than theology, and is dedicated to worldly, not divine, affairs"). According to the *Sátira*'s moral doctrine, prudence has as its object the understanding and is therefore an intellectual virtue, whereas the other virtues are "moral" in that their object is the appetitive part of the soul. Prudence's sovereignty consists in the fact that it acts upon both parts of the soul ("no solo tiene acto çerca de las intellectuales mas aun çerca de las morales"), determining on behalf of the appetitive part "quales son las cosas convenibles para proseguir, e quales para desechar" (51; "which things should be pursued, and which cast aside"). As such, prudence's psychological role bleeds into that of discretion, sorting out willful impulses to produce moral behaviour. By contrast, the theological virtues cannot be achieved through will or understanding, but only through grace (53), which is why they are mute in the *Sátira*.

Prudence, in her defence of the author's beloved, claims that her mistress has achieved – effortlessly – the "heroic degree" of strength (82). In the accompanying gloss on *Eroyco grado*, Don Pedro explains that there are four degrees of any virtue: perseverance, constancy, temperance, and the heroic degree (82–3). Emotion is the central element of this scale: the perseverant fall into vice but climb back out; the constant "feel the passions," but abstain from sin "with pain and sadness"; the temperate take pleasure in resisting temptations but are still subject to them; and finally, the heroic "do not feel the passions" (83). These last "son mas marmorinas estatuas inmutativas o dioses de la humana vida que mugeres o ombres" (84; "are more like immutable marble statues or gods of human life than women or men"). Such statuesque heroes are perhaps a bitter echo of the frozen rider crossing the Alps, equally stiff but for the opposite reason.[33] Continuing along these lines, Prudence explains that her mistress rejects the Epicureans in favour of the Stoics, and the gloss on the Epicureans explains that virtues should be valued in themselves, not for the pleasure ("delectaçion") we feel when acting on them (93). Finally, Prudence says that the lady has rid herself of desires based in the carnal, spiritual, and tepid will, and follows only her praiseworthy and virtuous will (98). The accompanying gloss hews closely to the theory of will we have seen articulated in Duarte's *LC* (see chapter three), adding that the heroic degree of virtue can only be achieved by those who follow their virtuous will (99). In essence, then, Prudence's argument and the glosses it engenders combine to paint the author's beloved as the embodiment of impassible virtue, the perfect realization of a dense field of emotionally ascetic moral systems. Totally free of emotion's pull – in Prudence's words, "ni puede faser tanto alguna passion que dexe de estar en un compas tan perfecto que, farto en pensarlo, esto maravillada" (123; "no passion can do enough to shake her from a composure so perfect that, having thought of it endlessly, I am amazed") – she is the opposite of the author, mortally subject to his will. Her perfect *compás*, Prudence argues, makes up for her lack of *compasión*. But this is just the view the author refuses to accept in the *Sátira*'s closing pages.

Toward the end of her defence, Prudence claims that her mistress would be found "syn yerro o reprehension" even if she had the capacity to sin imperceptibly (125) – but in the *Sátira*, the eyes examining her are those of compassion. This is why the author, whose brief response to his beloved's Prudence stands in contrast to his silence before his own Discretion, accuses his beloved only of cruelty: "Si esta mi sola e perpetua señora contra mi … fue llena de crueldat, como en tal estremo o grado qual dexistes sera perfecta e virtuosa?" (135; "If this, my only and perpetual lady … was filled with cruelty against me, how can she be as perfect and virtuous as you say?"). It is Pity, not Prudence, who answers this attack, "porque esta culpa a ella solamente o mas prinçipalmente tañia" (136; "because this accusation touched only or principally on her"). She repeats the charge that the author chose to enter his current predicament freely, and she adds, crucially, that having done so, he is now an "indigno juez" (137; "unworthy judge"). The indictment of the author is now complete: having subjected himself to his own will, he can no longer carry out the morally central task of judging. His brief *reprehensión* – rebuttal and condemnation – of his beloved's cruelty is empty because it is enunciated from a fatally compromised moral position.

It is precisely here, when his capacity to judge has apparently been completely undermined, that the author states his decisive reply – that he desires not his lady's love but her compassion:

> Mas, solamente, movida a clemençia, deseava que de mi mal se doliesse e que mi desigualado pesar sintiesse, pues non es alguna cosa mas convenible ni que mas cara deva ser al gentil, alto e virtuoso coraçon que aver merçed, dolor e sentimiento de los tristes infortunados. De aver compassion e piadat de mi, mucho mas que de todos los mortales, *razon lo mandava, virtud lo consentia.* (141–2; emphasis added)

> I desired only that she, moved to clemency, would grieve for me and feel my unparalleled suffering, for there is no more appropriate or dearer thing to the gracious, high, and virtuous heart than to feel pity, pain, and sadness toward the unfortunate. *Reason commanded, and virtue consented,* that she should have compassion and pity for me, more than any other mortal.

Compassion and pity are not depraved passions; rather, they are themselves both reasonable and virtuous. Furthermore, his beloved has not truly mastered her will:

> E que otra cosa, salvo su no piadosa voluntad, esto causava? Como no sea dubda que, ado ha e mora cruel voluntad, el serviçio buelve en deserviçio, el amor en desamor trastorna, porque tanto puede la voluntad llena de crueldat que çiega los ojos de la discreçion, judgando el bien por mal, la virtud por viçio, e la verdat por mentira o falsedat. (142)

> And what other thing than her pitiless will caused this? There can be no doubt that, where there is a cruel will, service becomes disservice, love is twisted into disdain [*desamor*], because the will filled with cruelty is so powerful that it can blind discretion's eyes, taking [*judgando*] good for evil, virtue for vice, and truth for lies or falsehood.

By introducing the element of willful cruelty, which blinds discretion and turns moral judgment around, the author disrupts the (former) binary that opposed virtuous reason to vicious will. In essence, malice replaces the ascetics' temptation as the primary moral risk, and its antidote is not restraint but compassion, which is why cruelty, not the passions, is now repeatedly associated with blindness.

These arguments vanquish Prudence, Pity, and the lady's other virtues, and the author argues that his victory was not merely rhetorical: "Claramente conosçi que, vençidas, de mi se partieron, no con eloquente e fermosa fabla, mas con verdat e justiçia que posseya, no con fraudulentas, sotiles o agudas questiones, mas con verdaderas" (153; "I saw them depart from me, clearly defeated not by eloquent or beautiful speech, but by truth and justice; not with fraudulent, sophistic, or sharp questions, but with true ones"). In a final reversal, the author accuses the fates of having frozen his lady's will against him: "Por que teneys elada, o fados crueles … la voluntad de aquella cuyo perpetuo esclavo so contra mi?" (153–4; "Why have you frozen against me, o cruel fates … the will of her whose perpetual slave I am?"). The author's will was frozen when his Discretion abandoned him, but it is the cruelty of the fates that freezes the will of his lady, already blinded by her own pitilessness. The author cannot make a decision; his beloved can make only one. It is from this perspective that the compounding indecision with which the *Sátira* comes to a close must be understood. The author's first indecision is whether to continue speaking at all:

> O dessentido, no se que faga, sy fable o si calle! Mi fablar nadie no oye, mi callar no me trahe provecho, sy fablare, no avera reposo mi pena, sy me callare, no se apartara de mi. Mas fablare yo, por çierto, contra vos mi soberana e obedesçida señora; dexare el fablar contra tan muchas passiones e varias afflicçiones mias, enderesçarlohe a la señoria vuestra. (155)
>
> Oh confusion, I do not know what to do, speak or be silent! No one hears my speech, silence does me no good; if I speak, my pain will find no rest, and if I stay silent, it will not leave me. But I will speak, certainly, against you, my sovereign and obeyed lady; I will stop speaking against my many passions and varied afflictions, directing it rather against your rule.

In the poem that follows, the author holds true to this promise; the culpability of his own emotions is rejected, and it is his beloved who is in moral peril:

> Doledvos de mi passion,
> e de mi gran perdimiento,
> quered vuestra perfecçion
> no queriendo mi tormento
> desygual,
> mi firme querer leal,
> vuestro muy mas que devia;
> libradvos, ydola mia,
> de dolor pestilençial (159, lines 19–27).
>
> Grieve for my passion and my great loss; desire your perfection not desiring my unparalleled torment, my own loyal desire, more yours than it should have been; free yourself, my idol, from pestilential pain.

In keeping with the numerous inversions of the *Sátira*'s precipitous conclusion, this stanza revisits a number of foregoing themes. First, "passion" here recuperates its connotation of suffering, rather than vice, so that it calls for compassion rather than condemnation. The perfect will, furthermore, is desirous of loyal service, not indifferent or hostile toward it. In fact, it is the beloved, not the author, who is a captive – to a painful fate. As such, the author's reference to his lady as his "idol" is a wry comment on her statuesque – and thus morally incomplete, inhuman – "perfection."

Having finished speaking, the author is met with a new, and final, dilemma:

> E yo, sin ventura, padesçiente, la desnuda e bicordante espada en la my diestra mirava, titubando, con dudoso pensamiento e demudada cara, sy era mejor prestamente morir o asperar la dubdosa respuesta me dar consuelo. La discriçion favoresçe e suplica la espera, la congoxosa voluntad la triste muerte reclama, el seso manda esperar la respuesta, el aquexado coraçon, gridando, acusa la postrimería. (174)

> And I, unfortunate, suffering, looked at the naked and double-edged sword in my right hand, doubting, with halting thought and palid face, whether it was better to die quickly or wait for the doubtful reply to console me. Discretion favours and pleads for waiting, the sorrowful will demands sad death, good sense commands to wait for the response, the suffering heart, crying out, warns of the approaching end.

This ending has been construed variously as a sign "that allegory's fundamentally heuristic function has failed" (Brownlee 126), an attempt to provoke compassion in the reader (Serés, "Ficción" 46), or as evidence that the courtly conflict between desire and honour is unresolvable (Gascón Vera 87–8). One could add to these interpretations another, consistent with a literal reading of the *Sátira*'s dedicatory letter, in which the author's bad end is evidence of his immorality, although of course the very existence of the letter would do away with this mortal fiction. The conflict described in this final indecision is between, once again, discretion and will, brain and heart. Compassion and cruelty, whose opposition had been added to this moral system, are once again absent. The opposition between will and discretion, which characterizes the moral thought of Duarte and the Infante Pedro, and whose fatal outcome is highly stylized in courtly poetry, is here compared to a double-edged sword. For Don Pedro, it is an inadequate moral palette, and further subjection to it – not just to the passionate side of it – is intolerable. A measured clemency had always been a desirable quality in a judge or king, but here, Don Pedro makes compassion an essential element of moral decision by dramatically laying bare the paralysis to which the conventional moral system leads. Rodríguez del Padrón's *Siervo* contains a similar scene of paralysis, immediately after the author has been abandoned by his understanding and feels himself to be in mortal peril (23). In *Siervo*, as we have seen, these circumstances introduce a new narrative element, the *Estoria de dos amadores*. The *Sátira*'s scene of indecision is, by contrast, definitive, bringing the narrative to an unsettling close.

Although Don Pedro's subject matter in the *Sátira* seems relentlessly personal, there is reason to believe that his ideas about cruelty and compassion are significantly broader in their targets.[34] His gloss on the pharaoh of Exodus, for instance, includes the following condemnation of cruelty:

> O detestable viçio enemigo de toda humana naturalesa, e muy contrario a toda natural razon, fiero a los amigos, amigable a los adversarios, muy poderoso no para fazer solamente subvertir el exerçito de pharao en las marinas ondas, mas de despoblar las poderosas çibdades, de destroyr los magnificos regnos, de annular los altos poderios e de distinguir las muy antiguas e esclaresçidas linages! El qual viçio en nuestros tiempos es usado e seguido como si fuesse virtud famosa e loable. (144)

> Oh detestable vice, enemy of all human nature, and very contrary to all natural reason, fierce toward friends, friendly to adversaries, powerful enough not only to subvert pharaoh's army in the waves of the sea, but also to depopulate powerful cities, to destroy magnificent kingdoms, to annihilate high dominions, and to extinguish the most ancient and noble lineages! This vice is customary in our times and followed as if it were a famous and praiseworthy virtue.

And in his poem of warning to his beloved, he calls cruelty "de todos los viçios reyna, señora,/ mal enemiga de real alteza" (169, lines 21–2; "queen of all the vices, lady, enemy of royal highness"). Cruelty is thus a political vice, particularly unbecoming in rulers and representing a mortal danger, not just to courtly lovers but to courts themselves, to cities, kingdoms, and lineages. It is tempting to explain this belief in biographical terms, since Don Pedro wrote in exile, his father having been killed in a civil conflict with his own nephew. It is also tempting to see Don Pedro's interest in compassion – especially in light of the rather more ribald treatment the *galardón* receives in much courtly poetry – as a youthful enthusiasm. But the fact remains that Don Pedro's destabilizing juxtaposition of courtly (lyrical), rhetorical, historical, and philosophical accounts of compassion and cruelty sought to expose the impasse at which a long-standing system of moral thought, whose logic dominates both the treatises of the Avis court and much courtly poetry, had arrived. The ascetic rationalists who envisioned a perfect will guided by discretion and the troubadours who exploited the creative force of erotic pessimism certainly viewed the poles of the reason-will binary differently, but in his *Sátira*, Don Pedro seeks to alter this system radically, calling for a personal and political ethics in which the granting of the compassionate *galardón* would be a real, collective possibility.

Satire and Tragedy as Modes of Consolation

Throughout Don Pedro's exile, his sister Isabel seems to have worked to soothe her husband Alfonso's anger, but in a cruel twist, she died (under suspicion of poisoning) soon after the exile was revoked.[35] Don Pedro's exile, then, is framed by two deaths, of his father in 1449 and his sister in 1455. It is also framed by two works, the *Sátira* and the *Tragédia de la insigne reina doña Isabel* (1457). In the same letter to Violante de Prades from which his definition of "satire" is drawn, Santillana defines "tragedy" as "aquella que contiene en sí caídas de grandes reys e príncipes … cuyos nasçimientos e vidas alegremente se començaron e grande tienpo se continuaron e después tristemente cayeron" (637–9; "the genre that contains the falls of great kings and princes … whose births and lives started joyfully and continued for a long time and after, sadly fell."[36] Both the *Sátira* and the *Tragédia* portray the author's attempt to emerge from despair, whether erotic or existential, through a literary reconstruction of a moral debate. In this sense, they are both works of consolation, regardless of the genres named in their titles.[37]

The *Tragédia*'s dedicatory letter addresses Don Pedro's brother Jaime, cardinal of Santestacio, explaining the unexpected and terrible grief that has characterized his return from exile:

> Creeran los mas, segund yo pienso, que seyendo revocado del injusto destierro venido a la paternal tierra, algund consuelo e descanso me fuesse la tal venida al grave dolor que ove con la fin de la reyna mi señora e hermana, cuya noble anima aya perpetua folgança, mas yo te juro por los soberanos çielos, reverendissimo señor, como a muy caro hermano mio, que el contrario me avino … Asy te digo, señor hermano, que yo sentia verdaderamente con mi venida al reyno de mi naturaleza mas dolor que consolaçion, e mas angustia que plazer. (63–4)

> Most will believe, as I see it, that, returned to my fatherland, my unjust exile having been revoked, my arrival would be some consolation and rest from the deep pain I felt at the death of the queen my lady and sister, God rest her soul, but I swear to you on the sovereign heavens, most reverend lord, as my very dear brother, that the opposite befell me … So I tell you, brother, that I felt upon returning to the kingdom where I was born more pain than consolation, more anguish than pleasure.

This suffering, as he explains it, led him to seek out a kind of literary compassion, searching for suffering comparable to his own in history because "consuelo es a los miseros, conpañeros aver de sus penas" (64; "it is a consolation to the miserable to have companions in their sorrows").

The *Tragédia*, although prosimetric, is simpler in formal terms than the *Sátira*. The text consists in an opening *planto*, when the author hears the news of his sister's death, and then a debate between the author, expressing his grief in verse of varying metres, and an unnamed interlocutor (possibly intended to be Petrarch) who tries to convince him, in Stoic prose, that he should not indulge in his grief. In the *planto*, the author again takes up the image of the impassible statue, here a representation of the shock from which the author is rescued by other mourners, whose formal gestures of grief return him to his own: "Por largo espacio estove trasportado/ como estatua que algo no siente, mas desque mi seso me fue retornado/ vi los circunstantes llorar agramente, e luego mis ropas romper fuy membrado; feriendo mi rostro inhumanamente/ comienço mi planto tan desesperado" (73–4; "For a long time I was transfigured like a statue that feels nothing, but since my sense was returned to me, I saw the others bitterly weeping, and later was reminded to tear my clothing; wounding my face savagely, I begin my despairing *planto*"). The formality of these gestures is not a sign of insincerity; rather, in a gesture underlain by the medieval assocation between memory and emotion (also active, as we have seen, in affective prayer and meditation), Don Pedro frames them as a mnemonic example. This example, in turn, prompts in Don Pedro the kind of introductory enunciation we have seen in *decires* and *canciones con citas*. Here, however, Don Pedro insists on the singularity and isolation of his suffering, from which he articulates, in his *planto*, a desire not for consolation but for annihilation: "His technique is to curse, full of anger and despair, as if he wanted to destroy the entire universe that permitted [his sister's] death" (Gascón Vera 154–5).[38]

It is at this moment of maximum despair that the old man who seeks to console him arrives. The old man's clothing is opulent, "bordada de ojos que fueron obrados/ por la gran Minerva con tal maestria,/ que jamas despiertos serian fallados" (76; "embroidered with eyes crafted by Minerva with such mastery that they would never be found awake [that is, they seemed to emerge from a dream]"); once again, the purveyor of wisdom is symbolized by a multitude of eyes. The consolatory material he spouts is a hodgepodge of medieval commonplaces, a fact he himself acknowledges (89). In another echo of the *Sátira*, he begins by suggesting that the author follow his discretion rather than his passions, a suggestion the author rejects as inadequate precisely because his grief has been provoked by the death of his sister's great discretion: "E como sera/ tanta discreçion/ assy olvidada?/ e no quedara/ en nuestra nasçion/ mas perpetuada? tanta gentileza/ e tanta virtud/ assy fenesçida/ con tanta crueza?/ e tal juventud/ no sera plañida?" (82; "And how should such discretion be forgotten? And no longer remain perpetuated in our nation? Such gentility, and such virtue, perished with such cruelty? And such youth will not be lamented?"). Not to mourn this loss would be unnatural because the peculiarly human combination of reason and feeling makes mourning virtuous: "Nas cocatrizes/ fieras çiertamente/ es bien congruente/ facer lo que dises;/ mas nos que tenemos/ sentir e rason/ sin tal reprehension/ plañir bien podemos" (83; "It is perfectly coherent that truly wild cockatrices do what you say; but we who have feeling and reason can very well lament without such condemnation"). Such grief is beyond reproach (*reprehension*): Christ, who wept for his friend and us all, is himself its model (83).

The old man, although he argues that it is "crazy" to feel grief over things that happen every day, concedes that, to the extent that feelings are natural, they should be experienced in moderation (84–6). After more traditional Stoic arguments, and in contrast to the *Sátira*, the author admits defeat – that his grief is not an appropriate response to his circumstances – and seeks advice, then, on how to feel happy, repeating the *Sátira*'s plea: "Sea piedad amiga,/ e crueldad lexos vaya" (108; "Let pity be a friend, and cruelty go far away"). The old man is given the final word in answering this question on happiness, and it is the very absence of the author's reply that makes this ending, like that of the *Sátira*, ambiguous. The old man himself, in the work's final passage, bridles at the author's silence: "Fabla, por que callas? di, por que no respondes, e no otorgas la verdad? E tu no has provado que la vida triste e malaventurada es peor de sofrir que la muerte? a ty mesmo fago juez desta cosa que muchas veses aborresçiste la vida tuya" (117; "Speak, why are you silent? Why do you neither respond nor admit the truth? And have you not proven that the sad and unfortunate life is worse to suffer than death? I make you yourself, who have abhorred your life many times, the judge of this question").

The author's closing silence in the *Tragédia* mirrors his closing paralysis in the *Sátira*. The Stoic and courtly discourses that oppose reason to the passions are inadequate to lived experience – a lived experience that, in this case, it should be noted, frames the consolatory debate in much clearer biographical terms than in the case of the *Sátira* – closing off all routes of escape through word or deed. Don Pedro's literary project, born in exile and framed by death, represents an effort to move courtly discourse and moral psychology out of stagnation by rehabilitating phenomena such as grief and compassion as reasonable foundations for both private and public virtue. He stages the failures of satire and tragedy as modes of consolation in order to reveal the resources of courtly literature, both narrative prose and lyric, to be a privileged site for this moral and aesthetic rehabilitation. Nevertheless, Don Pedro's approach remains diagnostic and suggestive: one searches in vain for an image of happiness realized through compassion or consolation, finding instead an aggrieved silence.

Chapter Seven

Confession, Consolation, and the Poetics of Hylomorphism

To this point, I have argued that Iberian poets from the late fourteenth century onward explored the creative potential of a compassion freed from the strictures of ascetic rationalism and the troubadours' erotic pessimism, and that the early authors of Castilian sentimental fiction sought to instil a new ethical force in the trope of compassion-as-reward through strategies of narrativization and the mobilization of both lyric epideixis and historical example. Furthermore, all of these discursive gestures implied an imaginative confrontation with death, through Christological identification, citational entombment, and the staging of consolatory debate. Such a confrontation clarifies the stakes of a conceptual framework, inherited from troubadour lyric and philosophical and religious asceticism, that takes the conflict between reason and the passions as the paradigm for moral deliberation. It reveals, above all, the paralysis to which this framework had led, a critique carried out through the resources of courtly lyric and with an eye toward alternate currents of religious thought.

The Valencian poet Ausiàs March (1400–59), widely admired throughout Iberia during his own lifetime, approaches similar problems and draws on similar (but not identical) intellectual resources in his 128 surviving poems,[1] yet emerges as the most idiosyncratic voice of this cultural milieu. As we will see, critics have perceived this idiosyncrasy to give psychological heft to March's frequent claims of individualizing sincerity, which in other poets appear highly conventional. To this exploration of lyric subjectivity we may add, as distinguishing features of March's poetry, the exhaustive development of a three-fold theory of love based on hylomorphic doctrine and the ordeal to which this theory is in turn subjected upon the death of the beloved, represented with moving literality.[2] March's poetry is also a superlative example of the lexical and conceptual focus that more broadly characterizes the poetry of fifteenth-century Iberia, Castilian and Catalan alike. His startlingly dense exploration of the lyrical possibilities of human love as a conceptual and moral problematic involving the mixture of the carnal and the spiritual is undertaken with a lexicon of about 700 words, much smaller than those of his

Valencian contemporaries (Casanova 137n7). This lyric focus, I argue, reveals not investment in the moral system but an attempt to exhaust its possibilities rhetorically. Through a poetics of introspection and confession (as self-judgment) and, ultimately, through an exploration of death and salvation, March shows that what is most intimate in us is shared, and that if the conflict between reason and the passions is real and deeply felt, it is not to be resolved individually. Rather, human love in its confrontation with mortality produces a shared subjectivity grounded in compassion, a subjectivity that March describes – exceptionally, in his oeuvre – in explicitly Christian terms. At a critical moment, March adopts this rhetoric of shared salvation as an alternative to the path of subject formation through confession that he appears to be treading in his foregoing love poetry.

March's social position is similar to, if not quite as exalted as, that of many of the aristocratic writers we have studied up to this point; he differs to a certain extent in terms of his interventions in public life and his immediate audience.[3] His grandfather, Jaume March, was knighted by Peter III of Aragon in 1360, and the family enjoyed noble status from then on. March participated as a representative of the military estate in the Valencian courts of 1415, was knighted himself in 1419, and participated in Alfonso V's expeditions to Sardinia, Corsica, Naples, Sicily, and Africa from 1419 to 1424; he was royal falconer from 1425 to 1428. After that, he seems to have retired to his lands in Gandia, administrating them and writing poetry; he nevertheless corresponded with King Alfonso into old age, and interacted with younger Valencian writers such as Bernat Fenollar and Joan Moreno (*Història* 357–9). March's poems, which survive in thirteen manuscripts, have since the sixteenth century been divided into four groups: the *cants d'amor*, the largest group, addressed for the most part either to *Plena de seny* ("Wise lady") or *Llir entre cards* ("Lily among thorns"); the *cants morals*; the *cants de mort*, a cycle of six poems responding prismatically to the death of his beloved; and the long *cant espiritual*.[4] Neither the chronological order of the poems' composition nor the poet's own arrangement of them can be definitively demonstrated (A. March, *Poesies* 7; Archer, *Pervasive Image* 6; *Història* 361); most critics follow Amédée Pagès's ordering in his 1912 *Auzias March et ses prédécesseurs* as, in Robert Archer's words, it is a "good working order" (*Pervasive Image* 6).[5] The primary audience for March's poetry is thought to have been Valencia's "local petty nobility" and "urban patricians" (Alemany 10). As Pere Bohigas writes, all indications are that, in life, March was a typical feudal lord, dedicated to protecting and increasing his possessions (A. March, *Poesies* 6). However, as Joan Fuster added with characteristic acuity, March was a feudal lord "with a problem of conscience" (*Ausiàs March* 12–13).

March's youth coincided with a time in which Catalan literature "was courtly in every sense" (Smith 297–8); indeed, as we have seen, March's uncle Jaume March was instrumental in the 1393 founding of the Barcelona Consistori. March married twice: his first wife, Isabel Martorell, was the sister of Joanot Martorell, author of *Tirant lo Blanc*. After her death in 1439, he married the Valencian lady Joana

Escorna, whom he also survived; neither marriage produced an heir, although his two wills reveal that he had five illegitimate children. The woman March addressed as *Plena de seny* – a *senhal* that associates her with prudence – remains unidentified; recently, however, strong evidence has been adduced to identify *Llir entre cards* as Teresa d'Híxar, a noblewoman widowed in 1421 who links March to Valencia's courtly milieu (*Història* 355, 358). This latter *senhal* alludes to Bernard of Clairvaux's interpretation of the Song of Songs 2:2, "As the lily among thorns, so is my love among the daughters" (Cabré et al. 74); broadly speaking, March's other chief influences are the Occitan troubadours, scholastic psychology and Aristotelian ethics, and Ovid, with occasional reminiscences of Dante and Petrarch (*Història* 365–71).[6]

The innumerable lyric manifestations of March's bad conscience have led critics to speak frequently of the poet's tendency toward sincere introspection or confession and of March's own assertions of exceptional individuality. The most celebrated of these assertions is found in the penultimate stanza of poem CXIV ("Retinga'm Déu en mon trist pensament"), which concerns the pleasure the poet, having abandoned human love, takes in his own sadness:

> Puix que lo món ne Déu a mi no val
> a rellevar la causa d'on só trist,
> a mi plau bé la tristor que yo vist:
> delit hi sent mentre yo·m trobe tal.
> Axí dispost, dolç me sembla l'amarch,
> tant és en mi enfeccionat lo gust!
> A temps he cor d'acer, de carn e fust:
> yo só aquest que·m dich Ausiàs March. (CXIV, lines 81–8)[7]

> Since neither the world nor God helps me to root out the reason for which I am sad, I am content with the sadness I wear; I feel joy, while I am in such a state. Thus disposed, what is bitter seems sweet to me: so corrupted is my taste! I have a heart of steel, flesh and wood, all in one. I am this man who is called Ausias March! (132)[8]

In a representative reading of this stanza, Bohigas writes that the last line in particular

> is of great significance in such a personal and concentrated poet. His works, so stark and arid, still suggest to us a certain pride consonant with his individualism. Perhaps it is a manifestation of his inclination toward making confessions, even unfavorable to himself, in which we can see, however, the desire to safeguard the integrity of his ego, whatever the judgment they might provoke. (A. March, *Poesies* 6)

March's introspection and sincerity are often asserted to differentiate him from the troubadours, whose metrical structures he never abandoned, or even to mark him as a "modern" poet.[9] The adoption of Catalan rather than Occitan is also considered a gesture of sincerity (Casanova 139) directed toward bourgeois Catalan culture (Sobrer, "Myth of Language" 331).[10] The poet's bitter attacks against his own person, his admissions against interest, are a tactic of persuasion: "The poet wants us to believe his confession literally, since he offers us his poems as a confession" (Fuster, *Ausiàs March* 61).

Recently, Barbara Rosenwein has reminded us that concerns about sincerity, in literature and beyond, are historically contingent (*Generations* 6); it is also worth recalling that demands for individual sincerity become urgent in the perceived absence of shared truth (Zambrano, *La confesión* 19). Yet here and elsewhere, March's lyric persona evinces disdain for "fals·opinió" (line 75) and seems to assert itself as a literal representation of the historical poet: "I am this man who is called Ausiàs March!" What is susceptible to analysis is not, in any case, March's historical sincerity, but rather the cycle of hyperbolic subjectivization and desubjectivization he carries out through lyrical introspection and confession.[11] As Marie-Claire Zimmermann has argued, March's lyric persona oscillates between narcissism and self-destruction: "The 'I' is raised to an Absolute that the poet never ceases to deny as such" (*Ausiàs March* 117). In poem CXIV, the sense of confession is strengthened by the poet's punning self-portrayal as a penitent: "the sadness I wear" (line 83) recalls his earlier declaration that "l'esperit meu tostemps està trist/ per l'àbit pres, que lonch temps és que vist/ d'un negre drap o celici molt gros" (lines 46–8; "my spirit is continually sad because of the kind of dress it has adopted, [and] which for a long time it has worn, of black material or coarse sackcloth").[12] The entire poem is framed as an almost literal confession, and its *envoi* takes the form of a prayer:

> A Déu suplich que·l viure no m'allarch,
> o meta·n mi aquest propòsit ferm:
> que mon voler envers Ell lo referm,
> perquè anant a Ell no trobe·nbarch. (lines 89–92)

> I pray God not to prolong my life, or (else) to instil in me this firm intention: to strengthen my will towards Him, so that, travelling towards Him, I shall meet with no obstacles. (132)

March confesses here, as elsewhere, that his desire is not naturally inclined toward God, nor does he wish to be severely tested if he is to journey toward the divine.[13] The poet's own surname provides the rhyme for both the wish for death ("que·l viure no m'allarch") and the obstacles to salvation ("no trobe·nbarch"). And, indeed, it is in the confrontation with death and its implications for salvation that March forges a lyric subjectivity whose desire for self-destruction is reformulated in terms of a shared resurrection.

If we accept Foucault's assertion that the moment "when the task and obligation of truth-telling about oneself [was] inserted within the procedure indispensable for salvation" was a crucial turning point in the history of subjectivity in the West, and that it was not just a matter of personal salvation but also "a necessary element in the individual's membership of a community" (*Hermeneutics* 363–4), then March's lyric subjection to moral scrutiny, read in a confessional mode, encodes his participation in literary community. March's admission in poem CXIV both that his will is misguided and that his senses themselves are corrupt – "infected" – places his own manner of truthful confession squarely within a scholastic ethical framework concerned with a particular model of the soul and the implications of that model, whose central principle Mark D. Johnston identifies as *recta ratio*, "right reason" (384), for proper worldly behaviour.[14] This hylomorphic model, reflected obliquely in the "steel, flesh and wood" of March's heart in poem CXIV, is most commonly expressed by March in terms of a tripartite typology of love: spiritual love, in which only the rational soul is engaged; carnal love, ruled by the body's appetites; and human or mixed (*compost*) love, in which the soul and the body participate together, if not always in cooperation.[15] Several scholars have noted that March is not truly consistent in this systematization throughout his works, while others have shown that the preoccupation with transcendence and immanence inherent in this paradigm, far from isolating him as an author, in fact puts March in dialogue with the songbook poets and other fifteenth-century Iberian writers.[16] The question of March's direct knowledge of Thomistic and other scholastic texts is less important here than his possibly "paradoxical" application of the scholastic ethical framework to the "implicitly immoral conduct of courtly love" (Johnston 387).[17] March's theory of love was also influenced in important ways by the mendicant preachers (Alemany 11), a fact reflected in his thoroughly Augustinian theory of mind and his use of the Augustinian powers of the soul (memory, will, and understanding) as an analytic (see later discussion).[18] In what remains, I will explore how March's assertions of exceptionalism, on the one hand, and rhetorical performance of moral self-scrutiny within a framework of scholastic hylomorphism, Augustinian theory of mind, and *fin'amor*, on the other, articulate through a confrontation with death (one's own and that of others) a particular form of intersubjective salvation. The thematic consistency and lexical density of March's oeuvre means that few poems would be entirely irrelevant to my argument, which will therefore necessarily proceed through analyses of a series of exemplary poems, concluding with two *cants de mort*, XCII ("Aquelles mans que jamés perdonaren") and XCVII ("Si per null temps creguí ser amador").

XXIII: "Lexant a part l'estil dels trobadors"

Like Dinis in "Proençaes soem mui bem trobar," March famously asserted his own fidelity to the truth through a declared abandonment of troubadour style:

> Lexant a part l'estil dels trobadors
> qui, per escalf, trespassen veritat,

e sostrahent mon voler affectat
perquè no·m torb, diré·l que trob en vós. (XXIII, lines 1–4)

Leaving aside the manner of the troubadours, who, carried away by passion, exceed the truth, and restraining my own amorous desire so that it does not distract me, I shall say what I find in you. (53)

Ultimately, March (again recalling Dinis) will undermine his own poem's claim to truth; the first point to consider, however, is precisely what March considered himself to be leaving behind as the "manner of the troubadours."[19] Troubadour poetry first arrived in the Crown of Aragon through the patronage of Alfonso II (1162–96), and its cultural foothold was reinforced with the arrival of the *faidits*, exiles fleeing the aftermath of the Albigensian Crusade in the early thirteenth century (M. Cabré 129, 133). The troubadours encode both feudal ties and religious devotion in a discourse of erotic love; it represents at its origin an "aestheticising of manners" and an "intense refinement in sentiment and emotion" that allow above all for increasingly subtle communication – whether genuine or deceitful – among a cultural and political elite (Jaeger 13). Chief among these refined sentiments was love, whose semantic field went far beyond the erotic. The word *drut*, "lover," connoted political as well as erotic love, describing the relationship between lover and lady but also between lord and vassal (Cheyette 235). This discursive codification (or aestheticization) of fundamentally political ties made them more visible, rather than obscuring them, in its use of erotic language. In this way, the troubadour poetic code – which, despite his disavowal, was undoubtedly March's fundamental lyric framework – came to define courtly communities: "The troubadours can be seen as determining the limits and members of polite society, and binding together an exclusive community in which an appreciation of the courtly lyric and practice of the courtly virtues of hospitality, generosity and affability were seen as marks of status and cultivation" (Harvey 20). The fact that courtly language serves to signal status does not mean, of course, that its "refined" emotions are false; rather, as we saw in the introduction, the management of deeply held attitudes toward emotion is common to a wide variety of rhetorical practices and cultural and institutional settings, all of which condition judgments of truth.

The troubadours' appropriation of the discourse of spiritual love must be approached with the same caution; the ambiguity of their apparently sacrilegious gestures arises at least in part from the erotic language of mystical texts and of Scripture itself, and its recontextualization within the courtly system should not lead modern readers to assume ironic intent, even if I have offered several examples in previous chapters that I believe were intended to elicit laughter. In fact, ironic and earnest images of devotion coexisted throughout the entire period of troubadour production (Gaunt, *Love and Death* 5), and in my view this aspect of troubadour poetry represents above all an open lyrical exploitation of this ambiguity rather than a secular challenge to religious doctrine. Still, it is undeniable that the professed willingness of the courtly lover to die for love (echoed frequently by March and the other Iberian poets we have been studying) increases the ethical stakes of the erotic beyond traditional questions of sin and chastity; as Simon Gaunt has argued, this lyrical sacrifice "engenders a space for an engagement with ethics that is removed from the sphere of organized religion" ("A Martyr to Love" 500). March certainly does not abandon this space in abandoning the troubadours. It is the space *par excellence* of the confessions entailed by his claims of difference.

The later troubadours tended to present themselves as love's initiates, privileged bearers of a knowledge born of rare experience (Wilhite 764). March also portrays himself as the bearer of special knowledge, but despite frequent critical references to his didacticism and its ties to courtly culture,[20] he is not confident in his ability to teach. Rather, shared emotional experience is the condition for understanding his poems: "Qui no és trist, de mos dictats no cur,/ o·n algun temps que sia trist estat" (XXXIX, lines 1–2; "Anyone who is not sad or has not at some time been sad should pay no attention to my works" [55]). This disavowal of abstract pedagogy is a crucial counterpoint to poem XXIII's opening claim, which I now quote in its entirety:

> Lexant a part l'estil dels trobadors
> qui, per escalf, trespassen veritat,
> e sostrahent mon voler affectat
> perquè no·m torb, diré·l que trob en vós.
> Tot mon parlar als qui no us hauran vista
> res no valrrà, car fe no y donaran,
> e los vehents que dins vós no veuran,
> en creur·a mi, llur arma serà trista. (lines 1–8)

> Leaving aside the manner of the troubadours, who, carried away by passion, exceed the truth, and restraining my own amorous desire so that it does not distract me, I shall say what I find in you. All my speech will be in vain to those who have not seen you, for they will not believe it; and those who see you, if they cannot see within, will be sad at heart when they believe me. (53)

At least one critic has read this opening as a "troubadouresque" assumption of authority (Sobrer, "Myth of Language" 333), while another notes that, elsewhere in March's oeuvre, sentiment and knowledge are complementary, not opposed (Ramírez i Molas, "El saber del sentiment" 340). In fact, however, the explicit opposition between affection (used here in a similar sense to Duarte and Pedro's *afeiçom*) and truth finds a deeper echo in the third line's juxtaposition of *torbar*, "to disturb," and *trobar*, literally "to find" but explicitly linked to literary invention here through the verb *diré*. Affection, the enemy of dispassionate judgment, precludes worthy speech, which also suffers in comparison to sight. This sight, which obviates the need for faith, is in turn inferior to the poet's *insight*, which can only be believed – in a process that leaves believers with their own spiritual sadness ("en creur·a a mi, llur arma sera trista").[21] But if the truth cannot be expressed by an affected soul, how can it be understood by one? This impasse between speech and sight, sight and insight, will be explored in hylomorphic terms throughout the rest of the poem.

Hylomorphism is presented as a problem of knowledge and speech in the poem's second stanza:

> Quant és del cors, menys de participar
> ab l'esperit, coneix bé lo grosser:
> vostra color y ell tall pot bé saber,
> mas ga del gest no porà bé parlar. (lines 13–16)

Whatever belongs to the body but does not share in the spirit, the coarse man knows well. He may be familiar with your colour and bearing, but he will not be able to speak properly of your gesture. (53)

This sentiment is reinforced in the next stanza in one of March's rare assertions of commonality: "Tots som grossers en poder explicar/ ço que mereix un bell cos e honest" (lines 17–18; "We are all coarse when we try to express what a fair and honest body deserves" [53]). The soul is thus associated with the lyrically inexpressible because of its role in movement (the "gest" that cannot be expressed by the coarse).[22] Belief is not at issue. Sarah Spence has argued that the troubadours rework the relationship between rhetoric and the body "so that the body can re-enter the field of rhetoric since desire is situated in the language of the body – or the vernacular – even as reason retains its connection to the tangible, visible world" (166). Here, however, March denigrates the lyrical value of the corporal. A more proper object for lyric praise, March suggests in the following stanza, is the lady's *seny* "wisdom" (notwithstanding that this poem belongs to the *Llir entre cards* cycle, rather than *Plena de seny*), which in this case is more peacefully ordered than the Venetian government (lines 33–4). The delight provoked by this well-ordered mind makes baser desires impossible:

> Tan gran delit tot hom entenent ha
> e occupat se troba·n vós entendre,
> que lo desig del cors no·s pot estendre
> a leig voler, ans com a mort està. (lines 37–40)

All who understand (these things) feel great delight and make it their occupation to understand you, since desire for the body cannot extend to base impulses: rather it is as though (it were) dead. (55)

We return here to the question of lyric understanding as March continues punning on *trobar* in line 38. Like the "understanding" man who finds or invents himself in attempting to understand the lady, March performs this process as he explicates it, dedicating his own lyric endeavour to spiritual matters in such a way that his own body appears dead. The carnal will is described in visual terms: it is *leig*, "ugly." It seems, then, that March's lyric is indeed up to the task of spiritual expression.

Here as elsewhere, however, March's *envoi* bears a contradictory, or at least oblique, relationship to the preceding stanzas:

> Lir entre carts, lo meu poder no fa
> tant que pogués fer corona·nvisible;
> meriu-la vós, car la qui és visible
> no·s deu posar lla on miracle stà. (lines 41–4)

> Lily among thorns: my power is not so great that it could make for you an invisible crown. You deserve one, since a visible crown should not be placed where there is a miracle. (55)

Thus, March's "power" (of invention, *trobar*) is in the end inadequate for the "invisible" praise merited by *Llir entre cards*. The final contrast between the visible and the invisible, a characteristically idiosyncratic instance of sacred hyperbole, is complicated by March's comparison of his lady to a miracle, etymologically related to wonder but bearing the phonic echo of *mirar*, a verb of sight. The return to the passion of sadness in the poem's opening stanza, which resulted from a belief in spiritual insight, finds its own thematic echo in the poet's inability, or unwillingness, to abandon sensation. Body and soul, passion and truth cannot be fully disentangled lyrically; sight and sadness resurface inevitably.

X: "De ffet que fuy a sa mercé vengut"

Poem X is a portrait of the mind of the poet in love according to the Augustinian powers of the soul. It opens with an extended simile, as March compares his mind to a king ruling over three cities and engaged in a long-running war with another king; the situation remains a stalemate until the enemy king hires a mercenary who helps him conquer all three cities. The conquered king is allowed to retain control, as the conqueror's vassal, of two of the cities, but he must abandon the third and avoid even thinking of it (lines 1–16). In the poem's third stanza, March reveals that Love is his enemy, and *Plena de seny* the mercenary:

> Lonch temps Amor per enemich lo sent,
> mas jamés fon que·m donàs un mal jorn
> qu·en poch instant no li fes pendre torn,

fforagitant son aspre pensament.
Tot m'ha vençut ab sol esforç d'un cors,
ne l·ha calgut mostrar sa potent força;
los tres poders qu·en l'arma són me força,
dos me'n jaqueix, de l'altr·usar no gos. (lines 17–24)

For a long time I have felt Love to be my enemy, but he has never given me a bad day without my instantly making him change, banishing from me his bitter thoughts. (Now) he has totally defeated me with the strength of a single body; he has had no need to display his mighty power: he overcomes the three faculties of my soul; he leaves me two, (and) I dare not use the other. (39)

We are confronted here with two kinds of allegory: the kind that seeks to "make the invisible visible" (Terry, "Introspection" 171), expressing the inner through the outer (the opening simile), and the familiar *psychomachia* of sentimental fiction, portraying the inner conflict between, in this case, allegorized powers of the soul and Love. This *psychomachia* makes an initial move away from the visibility of the opening simile in that Love's hidden power ("ne l·ha calgut *mostrar* sa potent *força*") overcomes (*força*) the powers (*poders*) of the poet's soul. The rest of the poem explores the moral consequences, for the lyric voice, of the expressive insufficiency of the *psychomachia*, which finds its echo in the poet's lost memory (the power forbidden to him).

The kind of psychological allegory deployed in poem X was also frequent in troubadour poetry, playing a key but ambiguous role in the development of troubadour subjectivity: "If the subject position is extended, by allegory, into a 'self' where Love and other forces interact, then the boundaries of this 'self,' and its relationship to other selves, are fundamentally unclear. Since the notion of the 'self' is obscure, the relationship to it of the first-person subject is likewise problematic" (Kay, *Subjectivity* 55). Through this process, "a rhetorical (and moral) scheme whose original purpose was the assertion of community can become a means of elaborating difference" (52), which is indeed what happens in poem X's next stanza:

Jamés vençó fon plaer del vençut,
sinó de mi que·m plau qu·Amor me vença
e·m tinga pres ab sa·nvisible lença,
mas paren bé sos colps en mon escut. (lines 29–32)

Defeat was never a pleasure for the defeated except in my case, for I am glad that Love should defeat me and keep me prisoner in his invisible net: his strokes fall gratefully upon my shield. (39)

Through an allegory of defeat, March declares himself an exceptional – indeed, unique – lover. He also, however, subtly recalls once more the image of the penitent, gratefully receiving Love's invisible lashes. Terry translates *lença* here as "net," but Bohigas glosses it as poetic licence for *lança*, "lance" (A. March, *Poesies* 97n31); the lance's *colps*, "blows," call to mind the poet's *colpa*, "guilt." Indeed, critics have read this poem as an admission of guilt, March's confession of having ceded moral judgment in ceding control of his memory (Pujol 308–9). However, March does not frame this concession in terms of absolute surrender, but rather of intersubjective participation.

Poem X does not describe, after all, an intact, discrete mind; rather, the poet's mind is "at the mercy of" another's will:

> De ffet que fuy a sa mercé vengut,
> l'Enteniment per son conseller pres
> e mon Voler per alguazir lo mes,
> dant fe cascú que may sera rebut
> en sa mercé lo conpanyó Membrar,
> servint cascú lealment son offici,
> sí que algú d'éls no serà tan nici
> qu·en res contrast que sia de amar. (lines 33–40)

> As soon as I fell into Love's hands, he took my Understanding as his adviser and appointed my Will executor, each promising that their companion Memory would never be admitted to their grace, each one loyally performing his duty, so that neither would be so foolish as to oppose anything which had to do with loving. (39–41)

The silencing of memory in particular in this portrayal of love as a disorder of the faculties points toward the intersection of ethics and emotion in this tradition of medieval thought.[23] As we have seen, memory does not just instigate cognitive processes in the Middle Ages; it also informs them morally, bearing "emotionally laden" intentions to the intellect along with, or rather as integral parts of, its images (Carruthers 14). We have also seen that a memory "captive," in the sense that it obsessively presents a misunderstood image of the beloved for the mind's contemplation, was central to the etiology of lovesickness. March's metaphor diverges from this diagnosis in its emphasis on the struggle with, and capitulation to, the will of the other – an ethical (voluntaristic) dimension that March figures in intersubjective terms as the withholding of "mercy" from their companion.

This figuration thus raises the question of subjectivity in terms of both self-consciousness, in its moral self-scrutiny, and subjection, the submission to Love's (and, by implication, the beloved's) will. In the Middle Ages, the Latin *subjectum* translated Aristotle's *hupokeimenon*, "substance" or "essence," which fused the physical subject as a "substrate for accidents" with the "logical subject" as a "support for the predicates in a proposition" (Balibar, Cassin, and Libera 1070). In a "transition from *subjectum* to *ego*," modern (Cartesian) notions of subjectivity make this *subjectum* "the basis of any psychology of the subject" (1073). What is remarkable about medieval psychology is that these two notions have yet to be fused:

> The Middle Ages had a theory of the ego or I-ness (*égoïté*), or a theory of the *subject* in the obvious philosophical sense of the term *mens*, but that theory did not require the implementation of the notion of a *subjectum*; it also offered a complete theory of subjectivity in grammar, logic, physics and metaphysics, but was reluctant to export it into pyschology in the form of a theory of *mens humana*. (1073–4)

Indeed, the Augustinian theory of *mens*, operative in poem X and throughout March's poetry, resisted this fusion as a matter of doctrine. This resistance is grounded in Augustine's theory of perichoresis or circumincession, "the mutual indwelling of the Persons of the Trinity" (1076), which explained how, in the Trinity, a substance could be both simple and multiple. Augustine famously argued, in books IX and X of *De Trinitate*, that the human mind was the (imperfect) image of this model of the Trinity's substance. God is not subject to accidents, differing in this essential way from the *subjectum* just discussed. If the *mens humana*'s faculties constitute, as the image of God, a single substance, then they also must not constitute a *subjectum*, and this latter concept must be "banished from the field of psychology, on pain of reducing mental acts to mere accidents that befall the mind … The *hupokeimenon* is incompatible with the transposition of the theological notion of mutual immanence to psychology" (Balibar, Cassin, and Libera 1076). In the *Trinity*, Augustine was spurred on toward developing this theory of the human mind by the Delphic injunction to "Know thyself" (X.12), and he makes self-certainty the main element of his argument for a similar reason: "The whole point of its [that is, the mind's] being commanded to know itself comes to this: it should be certain that it is none of the things about which it is uncertain, and it should be certain that it is that alone which alone it is certain that it is" (X.16). Self-certainty, then, is the mortal endpoint of human attempts to understand the nature of God, and it is essential to the human mind – but it is not a "subjective" quality as modernity understands the term.

The invocation of the Delphic injunction in the *Trinity* puts Augustine's thought in line with what Foucault has called the "ascetic-monastic" model of self-knowledge (*Hermeneutics* 255). This model calls for Christians to practise introspection as a search for moral truth:

> Self-knowledge is arrived at through techniques whose essential function is to dispel internal illusions, to recognize the temptations that arise within the soul and the heart, and also to thwart the seductions to which we may be victim. And this is all accomplished by a method for deciphering the secret processes and movements that unfold within the soul and whose origin, aim, and form must be grasped. An exegesis of the self is thus required. (255–6)

Readers will recognize in Foucault's exposition Cassian's model of discernment, the practical virtue that allows monks to identify the demonic, divine, or human sources of their affective "thoughts." This practice is in turn part of the broader practice of *mneme theou*, the "memory of God" (Carruthers 2). In this way, the monastic *mneme theou* and the particularly Augustinian approach to self-knowledge come together to form the crucial background for understanding March's confession, in poem X, that he has abandoned his memory and ceded control of – that is, subjected – his understanding and will to another.

For Augustine, the disordered will is the result of original sin, and those who through ascetic discipline have gained perfect control of their will have in fact given their will over to God (Burrus and MacKendrick 92). March's will, however, is at the mercy of Love, leading, in poem X's *envoi*, not only to a loss of memory but to a loss of the power of speech:[24]

> Plena de seny, vullau-vos acordar
> com per Amor vénen grans sentiments,
> e per Amor pot ser hom ignoscents,
> e mostre-u yo qui n'he perdut parlar. (lines 41–4)

> Wise lady: please remember how from Love there comes great suffering and that through Love one may be reduced to childishness: I, who have lost the power of speech, am evidence of this. (41)

Just as the *envoi* of poem XXIII adapts sacred hyperbole, March here takes the common trope of shyness in the beloved's presence as his starting point.[25] He invokes here, in one dense hemistich, his lady's will and memory ("vullau-vos acordar"). The poet has traded, unwillingly but also pleasurably, those powers for Love's *sentiments*, thereby becoming *ignoscents*, which can be understood, with Terry, as "childish," but which also serves as an ironic contrast to the penitent guiltily enjoying Love's harsh blows on his shield. This play of innocence and guilt is further emphasized in the poet's claim of his own visibility (and, therefore, sincerity) – "mostre-u yo" – as he is forced to submit to Love's invisible lance. Through the guilt of subjecting himself to Love's and his lady's will, March has lost the power of speech, and yet, as in XXIII, he retains his lyric voice.[26] In retaining control of his understanding and will, but not his memory, the "emotionally laden" and morally essential basis of human cognition and creativity, March presents himself as a lyrical subject moved primarily from without, at the mercy of his beloved. To be "at another's mercy" is here not a mere figure of speech, but a strong figure for intersubjective participation. Through this participation, the lover's silence is translated into lyric communication. How, then, and with whom, does this lyrical subject communicate?

XIII: "e vaja yo los sepulcres cerquant"

Poem XIII is March's most direct declaration of emotional isolation. In it, he contrasts public happiness with his macabre private sentiments:

> Colguen les gents ab alegria festes,
> loant a Déu, entremesclant deports;
> places, carrers e delitables orts
> sien cerquats ab recont de grans gestes;
> e vaja yo los sepulcres cerquant,
> interrogant ànimes infernades,
> e respondran, car no són companyades
> d'altre que mi en son contínuu plant. (lines 1–8)

> Let people celebrate feast days and be glad, praising God (and) playing games between times; let squares, streets and pleasant gardens be filled with tales of great deeds; and let me walk among tombs, questioning the souls of the damned; and they will reply, for they have no one but me to accompany them in their continual lament. (43)

In the Dantesque image of the poet interrogating damned souls, there is a conflation of empathy and communication: the dead respond because of March's accompanying laments. Perhaps, then, this is the communication that becomes possible after the "grans sentiments" of poem X have robbed the poet of his worldly voice. In fact, the image of March accompanying the dead in their "continual lament" recalls the invocation of a sympathetic audience in poems such as Macías's "Pues me falleçió ventura." In this context, the imperative that opens poem XIII ("Let people celebrate") is an ironic reversal of this poetic commonplace, and it is not coincidental that the other poets are to be found among the celebrating crowd, telling "tales of great deeds." March's emotional distance from these poets is reinforced by the repetition of the verb *cercar*, which meant both "to fill" or "surround" (as in the case of the other poets) and "to seek out" (in the case of March's visit to the cemetery). The popular praise of God that opens the stanza marks a further contrast with March's "damned" lamentations, similar to the play of guilt and innocence in poem X.

The assertion of difference in poem XIII's opening stanza gives way to a scholastic sentence about similarity:

> Cascú requer e vol a son semblant;
> per ço no·m plau la pràtica dels vius.
> D'imaginar mon estat són esquius;
> sí com d'om mort, de mi prenen espant. (lines 9–12)

> Everyone seeks and desires his like; thus I take no pleasure in the company of the living. They are reluctant to imagine my condition; they are terrified of me, as of a dead man. (43)

Similarity generates desire, and for this reason March takes no pleasure in the living. The *pràtica*, "conversation," of the living that March disdains continues his meditation on communication and renders the silence between March and the living as a failure of imagination ("D'imaginar mon estat són esquius"). As we will see, the confrontation with death in this poem seems to revive the poet's lyric imagination, as he here accuses the joyous crowds of the lack of imagination that plagued poem X's amnesiac version of himself.

The question of desire returns March, as always, to his hylomorphic schemes. His imagination may be intact, but love is attacking both his intellect and body, inflicting pain worse than that inflicted on Tityos by the vulture,

> car és hun verm qui romp la mia pensa,
> altre lo cor, qui may cessen de romper,
> e llur treball no·s porà enterrompre
> sinó ab ço que d'aver se defensa. (lines 21–4)

> for one worm gnaws my thoughts, another my heart, and neither rests, and their work can only be interrupted by that which is forbidden to me. (45)

Frustrated love – the absence of his lady's "mercy" – causes a suffering that overwhelms March in body and soul but somehow prevents the release of death. Meanwhile, the figure of the worm, which represents a pain more severe than the pagan vulture, recalls Bernard of Clairvaux's figuration of conscience in "On Conversion": "Let us not meanwhile resent the gnawing of that worm within. Nor let a dangerous tenderness of mind or pernicious softness persuade us that we want to hide our present trouble. It is far better for it to gnaw now, when it can be destroyed by gnawing itself to death" (V.7).[27] The "conversion" of Bernard's title marks a boundary between ascetic Christian self-knowledge and Platonic models of return to the truth: "The function of self-knowledge in Christianity is not to turn back to the self in an act of recollection in order to discover the truth it had once contemplated and the being that it is: rather … if we turn round on the self, it is essentially and fundamentally in order to renounce the self" (Foucault, *Hermeneutics* 256). Because the devouring worms of conscience, like the carnal desire they oppose, are doomed to dissatisfaction, March despairs of salvation and imagines death in apocalyptic terms:

> E si la mort no·m dugués tal offensa
> – ffer mi absent d'una tan plasent vista –,
> no li graesch que de tera no vista

lo meu cors nuu, qui de plaer no pensa
de perdre pus que lo ymaginar
los meus desigs no poder-se complir;
e si·m cové mon derrer jorn finir,
seran donats térmens a ben amar. (lines 25–32)

And (even) if death did not inflict such a penalty – to deprive me of so pleasant a sight – I should not thank it for not clothing in earth my naked body, which expects to lose no other pleasure than that of imagining that my desires will never be achieved; and if I must end my last day, there will also be an end to good loving. (45)

The lyric imagination that survives in the poet subjected to Love and his lady has, as its object, only the unfulfillment that animates courtly poetry. The lost "pleasant sight" of the lady's body – March is not praising here her invisible intellect – is the chief personal consequence of the poet's imagined death, while the poet's own body will be "clothed" in earth, the material of grief rather than the penitential sackcloth of poem CXIV. A pun on "vista" in lines 26 and 27 contrasts the pleasant sight of the lady with the invisibility of the poet's cadaver, naked but for the earth it "wears." This imagined invisibility, in turn, implies a true end to poetic composition as the verbal realization of *ben amar*, "good love." The articulate silence of the witness to a miracle becomes the imagined, but definitive, silence of the grave.

In fact, March persists in imagining the consequences of his death, and his beloved's imagined grief resurrects *fin'amor*'s conventional pleasure in pain through an image of compassion:

E si·n lo cel Déu me vol allogar,
part veur·a Ell, per complir mon delit
serà mester que·m sia dellay dit
que d'esta mort vos ha plagut plorar,
penedint-vos com per poqua mercé
mor l'ignoscent e per amar-vos martre:
cell qui lo cors de l'arma vol departre,
si ferm cregués que us dolrríeu de se. (lines 33–40)

And if God wishes me to dwell in Heaven, apart from seeing Him, for my pleasure to be complete, it will be necessary for them to tell me there that it has pleased you to shed tears at my death, repenting that, because of your meager favours, there dies an innocent man and a martyr to loving you: he who would (gladly) separate body from soul, if he could really believe that you would pity him. (45)

Pleasure and pain are joined here not only in the poet's vision of death as the culmination of his pleasure, but also in the alliterative "vos ha plagut plorar" (line 35). The poet's assumed salvation places the lady's salvation in question, as she takes on the penitent role elsewhere occupied by March. At the same time, the poet positions himself among the audience of the dead of the poem's opening stanza, receiving news from an unknown companion ("serà mester que·m sia dellay dit"). His community with the dead is in this way complementary to his beloved's grief, and this grief, in turn, has replaced the *mercé* of good love, as the fact of the poet's death again overwhelms hylomorphic *fin'amor* through the dense phonic group of *amar/martre/arma* (lines 38–9). Realizing the promise of the poem's Dantesque opening, the love martyr's sacrifice is recontextualized within the discourse of Christian salvation, and the poem's *envoi* turns around questions of belief and faith:

> Lir entre carts, vós sabeu e yo sé
> que·s pot bé fer hom morir per amor;
> creure de mi, que só en tal dolor,
> no fareu molt que y doneu plena fe. (lines 41–4)

> Lily among thorns: we both know that a man may well die of love; the least you can do is believe with all your heart that my suffering is as great as I say. (45)

The poet's plainspoken and emphatic "you know and I know" ("vós sabeu e yo sé") asserts that questions of desire (since "everyone seeks and desires his like") do not lose their relevance in the context of salvation. *Llir entre cards*'s belief here seems to stand in for that of the audience, who perhaps will now be able to imagine the poet's state of mind. The consolation March sought among the dead is imaginatively translated into penitential grief of which the poet is the object; presented as a way out of courtly love's hylomorphic tangle, this desired gesture of belated compassion is found in other Iberian troubadours.[28] March's solution to love's impossible contradictions will change, however, when that grief becomes his own.

XCII: "mescladament partirem nostres cossos"

March's *cants de mort* represent both the poet's deepest exploration of the conflict between reason and passion, body and soul, and also his most daring vision of an escape from the ethical and lyrical paradigms in which those conflicts were central. March brings his grief at his beloved's death to bear lyrically on all of the philosophical structures that have dominated his love songs: carnal, spiritual, and mixed love; memory, will, and understanding; confession and consolation. The analysis focuses sometimes on love, sometimes on grief; March considers the fate of his own and his beloved's souls and bodies. But what might seem like the apotheosis of March's scholastic inclination constitutes instead its exhaustion. Grief leads March's lyrical subject to a new self-awareness as a potentially *shared* subject, sharing in particular its will through its capacity for compassion. This shared, compassionate subject moves March beyond the ethical paradigms, courtly and scholastic, that had opposed virtuous spirit to sinful flesh, and the passions become a means to the salvation, rather than damnation, of body and spirit.

Poem XCII is the first of the *cants de mort* in Pagès's ordering, but some critics, citing its lexical style, formal structure, and treatment of the question of time, have argued that it was the last to be written.[29] The poem concludes with a striking image of a shared resurrection: "Lo jorn del Juhy, quant pendrem carn e ossos,/ mescladament partirem nostres cossos" (lines 249–50; "On the Day of Judgement, when we take on flesh and bone, we shall share out our bodies without distinction" [99]). This final image, I will argue, is March's attempt to escape the moral conflicts of courtly love through a reimagination of a will whose subject is the lovers, not the lover. It is certainly a heterodox vision, but perhaps there is an echo here of Christ, who, for monastic thinkers such as Bernard of Clairvaux, incarnated divine mercy more perfectly precisely because his body housed two natures (as we have seen, because Christ's human nature allowed him to suffer, it taught him to suffer with us). Analysing from a dizzying array of perspectives the forms of love available to a grieving lover, March ultimately imagines a kind of compassionate subjectivity made conscious of itself *as shared* through death. In order to see how March arrives at this image of resurrection in XCII, we must first examine another *cant de mort*, XCVII, whose overwhelming concern is the fate of the beloved's soul, reflecting the broader concern for salvation evident throughout this lyric cycle.

In poem XCVII, March does not present his anguish in altruistic terms, instead returning to the ethical examination of his own status as lover. Thus, the poem begins with the poet's self-accusation of insufficient love in the aftermath of his beloved's death:

> Si per null temps creguí ser amador,
> en mi conech d'amor poch sentiment.
> Si mi compar al comú de la gent,
> és veritat qu·en mi trob gran amor;
> però si guart algú del temps passat
> y el que Amor pot fer en loch dispost,
> nom d'amador solament no m'acost,
> car tant com dech no só passionat. (lines 1–8)

If at any time I thought myself a lover, I can recognize little feeling of love in myself. If I compare myself to the majority of people, it is true that I find great love within me; but if I consider any (lover) from the past and what Love can do in a place which is prepared (for it), I simply cannot aspire to the name of lover, for I am not as passionate as I should be. (109)

As this stanza reveals, March continues to consider idealized love through questions of what is and is not shared. This orientation is evident not only in the explicit comparison to the "common people," whose love pales in comparison to that felt by the poet, but also in the poet's consideration of his place in a tradition of lovers ("però si guart algú del temps passat") and in lexical choices around variations of *par*/*part*, as in line three's "compar." The experience of an apparently real death makes the question of a poetic tradition more, rather than less, salient in March's introspection. He wonders if he can consider himself a lover, but he aspires to the *name* of lover, to be *known as* a lover.

The lyric portrayal of the lady's death focuses, however, on what lovers can share. Here, a final memory occasions a reflection on compassion:

> Enquer està que vida no finí,
> com prop la mort yo la viu acostar,
> dient plorant: "No vullau mi lexar,
> hajau dolor de la dolor de mi!"
> ¡O cor malvat d'aquell qui·s veu tal cas,
> com pecejat o sens sanch no roman!
> Molt poc·amor e pietat molt gran
> degra bastar que senyal gran mostràs. (lines 17–24)

> (Her) life had still not come to an end when I saw her draw near to death, saying with tears: "Please do not leave me, have pity on my suffering!" O wretched heart of him who finds himself in such a situation, since it is not broken into pieces or left without blood! Little love and great pity should be enough for it to show great signs. (109)

March narrates here the lady's actual transition to spiritual invisibility. He sees his lady approach death fearfully ("prop la mort yo la viu acostar"), just as he, in lines seven and eight, is wracked with doubt in his own approach to the name of "lover." The theme is emphasized in his reference to the heart of him who sees himself ("qui·s veu") in a similar situation. The approach of death also reverses the traditional courtly roles, as the lady's direct speech (extremely rare throughout March's poetry) is a macabre imitation of the lover's plea for mercy: "No vullau mi lexar,/ hajau dolor de la dolor de mi!" Here, compassion becomes the figure for the subjected will, the latter emphasized in the command "no vullau."

In this moment of extremity, pity or mercy replaces love as the central unifier. Compassion is the matter of the final attempt to stay together. The rest of the poem, however, explores compassion's inadequacy (carved harshly into the poet's memory) to the task:

> ¿Qui serà·quell qui la mort planyerà,
> d'altre u de ssi, tant com és lo gran mal?

Sentir no·s pot lo dampnatge mortal,
molt menys lo sab qui mort jamés temptà.
¡O cruell mal, donant departiment
per tots los temps als coratges units!
Mos sentiments me trob esbalaÿts,
mon espirit no té son sentiment. (lines 33–40)

Who will mourn for death, his own or another's, such is the great evil? One cannot feel the mortal injury; he whom death never tempted knows still less of it. O cruel evil, for ever separating hearts (which were) united! I find my feelings stupefied; my spirit has lost its feeling. (111)

Both grief and self-pity are incommensurate with the pain of death, which furthermore is beyond our powers of perception ("Sentir no·s pot lo dampnatge mortal"), even if death has tempted us before – which presumably, March seems to be implying, is the case for any courtly lover. The cruelty of death lies in its splitting, *departiment*, of previously united *coratges*, this latter a term that could refer to any or all of the passions to which the heart was subject (Faraudo, "Coratge"). Death is no longer the occasion for hypothetical compassion, but rather for real separation: whereas before the lover proclaimed his willingness to die by separating his own soul from his body (XIII, lines 39–40), here death separates two united spirits. The poet's *sentiments* no longer silence him; rather, they themselves are "stupefied" in this separation.

These vanished *sentiments* are contrasted in the poem's final stanzas with the poet's passion, *passió*, which cannot be alleviated by his friends' compassion (*complanyiment*; lines 41–2). The poet is now only accompanied by his sad memory of his beloved's life, whose pain he tries to match with his own grief: "en tristor visch, de sa vida membrant,/ e de sa mort aytant com puch me dull" (lines 51–2; "I live in sadness, remembering her life, and I mourn her death as best I can" [111]).[30] The poet's will is subjected to that of his own grief: "No bast en més, en mi no puch fer pus,/ sinó·behir lo que ma dolor vol" (lines 53–4; "I cannot do more: all I can do is obey what my grief demands" [111]). The best state to which this self-subjection can lead, however, is absolute isolation, as the poem's *envoi* shows:

Tot amador d'amar poch no s'escús
que sia viu, e mort lo seu amat,
o que almenys del món visca·partat,
que solament haja nom de resclús. (lines 57–60)

No lover can escape the charge of loving little if he remains alive when the one he loves is dead; or he should at least live in retirement from the world and be known only as a hermit. (113)

The *envoi*'s "nom de resclús" is the obvious counterpart to the opening stanza's "nom d'amador." Ultimately, poem XCVII shows the poet's failed subjection to his dying lady's grief, and thereafter his realization that subjection to his own grief is insufficient for establishing empathetic continuity. This insufficiency is emphasized in the sentence that the failed lover should live as a hermit, *apartat* from the rest of humanity – echoing in life the *departiment* brought about by death. This poem narrates, then, the failure to overcome death through empathetic grief, and the hermit-lover of its *envoi* is a failed reflection of the anchorite. Poem XCII, by contrast, portrays an attempt to imagine postmortem unity in an altered soteriological context.

At 250 lines, XCII is among March's longest poems, and many critics have sought to explicate its complex structure. Some see a clear progression, from death to God and from the "bodily" to the "intellectual" (Sobrer, "Architecture" 274, 277), while others detect a pivot toward the middle of the poem, with *pietat* becoming central from the twelfth stanza on (Terry, "'Per la mort'" 235). Sobrer sees in the poem's many antitheses the structure of a church nave, along which the reader progresses toward God in a "process of conversion" ("Architecture" 274).[31] As we have seen, Christian processes of conversion in the ascetic-monastic model tend to lead toward self-abnegation. This is not the case, however, in poem XCII; rather, the poem ends with a striking affirmation, drawing on biblical and Augustinian models as an answer to the paradigms of courtly ethics, of a self shared eternally between two lovers.

The contradictory nature of this *cant de mort* cannot be denied, but neither can the poem be reduced to a series of antitheses. Rather, the poem has a cyclical structure, as the poet tries to explain the feelings of love that have survived his lady's death in hylomorphic terms, fails, and tries again. In the first stanza, March describes the role of grief in preserving memory:

> Aquelles mans que jamés perdonaren
> han ja romput lo fil tenint la vida
> de vós, qui sou de aquest món exida,
> segons los fats en secret ordenaren.
> Tot quant yo veig e sent, dolor me torna,
> dant-me recort de vós, qui tant amava.
> En ma dolor si prim e bé·s cercava,
> se trobarà que delit s'i contorna;
> donchs, durarà, puys té qui la sostinga,
> car sens delit dolor crey no·s retinga. (lines 1–10)

Those hands which never pardoned have now broken the thread which held the life of you who have left this world, as the fates secretly decreed. All that I see and feel turns to grief, reminding me of you, whom I loved so much. In my suffering, if one looks closely, one will find that pleasure is mixed with it; therefore my suffering will endure, since it has something to sustain it, for, without pleasure, I believe suffering does not remain. (85)

Alluding to Atropos, the poem's opening figures death's mercilessness in corporal terms ("Aquelles mans"), while the poet's sensations – particularly sight – are converted to grief. March discerns an element of pleasure in his grief, this conventional note accented by the appearance of *trobar* in line eight. This grief, epistemological in that sensations and memory are the roots of cognition in medieval psychology, becomes, appropriately enough, a matter for investigation ("si prim e bé·s cercava"). Once again, then, the fellowship March sought among the dead becomes a matter of introspection in his own moment of grief.

If passion and ascesis are linked through their ambiguous account of subjectivity and objectivity, materiality and immateriality, for March in the *cants de mort*, the term that condenses this ambiguity is "pain" or "grief," *dolor*. Indeed, March seeks the *comunaleza* Macías had required of Amor in Dolor: "O tu, Dolor, sies-me cominal!" (XCVI, line 35). And it is precisely the pain – but not, crucially, the expected *mortal* pain – provoked by his beloved's death that undoes the hylomorphic division of body and soul underlying March's theory of love. Each of poem XCII's next four stanzas repeats, with slight variations, the idea that now that March's beloved has died, carnal love is no longer possible, and mixed love will eventually die out despite its partial participation in the spiritual, so that only spiritual love will remain. Death has "clarified" all of the poet's confused wills: "Tots los volers qu·en mi confusos eren,/ se mostren clar per lur obra forana" (lines 21–2), causing his body pain ("ma carn se dol," line 23), but leaving his "pure" love intact (lines 29–30). March insists twice that his "honest" love will last forever (lines 19–20 and lines 29–30), but in his final reworking of the claim, his certainty disappears:

Aquell voler qu·en ma carn sola·s causa,
si no és mort, no tardarà que muyra;
l'altre per qui dol contínuu m'abuyra,
si·m deffaleix, no serà sens gran causa.
Ell pot ser dit voler concupiscible,
e sol durar, puys molt de l'arma toqua,
mas fall per temps, car virtut no invoca,
e d'un costat és apetit sensible.
Aquests volers l'amor honesta·m torben,
perqu·entre mal e bé mes penses orben. (lines 41–50)

That desire which arises from my flesh alone, if it is not dead, will not be long in dying; that other (desire) by which I am watered with continual suffering, if it fails in me, it will not be without great cause. It may be called concupiscible desire, and generally lasts, since it greatly concerns the soul, but it fails in time, since it does not

> call upon virtue, and in part is sensual appetite. These desires disturb honest love in me, since, between good and evil, they blind my thoughts. (87–9)

March's confident assertions of his spiritual love's survival are replaced here by an admission of confusion, instability, and blindness ("entre mal e bé mes penses orben"). Sight had earlier been associated with the carnal, but here the association is reversed: his blindness contradicts earlier claims that death has clarified the hylomorphic dilemmas of love. March's formal scholastic vocabulary cannot shape the confused matter presented to his mind by his grieving senses, which are preoccupied by dynamic and piercing pain:

> Lo loch on jau la dolor gran que passe,
> no és del tot fora de mes natures,
> ne del tot és fora de lurs clausures;
> lo moviment creu que per elles passe.
> Aquell voler qu·en mi no troba terme
> és lo mijà per on dolor m'agreuja;
> l'estrem d'aquest fora natur·alleuja,
> ffort e punyent, mas encansable verme.
> Oppinió falssa per tots és dita,
> que fora nós e dintre nós habita. (lines 71–80)

> The place where lies the great suffering I experience is not entirely beyond my own natures, nor is it entirely beyond their confines; I believe that the motive (for my suffering) passes through them. That (other) desire which in me has no limit is the means by which my suffering is increased: its opposite lies outside nature, a strong and piercing, but relentless, worm. A wrong opinion is voiced by people in general, since it dwells both outside and inside us. (89)

Here, the "purified" will or desire remaining after the death of the beloved is said to be the "medium" through which the poet's pain is felt; and yet, it is the "opposite" of this desire (which seems to mean carnal love) that is "outside of nature," that is, of the body, itself compared to a stinging, devouring worm (recalling poem XIII). Does this passage mean that spiritual love is the medium of carnal desire's pain? Is it thus that this composite pain and desire lives both within us and outside? Although March presents this stanza as a straightforward refutation of a widely held but false opinion, it is not immediately clear here how interiority and exteriority map onto the material and spiritual.

To begin to answer these questions, we should recall that, while March's theory of love combines courtly and scholastic ideas, his psychology is thoroughly Augustinian. The compositional approach of poem XCII, in which ideas are tried out, expressed fully, but eventually rejected or overwritten, recalls Augustine's search for the divine image in the *Trinity*. Augustine continually proposes and disqualifies Trinitarian structures he finds in the human mind and perception before settling on the self-conscious activity of the mind's three powers, and in the end he rejects even this final image, affirming humanity's fundamental dissimilarity from the divine (XV.39). The structure of the *Trinity*, then, anticipates the "*apophasis*-by-*kataphasis*" (Burrus and MacKendrick 81) of negative theology. Augustine, by saying everything about the Trinitarian structure of the mind, ultimately exposes its absolute incommensurability with the divine Persons. It is my argument that March engages in a similar manoeuvre in poem XCII, saying everything about the hylomorphic theory of love in order to demonstrate its final insufficiency, exposed by the experience of a fundamentally transgressive *dolor*.

Having established this insufficiency, March turns here to pity's role in grief and cognition:

> De pietat de sa mort ve que·m dolga,
> e só forçat que mon mal haj·a plànyer;
> tant he perdut, que bé no·m pot atànyer,
> Ffortuna ja no té què pus me tolga.
> Quant ymagín les voluntats hunides
> y ell converssar, separats per a sempre,
> penssar no pusch ma dolor haja tempre,
> mes passions no trob gens aflaquides;
> e si per temps elles passar havien,
> vengut és temps que començar devien. (lines 111–20)

> Out of pity I come to grieve for her death and I am compelled to lament my misfortune; I have lost so much that no good can reach me: Fortune has no more to take away from me. When I imagine our united wills and our conversation, now separated for ever, I cannot think my grief will ever know moderation: I do not find my sufferings have decreased at all; and if some day they were to pass, the time for this to begin has now arrived. (91)

Having rejected the received doctrine on ethical love in the preceding stanzas, March declares himself subject to the passions that should have faded with the death of his beloved's body. The poet's imagination (related, again, to memory and emotion through the concept of *intentio*) is in league with grief, as the poet laments the loss of a unity of will and conversation (lines 115–16). His grief remains intemperate and his passions strong; it appears that they are not going to give way to the spiritual love that should emerge victorious in the battle between "honest" reason and the passions.

It was not, then, during the time of earthly love that March's will was disordered; rather, disorder and confusion have emerged in the wake of his beloved's earthly demise. The stanzas that follow present a bewildering array of reversals and contradictions, perhaps the result of thoughts controlled by still-conflicting desires: “Mes volentats mos penssaments aporten/ avall y amunt, sí com los núvols l’ayre” (lines 121–2; “My feelings drive my thoughts up and down like clouds in the air” [91]). The false appears true, the true false (line 134); March’s heart may burst at any moment (line 140); yet such extremes are provoked by what is after all an everyday occurrence:

> Tan comun cas, ¿per què tan estrem sembla
> al qui per sort la Mort en tant lo plaga?
> ¿Per què·n tal cas la rahó d’om s’amaga,
> e passió tota sa forç·assembla?
> Déu piadós e just cruel se mostra:
> tant és en nós torbada conexença! (lines 171–6)

> Why does such a common case seem so extreme to one who by chance is so stricken by Death? Why, in such a case, does one’s reason hide and passion assemble all its forces? God, who is pitying and just, shows himself to be cruel: so confused is our knowledge of Him! (95)

This series of antitheses and reversals is framed by an overall oscillation between confusion and clarity, the latter of which is represented through images of separation: “Ço qu·en passat enbolt e confús era,/ és departit: lo gra no·s ab la palla;/ esperiment altre no·m pens hi valla;/ per la Mort és uberta la carrera” (lines 221–4; “What in the past was tangled and confused has gone: the grain is no longer with the straw; no other experience, I think, is of any value; the way has been cleared by Death” [97]). Death is thus aligned for and against discernment; it is paralyzing and freeing, provoking now extreme suffering, now a collapse into indifference. The apparent clarity of the path to spiritual love is belied by the jarring reversals of March’s verse, in which the wheat and chaff remain together resolutely. This unity is the final mercy March seeks from God:

> O Déu, mercé! Mas no ssé de què·t pregue,
> sinó que mi en lo seu loch aculles;
> no·m tardes molt que dellà mi no vulles,
> puys l’espirit on és lo seu aplegue;
> e lo meu cors, ans que la vida fine,
> sobre lo seu abraçat vull que jaga.
> Fferí’ls Amor de no curable plaga;
> separà’ls Mort: dret és qu·ella·ls vehine.
> Lo jorn del Juhy, quant pendrem carn e ossos,
> mescladament partirem nostres cossos. (lines 241–50)

> O mercy, God! But I do not know what to beg of you, except that you (should) gather me to her place; do not delay long in wishing me in the next world, (and) therefore take my spirit where her own resides; and, before my life ends, I wish my body to lie with its arms around hers. Love dealt them an incurable wound; Death separated them: it is right that she should bring them together. On the Day of Judgement, when we take on flesh and bone, we shall share out our bodies without distinction. (99)

As Virginia Burrus and Karmen MacKendrick have argued, Augustine's ideal resurrected will would not be bereft of the body: "The will thus reintegrated would harmonize not only with itself and with God's will but with the flesh as well" (84–5). Furthermore, as Caroline Walker Bynum has explained, medieval eschatology maintained a desire for "material and structural continuity" in the resurrected body, a materialism that "expressed not body-soul dualism but rather a sense of self as psychosomatic unity" (11). It was not until the thirteenth century that thinkers such as Albert the Great, Thomas Aquinas, and Giles of Rome "limited hylomorphism to the material world and maintained that there is a single form in man" (256–7), leaving us with a soul that could subsist on its own, but remained incomplete until the body should rise, giving it matter to inform. This view was attacked because the separated soul would not know particulars, meaning that "it would not know Christ's passion or its own individual sins" (274). Despite these objections, the doctrines of unicity of form and formal identity were widely accepted by about 1330 (277).

The doctrine of formal identity assures that, whatever matter is informed by the soul on Judgment Day, that matter *is* the soul's body. In this way, the matter shared between March's soul and that of his beloved would come to know the same particulars, but now sinless and released from the torment caused in life by the soteriological conflict of March's theory of love. Pere Ramírez i Molas has called this last image "rhetorical," an exaggeration meant to stoke the audience's emotion (*La poesia* 278); Arthur Terry, for his part, argues that, in this final image of the Resurrection, the poem's tensions between body and soul are resolved ("'Per la mort'" 240). They are not resolved, however, by removing or even purifying the body – the latter a goal traditionally pursued by Christian ascetics (Flood 145) – but rather by sharing it. The will, too, can be shared without subjection; it will retain and share material particularity even as identity resides in the soul. In this final image, through a mercy granted, the *departiment* of death can be envisioned as a future, eternal sharing: *partirem*, "we will share." For March, then, compassion is not just a possibility added to moral reasoning within hylomorphic structures; it explodes those structures once March's lyric has exhausted them through cyclical failures of discernment and confession.

Conclusion

Tragic Enclosure

Rather than words comes the thought of high windows:
The sun-comprehending glass,
And beyond it, the deep blue air, that shows
Nothing, and is nowhere, and is endless.

– Philip Larkin, "High Windows"

Although Ausiàs March's literary reputation would continue to grow well into the sixteenth century, inspiring numerous translations and borrowings, the ethical vision of compassion and consolation articulated in his poetry found few adherents even among his admirers. I wish to conclude with a brief reflection on the fading of this vision, taking as my central example Joan Roís de Corella's *Tragèdia de Caldesa* (c. 1458), which, I argue, both dramatizes and laments the incipient walling off of the formerly shareable self within discrete subjectivity.

In the generations immediately preceding and following that of March in Aragon, literary consolation in verse and prose was associated with friendship and conversation, collective modes of composition, and a misogynist framework parallel, but not identical, to that of Castile's "debate about women."[1] Consolation, death, and love were linked through the mortal stakes of lovesickness, whose medieval talking cure, *confabulatio*, called for the verbal intervention of a friend, physician, or other authority figure (Solomon 59–62). Literary representations of such interventions drew heavily on Ovid's *Remedia amoris* and on the lyric tradition of the *mala cansó* or *maldit*.[2] In the second half of the fifteenth century especially, the sentimental texts grouped under the heading of *prosa d'art* adapted Ovidian and other classical material more broadly, reframing it in terms of the courtly ethics that reached their greatest lyric elaboration in March's songs. Joan Roís de Corella (1435–97) drew not only on Ovid's *Metamorphoses*, *Ars amandi*, and *Heroides*, but also on Seneca's *Tragedies* and Boethius's *Consolation of Philosophy* in his remarkable sentimental lyric and prose, which was often elaborated in collective contexts, and which, as I will argue here, reacted sensitively but pessimistically to March's innovations.[3] In Corella's early adoption of a pose of disenchantment, he portrays with great subtlety the foreclosure of the spaces of friendship and compassion glimpsed by earlier Iberian courtly writers and still being explored by some of his contemporaries.

The *Consolació* or *Avís d'amor* of Lluís Icard (d. 1429) exemplifies the notion of consolation as verse *confabulatio*: its author offers advice to a formerly carefree friend in whom unhappy love has worked a terrible change.[4] In a mix of Catalan and Occitan characteristic of poetry from this period, the poet warns his friend that this change is the talk of the town:

> Donchs, ¿què pux de vós dir,
> que·z etz en aytal pas
> que ja lo vostra cas
> éz a mant hom notoris?
> E ja fan cossistoris
> de vós per mans lochs,
> disén: "Vegats le fochs
> d'amor, e com l'enflama!,
> que ten coralmens ama,
> que·l sen e sentimén
> han fayt transmudamén
> en la sua persona." (Molas 135, lines 38–49)

> So what can I say of you, who have arrived at such a state that your case is already notorious to many? And councils now meet in many places to discuss you, saying, "See the fires of love, how they enflame him! For he loves so sincerely that his sense and feeling are greatly agitated in him."

The sincerity of the friend's love ("ten coralmens ama"), which has caused his inner and outer senses ("sen e sentimén") to transmute him, is contrasted with the sincere friendship he maintained with the poet, wherein the latter spoke graciously despite love's ills:

> Car en lo temps passat
> per la nostr'amistat,
> qu'entr'ams és ten corals,
> per motz de crusels mals
> que vós, amichs, passàvetz,
> ges no·us descapdelhàvets
> de vostre franch donari (134–5, lines 13–19)

> For earlier in our friendship, so true between us, despite many cruel ills that you, friend, suffered, you never strayed from your affable wit.

Such friendly conversation has been replaced with the chattering of *cossistoris*, "councils," a word that, in recalling the Barcelona Consistori (whose founding was at the time fairly recent), emphasizes the artificial, poetic notion of love conditioning the public perception and description of the friend's suffering. This shared language is one of friendship's pleasures, to which the suffering lover has lost access.

Such a loss is the theme of Francesc Ferrer's *Lo conhort* (c. 1448), whose opening laments the great pain of hearing others talk of love "e no tenir què metre en joch!" (X, lines 1–3; "and have nothing to put in play"). In essence, Ferrer's poem dramatizes the opening lines of Torroella's *Tant mon voler*, inserting quotations from thirteen other poets who arrive at his door to console him, including Ausiàs March and an unknown Corella who may, as the poem's editor, Jaume Auferil, notes (Ferrer 243n133), be the governor of Valencia whose letter of advice from Ferrer was discussed in part one. Ferrer's crisis begins when, at the royal palace, he overhears a group of courtiers speaking joyfully of love (lines 26–37). They invite him to join them, and (as in Icard's *Consolació*) his unexpected silence betrays his suffering; he quickly leaves, anguished at having become "singular": "L'ànima tinch ja avorrida,/ pus só, e·m dolch, un singular" (lines 96–7; "I despise my soul, for I am, and it grieves me, singular"). The first of Ferrer's visitors to speak, Berenguer de Vilaragut, explains that if he cannot take joy in conversing about love, he need not be singular in sadness: "Ferrer,/ aquests senyors e yo·ndessemps .../ te som venguts aconortar,/ e més te deu aconsolar/ nostre conort que lo restant,/ que tot hom trist vol son semblant" (lines 150–6; "Ferrer, these men and I together ... have come to comfort you, and our comfort should console you more than the rest, for all sad men desire their like"). Toward the end of the poem, having heard from all of his visitors, Ferrer confirms Vilaragut's sentiment: "Cascú hac dit lo que sabia/ o part d'ellò per mon conort/ e per lo lur, car és confort/ dir passions entre·ls amics" (lines 627–30; "Each has said what he knows, or part of it, for my comfort and his own, for it is a comfort to speak of passions among friends"). Yet as Auferil notes (Ferrer 140), Ferrer's interlocutors, rather than urging him to bear his suffering with humility, launch into misogynist invective; all of *Lo conhort*'s inserted quotations are from *maldits*. Having narrowly escaped punishment at the hands of the king, the assembled poets part, promising, however, to offer similar "consolation" should the need present itself (lines 725–31). In this way, consolation as *consolació*, *conhort*, and *confort* represents not just a set of genres (individual and collective verse invectives against love and women such as Icard's *Consolació* and Ferrer's *Conhort*; consolatory letters and treatises; prosimetric texts based in part on Boethius), but also a theme apt for reflection on the causes and remedies of grief (*dolor*). As in the case of compassion, literary approaches to such grief involved the vision of death and collective modes of composition.

Joan Roís de Corella's best-known collective composition, the *Parlament en casa de Berenguer Mercader*, comprises short works of sentimental prose rather than verse, drawn from classical mythology. This work – and the rest of Corella's short prose – was likely composed between 1455 and 1463 (*Obres completes I* 28). However, between 1468 and 1471, Corella became a master in theology and was likely ordained; toward the end of his life he composed, along with Bernat Fenollar and Joan Escrivà, a versified Passion narrative, *Lo passi en cobles* (1493).[5] Corella's contribution to *Lo passi* is a final verse prayer to the Virgin, portraying the pietà; the preceding narrative is largely the work of Fenollar (c. 1438–1516), who himself also collaborated on satirical works such as *Lo procés de les olives*. *Lo passi* is dedicated to Isabel de Villena, whose *Vita Christi*, fundamental to the spread of a new form of Passion devotion throughout Iberia, was likely at least in part a response to Jaume Roig's *Spill* and the broader Catalan misogynist tradition (Piera 109). Albert Hauf has argued that *Lo passi*'s authors are sincere when they invite Villena to emend their work (311–12), and indeed, their text explicitly elicits affective contemplation through scripts attributed to a reader, *Lo Lector*. These contemplative scripts are in turn a vehicle for compassionate identification in terms that clearly recall both earlier works of sentimental prose and lyric, and the association of emotion, thought, and memory in monastic devotion.

One of the key metaphors for this kind of identification in *Lo passi* is that of transportation, for example in these lines attributed to *Lo Lector*:

> *Feu vós que·l recort en vós yo transporte*
> passant-hi la pena que vós hi pasàs.
> Lavòs seré tot fill verdader vostre
> penant yo per vós, com vós fes per mi,
> la vostra clemència tal gràcia·m mostre
> que dolrre'm lo cor en cert yo demostre,
> sentint lo greu mal que·l vostre sentí. (lines 1767–73; emphasis added)[6]

> *Transport my memory to you*, undergoing the pain that you underwent. Then I will truly be your son, suffering for you, as you did for me. May your clemency show me such grace that I demonstrate to you with certainty my heart's pain, feeling the grave affliction that yours felt.

Here, the memory is transported by virtue of Christ's grace, presented as a product of clemency. The identification itself is figured as undergoing or feeling the same suffering (lines 1768 and 1773, respectively) and also as reciprocal suffering (line 1770); saving sorrow is evinced by the Reader's grieving heart (line 1772). Although Fenollar, like San Pedro in the *Pasión trobada*, continues to play on "passion" as a general name for suffering and for Christ's suffering in particular,[7] this account of compassion as an act of mental "transportation" in fact formalizes the enclosed subjectivity of contemplative readers, who must travel beyond themselves in the act of compassion.

A similar formalization takes place in the verses directed toward, and attributed to, Mary, both in the Passion narrative and in Corella's final prayer. Mary's relation to the cross is initially described in musical terms: "Serà-us la creu arpa, essent encordada/ ab venes e nirvis del cos divinal,/ sonar-la eu vós ab fe concertada,/ la vostra veu dolça cantant concordada/ tostemps ab lo càntich del par·eternal" (lines 3067–71; "The cross will be a harp for you, strung with the veins and nerves of the divine body; you will play it with concerted faith, your sweet voice forever singing tunefully the eternal father's song").[8] Mary adopts the metaphor of song in wishing to be buried alive with her son: "Y aureu de tenir lavòs una cura/ dels dos, puix als dos ha mort una mort./ E si lo tal plànyer la mort no·m procura,/ posau-m·axí viva en la sepultura/ perquè fill e mare cantem d'un acort" (lines 4199–203; "And you will have to take care of both of us, for one death has killed us both. And if such grief does not bring me death, place me alive in the tomb, so that son and mother may sing together"). If, Mary seems to suggest, she cannot literally die the same death as her son, then she can harmonize with him in the grave (singing the same chord, rather than the same note).[9] The Reader's closing reflections echo Mary's wish: "Almenys pietat açò no·m contraste,/ lo meu esperit qu·en vós tot engaste/ ab vós en la tomba estiga reclòs" (lines 4274–6; "May pity at least not deny that my spirit be set into yours; may it be shut in the tomb with you"). In March's poem XCVII, ascetic reclusion was the lesser alternative to a death provoked by grief; here, reclusion with Christ in the tomb is possible for the soul "set into" (*encastar*) Christ. In *Lo passi*'s concluding prayer, Corella gives extended voice to Mary's grieving wish for entombment:

Puix no voleu que de present yo muyra,
estiga·b vós tancada·n lo sepulcre.
Yo us acollí en lo meu verge ventre,
ara vós, Fill, rebeu-me dins la tomba,
que no·s pot fer entre·ls vius yo conversse
puix que vós, mort, és ja ma vida morta.
En major loch no penseu yo m'estenga
del que vós, Fill, pendreu dins en la pedra.
Giten a mi primera dins la fossa,
que no us és nou dormir en los meus braços.
Cobrir vos ha lo mantell qu·a mi cobre
e si no us par vos baste tal mortalla,
la mia carn, que viu haveu vestida,
no us sia greu que, mort, encara us cobra. (lines 30–43)

Since you do not wish that I die at present, may I be shut with you in your sepulchre. I received you in my virgin womb, now you, Son, receive me in the tomb, for I cannot converse with the living; after your death, my life is dead. And do not believe that

> I will occupy more space than you in the stone. Let them toss me first into the grave, for it is not new for you to sleep in my arms. The blanket that covers me will cover you, and if you do not think such a shroud right for you, may it not upset you to be covered again by my flesh, which you took on when alive.

Mary's grief in these lines makes her "singular" in the sense that commerce with the living is now impossible ("que no·s pot fer entre·ls vius yo conversse"); at the same time, the courtly paradox of living death ("és ja ma vida morta") is here poignantly – but less paradoxically – reworked into jarring exchanges of birth and death. The hospitality of the womb is exchanged for that of the grave, and by the same token, the flesh that clothed Christ before birth is offered as a shroud. Corella presents Mary's desire to be buried with her son as a macabre reflection of the relationship that obtained between them during life. The emotional impact that these lines doubtless achieved should not obscure the fact that they are in this sense less transformative than March's heterodox vision of shared resurrection in poem XCII. Again, grief and compassion, as models for devotion, aspire to a layered form of enclosure.

In chapter five, I suggested that Diego de San Pedro's *Pasión trobada* takes up the courtly play of compassion and Passion but codifies them in atomistic terms. Folger has offered a similar view of *Cárcel de amor*, noting that the famously Christ-like Leriano represents an "'old' mode of courtly subjectivity" (*Escape* 113) in which "the hero is both object and subject of his passions" (115).[10] In contrast to Leriano's courtly subjectivity, *Cárcel*'s Auctor self-fashions a discrete masculine subjectivity enabling him to transcend his identification with Leriano, modelling "a new form of literary identification based on representation rather than reenactment" (152), the latter constituting, for Folger, a still-courtly strategy found in Rodríguez del Padrón's *Siervo* (147–8). I would only add to Folger's argument that it is significant, in this regard, that San Pedro in *Cárcel* abandons the *prosimetrum* of earlier works of sentimental fiction. San Pedro was a poet; *Cárcel* gives no indication that the same can be said of El Auctor.[11]

By contrast, Corella's earlier, concise masterpiece of sentimental fiction, *Tragèdia de Caldesa*, maintains a prosimetric structure and a secular, courtly frame in staging the enclosure of the passionate subject.[12] The *Tragèdia*'s simple plot, in which the protagonist first exchanges words of love ("enamorades raons") with the beautiful Caldesa, only for her to leave him in a dark room, from whose window he watches as she deceives him with another lover, stands in contrast to its extravagant rhetoric, which finds many and varied echoes throughout Corella's other works, lyric and prose, secular and religious.[13] This hyperbole extends to the title of the *Tragèdia*, which, as Jaume Torró ("El mite" 112) and Sol Miguel-Prendes (*Narrating* 214) point out, refers not so much to the downfalls of great men as to Nicholas Trevet's definition of tragedy as the denunciation in song of great crimes. In view of the protagonist's exaggerated sense of victimization, Miguel-Prendes reads the

Tragèdia in a primarily humorous vein, as a parody of the "lacrimose excesses" of courtly heroes such as the protagonist of Don Pedro's *Sátira* (*Narrating* 215). To the extent that courtly poetry emerged with an ironic awareness of its own artificiality, Corella's particular parodic gesture would consist in the resolutely prosaic depiction of Caldesa's betrayal, which includes the rival lover's coarse leave-taking, "Adéu sies, manyeta!" (68; "Good-bye, my little hussy!" [201]). Although there is no suggestion that the *Tragèdia* is autobiographical, its strategically earthy portrayal of amorous deception recalls March's decidedly anti-allegorical confrontation with his lover's death. Just as death in the *cants de mort* becomes a field for rethinking the hylomorphic underpinnings of March's love theory, Corella's "tragedy" does not merely turn the sublime conventions of courtly love on their head, but rather reflects on what is lost when those conventions are definitively undermined.

This reflection takes the form, I argue, of a lexical and conceptual translation that takes place between the fourth and seventh paragraphs of the *Tragèdia*, a translation from a world in which the *transposition* (*transpostació*) of an integral being between subjects is possible to another world in which the most radical intersubjective exchange is limited to the pious *transportation* (*transportació*) of a sympathetic listener. Clearly, the orthographic and semantic difference between these two terms – even the literal distance between the two on the manuscript folia – is minimal.[14] Yet the effort to interpret this small shift responds to the particular hermeneutic challenge of Corella's dense text and to the need to untangle the web of generic relations – sentimental fiction, troubadour poetry and the poetry of Ausiàs March in particular,[15] the *artes dictandi* (F. Rico, "Imágenes" 18), classical literature, and Corella's own later mythological and religious translations – in which the *Tragèdia* is situated. Indeed, the very brevity of the *Tragèdia*, which has elicited designations such as *novel·leta* (Riquer 294), seems to be a determining factor in the strange diachronic role attributed to its author: a writer of the "Pre-Renaissance," for Francisco Rico ("Imágenes"), who nevertheless represented a flowering that, in the words of Joan Fuster, "did not bear the subsequent fruit that we needed" ("Joan Roís" 242). Fuster also explained that Corella's work is particularly challenging for modern readers because of the "permanent sentimental shriek [*espinguet*] one perceives in it" ("Lectura" 289). Yet it is the very confluence of these two aspects of the *Tragèdia* – rhetorical concentration and hyperbolic sentimentalism – that is the key to interpreting the formal and expressive translation of an "ethical vision" (Cingolani 84) carried out by Corella. The translation of the *transpostació* of a being into the *transportació* of compassion encapsulates a new pessimism toward the ethical and stylistic potential of emotional identification.

Critics traditionally hold Corella's work to be dominated by moral and psychological concerns.[16] To these, I would add an interest in language and signification as such, made evident in Corella's translational practice, in his frequent wordplay (for example, the allusion to heat in the name "Caldesa"), and in philosophical reflections, to one of which I will turn shortly. The *Tragèdia*'s rubric in the Mayans manuscript, "Raonant un cas afortunat que ab una dama li esdevenc" ("Recounting an unhappy case that befell him with a lady"), condenses all three themes: *raonar* here refers, first and foremost, to the discursive and narrative nature of the text, yet as we have seen in part one, it also alludes to the text's moral and psychological content. The same set of concerns is manifest in the *Tragèdia*'s passage that refers to *transpostació*:

> Llarga història seria tenyir lo paper de les enamorades raons que entre nosaltres, ab mostra d'extrema benvolença, passaven: fengia la bella senyora tant contentament de mos passats servirs e presents paraules, que lo seu ésser en mi transpostava: tot lo que a sa volentat, persona e viure s'esguardaba, abandonadament deixà en discreció de ma coneixença. (67)
>
> It would be a long story, indeed, if I should expend my ink and paper in relating the sweet talk of lovemaking that we exchanged as a token of deep affection. My fair lady put on a good show as to how pleased she was with my past service and present conversation. Her very being, she said, was transported into mine; then added that she would surrender in total abandonment to my knowledge and discretion all that she treasured in her free will and private life. (199)

Here, then, we glimpse the possibility – even if a feigning one, on the part of Caldesa, who is after all following Baena's advice – of the *transpostació* of being, that is, according to Corella's taxonomy, of the lover's will, person, and life. As Lola Badia notes, Ausiàs March frequently uses the term *contentament* "to designate amorous plenitude" ("Ficció" 81), but Corella's taxonomy of human love is not as developed as that of his elder. Nevertheless, it is enlightening to trace the destinies of these three human components after Caldesa's betrayal.[17]

Precisely what Caldesa betrays is a state of "alta e delitosa concòrdia" (67; "joyful and harmonious dalliance" [literally: concord; 199]). As Josep Romeu i Figueras notes, Corella always insists on the necessity of "mutual possession" and of equality in human love (301); there is an example of this insistence in Corella's *Jardí d'amor*, a retelling of three stories from Ovid's *Metamorphoses*, in which Thisbe emphasizes that between her and Pyramus there was equality of beauty, age, and worldly fortune (*Obres completes I* 126–7) – equality sufficient not just for love, but for marriage. The "delightful concord" between the *Tragèdia*'s protagonist and Caldesa, meanwhile, is not lost through Caldesa's mere absence, but rather with the sight, through a "poca finestra" (67; "minuscule window" [200]), of another man concealing the "faenes secretes e de gran importància" (67; "private affair of utmost importance" [200]) in which Caldesa is occupied.

The possibility lost through this disturbing vision, of the amorous identification of will, person, and life, is a problem Corella returns to incessantly, and a consideration of it in the aforementioned *Jardí d'amor*, also known as the *Lamentacions de Mirra e Narciso e Tisbe*, will cast light on its particular articulation in the *Tragèdia*.[18] Specifically, in addition to some amplifications in Corella's translation, I will analyse briefly what Corella proposes with this particular mythological juxtaposition: discursive and emotional concord. Myrrha raises the problem of signification directly at the beginning of the *Jardí*, explaining that "si les paraules deuen ésser semblants a aquella cosa de què parlen, en gran part ne tinc io fallença, per no poder dir la causa de mon mal" (116; "if words should resemble the thing of which they speak, I am greatly lacking in this, for I cannot say the cause of my malady"). To lament a lack of similarity is, in Myrrha's case, ironic, given that the amorous obstacle she cannot overcome is precisely an excess thereof: she desires her father and, therefore, wishes to take her mother's place by his side. One of Corella's amplifications, criticized in aesthetic terms by Riquer (306), is of particular relevance here. Corella more than triples the four concise words with which Ovid had expressed Myrrha's incestuous desire: "Persona al món benaventurada sia no estime, sinó sola ma mare, que té Sinaras per marit" (119; "I do not believe there is any fortunate person in this world, except for my mother, who has Cinyras for a husband"). This loquacity and perverse resemblance are repeated, but as a way of concealing rather than revealing the truth, when Myrrha's confidante, her nursemaid, speaks with Cinyras: "No et desplàcia, Sinaras, acceptar en lo teu llit la donzella de qui io et parle, car no és menys bella que la tua filla Mirra" (120; "May it not displease you, Cinyras, to accept in your bed the maiden of whom I speak, for she is no less beautiful than your daughter Myrrha"). This lie of omission works through a lack of correspondence between words and their objects. The maid's words are literally an expression of absolute resemblance, a tautology – "Myrrha is no less beautiful than Cinyras's daughter, Myrrha" – and yet they deceive.

Another victim of deception in the *Jardí d'amor* is Narcissus, who also, of course, bears a perverse desire for excessive resemblance. In contrast to his poem "Desengany," where Corella writes "Amà Narcís a si mateix, en l'aigua" (48, line 11; "Narcissus loved himself in the water"), in the *Jardí* Corella emphasizes that Narcissus does not recognize himself in his reflection, but rather believes that he sees a beautiful nymph.[19] And it is precisely in failing to recognize himself, or his own solitude, that Narcissus despairs of a lack of harmonious desire: "Aquesta era la major dolor que ma pensa soferia, que no sé qual desaventura nostres voluntats concordes separava" (124; "This was the greatest pain suffered by my thought, that I did not know what misfortune separated our harmonious wills"). As we have seen, Thisbe and Pyramus satisfy the requirements of amorous concord and, therefore, of *contentament*. It is for this reason that Thisbe considers herself the most unfortunate lover in Corella's *Jardí*, and as in the case of the *Tragèdia*, the tragic end of her deceiving contentment is set in motion when she peers through a "secret window" (127). At the climax of Thisbe's story, just before her suicide, she makes two requests of the gods. First, she asks that the fruit of the mulberry tree, stained with Pyramus's blood, keep forever the colour of "lo dol de nostra desaventura" (131; "the pain of our misfortune") – that is, that there be an eternal correspondence between her experience of suffering and its sign. But she also asks that her body share Pyramus's tomb (131).

This possibility, of shared entombment, is also considered in the verses that form, in Badia's words, the "lyric nucleus" of the *Tragèdia* ("Ficció" 87). Like several writers studied in part two, Corella was interested in tombs and epitaphs; the epitaph he composed for Hero appears in *Tirant lo Blanc* as the epitaph of Tirant and Carmesina.[20] In his poem "La sepultura," Corella explores the impossibility of honest love:

> En lletres d'or, tendreu en lo sepulcre
> la mia mort per excel·lent triümfo,
> on clar veuran m'haveu llançat del segle,
> ab honestat matant ma vida morta.
> E io, esculpit, als vostres peus, en marbre,
> agenollat, mostraré gest tan simple,
> que tots diran, ab los ulls corrents aigua:
> "Cruel virtut, que no la pogué vençre
> Gest tan humil" (53, lines 1–9)[21]

> In golden letters, you will have my death on your tomb as an excellent triumph, where they will clearly see that you tossed me from this world, killing my life dead with honesty. And I, sculpted at your feet in marble, kneeling, will show such a simple countenance, that all will say, their eyes running with water: "Cruel virtue, that such a humble countenance could not conquer it."

In light of this rejection of honesty – which bears a close relationship to conventional troubadour complaints about cruelty – we can interpret the author's desire, at the end of the *Tragèdia*, to divide Caldesa in two: "E fóra més alegre, aquesta bella senyora en parts de singular partida, la sua gentil persona ab tan subtil enteniment fos la part mia, e la sua fall e moble voluntat, de falsa estima guiada, cercàs un cos lleig e diforme, en part d'aquell qui indignament l'havia tractada" (70; "How happy would I be if this beautiful woman could be divided into two parts and her noble person, endowed with subtle understanding would be my portion, while her deceitful and fickle will, swayed by misguided preference, would inhabit an ugly deformed body to be allotted to the man that had dealt with her in such a scandalous fashion" [204]). What is shown to be impossible in this desire, which is not to separate the desiring body and the understanding, but rather to separate, as Rosanna Cantavella emphasizes ("Aspectes" 303), in two bodies the "gentil *persona* ab tan subtil enteniment" and the "moble *voluntat*,"[22] is precisely the illusory *transpostació* of the *Tragèdia*'s opening, which I repeat here: "Lo seu ésser en mi transpostava: tot lo que a sa volentat, persona e viure s'esguardaba, abandonadament deixà en discreció de ma coneixença" (67).

We have seen that Ausiàs March's poem XCII concludes with a redemptive vision of shared resurrection; this image of plenitude is exactly what Corella has rejected in his *cobles*:

> E, si per cas, del meu cos, gens ne resta,
> sia menjar als animals salvatges:
> prenga'n cascú la part d'una centil·la,
> perquè en tants llocs sia lo meu sepulcre,
> que, el món finit, no es trobe la carn mia,
> ni es puga fer que mai io ressuscite. (69, lines 23–8)
>
> And should but a piece of flesh be left of me,
> be it repast of beasts both fierce and wild
> till they devour my body bit by bit.
> Thus, as in many a place I shall be entombed,
> the finite realm shall see no trace of me:
> no part of me there'll be to resurrect! (203)

It is thus too late when an apparently apologetic Caldesa responds, in her own verses, "És-me la mort més dolça que no sucre/ si fer se pot en vostres braços muira" (69–70, lines 5–6, punctuation slightly modified; "Now death to me would taste as sweet as honey,/ if I should chance to die in your embrace" [204]). The *Tragèdia* ends, then, with an expression of terrible grief provoked by these words and the impossibility of accepting them – that is, grief at the definitive loss of *transpostació*. It only remains to be considered to what extent Corella viewed *transportació* as a consolatory substitute.

Recall that, in Corella's *Jardí*, Thisbe considers herself the most unfortunate lover. She argues her case before Myrrha and Narcissus in the following terms: "Les vostres nafres són invisibles, e les mies porten ferea d'ésser mirades. Los vostres mals demanen piadosos recitadors, perquè als qui els oiran moguen a misericòrdia; los meus, ells se manifesten, e no consenten ésser oïts, sinó ab ulls de piadoses llàgremes" (126; "Your wounds are invisible, and mine bear the horror of being seen. Your ills require piteous reciters in order to move listeners to mercy; mine manifest themselves, and they cannot be heard but with eyes filled with tears of pity"). Like the protagonist of the *Tragèdia*, Thisbe insists on the pain of the visible. When the *Tragèdia*'s protagonist, in turn, speaks of *transportació*, he seems to identify implicitly with Thisbe's "piadosos recitadors": "O piadosos oints!

Transportant vostres misericordes penses en mi, diga cascú si semblant dolor a la mia jamés ha sofert, e ab adolorit pensament mirau la tristor que a tal hora ma trista pensa combatia, esperant quina seria la fi que de tan dolorós principi esdevendria" (67; "I ask all those who may be inclined to listen to me in sympathy: turn to me your merciful attention! Tell me if any of you has felt a pain as intense as mine. Put yourselves in a cheerless mood and consider the sadness that on that afternoon assailed my wretched heart as I wondered what would be the outcome of such a woeful beginning" [200]). This invocation of an empathetic audience is, of course, part of a long tradition,[23] but it is a varied tradition that does not always reproduce all of the elements present here: pity, compassion, "semblant dolor," but also thought and vision ("mirau la tristor"). The passage represents, taken together, an attempt to recompose the absolute identification of *transpostació* through the *transportació* of pity.

Corella received a *demanda* from Bernat Fenollar, enquiring "si mata pietat,/ ni pot matar, així com vida créixer" (55, lines 7–8; "if pity kills or can kill, as it can give life"). In his response, Corella defines pity as "dolor de mal ab bona voluntat" (55, line 9; "sympathetic pain with good will") and gives two examples, that of the inhabitants of Sagunt, who "moriren tots per haver llibertat;/ d'on s'esdevé se causa pietat/ en lo matar, com en la vida créixer" (55, lines 14–16; "died to have liberty, whence it proceeds that pity can cause death, as it grows in life");[24] and that of Dido, who "morí per la gran pietat/ que Juno hac de la sua fort pena" (55, lines 21–2; "died for the great pity that Juno felt for her great pain"). In view of these two examples, we can say that Corella approaches pity with an ironic scepticism, recognizing that death provokes pity and that pity – and not just the "cruel virtue" of honesty – can provoke death. In the end, Corella does not seek consolation from his "piadosos oints," but rather, as Fuster notes ("Lectura" 313), from the very act of writing. Like the correspondence between Pyramus and Thisbe's tragic end and the colour of the mulberry's fruit, a correspondence between the blood used by the protagonist as ink and the pain he describes ("dolor que raona") closes the *Tragèdia*.

This work was not, however, Corella's final word on the matter of Caldesa. He wrote a consolatory letter to a friend who, like the *Tragèdia*'s protagonist, had discovered he was not the only object of his lover's affections. Here, Corella finds consolation, rather than affliction, in the partiality of human love: "Car, si les paraules de vostre escrit a mi són clares, aquella part que abans teníeu no us és tolta en la *possessió de la sua bella persona*, puix l'acollir-hi ella altre no minva la sua bellea *ni la part vostra*" (95, emphasis added; "For, if I understand clearly the words of your letter, that part you had before is not lost to you in the *possession of her beautiful person*, for the fact that she receives another there diminishes neither her beauty *nor the part that is yours*"). The ideal of absolute identification vanishes completely. What is lost with the failure of *transpostació* and the rejection of *transportació* is the psychologically beneficial and morally normative role played by shared or collective emotion in Iberian courtly poetry and prose. From one perspective, then, this shift confirms an image of Corella as a figure of the "Pre-" or "Proto-Renaissance." We cannot fail to see, however, that it was only from a critical and darkly mournful stance that he narrated the definitive enclosure of the courtly subject.

Notes

Introduction: Courtly Conflict and the Passions

1 The Avis dynasty took power in Portugal with the proclamation of John I as king in 1385, the Trastámara dynasty in Castile with the ascension of Henry II in 1369 and, after the 1412 Compromise of Caspe, with that of Ferdinand I in Aragon (Ferdinand's successor, Alfonso V, would also be king of Naples from 1442 to 1458).

2 These broad descriptions will each receive a more nuanced treatment later; on the installation of the Trastámara dynasty in Aragon as a factor of "Catalanization," see Torró, "Una cort" 113–14.

3 The violence of the nobility was particularly widespread in Castile, whereas in Aragon conflict occurred throughout the social hierarchy, as well as with Castile directly (Ruiz, *Spain's Centuries of Crisis* 86–7). For a concise account of the labyrinthine conflicts between John II of Castile and his cousins, the Infantes of Aragon, during this period, see Ruiz, *Spain's Centuries of Crisis* 87–94. On the causes of violent behaviour on the part of both urban and rural nobles in the Crown of Aragon, see Ryder 66–8. In Portugal, the House of Avis sought to solidify its hold on power by presenting John I's sons as "mirrors of virtue" and exemplary rulers (Dias 309); nevertheless, this cultural effort would prove fragile in the face of tensions with both the high nobility and urban representatives, on whose support kings, queens, and regents alike depended (Mattoso 421).

4 Throughout this discussion, I cite Ángel Gómez Moreno's edition of the exchange ("La *Qüestión*"), whose importance, Gómez Moreno notes, is underscored by the fact that it survives in seven fifteenth-century manuscripts (336). For a description of the manuscript tradition, see Gómez Moreno, "La *Qüestión*" 340–2.

5 Translations throughout are my own unless otherwise noted.

6 For an introduction to the *galardón* as commonplace in *cancionero* poetry, see Green 60–4. The effects of unreciprocated love make up the most common theme for questions and answers in the *cancioneros*, constituting just over one quarter of the entire corpus (Chas Aguión 110–11). For the increasing dominance of love poetry over doctrinal poetry in the *cancioneros*, see Beltran, *La canción* 43–6.

7 The Constable's father knew some of Mena's works and himself wrote to Mena asking for a copy of others (Dias 317).

8 I cite Ángel Gómez Moreno's edition of the *Prohemio* throughout.

9 See, for example, Miriam Cabré on the presence of Occitan poets at the courts of Alfonso X in Castile and Alfonso II and his great-grandson, Peter III, in Aragon.

10 On the use of the name "España," "Hispania," and "las Españas" for the entire territory of the Iberian Peninsula, see Maravall 53–102.

11 The possibly Semitic origins of troubadour lyric remain a vexed question that is both too complex to treat here fully and beyond my competence; an array of diverse views and further bibliography can be found in Menocal; Monroe; Zwartjes, especially 94–124 and 242–52; and Corriente.

12 On this early critical rejection, see Weiss, "Introduction" 3.

13 In his study of this vocabulary, Keith Whinnom notes that, of the 297 different nouns in his corpus, just 25 account for over half of all occurrences ("Towards" 117); he continues: "This poetry is limited conceptually to abstractions, and there are singularly few concrete terms … Although theoretically it is the lady's beauty which awakens the poet's desire and is the prime cause of love, the lady's 'merit' (*merescimiento* or *merescer*) is mentioned far more frequently than her beauty" (117–18). Already in 1962, Rafael Lapesa had noted that Castilian poets tended to avoid the physical portrayal of the beloved ("Poesía de cancionero" 150).

14 Fifteenth-century poetry in Catalan has not suffered the same critical rejection as its Castilian counterpart, despite their common tendency toward emotional abstraction and lexical repetition, but, as Jaume Torró has argued (*Sis poetes* 26–7), the towering figure of Ausiàs March has often eclipsed or distorted the legacy of a much broader poetic movement linked to the court of Alfonso V of Aragon.

15 Compare James Hillman's similar statement: "Yet when we come home to systematic (academic or theoretical) psychology to inquire quite naïvely: 'What is emotion; how is it defined; what is its origin, nature, purpose; what are its properties and laws; everyone uses this concept "emotion" – what are we speaking about?', we find a curious and overwhelming confusion" (5). See also Trigg, who acknowledges that these terms are frequently used interchangeably, but argues that, from the perspective of historical development, "the rise and fall in popularity and significance of these terms becomes an important part of the story" (5).

16 "I use the term emotions in this book with full knowledge that it is a convenience: a constructed term that refers to affective reactions of all sorts, intensities, and durations" (Rosenwein, *Emotional Communities* 4); "In emphasizing the term *emotions* in this book, we are asserting that this concept subsumes the phenomena denoted by other labels – sentiments, affect, feelings, and the like – which are often employed by theorists and researchers" (Turner and Stets 2).

17 In the rest of her fascinating study, Bordelois makes clear that there are indeed deep etymological roots for particular emotions, such as anger and love (29).

18 As Trigg remarks, "historically-oriented studies, where we cannot accurately map, chart, or measure somatic or cognitive affect, must rely on textual and material traces and representations of feelings and passions: the emotions *as they are processed, described, and performed by human subjects*" (7; emphasis in original).

19 The division between emotion as feeling and emotion as behaviour is ancient as well: "The Emotions are all those feelings that so change men as to affect their judgements, and that are also attended by pain or pleasure" (Aristotle, *Rhetoric* 1378a). One might object that the disappearance of the concept of soul (rather than mind) marks an important contemporary break with ancient and medieval thought, but as Hillman reminds us, the soul has lived on in concepts of psychic "energy": "Where the soul is often denied a place in modern psychology, the soul is still represented in all its classic ambiguity by such concepts as psychonic energy, vital energy, bio-energy, nervous energy and the like, all combinations of mind and matter … In short, it is our contention that the flow of energy model as an explanation of emotion has replaced the soul model and that the energy model, untenable logically and empirically, is only intelligible on the basis of the earlier model, the soul" (77). Amélie Oksenberg Rorty, echoing Hillman, describes modern emotion theorists as "a veritable walking archaeology of abandoned theories, even those that have claimed to vanquish one another" (172).

20 English quotations from the *Tusculan Disputations* are from Graver's translation; Latin references are to the Loeb Classical Library edition.

21 For an excellent diagram of this system, see Knuuttila 52; cf. Rosenwein, *Emotional Communities* 39.

22 The term "emotion" here translates the notion of disturbance or disorder of the soul, *perturbatio animi*.

23 Pity has earlier been defined along Aristotelian lines as "distress over the misery of another who is suffering unjustly" (IV.18).

24 This argument does not mean that empathy is never useful. Those seeking to soothe the distress of others will, like good rhetoricians, adapt their consolation to the nature of the situation and of their audience: "In soothing distress we must consider what sort of cure each hearer is able to accept" (Cicero, *Tusculan Disputations*, III.79).

25 Cooper and Procopé note that this account is "more articulated than anything to be found in our sources for early Greek Stoics" (Seneca, *Moral and Political Essays* 45n4).

26 Latin references are to the Loeb Classical Library edition of Seneca's moral essays (Seneca, *Moral Essays*).

27 Aquinas's theory of the passions was summarized in Alfonso de la Torre's c. 1440 *Visión deleytable de la filosofía y las artes liberales, metafísica y filosofía moral*, which follows Aquinas's own exposition very closely (Girón-Negrón 185–6). De la Torre also adapts Aristotle's *Rhetoric* 2.12–17, as Razón (Reason) voices "Aristotle's taxonomy of human characters according to emotional and moral qualities" (Girón-Negrón 186). Razón will later speak of a "textbook definition" of Aristotelian *akrasia*, an "excess of passion [that] inclines the will to wrongdoing" (187).

28 See Reddy xii and Rosenwein, *Emotional Communities* 16–17.

29 "As opposed to the philosophy that posits language as a mirror of nature, rhetoric is an inventive attitude toward language and the world, where 'emotion' names one important way in which language and the world connect" (Gross 15).
30 As Damien Boquet and Piroska Nagy note, medieval medical discourse about the emotions tended to reinforce their function as social signifiers: "Medical doctors proposed remedies for the emotional disorders that were aligned with the class of their wealthy patients: listening to delicate music, reading poetry, or drinking good wine would have been available to or suitable for only the most affluent individuals. Stereotypes about the emotional agitation and instability of common people were thus strengthened as a result, while other emotions, like melancholy, became a mark of the elites. In fact, one might say, strangely enough, that the medical consideration and treatment of emotions reinforced social discrimination and caused emotions to be further used as a tool of social distinction" (34).
31 See, for example, Sarah Kay's clarifying discussion of *subject of* and *subject to* in troubadour poetry (*Subjectivity* 43).
32 As Jonathan Culler explains, however, even for Hegel lyric subjectivity is not a basis for individuation: "Although the essence of lyric for Hegel is subjectivity attaining consciousness of itself through self-expression, he stresses that the lyric process is one of purification and universalization … Thus, despite the centrality of subjectivity to his account of the essential nature of the lyric, subjectivity functions as a principle of unity rather than a principle of individuation: what is essential in this theory is not that the formulations of a lyric reflect the particular experience of an individual but that they be attributed to a subject, which brings them together" (*Theory* 94–5). In the terms of Balibar, Cassin, and Libera, Hegelian lyric subjectivity is a matter of "subjectness," where the lyric "I" is grounds for predication but cannot be identified with the individual ego. Such a reading is also in line with Kay's reading of the troubadour's "I" as a *representation* of self-awareness.
33 I cite Julia Castillo's edition (Sánchez de Badajoz, *Cancionero*). Wherever possible, I will include the Dutton ID of Castilian poems (in this case, ID6802), which, in conjunction with Dorothy S. Severin's *Electronic Corpus of 15th Century Castilian* Cancionero *Manuscripts* (http://cancionerovirtual.liv.ac.uk/), allows readers to compare multiple manuscript witnesses.
34 I cite Rodríguez Risquete's edition of Torroella's complete works (*Obra completa*).
35 Poem 6 in the *Cancionero de Estúñiga*, ed. Manuel Alvar and Elena Alvar; ID0016.

1 Classical Rhetoric and Vernacular Theories of Social Integration

1 Ottavio di Camillo considers the vernacular translation of rhetorical treatises, along with other works by Cicero, Virgil, and Seneca, to be a "distinctive feature of Spanish cultural life" during Cartagena's lifetime (50).
2 Juan Alfonso de Zamora had made a broad request for Cartagena to translate some classical work, not even specifying Cicero as author (*Libros de Tulio* 207). Nieto Soria

has noted the "extraordinary diffusion" of Cartagena's works in the fifteenth century (*Iglesia y génesis* 218), and Cartagena was remarkably active in royal and ecclesiastical politics. For Cartagena's 1441 attempt to mediate between the crown (and Álvaro de Luna) and rebellious forces, see Serrano 166–70; for a recent assessment of Cartagena's relationship with humanism, see Fernández Gallardo.

3 Guzmán also commissioned translations of Cicero's *De oratore*, the *Declamationes* (attributed to Quintilian), and Leonardo Bruni's *Cicero novus* (a biography of Cicero) and was himself the author of a *refundición* of the Alfonsine translation of Seneca's *De ira* and, possibly, of an epitome of the *Nicomachean Ethics*, among other works (Lawrance, "Nuño de Guzmán" 56–67). Although Lawrance refutes M. Schiff's (anyhow cautious) hypothesis that Guzmán had aided in the formation of Santillana's library (57–8), he shows that Guzmán was present at the 1440 wedding of Prince Henry (later Henry IV of Castile) and Blanca of Navarre, and thus travelled in circles overlapping with those of Santillana and Cartagena, whose palaces hosted festivities in the months leading up to the wedding (60–1).

4 I cite Frank Anthony Ramírez's edition throughout. The *Tratado* survives in a single fifteenth-century manuscript held by the Escorial (MS &-II-8) and is based largely on Juan García de Castrojeriz's *Glosa castellana al "Regimiento de príncipes"* (c. 1344; *Tratado* 10). It is bound with several other didactic works; for a list, see *Tratado* 10–11.

5 I will cite the Real Academia de la Historia's 1807 edition of the *Partidas* throughout (Alfonso X). On the development of medieval notions of the republic as a mystical body (*Corpus Reipublicae mysticum*), see Kantorowicz 207–32; on the notion of the "body politic" in particular, see 210–12. As Kantorowicz notes, Aristotle's influence led to the parallel development of notions of the "body moral" and the "body ethical" (210). Originally an ecclesiological term, "mystical body" came to be used almost interchangeably with "moral and political body" in political thought after Aquinas (211–12). On invocations of the body politic in medieval and early modern texts from Portugal, Castile, and Aragon, see F. Rico, *El pequeño mundo* 108–10.

6 A similar conceptualization of the body politic in terms of mutual love and aid is found in Francesc Eiximenis's 1383 *Regiment de la cosa pública*, dedicated to the *jurats* of Valencia and later incorporated, in a slightly modified version, into the *Dotzè llibre del Crestià* (Eiximenis 7). In defining the *cosa pública*, the Franciscan writes that such a community "deu ésser composta de diverses persones ajudants la una a l'altra segons llurs necessitats. Açò per tant car com lo lligament de cascuna bona comunitat haja a ésser unitat e benivolència dels habitants e sia fundada e lligada en amor e en concòrdia" (40; "should be composed of different people helping each other according to their needs. And this because what joins each good community must be the unity and goodwill of its inhabitants, and that it be based on and connected by love and concord"). On Eiximenis's influence on the piety of the Catalan court, see Silleras-Fernández 21–58.

7 This is likely an adaptation of the Senecan commonplace, widely cited by authors in this milieu, that a friend is "another I."

8 For an incisive overview of ideas about friendship in Iberia in earlier centuries, see Liuzzo Scorpo.

9 On classical attempts, by Aristotle and others, to construct a "politics of love," see Nirenberg, "Politics."

10 Walsh notes that this doctrine is itself adopted from Aristotle (Cicero, *On Obligations* 136n50).

11 See the discussion further on of Cicero's related account of the origins of human community in his youthful rhetorical treatise *De inventione.*

12 Latin references are to the Loeb Classical Library edition (Cicero, *De Officiis*).

13 See, for example, *De beneficiis* I.6.(1) and the discussion further on of the *Livro da vertuosa benfeytoria.*

14 For a list of Iberian translations of Seneca from the thirteenth to seventeenth centuries, see Blüher 597–601.

15 Translations of this text, thought to be Syrian in origin and to date from the eighth century, are to be found throughout medieval Iberia; the earliest is a thirteenth-century Castilian translation known as the *Poridat de las poridades*, in turn a key source for the *Llibre de saviesa/Llibre de doctrina*, attributed, albeit doubtfully, to James I of Aragon (*Secreto* 2–6). There are also several Portuguese translations; this Castilian version, which is a translation of the longer "Eastern" version of the text, dates from the late fourteenth century (*Secreto* 47).

16 In his *Regiment*, Eiximenis extends this argument beyond the relationship between ruler and subjects to all members of a community: "Semblantment, pots veure que si la un membre sofir mal, los altres se'n complanyen, car si percuts a nengú en lo cap o en qualque altre membre se vulla, tantost lo braç s'hi para e li fa escut, e la boca crida ajuda e dóna senyal de dolor. E si a vegades, per ventura, un membre nafra a l'altre e li fa mal, lo membre ferit o nafrat no demana venjança, ans tot lo cos està trist e es complany del mal que el membre nafrat haurà pres" (43; "Similarly, you can see that if one member suffers harm, the others commiserate, for if you strike someone in the head or anywhere else, the arm moves right away to act as a shield, and the mouth cries for help and to signal pain. And if sometimes, by chance, one member wounds another and harms it, the harmed or wounded member does not seek vengeance; rather the whole body is sad and bemoans the harm done to the wounded member"). When the focus is no longer specifically on governance (this passage is part of Eiximenis's definition of the *cosa pública*, not yet his advice to Valencia's *jurats*), what in other texts is a question of clemency becomes a question of compassion ("tot lo cos està trist e *es complany* del mal").

17 Curiously, one of Seneca's strongest arguments for mercy comes toward the end of *On Anger*, in the metaphor of the bull and the bear: "We regularly see, in the morning show at the amphitheatre, the match between bull and bear tied together; when the one has worn down the other, the slaughterer awaits them both. Our act is the same; we assail an opponent who is tied to us, while the end, and that right early, looms alike over victor and vanquished" (III.43.2). Here, the previously important

distinction between the human and the animal is overshadowed by the assertion of absolute human unity in death. What is left unclear is whether this "tie" could bear a positive ethical program or merely an ethics of (at best) tolerance and (at worst) indifference.

18 For a concise biographical sketch of Diego de Valera, see Rodríguez-Puértolas 15–18; for a selection of recent approaches to Valera's work with a comprehensive bibliography, see Moya García, *Mosén Diego de Valera.*

19 Quoting Augustine, Valera immediately relates this debt of love to familial love, since all men, as descendants of Adam and Eve, are *fratres* (*Exortación* 84).

20 I will cite Adelino de Almeida Calado's 1994 critical edition throughout; on the date of the text's final version, see his introduction (Pedro and Verba XXXVI). Pedro composed a first redaction of the *LVB* in 1418 and likely composed the first four chapters of what would become the final redaction, plotting the remainder of the text with Verba, who then completed it, save for a final retouching by Pedro himself around 1430; on the text's authorship, process of composition, and manuscript history, see Calado's introduction (Pedro and Verba XXIII–LXXXIX). At Duarte's request, Verba also translated Cicero's *De amicitia* (Dias 314).

21 As Francisco Elías de Tejada notes in comparing the *LVB* and *De beneficiis*, "the shared theme gives rise to many common perspectives and inevitable parallels; but, in general, [Pedro's] argument follows independent paths, developing along its own lines" (Tejada 8). On the influence of the *De regimine principum*, which Pedro would likely have known through Castrojeriz's *Glosa castellana*, see Carvalho 105 and 113.

22 Pedro cites Pseudo-Dionysius's *Divine Names* in claiming that the will's desire is inherently good – all *querença* is *bemquerença* – because "o mal he sen voõtade" (Pedro and Verba 26; "evil is without will").

23 In their introduction to *On Favours*, John M. Cooper and J.F. Procopé write: "*On Favours* is a work about acts of kindness by individuals to other individuals. Seneca is not concerned with the spectacular benefactions – the erection of lavish public buildings, the financing of festivals and so forth – by monarchs, magistrates, and local notables – to entire communities, important though these were in the ancient world" (Seneca, *Moral and Political Essays* 186).

24 Later in the text, Pedro insists on this point: "E consyrando nos que o bem comuũ he melhor que o perssoal prinçipalmente acorreremos a elle" (Pedro and Verba 93; "And considering that the common good is better than the personal, we will attend to the former principally").

25 For Tejada, Pedro's concrete social analysis is the source of the political in the text: "The political manifests itself in the conception of the theory of political community as the exchange of external benefits, as the weaving-together of men appreciative of concrete and palpable favors" (Tejada 17).

26 Pedro's brother Duarte defines *bemquerença* as a kind of love in his *Leal Conselheiro* (Duarte 176).

27 Describing the participatory nature of friendship, Pedro goes so far as to say that two friends should have no fear in counselling each other, "pois homem strangeyro non stá antre elles, mas cada hũu he tornado en outro, *e ambos son feytos hũa persoa*" (Pedro and Verba 113, emphasis added; "since there is no discrete man between them, but rather, each has become another, *and both have become one person*").
28 As Josiah Blackmore has shown, *afeiçom* was a crucial term for fifteenth-century Portuguese thinkers. Blackmore notes several occurences of *afeiçom* connoting goodwill in the *LVB* ("*Afeiçom*" 16) and points out that it is explicitly opposed to reason in Duarte's *Leal Conselheiro*, where it furthermore "clouds the mind that must act judiciously" (17).
29 As we have seen, a less articulated form of this same psychological unity is at the heart of the *Tratado de la comunidad*, whose definition of "community" reproduces not only the connection between shared will and good governance but also, in referring to "personas mayores e medianas e menores" (87), Pedro's concern for social and moral hierarchy.
30 It cannot be said that this conflict is completely absent; early in the *LVB*, Pedro makes the familiar assertion of the understanding's superiority among our faculties: "Segundo que veemos que o entender porque he fundado em natureza spiritual he mais perffeyto que o sentir, o quall em a corporall sensualidade tem seu naçimento" (Pedro and Verba 67–8; "We see that the understanding, because it is grounded in our spiritual nature, is more perfect than perception, which is born of bodily sensation").
31 For Pedro's brother Duarte, conversation among rulers and their friends is at once a principal cause of personal change and the route by which those changes spread in a polity: "Da converssaçom do senhor e amygos como se muda nossa condiçom, per speriencia bem se mostra nas cortes dos senhores, Reynos e moesteiros como grande parte dos sobdictos seguem seu senhor e amygos" (Duarte 156). The grouping of court, kingdom, and monastery exemplifies the dominance of these spaces in contemporary analyses of emotion and social ethics.
32 The *Suma* survives in a single manuscript held by the Biblioteca Nacional de Madrid (Ms. 1221).
33 As Francisco Rico has noted, Sánchez de Arévalo, in his *Vergel de los príncipes* – also dedicated to Henry IV – does recommend music as a leisure activity through which rulers can achieve a politically beneficial inner harmony (*El pequeño mundo* 114).
34 It should be noted that the *Suma* also contains a more traditional image of the ruler as the city's "heart" (Sánchez de Arévalo 127).

2 Alfonso de Madrigal, el Tostado, on the Politics of Friendship

1 On the relationship between metaphysics, split subjectivity, and reflection in Gracián and in modernity more broadly, see Egginton, particularly 159–62.
2 It is tempting to translate Gracián's masculine *ánimo* as "mind," but the 1726 *Diccionario de autoridades* lists "el alma" as the first definition of "ánimo," making specific

reference to Latin *animus* (not *anima*) as the source of this meaning. Recently, Suzanne Verderber has challenged the notion that modern subject formation differs from its medieval counterpart in that the former excludes dependence on or imitation of an external model (10–11); here, I address the questions of *how* that dependence was conceived (as a form of friendship) and *what form* of political subjectivity such dependence implies.

3 The analogy among natural, civil, and personal order arises with some frequency in medieval political texts from Portugal, Castile, and Aragon in authors such as Ramon Llull, Castrojeriz, and Sánchez de Arévalo; see F. Rico, *El pequeño mundo* 111–15.

4 On this point, see Étienne Balibar, Barbara Cassin, and Alain de Libera 1073–74; the authors associate consciousness and self-knowledge with Augustine's Trinitarian model of the human soul and thought as such with a non-Trinitarian, Averroist model of subjectivity based on Aristotle's *hupokeimenon*. One of my key hypotheses here is that Alfonso de Madrigal's political thought imports an Augustinian model of subjectivity into an explicitly Aristotelian ethical framework. The bibliography on the formation of modern subjectivity is, of course, vast; texts that I have found particularly valuable on the transition from the medieval to the modern subject include Aers; Balibar, Cassin, and Libera; Cascardi, "Afterword" and *Subject of Modernity*; Foucault, "About the Beginning" and "Technologies"; Haidu, *The Subject*; Kay, *Subjectivity*; Morris; Stone; and Verderber.

5 I use Nuria Belloso Martín's edition with Spanish translation, *El gobierno ideal (De optima politia)*.

6 This biographical information is drawn largely from Belloso Martín (13–35). The nickname "Tostado" most likely refers to Madrigal's dark hair (Belloso Martín 13); among his early biographers, Madrigal's capacity to work and study long hours gave rise to another nickname, "entrañas de bronce" (González Maeso 159).

7 A 2004 critical cluster on Madrigal in *La corónica*, edited by Roxana Recio and Antonio Cortijo Ocaña, does much to counteract modern critical neglect of Madrigal and provides an excellent starting point and bibliography for interested scholars.

8 In his 1486 collection of brief biographies, *Claros varones de Castilla*, Fernando del Pulgar wrote of Madrigal: "Puédese creer dél que en la ciencia de las artes e theología e filosofía natural e moral, e asimismo en el arte del estrología e astronomía, no se vido en los reinos de España ni en otros estraños se oyó aver otro en sus tienpos que con él se conparase" (qtd. in Cátedra, *Amor y pedagogía* 17; "It can be believed that in the knowledge of the arts and theology and natural and moral philosophy, as well as in the art of astrology and astronomy, there was never seen in the realms of Spain, nor was there heard of abroad, another in his times who could compare with him").

9 This edition spans 34 volumes in folio and was printed between 1507 and 1531 in Venice by Peter Liechtenstein (Recio and Cortijo Ocaña, "Alfonso" 7).

10 On Madrigal's knowledge of Hebrew, see Santiago García, who notes that one source of Madrigal's knowledge may have been disputational literature (92).

11 This last text is a commentary on book one, chapter eleven of Aristotle's *Nicomachean Ethics*, which, it should be noted, is devoted to the question of whether the "good or bad fortunes of friends" have an effect on the dead (1101b).

12 These texts are discussed at length in chapter six. On Madrigal and Rodríguez del Padrón, see Gregory B. Kaplan (18); for the influence of Madrigal's *Catorze questiones* on Pedro's *Sátira*, see Serés, "Don Pedro" 977.

13 If "Antiquity and the Middle Ages treated love in any public discourse as an ethical subject" (Jaeger 27), the predominance in Iberia of this parallel moral tradition illustrates the need to be sensitive to generic variation (and all the difference it implies) in the broad field of ethical discourse.

14 For a concise overview of *De optima politia*'s contents, see Tomás Carreras y Artau and Joaquín Carreras y Artau (2: 551–8).

15 I cite Ernest Barker's translation (Aristotle, *Politics*).

16 "Politia est quaedam communicatio." My translations are based on Belloso Martín's edition of the text (Madrigal, *De optima politia*), whose Spanish translation I also consulted in carrying out my own.

17 "Causa, ergo, verissima huius turris magnae, secundum quod in littera *Genesis*, 11 capite exprimitur, fuit quia homines iam multiplicati in diversas orbis partes discedere moliebantur, ut aliquid magnum atque admirabile maneret quod totum genus fecisset humanum, turrem illam magnam et civitatem fortissimam facere inceperunt. Et ista quidem intentio satis honesta videbatur, saltem in cortice ut, dato quod postea multa opera ab hominibus fierent, nullum tamen ita excellens esset sicut illud quod totum genus simul condidisset humanum" (Madrigal, *De optima politia* 140–1).

18 "Aliter autem habet hic littera hebraica, scilicet, celebremus nomen nostrum, no dividamur in terras. Quod quidem aliam longe distantem sententiam facit, scilicet, quod homines illius temporis volebant simul morari, quia cognati erant et ex similitudine speciei se diligebant" (Madrigal, *De optima politia* 141). It is worth noting that the *Biblia medieval romanceada*, a fifteenth-century translation of the Hebrew Bible, echoes this account of the tower's purpose: "e fagamos a nos nombradia, porque no nos derramemos sobre la faz de toda la tierra" (12–13; "and let us make a name for ourselves, so that we may not be scattered across the face of the whole earth"). As Simone Pinet has argued, the question of *nombradia* in the Babel episode is also key to understanding Alexander's ultimate punishment in the *Libro de Alexandre* ("Babel historiada" 385).

19 "Ego autem, ut in Procemiolo huius operis proposui, sensum literalem prosequi intendo; quia moralitatibus, & allegoriis omnes libri repleti sunt, sensus autem literalis difficilior est" (Madrigal, *Commentaria* IV).

20 I quote the 1545 Burgos edition of the text, having resolved its abbreviations (Madrigal, *Catorze questiones*).

21 "Cum in antiquis saeculis homines sine ulla comunicatione, sine ullo foedere vitam solitariam agerent, aliquis cui natura parens ingenium altum et ingenio accommodate verba tribuerat, rude illud saeculum et nimis barbaras gentes eloquentiae viribus ad communicationem politicam invitavit" (Madrigal, *De optima politia* 137–8).

22 "Cum, ergo, optima politia sit quae maxime a malo vetat et maxime ad virtutem incitat et promovet, et nulla lex sive constitution sit quae magis hoc faciat quam constitutions monachorum et fratrum in quibus quisque profitetur obedientiam, continentiam et paupertatem, qui voluerit dare alicui politiae optimas leges, det eis leges monachorum. Quo quid stultius excogitari potest quam facere aliquam talem politiam?" (Madrigal, *De optima politia* 145).

23 "Si tamen velimus eum reducere ad simpliciorem unitatem auferendo tantam partium compositionem aut personarum pluralitatem, iam non erit homo; quia unitas eius tantam requirit diversitatem. Ita de civitate. Civitas namque non est unum per se, sed per aggregationem. Si, ergo, velimus reducere eam ad tantam unitatem ut sit unum ens per se, excedemus naturam civitatis" (Madrigal, *De optima politia* 163).

24 Eiximenis, in the *Regiment*, incorporates this necessary diversity into his fundamental definition of the *cosa pública* as its third condition: "Tots los hòmens de la comunitat no poden ésser eguals" (40; "All men of the community cannot be the same").

25 The *Brevyloquyo* survives in three late-fifteenth-century manuscripts and one copy made c. 1600; see PhiloBiblon texid 1607 (https://bancroft.berkeley.edu/philobiblon/index.html). I have consulted the Escorial manuscript, h.II.15, and will cite my own transcriptions. The text has not been published in its entirety, but some excerpts (drawn from the Escorial manuscript) have been published by Belloso Martín as *Brevyloquyo de amor e amiçiçia*. For an overview of the *Brevyloquyo*'s contents and codicological descriptions, see Belloso Martín's introduction to her edition (Madrigal, *Brevyloquyo* 28–50). Madrigal's interest in addressing courtly audiences beyond the university leads Emiliano Fernández Vallina to compare him to the Italian humanists (288).

26 As Pedro M. Cátedra has noted, Madrigal may have encountered this saying in the *Bocados de oro* or a related text of wisdom literature (*Amor y pedagogía* 27).

27 I have maintained the manuscript's orthography, but, as in the case of the *Catorze questiones*, resolved its abbreviations.

28 For Hernán Núñez de Toledo's slightly later (1499) typology and analysis of love as a social phenomenon, see Antonio Cortijo Ocaña, "La Orden de Venus" 113–14.

29 Cortijo Ocaña has noted that, in the fifteenth century, the analysis of love as a passion felt by individuals tended to follow psychological and medical lines, whereas a parallel analytical tendency examined love's social implications ("Notas" 68–9). Here, as elsewhere, Madrigal's analysis refuses to distinguish clearly between the individual and the social. For an excellent account of the medical theorization of love during this period, see Folger, *Images* 27–56.

30 In his *Breve forma de confesión*, Madrigal uses *piedad* and *misericordia* interchangeably in discussing the Works of Mercy; see, for example, 53r. *Piedad* also arises specifically as pity in *Partida* II.X.II, as a form of love owed by the king to all subjects when imposing punishments (2: 87).

31 On this problematic during an earlier period, see Liuzzo Scorpo 128–34.

32 In *The Politics of Friendship*, Jacques Derrida points to quantity ("counting") as a key element of historical thought on friendship (20–4). David Nirenberg has shown that, in Aristotle's *Eudemian Ethics*, "civic" friendship may be "strictly legal" or moral but is

"always governed by an economic calculus" ("Politics of Love" 588). As Nirenberg goes on to explain, Aristotle shows great confidence in the possibility of calculating "equivalencies" in exchanges governed by love or friendship (589).

33 Indeed, in Michel de Montaigne's "Of Friendship," the difference between friendship and the love between fathers and their children hinges on communication: "Friendship feeds on communication, which cannot exist between them [that is, fathers and children] because of their too great inequality, and might perhaps interfere with the duties of nature" (136).

34 On this point, see Dale Kent (23). As Brian Patrick McGuire has noted, medieval invocations of Christ as the perfect friend tended to militate *against* the desirability of human friendship (414).

35 Interestingly, Cicero figures this identity in terms of reflection: "He who looks upon a true friend, looks, as it were, upon a sort of image [*exemplar aliquod*] of himself" (*On Friendship* VII.23). Castrojeriz's *Glosa castellana* makes reference to this point in Cicero and goes on immediately to explain that "tal amigo fue el Fijo de Dios, como el fue sobre todos los ommes, fízose igual de ellos, e estaba en medio de los discípulos así como servidor" (1: 209; "such a friend was the Son of God, for being above all men, he made himself equal to them, and was among the disciples like a servant").

36 This interpenetration of identity and diversity is why, as Belloso Martín explains, Madrigal's notion of *amiçiçia çivil* "no se reduce a una convivencia ordenada que permite a cada miembro su personal desarrollo y perfeccionamiento" (112; "cannot be reduced to an orderly coexistence permitting each member his personal development and perfection"). The Italian scholar and rhetorician Boncompagno da Signa, active before and after the turn of the thirteenth century, whose influence on late medieval Castilian culture has been demonstrated by Cortijo Ocaña, also considered friendship a "civil" virtue, distinguishing nevertheless between "celestial friendship" and the diabolical "worldly friendship," whose indomitable immoderation is in fact a source of discord (Cortijo Ocaña, "*De amicitia*" 39–42).

37 See Aristotle, *NE* 1166a-b. The question of friendship and self-love in Aristotle is fruitfully analysed in Jean-Claude Fraisse (232–7); see also Morrison 8.

38 As Fraisse explains, Aristotle's wicked man finds sorrow in introspection to the extent that, unlike the good man, he cannot unify the alterity that he embodies (234). In this sense, for Madrigal the *fabla* sought by those who lack virtue is not a form of communication, but rather one of verbalized discord.

39 See Aristotle, *NE* 1166a.

40 See, among many possible examples, Morris 73 and Le Goff 214.

41 Evelyn Birge Vitz has written that, in the Middle Ages, "individuation was a *spiritual* principle not a *psychological* one; that is, it was based on the *soul* (only individual souls could be saved), not on what we call the *personality*" (85). More recently, Verderber notes that attempts to distinguish between "individuality" and "personality" in discussions of medieval subjectivity are hopelessly fraught (6–7). However, if penitence after the Gregorian Reform could produce "accountable, guilty, interiorized subjects"

(Verderber 42), Madrigal emphasizes the priority of virtuous behaviour and of sentimental to sacramental practice.

42 Here, at least, Madrigal is within the medieval mainstream from the Fourth Lateran Council onward; see Aers 185.

43 In the case of Aristotle, Martin Heidegger goes so far as to argue, for example, that the "right reason" (*orthos logos*) of the *NE* should be translated as "right discussion" (Heidegger 103–4). For other points of theological and metaphysical contrast between Madrigal and Aristotle, see Fernández Vallina (306–7).

44 As Cascardi has argued, it was precisely the association of the passions with individuals who must be controlled socially and politically that led to the "formation of the subject-self" in Counter-Reformation Spain ("Afterword" 245).

45 See Coleman 14.

46 As Karl Kohut notes, because these commentaries were produced simultaneously, it is impossible to detect a development of Madrigal's opinion of literature from negative to positive or vice versa ("Der Beitrag der Theologie" 217).

47 On this assessment of Cartagena, see Pagden 306.

48 On this final point, see Cortijo Ocaña, who notes Madrigal's influence not just on sentimental fiction but also on exemplary works such as Alfonso Martínez de Toledo's *Corbacho* and even on later *comedias* ("Notas" 78–9).

3 Reason and Its Discontents

1 On the *LC*'s sources, see Dias 312.

2 As noted by the text's editor, Joseph M. Piel (Duarte 14n3). I explore Duarte's debt to Cassian in Berlin, "Willing Reader"; see also Dionísio, "D. Duarte, leitor de Cassiano." Cassian, the authority most frequently cited in the *LC* (Gama, *A filosofia* 149), was enjoying a vogue during this period (Gama, "Análise" 393), and his texts were widely copied and translated throughout Iberia (for a bibliography, see M.J.T. Rico, "A projecção" 124–30).

3 Cassian, in condemning the spiritual will, has in mind those monks tempted by demons into self-destructive acts of extreme asceticism. In his conference "On the Goal and End of the Monk," he names God, demons, and ourselves as the three possible sources of thoughts (that is, emotions; I.xix.1). Discretion "holds the supreme and first place" (I.xxiii.1) among the virtues precisely because it allows us to surmise the source of a particular thought and act accordingly. It is important to keep in mind that the thoughts themselves, even those of demonic origin, are not sins and cannot be avoided altogether: "It is, indeed, impossible for the mind not to be troubled by thoughts, but accepting them or rejecting them is possible for everyone who makes an effort. It is true that their origin does not in every respect depend on us, but it is equally true that their refusal or acceptance does depend on us" (I.xvii.1). In later thinkers such as Duarte, discretion is conceived of not so much as a way to identify the source of thoughts (or emotions), but as a way to react appropriately to them.

4 The social implications of the *LC* have long been a subject of critical debate. António José Saraiva viewed Duarte's "mental schemes" as expressive of social values but not of actually existing social structures (235), whereas José Gama describes the text as a reflection of both "the dominant society and thought of the Portugal of the first half of the fifteenth century" and the forward-looking "motivating spirit" of the so-called *Ínclita Geração* (*A filosofia* 50). Armando Luís de Carvalho Homem and Isabel Beceiro Pita contrast Duarte as a "modernizing exponent of fifteenth-century Portuguese political thought" with his brother Pedro, whose "archaizing" theory of favours in the *LVB* is tied to decadent feudal structures (943, 943n66).

5 In his seminal study of feudal social structure, Georges Duby notes that the "expansion of the monetary economy" at the end of the twelfth century caused shifts in the traditional social power structures described by the three traditional orders; in particular, the merchants and money changers on whom rulers depended grew in importance (323). In Duby's terms, what had been *labor* became *negotium* (323), and the knights, in turn, "were being reduced to supplicants living by the good graces of the prince," as the nobility "had to spend more and more money, while their subjects in the villages were yielding less and less of it" (324). Faced with such changes, "the nobility fled to what refuge it thought there was: in etiquette, worldly pleasures, ideology – making its last stand on the ramparts of the imaginary" (324–5). Duby's argument is thus consonant with that of Boase (see introduction), but Duarte shows no signs of discomfort in his description of a more complex economic and social arrangement.

6 Robert Folger has noted that, for Aquinas, "it is a moral obligation that the 'intellect' controls the senses and the resulting 'emotions,' which, in the words of Aquinas, 'leads one towards sin insofar as it is uncontrolled by reason; but insofar as it is rationally controlled, it is part of the virtuous life'" (*Images* 47–8; the citation is to the *Summa theologiae* 1a.2ae. 24, 2). Duarte's account of the free will's role responds to the requirement in Aquinas that "in order to be morally good the emotions must be voluntary" (Folger, *Images* 48).

7 The sensitive will is itself divided into two parts, desiring ("desejador" – what others call "concupiscible") and irascible ("hiracivel"). To the *desejador* belong, on the positive side, love, desire, and delight; and on the negative side ("enna parte do mal"), hate, abhorrence, and sadness. To the *iracivel* belong, on the positive side, meekness, hope, and daring; and on the negative side, anger, desperation, and fear (Duarte 26).

8 In his 1423–24 *Tratado de la consolación*, Enrique de Villena similarly argues that it is "healthy" to have an understanding of the passions of the soul, especially anger and fear, even if ultimately it is best to remove the passions and be governed by natural reason (29–31).

9 The entire inventory of Duarte's library can be found in Nascimento 284–6.

10 In part two, I discuss the role of exemplarity in Cassian's hermeneutics. One way in which Duarte's emphasis on familiar exemplarity manifests itself in the *LC* is the repetitive presence of the verb *filhar*. According to José Pedro Machado's *Dicionário*

etimológico da língua portuguesa, the original meaning of *filhar* was to attract or adopt (as a child); it later came to mean "take account of" or "come over to" ("apossar-se"), and its final meaning was to rob or kidnap (1042). Joaquim de Santa Rosa de Viterbo's *Elucidário* (1798) defines it as "Tomar, receber, conquistar" and notes that it is "do século XIII, XIV e XV" (271). Duarte uses the verb to describe his inclusion of passages from Cassian's *Conferences* (Duarte 14), the onset of certain emotions ("suydade propriamente he sentydo que o coraçom filha por se achar partydo da presença dalgũa pessoa" [95]), the adoption of virtues such as patience (26), and the conquest of cities (50–1). As such, the filial metaphor operates inwardly and outwardly, once again reflecting the implicit analogy between private and public governance.

11 This chapter, "Da tristeza," is largely a close translation of Cassian's *Institutes* IX.ix-xiii, *De spiritu tristitiae* (Duarte 64n1); however, the closing disquisition on the sources of sadness is Duarte's own.

12 Thus recalling Augustine's sentence, discussed in part two, that "the consequence of a distorted will is passion" (*Confessions* VIII.v.10).

13 Indeed, the manuscript of the *LC* is accompanied by another work by Duarte, the unfinished *Livro da ensinança de bem cavalgar toda sela.*

14 For a concise overview of lovesickness in Latin and vernacular sources, see Folger, *Images* 33–51; as Folger notes, melancholy and lovesickness were associated in Gerard of Berry's *Glosule super Viaticum* and its chief source, the *Canon medicinae* of Avicenna (Ibn Sina, d. 1037; Folger, *Images* 35–6). Furthermore, in his 1498 *Sumario de la medicina*, Francisco López de Villalobos (the personal physician of Ferdinand II of Aragon and Carlos I, among others) "associates *amor hereos* explicitly with love as expressed in courtly poetry," defining it as a "damage of the imagination" (Folger, *Images* 43–4). For a more extensive account of medieval lovesickness, see Wack. In his *Tractatus de amore heroico* (c. 1270–80), Arnau de Vilanova describes lovesickness as an affliction that, if left untreated, can give rise to melancholy (76).

15 The term also appears in Pedro's *LVB*, referring to both ethical inclinations and emotional attachments; both Duarte and Pedro would have encountered the term in Cartagena's *Rethórica* (Blackmore, "*Afeiçom*" 16).

16 Similarly, Saraiva contrasts Duarte's "subjectivism" with Pedro's "scholasticism," noting the relative absence of lived experience from the *LVB* (220–1).

17 Duarte's cautious approach to humoral management thus echoes his scepticism toward the moral efficacy of "books of stories," which place insufficient demands on the understanding.

18 Duarte famously writes of the word *saudade* (*suydade* in the *LC*) that "me parece este nome de ssuydade tam proprio, que o latym nem outro linguagem que eu saibha nom he pera tal sentido semelhante" (95; "this word *saudade* seems so unique to me that neither Latin nor any other language known to me has a name for such a feeling"). The word's etymology is still subject to debate; many relate it to the Latin *solitas* (pl. *solitates*), describing a gradual shift from *soidade* to *saudade* under the influence of the verb *saudar*, "to greet," and the words *salvo*, "safe," and *saúde*, "health"

(Santoro 930). Alfredo Antunes posits that the shift may also be related to *saludade*, an antiquated form related to *salvação*, "salvation" (29); this particular connotation would rise to prominence during the Portuguese renaissance movement of the early twentieth century (Santoro 930). Still others have suggested a relationship to Arabic *saudá* (and related forms *suad* and *suaidá*), which signifies profound sadness or, more literally, "bruised and black blood in the heart" (Antunes 31), in which case the term would bear a specific relationship to humoral theory and not just a broad one to health (Blackmore, *Moorings* 143).

19 Saraiva, by contrast, concludes that the *LVB* aims at "social solidarity" based on love of God and neighbour – and also on the acceptance of pre-established social hierarchies and one's place therein (226).

20 In a chapter drawn largely from Cicero on forms of love, Duarte briefly describes erotic love, *amores*, as an excessive, inconstant, blind, or unwilling need to attain the affection, *afeiçom*, of another (176).

21 It is also the theme developed at length in Ausiàs March's "Axí com cell qui·n lo somni·s delita" (*Poesies* 78); I am grateful to Reader 1 for reminding me of this connection.

22 Witnessing or participating in courtly conversation implies its own perils: the sixth and final source of sadness identified by Duarte is "per fallas, converssaçom de tristes perssoas, ou desconcertado cuidado que a desperaçom de cobrar boa nem leda vida nos derrubam" (67; "through speech, conversation with sad people, or disordered care that demolish our hope of regaining a good or happy life").

23 "In the philosophical tradition dominated by Stoicism, *askēsis* means not renunciation but the progressive consideration of self, or mastery over oneself, obtained not through the renunciation of reality but through the acquisition and assimilation of truth … It is a set of practices by which one can acquire, assimilate, and transform truth into a permanent principle of action … It is a process of becoming more subjective" (Foucault, "Technologies" 35).

24 ID0192; I cite César Hernández Alonso's edition (Rodríguez del Padrón, *Obras Completas*). This difficult poem, to which I return in part two, was nonetheless "an authentic classic of *cancionero* poetry," surviving in fifteen manuscripts (Beltran, "Los *Gozos*" 93). The doctrine of first movements is also expressed with admirable clarity by Leriano in Diego de San Pedro's *Cárcel de amor* (discussed later): "Como los primeros movimientos no se puedan en los honbres escusar, en lugar de desviallos con la razón, confirmélos con la voluntad" (89; "As men cannot avoid the first movements, instead of turning them away with reason, I confirmed them with my will"). As Whinnom notes in his edition of *Cárcel*, Leriano follows Aquinas's *Summa theologica* 1–2.74.3 to the letter (San Pedro, *Obras completas, II* 89n48); his precision includes the nuance that the first movements are confirmed (and thereby transformed into sins) by the rational will.

25 ID1955; this song was glossed by both Gregorio Silvestre and Luís Vaz de Camões.

26 ID0276; I cite Jesús-Manuel Alda Tesán's edition (Manrique, *Poesía*).

27 ID2910; the poem, addressed to Enrique IV of Castile, is found in the *Cancionero de Oñate Castañeda* (c. 1485). On Montoro's place in the *cancionero* corpus, see Gómez-Bravo, *Textual Agency* 205–13.

28 ID0654.

29 ID2262.

30 As the final quoted verse indicates, the entire will ("do non *quería*") is incapacitated.

31 ID1437; I cite Azáceta's edition (*Cancionero de Juan Alfonso de Baena*).

32 ID0717.

33 ID2506.

34 As Francisco Rodríguez Risquete notes, Santa Fe was one of the Castilian predecessors for whom Torroella felt a "special admiration" (Torroella, *Obra completa* 1: 98; the others are Villasandino, Alfonso de la Torre, Lope de Estúñiga, and Santillana).

35 I cite Jaume Torró's edition in *Sis poetes del regnat d'Alfons el Magnànim*. Elsewhere, Dies describes *sentiment* as a derivation of thought: "La mia mà a la vostra rescriu/ lo sentiment que de ma pensa trau" (*Sis poetes* III, lines 3–4; "My hand responds to yours/ the sentiment it draws from my thought").

36 Torró glosses "voler ab moviment" as "una voluntat moguda per la passió" (*Sis poetes* 190nn14–16; "a will moved by passion").

37 For a brief account of Llull's life, see Torró's [Turró's] edition of Llull's *Obra completa* (Llull 15–18). Llull's works are conserved in the *Jardinet d'orats* (*Garden of Fools*; Biblioteca Universitària de Barcelona, ms. 151), which also contains poetry and prose by Joan Roís de Corella, Bernat Fenollar, and Francesc Alegre, among others.

38 All of Alegre's sentimental works survive, like the works of Romeu Llull, in the *Jardinet d'orats*; Alegre also wrote three religious works, of which only the *Passió de Jesucrist* (1488) survives (*Obres de ficció sentimental* 9–11).

39 As in the case of its Castilian counterpart, the ascetic rationalism that opposed reason and the passions constitutes the conventional wisdom of the Catalan lyric tradition, which provided the key affective terms of Catalan sentimental fiction in the second half of the fifteenth century. Thus, in the last decades of the fourteenth century, Jaume March writes in his "Cobles de Fortuna" that "la rahó pot e deu ben regir/ lo cors" (*Obra poètica* IV, lines 9–10; "reason can and should govern the body well"), and his brother Pere March (father of Ausiàs), in his lengthy "Arnés del cavaller" ("The Knight's Armor"), advises that "sitot natura·ns dóna/ ceyll voler e desir,/ nós devem corregir/ lo voler per rahó" (*Obra completa* 211, lines 360–3; "although nature gives us this will and desire, we should correct the will through reason"). And if Pere March's model of exemplary knighthood draws on "Gregorian moralism" and "medieval Senecanism" (43), his contemporary Antoni Canals, who can be linked, like Pere and Eiximenis, to the Gandia of Alfons el Vell (Canals 34), could cite the ancient authority of Plato, who wrote in the *Phaedrus* that "aquela mort és bona com la persona mata en si les passions e delectacions carnals, car la ànima de aquel, estant en lo cors, se'n puja en lo cel per pura contemplació, sedades e reposades les passions" (Canals

40–1; "that death is good in which the person kills in himself the passions and carnal delights, for the soul of that one, being in the body, rises up to the sky in pure contemplation, the passions having been sedated and put to rest").

40 The correspondence between Torroella and Ferrer seems to date from 1468, whereas Ferrer's love poetry, in which *grat* plays an outsized role, is likely from the mid-1440s (Ferrer, *Obra completa* 183–4).

41 As Rodríguez Risquete notes (Torroella 2: 233nn14–15), different historical accounts of the faculties of perception make it difficult to pinpoint the exact role of each one; the important point is once again the identification of *grat* with the understanding's judgment that the perceived object is good ("mira l'enteniment aquelles [coses] qu·estima bones").

42 This Joan Roís de Corella is not the well-known writer of the same name (a key figure in the conclusion of this book), but Joan Roís de Corella i Llançol de Romaní, governor of Valencia from 1448 until his death in 1479.

43 I discuss *transpostació* as an ideal of absolute identification in the conclusion.

44 As Rodríguez Risquete notes, versions of this paradox of *poder* and *força/fuerza* are found in poems by Ausiàs March and Juan de Villalpando, among others (Torroella 1: 233n1).

45 Coimbra, Biblioteca da Universidade, ms. 1011. On the context of this debate and, in particular, the influence of Ausiàs March therein, see Lluís Cabré, "Dos lectors." Unlike Ferrer, a merchant, Urrea was a nobleman from one of the most powerful Aragonese families; Cabré perceives a telling contrast in how Torroella addresses his social inferior and superior (60).

46 As Rodríguez Risquete notes (Torroella 2: 286nn107–12), this quotation corresponds to lines 98–103 of Rodríguez del Padrón's poem (I cite, however, Rodríguez Risquete's edition of Torroella's letter).

47 See L. Cabré, "Dos lectors."

48 Torroella does not cite them directly, but creates a hyperbolic list of antitheses such as friendly war, moderate furor, painful joy, and hateful affection (2: 293).

49 Once again, I cite from Rodríguez Risquete's edition of Torroella's letter.

50 Ausiàs March is the central figure of chapter seven; I therefore limit my remarks here to the most relevant passages of this doctrinal poem.

51 It is interesting to note here that Ausiàs March's account of virtuous love adopts the metaphor of armament developed so thoroughly in his father's "Arnés del cavaller."

52 I have cited Arthur Terry's translations for Ausiàs March's poems (A. March, *Selected Poems*), but Terry did not include this poem in his selection, so I cite Robert Archer's translation here instead (A. March, *A Key Anthology*).

53 Ausiàs March's doctrine here recalls Duarte's warnings about the sinfully tepid will.

54 It is also instructive that they set their exemplary inner conflict in the mind of a woman; this setting will become an increasingly important resource in the development of sentimental fiction. As Toril Moi has argued in her seminal reading of Andreas Capellanus's *De amore*, the courtly lover tends to understand his problem as one of correctly interpreting women's words (27). Moi goes on to note that the role of

the active male reader is in keeping with Capellanus's "insistence on male lust and female passivity" (27). As we have seen, Torroella, despite being perhaps the best known misogynist in fifteenth-century Iberia, certainly in the songbook tradition (Archer, *The Problem of Woman* 170), did not insist on female passivity in erotic matters, and it is perhaps for this reason that he could understand his central problem as one of effective self-expression (although this remains, of course, an active rather than passive stance). Robert Archer has shown that Torroella's so-called "Maldezir de mugeres" (ID0043) constituted "an act of cultural transference," importing into Castilian poetry the Occitan-Catalan *maldit* tradition (*The Problem of Woman* 182).

4 Impassibility, Pity, Community

1 For an excellent overview of references to the Passion in *cancionero* verse, see Tillier.
2 San Pedro, *Obras completas, III: Poesías*, ed. Severin and Whinnom; ID6188.
3 I cite Whinnom's edition, San Pedro, *Obras completas, II: Cárcel de amor.*
4 Latin references are to the Loeb Classical Library edition (Augustine, *Confessions*, vol. 1).
5 The idea that true compassion is inextricably tied to action persists in modern criticism: "There is nothing clear about compassion," writes Lauren Berlant, "except that it implies a social relation between spectators and sufferers, with the emphasis on the spectator's experience of feeling compassion and its subsequent relation to material practice" (1).
6 For a critique of the "impassioned 'I'" as a sign of the development of "personal" devotion or individuality in medieval prayer, see McNamer 67–73.
7 On Evagrius's life and thought in general, see Sinkewicz xvii–xl. These eight thoughts, reduced to seven and lightly modified, would eventually be codified by Gregory the Great as the Seven Deadly Sins (Knuuttila 141–2).
8 Richard Sorabji has noted the similarity between Evagrius's doctrine and the Stoic doctrine of unavoidable "first movements" that become emotions only with reason's assent (359–60).
9 As Geoffrey Galt Harpham has noted, early cenobites were well aware that they could not achieve divine impassibility, and so the ascetic practices meant to facilitate divine contemplation constituted "a quest for a goal that cannot and must not be reached, a quest with a sharp caveat: 'seek but do not find'" (43). In this way, they are similar to the courtly lover's erotic quest, defined in lyric practice by its constitutive unfulfillment.
10 Knuuttila has noted a similarity here to Schleiermacher's hermeneutics (150), although one of the German theologian's recent editors has rejected this "empathetic" reading (Schleiermacher xxix). Schleiermacher held that every utterance must be understood as both "derived from language" and "a fact in the thinker" (8). The first understanding leads to "grammatical interpretation," whereas in "psychological interpretation," "every utterance is to be understood only via the whole life to which

it belongs, i.e., because every utterance can only be recognised as a moment of the life of the language-user in the determinedness of all the moments of their life, and this only from the totality of their environments, via which their development and continued existence are determined, every language-user can only be understood via their nationality and their era" (9). The broader areas of investigation implied by this last clause lead Schleiermacher to go further than Cassian, suggesting that interpreters can come to understand utterances better than their original speakers did (23). But Schleiermacher's method proceeds through critical self-abnegation: "To the extent, therefore, that one wants to understand completely one should free oneself from the relation of what is to be explicated to one's own thoughts, because this relationship precisely does not at all have the intention of understanding, but instead of using as a means that which in the thought of the other relates to one's own thoughts" (135). Cassian's empathetic monk does not vanish in becoming prophet; rather, the monk remains essential to prophetic subjectivity as the *subjectum* to whom accidents occur and predicates accrue (cf. Balibar, Cassin, and Libera 1070).

11 Mary Carruthers has noted the intensely rhetorical nature of this model of sin (107–8).

12 There is, nevertheless, as Gavin Flood has shown, a paradoxical place for the will in the formation of ascetic subjectivity: "Yet the eradication of subjectivity in ascetic pursuit entails the assertion of subjectivity in voluntary acts of will. Asceticism, then, is the performance of this ambiguity, an ambiguity that is absolutely central to subjectivity" (2–3).

13 Jean Leclercq drew a distinction on this basis between scholastic and monastic reading practices: "The scholastic *lectio* takes the direction of the *quaestio* and the *disputatio*. The reader puts questions to the text and then questions himself on the subject matter: *quaeri solet*. The monastic *lectio* is oriented toward the *meditatio* and the *oratio*. The objective of the first is science and knowledge; of the second, wisdom and appreciation. In the monastery, the *lectio divina*, which begins with grammar, terminates in compunction, in desire of heaven" (72).

14 It should also be noted that the medieval theory of the four levels of meaning "received its definitive formulation" from Cassian (Grondin 31).

15 This doctrine is also taken up by Isidore in his *Etymologies* (II.xvi).

16 "Tantum enim valet animi compatientis affectus, ut cum illi afficiuntur nobis loquentibus, et nos illis discentibus habitemus in invicem; atque ita et illi quae audiunt, quasi loquantur in nobis, et nos in illis discamus quodam modo quae docemus" (Augustine, *De catechizandis* 12.17).

17 As Leclercq notes, experience is also a key element of Bernard's hermeneutics in his celebrated sermons on the *Song of Songs*: "The important word is no longer *quaeritur*, but *desideratur*; no longer *sciendum*, but *experiendum*" (5).

18 For a substantial overview of Pérez de Guzmán's life, library, and place in fifteenth-century culture, see Vaquero. Pérez de Guzmán's poetry is found in *Baena*, *San Román*, the *Cancionero general*, and several other songbooks. His *Floresta* compiles sayings from Seneca, Cicero, Boethius, and Augustine, alongside Bernard and many others.

19 I cite Raymond Foulché-Delbosc's 1904 edition of Pérez de Guzmán's text and share Miguel Pérez Rosado's hypothesis that the *Floresta*'s sentences follow their order of appearance in their respective sources (153). On the relationship of the Castilian and Catalan wisdom traditions, and on the uses to which wisdom texts such as the *Floresta* were put, see Taylor.

20 The sentence immediately following this one lists the nine works of mercy, the first five of which ("las cinco corporales") involve the care of the poor and infirm (Pérez de Guzmán 113).

21 "2138. En vano lee o contempla la persona si a Dios non ama" (Pérez de Guzmán 101).

22 For an overview of ecclesiastical involvement in fifteenth-century Castilian politics, see Nieto Soria, *Iglesia y genesis* 262–72.

23 For an introduction (including images) to this altarpiece and its history, see Silva Maroto.

24 Berceo was likely aware of Bernard of Clairvaux's sermons on the Virgin (Saugnieux 61–2). Marina Warner's *Alone of All Her Sex* remains a helpful introduction to the broad phenomenon of Marian devotion. On representations of Mary in medieval Passion narratives, see Bestul 111–44.

25 The seven traditional Joys of the Virgin are the Annunciation, Christ's Nativity, the Adoration of the Magi, Christ's Resurrection and Ascension, the Pentecost, and the Coronation of the Virgin in Heaven. Santillana expands the list to twelve through the inclusion of the virgin birth, the presentation of Christ at the Temple, the return from Egypt, the Disputation ("Christ among the Doctors"), and the wedding at Cana's transformation of water into wine. For an exhaustive study of the Joys in the *LBA*, see Morreale, who notes that, in the New Testament, joy is frequently counter-posed to pain "as participation in the suffering of the Redeemer" (32). Serra i Baldó offers a brief overview of the genre across the European vernaculars (367–8) and traces its development in Catalan poetry through the end of the fifteenth century (368–86).

26 The bibliography devoted to this outstanding genre of medieval Castilian literature is, of course, vast. Alongside Francisco Rico's seminal article "La clerecía del mester," Julian Weiss's *The Mester de Clerecía* and, more recently, Simone Pinet's *Task of the Cleric* offer insight into several major works of the genre's first century and can be consulted for further bibliographic references. Here, I am principally interested in the emergence of intercalated lyric, devotional and otherwise, in the genre's later works.

27 On Ayala's life and work, see Michel Garcia. According to Kenneth Adams, there is no strong evidence in the *Rimado* of direct borrowings from Ruiz (30).

28 The first to do so was José Amador de los Ríos (Coy 71).

29 I cite Kenneth Adams's edition of López de Ayala's *Libro rimado de Palacio*.

30 Eugenio Asensio identified *coita* as the Galician-Portuguese counterpart to Occitan *joi* (108); for an overview of *coita*'s historical roots, role in the *cantigas*, and relationship to melancholy and lovesickness, see Blackmore, "Melancholy."

31 Richard P. Kinkade has argued that Ayala was influenced by emerging Hieronymite practice; in the last years of his life, Ayala was a benefactor of the Hieronymite

monastery at San Miguel del Monte and spent a significant amount of time there (Kinkade 165, 174–5). Michel Garcia, by contrast, views the affinities between Ayala and the early Hieronymites as part of an epochal spiritual turn involving "a return to Scripture, with a predilection for the poetic Books, better suited to personal expression; greater attention paid to the speculative literature of the Doctors; [and] renewed interest in the practical norms of the Christian life" (269). Ayala's identification with the Hieronymites would therefore be based on the order's instantiation of spiritual principles to which Ayala already subscribed (M. Garcia 269).

32 Ayala's adherence to the counsel of mercy can in part be explained by his view that powerful rulers are naturally inclined to cruelty: "Los reyes poderosos, si catan su alteza,/ naturalment se inclinan a fazer toda crueza" (277ab; "Powerful kings, if they regard their highness, are naturally inclined to commit all cruelty").

33 As Gómez-Bravo has argued, the traditional distinction between the *cantar* or *canción* as a poem set to music and the *dictado* or *decir* as a poem meant to be recited without music is untenable, given current research on the polyphonic music of the late Middle Ages, along with the increasing dominance of private, silent reading beginning in the late fourteenth century ("Retórica y poética" 137–9). On the relation of the generic name *decir* to rhetorical terms such as *dictado*, *deytado*, and *dictar*, see Gómez-Bravo, "Retórica y poética" 141–4. Gómez-Bravo notes that the *artes dictaminis*, although now associated with prose letters, in fact enumerate three kinds of *dictamen*, prose, rhythmic, and metrical; as such, *dictamen* could signify a poetic composition (143). The *dictamen* (and thus the *decir*) would also be linked to poetry because of the porous distinction between rhetoric and grammar in the Middle Ages, with the *ars poetriae* as a grammatical genre (144). If the *decir* can be traced to the *artes dictaminis* and the *cantiga* to vernacular sources, that might explain "the well-known 'learned' character of the *decir*" (Gómez-Bravo, "*Decir canciones*" 167); the shift in terminology away from *decir* and toward *coplas* in the second half of the fifteenth century can be partly explained by a shift in prestige away from the *dictamen* and toward Ciceronian rhetoric (172–3).

34 Noting the great formal variety of the *Rimado*'s lyrics and their widely varying periods of composition, Garcia describes Ayala's "inability to separate lived experience from the experience of writing," which led the writer to incorporate disparate pieces, "assign[ing] each one the vital frame that surrounded it" (302). On the periods in which the lyrics were produced, which Garcia deduces from the biographical allusions they contain, see 297–8.

35 Context makes clear that "pero que" has a coordinating rather than concessive function in this stanza. Ayala thus maintains a distinction between the *deitado* and *cantar* as *arte mayor* and *menor* verse forms, respectively. Joaquín Gimeno Casalduero describes Ayala as a conservative in comparison to the next generation of *cancionero* poets, maintaining a "moral" rather than "poetic" sensibility (2). However, in describing the same poetic debate on free will discussed by Gimeno Casalduero (the poems in question are *Baena* 517–25), Weiss argues that "elegant discussion," and not

"philosophical inquiry undertaken for its own sake," was the overriding concern of all involved (*The Poet's Art* 16).

36 This trope persists, for example, in *Cárcel de amor*: "Desesperado havría, segund lo que siento, si alguna vez me hallase solo, pero como sienpre me aconpañan el pensamiento que me das y el deseo que me ordenas y la contenplación que me causas … consuélanme acordándome que me tienen conpañía de tu parte" (San Pedro, *Obras completas, II* 152).

37 ID6282.

38 It was not until the final decade of the fifteenth century that Castilian translations of the *Meditationes vitae Christi*, Bonaventure's *Lignum vitae*, and Ludolph of Saxony's *Vita Christi* were produced, and "these texts are only sparsely and belatedly represented in Latin in a Castilian context" (Robinson 10).

39 "Juan Alfonso and his colleagues in the Cancionero accused each other of Jewish ancestry, of having too small a foreskin or too big a nose, of heterosexual and homosexual intercourse with Jews. They also accused each other of sexual intercourse with Muslims and prostitutes, of cowardice, ignorance, greed, and mendacity, of letting themselves be sodomized by shepherds and Muslim slaves, and even of renouncing their Christianity in favor of Islam" (Nirenberg, "Figures" 403).

40 On the notion of divine grace in Baena's prologue, see Kohut, "La teoría de la poesía cortesana" 130–5 and Weiss, *The Poet's Art* 25–40.

41 Kay argues that, for Ermengaud, a Franciscan friar, all love poets "participate in the same knowledge as the God of Love," an "intersubjectivity" of which they may be unaware ("Grafting" 364–5).

42 As Michael Camille notes, this "doubling" of compassion is ever-present in visual depictions of the Passion in the Middle Ages, manifested in "the mournful face of Christ, whose sad look is exactly that of the Virgin in countless contemporary Passion images" (198).

5 Passionate Quotation

1 For a critical overview of the poems that have been attributed to Macías and their textual tradition, see Casas Rigall, "El enigma literario" 12–33; Andrea Zinato has published an excellent critical edition as *Macías: l'esperienza poetica galego-castigiliana*. The five poems Zinato attributes to Macías with certainty are those compiled by Baena, that is, "Cativo de miña tristura" (ID0131), "Ay, señora en qué fiança" (ID0447), "Amor cruel e bryoso" (ID0128), "Con tan alto poderío" (ID0130), and "Provė de buscar mesura" (ID1437). Kenneth Hale Vanderford's "Macías in Legend and Literature" remains a useful introduction to the Galician troubadour's literary afterlife; see also Zinato 18–31. In Aragon, the poet Pau de Bellviure, active around the turn of the fifteenth century and mentioned in Santillana's *Prohemio*, came to play a similar role to Macías as love martyr; of his works, only one misogynist poem and one stanza incorporated into Francesc Ferrer's *Lo conhort* (see later discussion) survive (L. Cabré, "Notas sobre la memoria" 33–5).

2 I cite from Azáceta's edition of the *Cancionero de Baena*, but for lines 17 and 18, I have adopted the punctuation of Ricardo Polín's *Cancioneiro galego-castelán.*
3 I have chosen this capacious translation of *non fases comunalesa* in order not to foreclose shades of meaning that emerge in my subsequent discussion of *comunalesa* as a poetic and ethical concept.
4 Macías's poems were likely heavily Castilianized by their copyists and may date from much earlier than those of the first generation of Baena poets (see note 10, below).
5 Beltran, "La *cantiga*" 259.
6 Deyermond, "Baena, Santillana, Resende."
7 In Rennart's *Macias, O Namorado*, published in 1900.
8 In Lang's *Cancioneiro Gallego-Castelhano*, published in 1902.
9 See, for example, Lapesa, "La lengua" 51–5.
10 Although Macías's literary activity is generally located between the reigns of Alfonso XI and Pedro I of Castile (1340–69), it is now considered likelier, owing to recently discovered archival evidence, that he flourished in the thirteenth century (Perea Rodríguez 84–5).
11 Davies and Ferreira, *Corpus do Português*, https://www.corpusdoportugues.org/hist-gen/; consulted 24 September 2019.
12 The *Corpus del Nuevo diccionario histórico del español* lists twenty-two occurrences of *comunaleza*, drawn largely but not exclusively from Alfonsine legal and lapidary texts; the main meaning one can derive from this small corpus is that of a shared quality or (as in the case of excommunication) shared belonging to a group.
13 In this context, it is interesting to note that, in Castrojeriz's *Glosa castellana, medianeros* are contrasted with flatterers and the taciturn in that they "saben tener buena manera en vivir con los ommes" and, therefore, "son de alabar e llámalos el Filósofo amigables, porque son de buena conversación entre los ommes" (1: 207). This first definition of *comunaleza* thus links it not only with communication and conversation (as in the second *Autoridades* definition) but also with friendship as an ethical ideal.
14 On Juan Ruiz's description of one of the *LBA*'s *cánticas de serrana* as neither beautiful "nin comunal" (986b), see Galvez 43.
15 Dutton ID0146. The poem appears in *cancioneros* PN8 and PN12 (Bibliothèque nationale de France, esp. 230 and 313); I cite the Severin-Maguire edition of PN8 from Severin, *An Electronic Corpus of 15th Century Castilian* Cancionero *Manuscripts.*
16 This definition of "religion" is Cartagena's third; interestingly, the first is *releer* or *relecçion*, the diligent re-reading of Scripture that Cartagena sees as central to worship (*Oracional* 83).
17 Dinis is the author of one out of every twelve surviving *cantigas*, so it is of course not rare for him to have used any given word more often than the other *trovadores.*
18 For all Galician-Portuguese *cantigas*, I cite Graça Videira Lopes's 2016 edition, *Cantigas medievais galego-portuguesas:* Corpus *integral profano.*
19 See, for example, Deyermond, "The Love Poetry"; Ferreira 35; Hart, "New Perspectives," "The *cantigas*," and *En maneira* 23; and Weiss, "On the Conventionality."

20 As Eugenio Asensio notes, *coita* is often qualified as *descomunal* in the Galician-Portuguese songbooks (108; other common qualifiers are *forte*, *grande*, and *mortal*).
21 Dutton ID1158. I cite here Azáceta's edition of the *Cancionero de Juan Alfonso de Baena.*
22 This sense is still its second meaning in the 1729 edition of the *Diccionario de autoridades.* On Villasandino's adaptation of key words and phrases from the Galician-Portuguese songbooks in his Galician poems, see Vallín.
23 On the relationship of the Castilian tradition to these earlier texts, see Martinengo 161–7, Caravaggi 108–25, and Tomassetti, "Tra intertestualità."
24 For Sant Jordi's reliance on the *Perilhos tractat,* see *Poesies* 199–200; for Ferrer and Torroella, see Cantavella, "Del *Perilhos tractat*" 453–8 and Avenoza 25–8. According to Cantavella ("Del *Perilhos tractat*" 455–7), the *Breviari* circulated in two versions in the Crown of Aragon: a complete version in the original Occitan and a Catalan prose translation that omitted the *Perilhos tractat.*
25 At an extreme, *acomodación* becomes parody (Casas Rigall, *Agudeza* 172).
26 Tomassetti is drawing, in turn, on T. Navarro Tomás, who described the genre as a whole under the rubric of *decires de refranes,* specifying texts with lyric insertions as *decires de estribillos* (Tomassetti, "Sobre la tradición" 1708n3).
27 As Rodríguez Risquete notes (Torroella I: 374n1), this first line is inspired by Ausiàs March, *Poesies,* poem LIII, l. 21: "Tant mon voler Amor ha hobeÿt" ("My will has so obeyed Love").
28 In the poem's first citation, of Jaume March's "Un sobtós pler," love itself is both the initial "sudden pleasure" and a "strany voler" that deprives the lover of his "sense, feeling, and knowledge" ("seny, sentiment he saber"; here, lines 56–8). The "strany pler" described by Torroella is not love itself, but the close relationship between the two is implied in this rhyming citation.
29 For an overview of this subgenre, several examples of which are discussed further on, see Martinengo. The Castilian and Catalan poems cited by Torroella are: Jaume March, "Un sobtós pler" (lines 52–9); Lluís de Vila-rasa, "Començ de cas" (lines 108–15); Arnau March, "Tot hom se guart" (lines 128–34; this quotation is the only surviving fragment of this poem); Ausiàs March, "Alt e amor" (lines 169–76); Lope de Estúñiga, "Si mis tristes pensamientos" (lines 186–97; ID0020); Martí Garcia, "Lo Voler pot bé son dan" (lines. 262–9; another unique witness); Álvarez de Villasandino, "De lo qual" (lines 281–94; ID1152); Santillana, "Por amar non sabiamente" (lines 322–5; ID0310); Juan de Torres, "O, maldita fermosura" (lines 417–20; ID1736); Francesc Ferrer, "Enamorats, doleu-vos de ma vida" (lines 488–95); Juan de Mena, "Ya no sufre mi cuydado" (lines 523–31; ID0010); Macías, "Ay, señora en qué fiança" (lines 552–9; ID0447); Juan de Dueñas, "Amor, temor y cordura" (lines 603–6; ID0485); Joan de Castellví, "Amor és tal que son poder" (lines 624–8); and Pedro de Santa Fe, "Como yo, mi amor caya" (lines 637–45; ID2239). For a complete list of citations and corresponding manuscript witnesses and variants, see Rodríguez Risquete (Torroella I: 370–4). Torroella's poem draws on at least two earlier Catalan songs of this type, Jordi de Sant Jordi's *Passio amoris* and Francesc Ferrer's *Conhort* (*Obra completa* I: 349), both

of which are discussed later. On songs of this type in Garcia de Resende's *Cancioneiro Geral* (1516), see Tomassetti, "Tra intertestualità."

30 I thus agree with Rodríguez Risquete (Torroella I: 375n10) that the "tròban" of line 10 "seems to have the etymological sense of *invenire*" as "to compose." Zumthor has described the practice of inserting *versus cum autoritate* in bilingual poems – an authoritative Latin verse in a Romance song or, "generally with ironic intent," a vernacular verse in a Latin poem – with examples from Occitan (Marcabru) and Old French (*Langue et techniques* 102–3).

31 The first four senses in Alcover i Sureda and Borja Moll's *Diccionari català-valencià-balear* (henceforth *DCVB*) relate to foreignness, the fifth to familiarity; all are attested as early as the thirteenth century.

32 Rodríguez Risquete points readers to this sense of *invenció* in the *DCVB* (Torroella I: 380n208).

33 As noted above, Ferrer is the author of an earlier citation song, *Lo conhort* (discussed later), which, Rodríguez Risquete points out, is an important Catalan antecedent of *Tant mon voler* (Torroella I: 349).

34 Sant Jordi would later participate, alongside Andreu Febrer and Ausiàs March, in the king's 1420 military campaign in Sardinia and Corsica; in 1423 he fell prisoner to Muzio Attendolo Sforza in Naples, his brief captivity giving rise to the poem "Deserts d'amichs, de béns e de senyor," known more familiarly as *Presoner*. Born at the very end of the fourteenth century, Sant Jordi died on 12 June 1424 (*Història de la literatura catalana* 334–5); for a recent account of Sant Jordi's life, see Sant Jordi, *Poesies* 9–20. Other prominent literary figures Sant Jordi would have encountered at the court of Alfonso V include Lluís Icard, Pedro de Santa Fe, and, from an earlier generation, Enrique de Villena (*Història de la literatura catalana* 334).

35 As noted earlier, this is also the theme of Dinis's "Proençaes soem mui bem trobar." *Refrezir*, "become cold," is the reading in all but one manuscript of Berguedà's song; the exception is a copy from the early nineteenth century that, like the *Passio*, reads *brunezir*, "darken" (Sant Jordi, *Poesies* 212nn1–2).

36 See D. Turner, *Eros and Allegory*.

37 Fratta finds reminiscences of Giraut de Bornelh, Cerverí de Girona, mossèn Avinyó, Ramon Boter, Guiraut Riquier, Aimeric de Peguilhan, and Perdigon in Sant Jordi's definition (Sant Jordi 213nn11–29).

38 It is because of his willingness to undergo this suffering that the protagonist invokes Ovid, whose *Amores* (3.11a.1–7) taught perseverance in the expectation of a future reward (Sant Jordi 200).

39 Dutton ID0195; I cite from Ana María Álvarez Pellitero's edition of the *Cancionero de Palacio*, slightly modified to indicate directly that the refrains are crossed out in the manuscript. As Álvarez Pellitero notes (*Cancionero de Palacio* 232), this *decir* is attributed to Villalobos in MN54 (the *Cancionero de Estúñiga*), PN12, RC1 (the *Cancionero de Roma*), and VM1 (the *Cancionero de Venecia*), all fifteenth-century witnesses, albeit none as early as *Palacio*. Zinato concludes that the correct attribution is indeed to

Villalobos (44); however, as I show further on, there is evidence that Santillana, at least, accepted the attribution to Macías.

40 See Lida de Malkiel, "La hipérbole sagrada."

41 See Gerli, "La 'Religión del Amor.'"

42 Casas Rigall, *Agudeza y retórica* 176–86.

43 I cite from Julio Rodríguez-Puertolas's edition of Mendoza's *Cancionero*.

44 A group of Portuguese and Castilian poets mostly associated with the court of Alfonso X – Pero Garcia Burgalês, Gil Peres Conde, João Lobeira, Vasco Gil, and Pero Guterres – attack God directly for their erotic misfortune; perhaps the most representative of these *cantigas* is Pero Garcia Burgalês's "Nunca Deus quis nulha cousa gram bem." On this group of texts, see Pilar Lorenzo Gradín, "*Adversus Deum.*"

45 This version of the line appears in MN54 (*Cancionero de Estúñiga*), RC1 (*Cancionero de Roma*), and VM1 (*Cancionero de Venecia*). In the last of these, the poem is attributed to Santillana ("El marques").

46 As noted by Tillier 71.

47 The Psalms were central to the celebration of the Divine Office, and verses therefrom were chanted as antiphons during the Mass (Pierce); as Tomassetti has noted, the penitential psalms in particular were included in books of hours and "formed part of the canonical repertoire of prayers" ("Los *Salmos*" 270).

48 The penitential psalms are 6, 31, 37, 50, 101, 129, and 142; other poets who composed *contrafacta* or glosses of the psalms in Castilian are Francisco de Villalpando, Pero Guillén de Segovia, Juan del Encina, Juan de Luzón, and Jaume Gassull (Tomassetti, "Los *Salmos*" 264–5).

49 Valera's *Salmos* survive in a single manuscript, SA10 (Biblioteca Universitaria de Salamanca, ms. 2763). As Rodríguez-Puértolas notes, both this poem and a companion, the *Letanía de Amores* (ID0535), were harshly received, as blasphemous or simply in bad taste, by modern critics such as Menéndez Pelayo and Mario Penna (Rodríguez-Puértolas 31). Lida de Malkiel defends Valera and other authors of "sacred hyperbole" from accusations grounding their heterodoxy in their status as *conversos*, arguing that poetry of this type resulted from Castilian society's "general state of crisis" during this period ("La hipérbole sagrada" 126–7).

50 The Hebrew version of the psalm, by contrast, refers to Sheol (where both the righteous and unrighteous go after death) rather than Hell and to remembrance rather than confession (*HarperCollins* 804, 804n6.5).

51 These lines, while not a direct translation, follow the Vulgate rather closely: "Laboravi in gemitu meo; lavabo per singulas noctes lectum meum: lacrimis meis stratum meum rigabo" (Ps 6:7).

52 This psalm thus repeats the opening verse of Psalm 6.

53 This reasoning, with its allusion to Cupid, draws daringly on a metaphor from the original psalm: "quoniam sagittae tuae infixae sunt mihi" (Ps 37:3).

54 Francisco de Villalpando's parody of this psalm, *Cancionero de Palacio* XCIV (ID2484), is entirely crossed out in the manuscript (78).

55 It also alludes not only to the cry of Macías's "Pues me falleçió ventura" but also to "Cativo de miña tristura," which, as we will see, thematizes the inarticulate but revealing cry of the frustrated lover sworn to secrecy.

56 It is worth recalling in this vein that, in early *cancionero* poetry, "señor," like the Galician-Portuguese "senhor," referred to the female beloved.

57 The "Querella" underwent numerous revisions and appears in different forms, with different quotations, throughout the manuscript tradition; for a recent analysis of the poem's transmission, see Russo. I will cite from Kerkhof and Gómez Moreno's edition (Santillana, *Poesías completas*), based on SA8, a c. 1455 manuscript generally held to have been produced in Santillana's own *scriptorium* (Cátedra, *Cancionero del Marqués de Santillana* XXIII). This is likely the final version of the poem (Russo 38) and is the only one to cite (without attribution) "Pues me falleçió ventura." The version in the *Cancionero de Palacio* substitutes the opening lines of Macías's "Con tal alto poderío," although, as Álvarez Pellitero notes (*Cancionero de Palacio* 85nn33–6), in his *Prohemio*, Santillana attributes these lines to Alfonso González de Castro. In both *Palacio* and SA8, the first quoted lines are the opening of Macías's "Amor cruel e bryoso." The version of the "Querella" in SA8 also cites lines by unknown authors (lines 21–4, 80–3), by Santillana's grandfather, Pero González de Mendoza (lines 57–9), and by either Villasandino or the Duke of Benavente (lines 68–71; in the *Prohemio*, Santillana attributes these lines to the Arcediano de Toro).

58 "Jamás" is used here in its antiquated sense of "always."

59 Macías's birthplace is also prominent when he appears in the Third Order of Mena's *Laberinto de Fortuna*: "Lleguéme más çerca, turbado ya quando/ vi ser un tal ombre de nuestra nación" (Mena, *Obras completas*, lines 837–8). Macías is overheard in song, urging others to avoid passionate love: "Fuid un peligro tan apassionado,/ sabed ser alegres, dexad de ser tristes" (lines 849–50; as is clear from these lines, the Galician troubadour's poetic prowess has suffered somewhat in his postmortem transition to *arte mayor* verse).

60 On Santillana's knowledge of Dante, in addition to Mario Schiff's seminal study *La bibliothèque du Marquis de Santillane* 271–307, see Hartnett 121–32. Schiff indicates that Santillana took particular note of these verses (290n6).

61 As Pau Cañigueral Batllosera notes, Macías applies Dante's phrase to the community of lovers, whereas in the *Inferno* Francesca speaks for all condemned souls and not just those guilty of lust (14).

62 A similar phrase appears in Joan Roís de Corella's *Jardí d'amor* (*Obres completes I* 131), discussed in the conclusion.

63 Drawing on the maiden's self-identification, "Lo meu nom es dels amants Conaxença" (line 281), Heaton translates *conaxença* as "Acquaintance with Lovers" (Rocabertí 22, 22n1). This sense of familiarity is certainly appropriate to the role of guide, but to the extent that the narrator embodies the lover whose service goes unrecognized – his beloved ("aymia") shows him "Gran desfavor e poch voler" (line

32) – the name *Conaxença* likely refers to the (always illusory) possibility of the gracious lady who grants the lover's just reward, that is, who does not refuse to recognize (*desconèixer*) his worth.

64 Nero is also, of course, associated with a conflagration, so it is doubly meaningful that he should be moved by the "strange fire" wielded by Aphrodite ("Citarea") against the narrator. According to Heaton, "Pirrus" refers not to the Greek general famous for taking unacceptably heavy losses, but to the son of Achilles who killed Priam and sacrificed Polyxena; Rocabertí could have been familiar with this figure from the *Roman de Troie* (Rocabertí 106n16).

65 Cf. *Posar els pensaments en una dona*, "enamorar-se'n, patir de l'amor d'ella" (*DCVB*, fourth sense of *pensament*).

66 These lines do not appear in any other manuscript, and Macías is not clearly identified as their author (he may, for example, be reciting the lines he was reading when interrupted by the *Glòria*'s protagonist).

67 Book III of Capellanus's *De amore* famously repudiates the teachings on courtly love of Books I and II; on the critical debate surrounding the interpretation of Book III and Capellanus's true attitude toward courtly love, see Moi 13–15.

68 Macías's poem is number 306 in the *Cancionero de Juan Alfonso de Baena* (ed. José María Azáceta).

69 *Cancionero de Palacio* CXIX; ID2503.

70 Reading "Quen ben see nunca devria/ ál pensar, que fas folia" (lines 8–9, slightly modified; "He who is well should never think of something else, for that is folly").

71 A later poem by Torquemada in the *Cancionero de Palacio* repeats the premise of Santillana's "Querella" in that the lyric voice, having wandered into a dark valley, happens upon "hun hombre desesperado/ cantando desaguisado/ un cantar con amargura" (CXXIII, lines 6–8). The song is "Cativo de miña tristura," and the singer soon addresses the lyric voice: "E díxome a poco estado:/ 'Vet que escomunaleza/ de su corte m'á hechado/ por servir bien su nobleza'" (lines 13–16). A later hand has corrected line 14 to read "d[e]scomunaleza" (127n14). Although only one other quoted refrain is from Macías, these first lines of dialogue reveal his identity to an initiated audience and suggest that, while "descomunaleza" retained a certain strangeness, it was associated with the Galician troubadour through "Amor cruel e bryoso," here indirectly quoted.

72 ID6127. I cite Rodríguez del Padrón's *Obras Completas* (ed. César Hernández Alonso) for this and the following poems (poems III, I, and V).

73 It should be noted that Rodríguez del Padrón's reinterpretation of Macías's song takes advantage of the polysemous nature of the verb *trabar*, which in the earlier poem may have the metaphorical sense of "censurar, notar, ò mormurar" (the sixth definition in the 1739 edition of the *Diccionario de autoridades*), but to which the later poet gives the sense of grasping ("prender, agarrar, ò asir").

74 Severin is elaborating on Beltran's observation that the poet of the "Gozos" insists on his own exemplarity as lover despite his failure to achieve the joys he enumerates

(Beltran, "Los *Gozos*" 93), although it is worth recalling here that courtly love is paradigmatically frustrated.

75 ID0017; this song is found in the *Cancionero de Estúñiga* (the version here transcribed) and *de Roma*, among others.

76 Beltran notes that lover's wills such as this have medieval Latin antecedents and that the *Cancionero de Baena* includes earlier examples by the Arcediano de Toro and Villasandino ("El *Testamento*" 66–8).

77 This reference to the archbishop of Lisbon allows Vicenç Beltran to date this poem and identify its author. The archbishop referred to is Pedro de Noroña, archbishop from 1423 to 1452, who was exiled along with Leonor of Aragon from 1440 to 1442 (Beltran, "El *Testamento*" 69); this latter date range, during which the *Testamento* was composed, permits the identification of the poem's author with an "Alfonso Enrriques" mentioned in the *Crónica del Halconero* as a partisan of the infantes of Aragon defeated by the maestre de Alcántara in 1441 (70).

78 ID2519.

79 Montoro may not have attributed "Pues me falleçió ventura" to Macías, although, as noted earlier, that attribution is found in this same songbook.

80 The *Pasión trobada* was likely the earliest of San Pedro's works and remained the most popular Castilian text of its kind into the nineteenth century (San Pedro, *Obras completas, III* 10–15). As Severin has noted, although there is a "Sepultura de Macías" attributed to Diego de San Pedro in SA10b, its earlier attribution to the more obscure Juan de San Pedro in PN6 is likelier to be correct ("The *Sepultura*" 306).

81 The reign of Isabel I has also been characterized as a period of increased decorum and orthodoxy, hostile to the "exaggerations" of the *religio amoris* in the preceding decades (Rodríguez-Puértolas 29–30).

82 "Aquella gran conpasión,/ aquel amor entrañal/ que por nuestra salvaçión/ hizo sofrir tal passión/ a tu fijo natural" (Mendoza, 1–2).

6 The Impasse of the Courtly Reward

1 For those interested in the broader debate surrounding sentimental fiction, a good starting point is Whinnom's *The Spanish Sentimental Romance, 1440–1550: A Critical Bibliography*, since it establishes a canon of twenty-one works belonging to the genre (of which *Siervo* is the first and *Sátira de infelice e felice vida* by Pedro, Constable of Portugal, discussed later, is the third, chronologically). A good recent summary of the debate can be found in Cortijo Ocaña, *La evolución genérica* 7–18. Other important contributions to the debate are Brandenberger, Blay, the essays collected in Gwara and Gerli's *Studies on the Spanish Sentimental Romance*, Rohland de Langbehn (*La unidad genérica*), Deyermond (*Tradiciones*), and recent special issues of *La corónica* (29.1) and *Ínsula* (651).

2 Deyermond also lists the four main sources of the genre: books of chivalry, Italian fiction (especially Boccaccio's *Fiammetta*), Ovid's *Heroides*, and *cancionero* poetry (*Tradiciones* 49).

3 In this sense, Gerli's article is also an entry in the debate on the modernity ("proto-humanism") or atavism (aristocratic clinging to fading social structures) of courtly culture in fifteenth-century Castile.

4 This collectivity is particularly evident in their frequent recourse to internal, allegorized debate: "If the subject position is extended, by allegory, into a 'self' where Love and other forces interact, then the boundaries of this 'self,' and its relationship to other selves, are fundamentally unclear. Since the notion of the 'self' is obscure, the relationship to it of the first-person subject is likewise problematic" (Kay, *Subjectivity* 55). Recently, Ricardo Matthews has made the inverse argument, namely, that "by narrating each song's fictional circumstances, the prosimetrum undermines any idea of song's fundamental anonymity and autonomy" (302). Matthews moves on, however, to frame the *prosimetrum*'s confrontation between prose and lyric more dialectically: "Song's conventionality enters into the contingencies of historical time while narrative's gallop is halted by reflective moments of individual self-expression" (303).

5 As Brownlee notes, the titles of the three first works of sentimental fiction, *Siervo libre de amor*, *Sátira de infelice e felice vida*, and *Triste deleytaçion*, are all paradoxical (13).

6 I cite Enric Dolz's critical edition of the text (Rodríguez del Padrón, *Siervo*); here, 10.

7 The path of neither loving nor being loved, that is, of "la vida contemplativa de no amar," is also identified with Minerva (Rodríguez del Padrón, *Siervo* 19); as Emily C. Francomano notes, Synderesis and Minerva were but two of a "familiar cadre of metonymically related and specifically feminine tropes representative of man's higher intellectual faculties and the knowledge those faculties may attain and retain" (1). In early sentimental fiction, these feminine allegories of wisdom were central not just to the portrayal of masculine intellect but to an ambivalent idealization of the beloved whose other side, as we will see, was an unfeeling cruelty.

8 On this debate, see Folger, *Images in Mind* 108–10.

9 Whether the same applies to personifications of virtues (and vices) that are not psychological faculties – such as Pity, who spars with the narrator of the *Sátira* (see later discussion) – remains to be seen.

10 See Herrero 752 for a similar conclusion.

11 Cartagena's explanation rests on the double meaning of *piedad* in Castilian, which must be rendered with two different words ("piety" and "pity") in English.

12 Padilla's song (ID0577) is part of a debate with Sarnés.

13 Rubrics such as "Fabla el autor" (Rodríguez del Padrón, *Siervo* 28) indicate (perhaps erroneously) that the author is recounting the story, but the narration itself remains in the third person.

14 Folger, noting Ardanlier's acceptance of the key and later admission, after Liessa's death, of his love for Irena ("siempre ardí en intrínseco amor de ti"), argues that it is the contrast between frustrated (Irena) and consummated or mixed (Liessa) love that makes the *Estoria* exemplary for the author (*Images in Mind* 120–1).

15 The rhetorical manipulation of popular sayings would become central in Rojas's *Celestina*, in which, as Theodore L. Kassier has argued, many conventions of troubadour lyric are satirized or otherwise condemned through a process of "literalization" in narrative (19–20).

16 This inversion can be fruitfully compared to the moment in Rojas's *Celestina* when the titular character, bragging of her ability as a go-between and expecting to please her client, describes Melibea as Calisto's servant ("más está a tu mandado y querer que de su padre Pleberio"). Calisto, alarmed, reminds her that she has overstepped the limits of courtly discourse: "Habla cortés, madre; no digas tal cosa … Melibea es mi señora, Melibea es mi Dios, Melibea es mi vida; yo su cativo, yo su siervo" (460).

17 The idea that synderesis might help achieve psychic balance rather than reason's triumph distances the text from Aquinas's notion of the virtuous will, which drew on an Aristotelian ethics according to which "internal division is a condition human beings can and should overcome" (B. Kent 204).

18 On the *Sátira*'s date of composition, see Gascón Vera 75; I will refer to Pedro throughout as either "Don Pedro" or "the Constable" in order to distinguish him from his namesake father. On the *Sátira*'s debt to the *Siervo*, see also Castro Lingl, who argues that Don Pedro "wished to use his text as a form of criticism of the ambiguity of certain parts of *Siervo*" (78).

19 In "A New Reading of *Sátira de infelice e felice vida* by Don Pedro, Constable of Portugal," Ana M. Montero also notes the thematic dominance of cruelty in the *Sátira* (107), demonstrating conclusively the influence of Seneca's *De clementia* on Don Pedro; I take up some of her arguments later.

20 This theory and the biographical details that follow are drawn from Gascón Vera 7–32; for a full biography, see Adão da Fonseca, *O Condestável*.

21 In fact, despite Don Pedro's own literary activity, he is still perhaps best known as the recipient of Santillana's *Prohemio*.

22 The war would end with John II's victory in 1472, although many of the underlying conflicts between the crown and other foci of institutional power would persist. For a complete historical account, see Sobrequés Vidal and Sobrequés i Callicó, and Ryder.

23 I reserve uppercase letters for concepts and faculties that are explicitly personified in the text.

24 He experiences this dilemma, even though, as Ana M. Montero notes, he claims to have accepted love servitude out of his own free will and not in expectation of a reward ("A New Reading" 111).

25 On the ambiguous relationship of the *Sátira*'s glosses to medieval notions of *auctoritas*, see Agnew.

26 Santillana offers a similar definition in a letter to the noblewoman Violante de Prades accompanying some of his poetic works: "satire" is "aquella manera de fablar que tovo un poeta que se llamó Sátiro, el qual *reprehendió* muy mucho los viçios e loó las virtudes" (*Poesías completas* 639; emphasis added; "the manner of speaking of a poet named Sátiro, who *condemned* mightily the vices and praised the virtues").

27 For a survey of these debates in the Castilian *cancionero* tradition, see Green 83–91.

28 For the *colores grammatici* and *colores rhetoricae*, see Murphy 20n38 and 189–90.
29 As Julian Weiss notes, Don Pedro's enthusiasm for the autonomous literary potential of the gloss stands in contrast to the restrained approach of Santillana's *Proverbios* ("*Fermosas e peregrinas*" 104–8).
30 Don Pedro makes a similar claim about the necessity of the work as a whole in his gloss on Luçio Sila: "Lo fago mas como cosa neçessaria que voluntaria" (*Sátira* 30).
31 The understanding's exasperation is almost certainly an echo of *Siervo*.
32 It is useful to recall here Pedro's pronouncement in the *LVB* that those who have compassion for their own suffering are not to be called *piedoso* (Pedro and Verba 41).
33 In a sixteenth-century coda to this image of impassible virtue, Juan Luis Vives would violently condemn the Stoics, and Cicero and Seneca in particular, for their views on pity, arguing that "nothing is more human than to sympathize with those who suffer" and concluding: "But let us forget the Stoics, who through pedantic cavils tried without success to convert their human natures into stones" (46–7).
34 Montero notes that the "unrestrained brutality" recounted in a series of glosses on historical and biblical figures both explains the extremity of the lover's suffering ("A New Reading" 109) and extends the work's commentary on cruelty into "the unexpected field of political ethics" (116).
35 For a helpful biographical sketch of Doña Isabel that also articulates the political situation of the family from the regency of the Infante Pedro to Isabel's death, see Montero, "Durmiendo" 178–84.
36 The letter's editors note that Santillana draws these definitions from Benvenuto Rambaldi da Imola's commentary on the first seven cantos of Dante's *Inferno* (Santillana 637n4). Santillana was joined by writers such as Juan de Mena and Enrique de Villena in these understandings of satire and tragedy (Gascón Vera 145).
37 In her introduction to the *Tragédia*, Carolina Michaëlis de Vasconcelos notes that "*Auto-Consolatória*" would have been another appropriate name for the work (Pedro, *Tragédia* 22). In a recent groundbreaking study, Sol Miguel-Prendes argues for a new interpretation of the genre of sentimental fiction, emphasizing the influence of Christian penitential works and delineating two dominant groups of texts: "moral consolations and their sentimental distortions" (*Narrating Desire* 27). In what follows, drawing on Don Pedro's use of the term, I emphasize what might be termed "vulgar," emotional rather than generic consolation.
38 As Montero shows, the praise of Isabel in the *Tragédia* is significantly less ambiguous than in the *Sátira* ("Durmiendo" 197–8).

7 Confession, Consolation, and the Poetics of Hylomorphism

1 A recent critical consensus considers the last of these poems to be apocryphal (*Història* 359).
2 It thus differs from, for example, the allegorized death of Belh Deport in the songs of Guiraut Riquier (fl. 1254–90; on Belh Deport's death as an element of Riquier's self-presentation, see Holmes 111–12).

3 In what follows, I draw principally on Lluís Cabré's biographical sketch in the *Història de la literatura catalana* (353–9), which contains ample bibliographic references for a deeper exploration of March's life.
4 This division first appeared in the first edition of March's poems, published by Baltasar Romaní in Valencia in 1539. On the editorial shaping of March according to Petrarchan models in the sixteenth century, see Lloret 157–209.
5 For a recent synthesis of the transmission and order of March's poems, see *Història* 359–65. My argument does not depend on a chronological development of ideas in March's poetry, but rather draws on themes that arise repeatedly, in varied guises, throughout the poems. For a brief history of the publication, translation, and reception of March's poetry, see Fuster, *Ausiàs March* 44–52.
6 On the influence of Ovid, see Cabré et al. 98–104; the other influences will be discussed later in this chapter, with relevant bibliographical references.
7 All quotations of March's poems are from Pere Bohigas's edition (A. March, *Poesies*), which follows Pagès's ordering.
8 All translations of March's poems are by Arthur Terry (A. March, *Ausias March: Selected Poems*).
9 On the first point, see Archer, *Pervasive Image* 2; Archer notes that it is not a question of absolute difference, but of degree. For the "modernity" of March's introspection, see Bohigas's and Terry's remarks in A. March, *Poesies* 33 and *Selected Poems* 20, respectively.
10 Recently, without denying March's towering reputation among his contemporaries, critics have situated his use of Catalan within a broader process of cultural and linguistic transformation that includes some poets older than March himself; this process is associated with the court of Alfonso V between his two trips to Naples and became dominant through March's prestige (*Història* 269–72). For a contrasting view on the utility of sincerity as a critical concept, see Zimmermann, "Metàfora" 123–4.
11 I adopt here Sarah Kay's neutral conception of lyric subjectivity as "the elaboration of a first-person (subject) position" (*Subjectivity* 1).
12 "Habit" ("l'àbit") here also conveys the sense of custom.
13 On the rejection of Neoplatonism in March, see Lledó-Guillem.
14 *Recta ratio* is associated in scholastic ethics with both synderesis and the intellectual virtue of prudence (Johnston 384).
15 March's most famous explication of this system is found in poem LXXXVII (discussed in part one), although there he uses different terminology: spiritual love is *honest*, carnal love is *delitable*, and mixed love is *profitable*.
16 On the first point, see Archer ("Theorist of Love" 4); Fuster (*Ausiàs March* 96); and Terry (A. March, *Selected Poems* 14). On the second, see Cocozzella ("Ausiàs March's *Imitatio Christi*" 428–9).
17 Arthur Terry notes, however, that, despite their apparent rigidity, the moral vocabularies of scholasticism and *fin'amor* are in practice almost infinitely flexible ("Introspection" 169–70). For a brief overview of Aristotelian thought in medieval Aragon, see L. Cabré, "Aristotle" 50–3.

18 The authors most commonly cited as philosophical sources for March are Aquinas, Aristotle, Ramon Llull, Seneca, and Augustine; Dante and Petrarch are also named with some frequency. For a critical appraisal of the literature on these sources in March, see Archer (*Pervasive Image* 11–20). The critical tendency is to downplay Italian influence; see, for example, Bohigas (A. March, *Poesies* 28) and Fuster (*Ausiàs March* 15–17), although both critics do admit certain similarities.

19 In an important article, Antoni M. Espadaler argues that the reference to "trobadors" in XXIII.1 is to other contemporary poets whose desire is fired by Teresa, not to the troubadours of the past (125). The poem would thus belong to the genre of "elogi cortesà," in which poets praise the physical and spiritual qualities of their ladies; March's distinction would lie not in his lack of "escalf," but in the object of his praise, the harmony in which Teresa surpasses Venetian government (125). Espadaler suggests that March's other references to the troubadours (in poems LV, LXXXVII, and XCI) are less combative and portray the troubadours as superficial rather than excessively heated, but I do not think that is the case in LXXXVII, where, as we have seen, March describes the troubadours as excessively tied to the sensual appetite (lines 43–4), an accusation perfectly coherent with poem XXIII's *escalf.* I am also unconvinced that March's use of the present tense (*trespassen*) here in connection with the troubadours, but the past tense in poems LV and XCI, implies that March refers here strictly to his contemporaries (Espadaler 124–5). Espadaler does not take into consideration that disavowals such as March's were a troubadour commonplace, although this omission in no way undermines his subsequent argument that poem XXIII is based on the conversion of Teresa into an image, which is then described (127).

20 See, for example, Sobrer, *Doble soledat* 22.

21 D. Gareth Walters notes the tension between the expectation of dispassionate realism created by the poem's opening lines and the need for "visionary, even mysterious, perception" expressed at the end of the stanza (46).

22 In medieval Catalan, *gest* could refer to a body's movement, attitudinal disposition, and appearance (Faraudo, "Gest," def. 1 and 2; *DCVB*, def. 1.1–2).

23 On the question of disorder in poem X, see Rubio, "Les tres potències" 167.

24 For a survey of March's invocations of his own silence, see Sobrer, *Doble soledat* 11–40.

25 I am grateful to Reader 1, who prompted me to think through this conventional aspect of the *envoi.*

26 This poem thus finds echoes in Macías's "Cativo de miña tristura" and Rodríguez del Padrón's "¡Ham, ham, huíd que ravio!" both of which contrast the articulateness of lyric with the silence or raving of the suffering lover.

27 On the Ovidian origins of this passage, see Torró, "Ausiàs March no va viure" 192–6.

28 The clearest example is Rodríguez del Padrón's "Sólo por ver a Macías," where the beloved's reaction to the poet's imagined death is framed as a question; the almost sacrilegious understatement of March's "part veur·a Ell" (line 34; "apart from seeing Him"), furthermore, recalls Rodríguez del Padrón's initial wish to die "sólo por ver a Macías" rather, it is implied, than the face of God.

29 See, for example, Ramírez i Molas, *La poesia* 296. For a contrasting view, see Terry, "'Per la mort'" 231.

30 Rubio calls this state the "tragic" memory of the *cants de mort* ("De Llull a March" 121), arguing elsewhere for an exact equation between memory and grief in this series of poems ("Les tres potències" 158). As this poem in particular shows, however, March's grief is inadequate, in his own estimation, to the tragic memory of his lady's life and death. Because the consolatory genre was aimed at curtailing mourning, whereas for March memory is preserved through grief, Archer views this poem as a rejection of consolation as such ("Against Consolation" 149–50).

31 More broadly, Cocozzella sees in all of March's poetry the intuition that "the symbiosis between the human and the divine is effected, metaphysically, through the mediacy of suffering," allowing erotic love to be perfected, through the human lover's *imitatio Christi*, into a kind of *agape* ("Ausiàs March's *Imitatio*" 433).

Conclusion: Tragic Enclosure

1 On this debate, see Weiss, "Álvaro de Luna" and "¿Qué demandamos?" The latter article includes a helpful bibliography of primary texts (275–81). In "Álvaro de Luna," Weiss lays bare how a debate ostensibly about female virtue and vice was in fact a proving ground for the public display of a violent masculine identity. On developments in this debate toward the close of the fifteenth century, see Weissberger, "Deceitful Sects."

2 On these genres as the background for Torroella's *Maldezir*, see Archer, *Problem of Woman* 178–82. Ausiàs March also composed a *maldit*, poem XLII, in which he scandalously named the target of his invective; on this poem, see Archer, "Tradition," and on March's attitude toward women as expressed more broadly throughout his poetry, see Coderch, especially 177–226.

3 On Corella's sources, see Carbonell's introduction to Roís de Corella, *Obres completes I* 26; and Cabré et al. 83. Among medieval writers in the vernacular, Boccaccio seems to have been Corella's most significant influence (Cabré et al. 110–16).

4 On the life and works of Icard, see *Història* 316–24. Molas believes the *Consolació* dates from 1409–10 (132).

5 Fenollar and Escrivà also composed together a *Contemplació a Jesús crucificat*, preserved in the *Jardinet d'orats*.

6 I will cite Marinela Garcia Sempere's edition of *Lo passi* (Fenollar, Escrivà, and Roís de Corella, *Lo passi en cobles*).

7 "De grans passions és tota brodada/ la greu Passió que vós comportàs" (lines 4053–4; "The grave Passion that you bore is embroidered with great passions").

8 As Garcia Sempere notes (357–8, n324), this metaphor is found in Bonaventure's *Officium de Passione domini* and has its roots in Augustine's homilies and Isidore's *Etymologies*; the seven strings of the ancient zither were said to coincide with the seven words Christ spoke on the cross.

9 Mary's admission that she may not die of grief recalls both the conclusion of Ausiàs March's poem XCVII (see chapter seven) and Pleberio's final lament in *Celestina*,

in which he berates his own "hard heart" for not breaking at the sight of his dead daughter (Rojas 609).

10 On the scholarly debate surrounding Leriano's *imitatio Christi*, see Miguel-Prendes, "Reimagining" 12 and 12n12; this article gives a compelling account of *Cárcel de amor* as a product of, and object for, medieval contemplative practices.

11 As José Francisco Ruiz Casanova notes in his edition of *Cárcel*, Leriano does incorporate lines 64–5 of San Pedro's "Dama que mi muerte guía," as prose, into a letter to Laureola (San Pedro, *Cárcel* 88n48).

12 I will cite Jordi Carbonell's edition of the *Tragèdia* and Corella's secular lyric (Roís de Corella, *Obres completes I*) throughout the chapter, and I will cite Peter Cocozzella's English translation of the *Tragèdia* (*Text, Translation*). Lyric translations are my own.

13 Rosanna Cantavella describes the *Tragèdia*'s rhetoric as "hyperbolic" ("On the Sources" 76), and Francisco Rico has noted the bombastic nature ("ampulosidad") of vernacular translations of classical material such as those in the *Parlament* ("Imágenes" 16–17). On rhetorical ties between Corella's secular and religious works, see Garcia Sempere 177–9.

14 According to the *DCVB*, *transpostació* derives from the antiquated *transpostar*, that is, to transfer or simply move. The verb "transpostava" appears in the version of the *Tragèdia* found in the *Jardinet d'orats*; the version in ms. R 2804 of the Biblioteca Universitaria de València reads "deixà." The *Jardinet*'s version seems to be the first redaction (Rico, "Imágenes" 22), a fact coherent with my view that Corella in the *Tragèdia* affirms the impossibility of *transpostació*, leading to an abandonment of the concept in later works such as the *Oració*.

15 See Badia, "Ficció" 89–90; Annicchiarico 78n51; and Cantavella, "Aspectes" 305–6.

16 For the former, see Fuster, "Lectura" 306 and Cingolani 95; for the latter, see Cocozzella, *Text* 53.

17 It is also worth noting the ambiguity of "coneixença" in this passage, which allows for both intellectual and physical interpretations that would correspond, respectively, to Caldesa's "volentat" and "persona."

18 Badia includes the *Jardí* among Corella's "amatory parables," which constitute "an extensive reflection taken from the teachings of antiquity about the disasters that result from love-passion [*l'amor-passió*]" (*De Bernat Metge* 171).

19 Riquer argues that it is unlikely that this change is an error, given the presence of the word *puer* in Ovid's text (307).

20 Cf. Riquer 287–90.

21 Romeu i Figueras argues that the distinction between honest and dishonest love is central to Corella's moralism (300), drawing attention to this definition of honesty as a "cruel virtue" (307).

22 On the impossibility of this desire, see Terry, *Three* 54.

23 Cf. Badia, "Ficció" 82.

24 *Pietat* here thus recalls the sense of fellow-feeling described by Madrigal and Cartagena.

Works Cited

Adams, Kenneth. "'Plógome otrosí oír muchas vegadas libros de devaneos': Did Pero López de Ayala Know the *Libro de buen amor*?" *Essays on Hispanic Themes in Honour of Edward C. Riley*. Ed. Jennifer Lowe and Philip Swanson. Edinburgh: Dept. of Hispanic Studies, U of Edinburgh, 1989. 9–40.

Adão da Fonseca, Luís. *O Condestável D. Pedro de Portugal*. Porto: Instituto Nacional de Investigação Científica, Centro de História da U do Porto, 1982.

Aelred of Rielvaux. *Spiritual Friendship*. Ed. Marsha L. Dutton. Trans. Lawrence C. Braceland. Collegeville, MN: Liturgical Press, 2010.

Aers, David. "A Whisper in the Ear of Early Modernists; or, Reflections on Literary Critics Writing the 'History of the Subject.'" *Culture and History, 1350–1600: Essays on English Communities, Identities, and Writing*. Ed. David Aers. Detroit: Wayne State UP, 1992. 177–202.

Agamben, Giorgio. *Stanzas: Word and Phantasm in Western Culture*. Trans. Ronald L. Martinez. Minneapolis: U of Minnesota P, 1993.

Agnew, Michael. "The 'Comedieta' of the *Sátira*: Dom Pedro de Portugal's Monkeys in the Margins." *Modern Language Notes* 118 (2003): 298–317.

Alcover i Sureda, Antoni Maria, and Francesc de Borja Moll. *Diccionari català-valencià-balear* (*DCVB*). Institut d'Estudis Catalans and Institució Francesc de Borja Moll. https://dcvb.iec.cat/.

Alegre, Francesc. *Obres de ficció sentimental*. Ed. Gemma Pellissa Prades. Alessandria: Edizioni dell'Orso, 2016.

Alemany, Rafael. "Ausiàs March i el context literari valencià del segle XV." *Ausiàs March (1400–1459): Premier poète en langue catalane*. Ed. Georges Martin and Marie-Claire Zimmermann. Paris: Séminaire d'études médiévales hispaniques de l'université Paris 13, 2000. 7–26.

Alfonso X. *Las Siete Partidas*. Madrid: Real Academia de la Historia, 1807.

Álvarez Palenzuela, Vicente Ángel. "Expansión de las órdenes monásticas en España durante la Edad Media." *III Semana de Estudios Medievales: Nájera, 3 al 7 de agosto de 1992*. Ed. José Ignacio de la Iglesia Duarte. Logroño: Gobierno de la Rioja, Instituto de Estudios Riojanos, 1993. 161–78.

Annicchiarico, Annamaria. "Perché 'tragedia'?: il gioco delle 'ambiguità' nella *Tragèdia di Caldesa* di Joan Roís de Corella." *Boletín de la Real Academia de Buenas Letras de Barcelona* 43 (1991–92): 59–79.

Antunes, Alfredo. *Saudade e Profetismo em Fernando Pessoa: Elementos para uma Antropologia Filosófica.* Braga: Publicações da Faculdade de Filosofia, 1983.

Archer, Robert. "Against Consolation: Ausiàs March's Sixth Death-Song." *Mediaevalia* 22, Special Issue (2000): 145–55.

– "Ausiàs March as a Theorist of Love." *The Discerning Eye: Studies Presented to Robert Pring-Mill on His Seventieth Birthday.* Ed. Nigel Griffin et al. Llangrannog: Dolphin Book, 1994. 3–15.

– *The Pervasive Image: The Role of Analogy in the Poetry of Ausiàs March.* Amsterdam: John Benjamins, 1985.

– *The Problem of Woman in Late-Medieval Hispanic Literature.* Woodbridge: Tamesis, 2005.

– "Tradition, Genre, Ethics, and Politics in Ausiàs March's *maldit.*" *Bulletin of Hispanic Studies* 68.3 (1991): 371–82.

Aristotle. *De Anima (On the Soul).* Trans. and ed. Hugh Lawson-Tancred. London: Penguin, 1986.

– *Nicomachean Ethics.* Trans. Martin Ostwald. Englewood Cliffs, NJ: Prentice-Hall, 1962.

– *Politics.* Trans. Ernest Barker. Oxford: Oxford UP, 1995.

– *Rhetoric.* Trans. W. Rhys Roberts. *The* Rhetoric *and* Poetics *of Aristotle.* Ed. Edward P.J. Corbett. New York: Modern Library, 1984. 3–218.

Asensio, Eugenio. *Poética y realidad en el cancionero peninsular de la Edad Media.* 2nd ed. Madrid: Gredos, 1970.

Auerbach, Erich. "*Passio* as Passion." Trans. Martin Elsky. *Criticism* 43.4 (2001): 288–308.

Augustine. *De catechizandis rudibus.* Ed. H. Hurter. London: David Nutt, 1895.

– *Confessions.* Trans. Henry Chadwick. Oxford: Oxford UP, 2008.

– *Confessions.* Vol. 1. Trans. William Watts. Loeb Classical Library 026. London: William Heinemann, 1912.

– *The First Catechetical Instruction.* Trans. Joseph P. Christopher. Westminster, MD: Newman Bookshop, 1946.

– *On Christian Doctrine.* Trans. J.F. Shaw. Mineola, NY: Dover, 2009.

– *The Trinity.* Trans. Edmund Hill, O.P. Hyde Park, NY: New City Press, 1991.

Avenoza, Gemma. "Poetas catalanes del XV y trovadores. Pere Torroella y el *Perilhos tractat.*" *Scène, évolution, sort de la langue et de la littérature d'oc: actes du septième Congrès international de l'Association internationale d'études occitanes, Reggio Calabria-Messina, 7–13 juillet 2002.* Ed. Rossana Castano, Saverio Guida, and Fortunata Latella. Rome: Viella, 2003. 25–40.

Badia, Lola. *De Bernat Metge a Joan Rois de Corella: Estudis sobre la cultura literària de la tardor medieval catalana.* Barcelona: Quaderns Crema, 1988.

– "Ficció autobiogràfica i experiència lírica a la *Tragèdia de Caldesa*, de Joan Roís de Corella." *Homenaje al profesor Antonio Vilanova.* Ed. Antonio Vilanova, Adolfo Sotelo Vázquez, and Marta Cristina Carbonell. Vol. 1. Barcelona: Departamento de Filología

Española, Facultad de Filología, División de Ciencias Humanas y Sociales, Universidad de Barcelona, 1989. 75–93.
Balibar, Étienne, Barbara Cassin, and Alain de Libera. "Subject." *Dictionary of Untranslatables: A Philosophical Lexicon*. Ed. Barbara Cassin. Trans. Steven Rendall et al. Trans. ed. Emily Apter, Jacques Lezra, and Michael Wood. Princeton, NJ: Princeton UP, 2014. 1069–91.
Baraz, Daniel. *Medieval Cruelty: Changing Perceptions, Late Antiquity to the Early Modern Period*. Ithaca, NY: Cornell UP, 2003.
Belloso Martín, Nuria. *Política y humanismo en el siglo XV: el maestro Alfonso de Madrigal, el Tostado*. Valladolid: U de Valladolid Secretariado de Publicaciones, 1989.
Beltran, Vicenç. *La canción de amor en el otoño de la Edad Media*. Barcelona: PPU, 1988.
– "La *cantiga* de Alfonso XI y la ruptura poética del siglo XIV." *El Crotalón: anuario de filología española* 2 (1985): 259–73.
– *La corte de Babel: Lenguas, poética y política en la España del siglo XIII*. Madrid: Gredos, 2005.
– "La encrucijada de Santillana." *Comedieta de Ponza, sonetos, serranillas y otras obras*. Ed. Regula Rohland de Langbehn. Barcelona: Crítica, 1997. IX–XXX.
– "Los *Gozos de amor* de Juan Rodríguez del Padrón: edición crítica." *Studia in Honorem Germán Orduna*. Ed. Leonardo Funes and José Luis Moure. Alcalá de Henares: U de Alcalá, 2001. 91–109.
– "El *Testamento* de Alfonso Enríquez." *Convergences médiévales: épopée, lyrique, roman: mélanges offerts à Madeleine Tyssens*. Ed. Nadine Henrard, Paola Moreno, and M. Thiry-Stassin. Brussels: De Boeck U, 2001. 63–76.
Benedict. *The Rule of Benedict*. Trans. Carolinne White. London: Penguin, 2008.
Berlant, Lauren. "Introduction: Compassion (and Withholding)." *Compassion: The Culture and Politics of an Emotion*. Ed. Lauren Berlant. New York: Routledge, 2004. 1–13.
Berlin, Henry. "The Willing Reader of Duarte's *Leal conselheiro*." *Journal of Medieval Iberian Studies* 5.2 (2013): 204–19.
Bernard of Clairvaux. "On Conversion." *Selected Works*. Trans. G.R. Evans. New York: Paulist Press, 1987. 65–97.
– "On the Steps of Humility and Pride." *Selected Works*. Trans. G.R. Evans. New York: Paulist Press, 1987. 99–143.
Bestul, Thomas H. *Texts of the Passion: Latin Devotional Literature and Medieval Society*. Philadelphia: U of Pennsylvania P, 1996.
Biblia medieval romanceada. Ed. Américo Castro, Agustín Millares Carlo, and Ángel J. Battistessa. Buenos Aires: Facultad de Filosofía y Letras, 1927.
Bishko, Charles Julian. *Spanish and Portuguese Monastic History, 600–1300*. London: Variorum Reprints, 1984.
Blackmore, Josiah. "*Afeiçom* and History-Writing: The Prologue of the *Crónica de D. João I*." *Luso-Brazilian Review* 34.2 (1997): 15–24.
– "Melancholy, Passionate Love, and the *Coita d'Amor*." *PMLA* 124.2 (2009): 640–46.

– *Moorings: Portuguese Expansion and the Writing of Africa*. Minneapolis: U of Minnesota P, 2009.

Blay, Vicenta. "La conciencia genérica en la ficción sentimental (planteamiento de una problemática)." *Historias y ficciones: Coloquio sobre la literatura del siglo XV*. Ed. Rafael Beltrán Llavador, José Luis Canet Vallés, and Josep Lluís Sirera. Valencia: U de València, Departament de Filologia Espanyola, 1990. 205–26.

Blowers, Paul M. "Pity, Empathy, and the Tragic Spectacle of Human Suffering: Exploring the Emotional Culture of Compassion in Late Ancient Christianity." *Journal of Early Christian Studies* 18.1 (2010): 1–27.

Blüher, Karl Alfred. *Séneca en España: Investigaciones sobre la recepción de Séneca en España desde el siglo XIII hasta el siglo XVII*. Trans. Juan Conde. Madrid: Gredos, 1983.

Boase, Roger. *The Troubadour Revival: A Study of Social Change and Traditionalism in Late Medieval Spain*. London: Routledge & Kegan Paul, 1978.

Boquet, Damien, and Piroska Nagy. "Medieval Sciences of Emotions during the Eleventh to Thirteenth Centuries: An Intellectual History." *Osiris* 31.1 (2016): 21–45.

Bordelois, Ivonne. *Etimología de las pasiones*. Buenos Aires: Libros del Zorzal, 2006.

Botelho, Afonso. *Da Saudade ao Saudosismo*. Lisbon: Instituto de Cultura e Língua Portuguesa, 1990.

Brandenberger, Tobias. "La genericidad de la ficción sentimental." *Actas del IX Congreso Internacional de la Asociación Hispánica de Literatura Medieval (A Coruña, 18–22 de septiembre de 2001)*. Ed. Mercedes Pampín Barral and M. Carmen Parrilla García. 2 vols. A Coruña: U da Coruña, Departamento de Filoloxía Española e Latina, 2005. 527–41.

Brown, Catherine. *Contrary Things: Exegesis, Dialectic, and the Poetics of Didacticism*. Stanford: Stanford UP, 1998.

Brownlee, Marina Scordilis. *The Severed Word: Ovid's* Heroides *and the* Novela Sentimental. Princeton, NJ: Princeton UP, 1990.

Burrus, Virginia, and Karmen MacKendrick. "Bodies without Wholes: Apophatic Excess and Fragmentation in Augustine's *City of God*." *Apophatic Bodies: Negative Theology, Incarnation, and Relationality*. Ed. Chris Boesel and Catherine Keller. New York: Fordham UP, 2010. 79–93.

Burton-Christie, Douglas. *The Word in the Desert: Scripture and the Quest for Holiness in Early Christian Monasticism*. Oxford: Oxford UP, 1993.

Bynum, Caroline Walker. *The Resurrection of the Body in Western Christianity, 200–1336*. New York: Columbia UP, 1995.

Cabré, Lluís. "Aristotle for the Layman: Sense Perception in the Poetry of Ausiàs March." *Journal of the Warburg and Courtauld Institutes* 59 (1996): 48–60.

– "Dos lectors antics del mestre Ausiàs March i un context." *Ausiàs March: textos I contextos*. Ed. Rafael Alemany Ferrer. Alacant and Barcelona: Institut Interuniversitari de Filologia Valenciana and Publicacions de l'Abadia de Montserrat, 1997. 59–71.

– "Notas sobre la memoria de Santillana y los poetas de la Corona de Aragón." *Cancionero Studies in Honour of Ian Macpherson*. Ed. Alan Deyermond. London: Queen Mary and Westfield College, 1998. 25–38.

Cabré, Lluís, et al. *The Classical Tradition in Medieval Catalan, 1300–1500: Translation, Imitation, and Literacy*. Woodbridge: Tamesis, 2018.

Cabré, Miriam. "Italian and Catalan Troubadours." *The Troubadours: An Introduction*. Ed. Simon Gaunt and Sarah Kay. Cambridge: Cambridge UP, 1999. 127–40.

Camille, Michael. "Mimetic Identification and Passion Devotion in the Later Middle Ages: A Double-Sided Panel by Meister Francke." *The Broken Body: Passion Devotion in Late-Medieval Culture*. Ed. A.A. Macdonald, H.N.B. Ridderbos, and R.M. Schlusemann. Groningen: Egbert Forsten, 1998. 183–210.

Canals, Antoni. *Scipió e Aníbal. De providència (de Sèneca). De arra de ànima (d'Hug de Sant Víctor)*. Ed. Martí de Riquer. Barcelona: Barcino, 1988.

Cancionero de Estúñiga. Ed. Manuel Alvar and Elena Alvar. Zaragoza: Institución "Fernando el Católico," 1981.

Cancionero de Herberay [*Le chansonnier espagnol d'Herberay des Essarts (XVe siècle)*]. Ed. Charles V. Aubrun. Bordeaux: Féret et Fils, 1951.

Cancionero de Juan Alfonso de Baena. Ed. José María Azáceta. 3 vols. Madrid: CSIC, 1966.

Cancionero de Palacio: Ms. 2653, Biblioteca Universitaria de Salamanca. Ed. Ana María Álvarez Pellitero. Valladolid: Junta de Castilla y León, 1993.

Cañigueral Batllosera, Pau. "La sentimentalització de Dante a la poesia cortesana del segle XV: La *Glòria d'amor* de fra Bernat Hug de Rocabertí i l'*Infierno de los enamorados* del marquès de Santillana." *La corónica* 45.1 (2016): 9–36.

Cantavella, Rosanna. "Aspectes argumentals de la *Tragèdia de Caldesa*." *Ausiàs March i el món cultural del segle XV*. Ed. Rafael Alemany Ferrer. Alacant: U d'Alacant, Institut Universitari de Filologia Valenciana, 1999. 299–318.

– "Del *Perilhos tractat* al *Conhort* de Francesc Ferrer." *Actes del Vuitè Col·loqui Internacional de Llengua i Literatura Catalanes, Tolosa de Llenguadoc, 12–17 de setembre de 1988*. Ed. Antoni M. Badia i Margarit and Michel Camprubí. Vol. 1. Barcelona: Associació Internacional de Llengua i Literatura Catalanes, 1989. 449–58.

– "On the Sources of the Plot of Corella's *Tragèdia de Caldesa*." *The Medieval Mind: Hispanic Studies in Honour of Alan Deyermond*. Ed. Ian Macpherson and Ralph Penny. Woodbridge: Tamesis, 1997. 75–90.

Cantigas medievais galego-portuguesas: Corpus *integral profano*. Ed. Graça Videira Lopes. 2 vols. Lisbon: Biblioteca Nacional de Portugal, Instituto de Estudos Medievais, and Centro de Estudos de Sociologia e Estética Musical, 2016.

Caravaggi, Giovanni. "La canzone con 'refranes' di Francisco Bocanegra e un fenomeno romanzo d'intertestualità poetica." *Studi di cultura francese ed europea in onore di Lorenza Maranini*. Ed. Lorenza Maranini et al. Fasano di Puglia: Schena, 1983. 101–25.

Carreras y Artau, Joaquín. "Las 'repeticiones' salmantinas de Alfonso de Madrigal." *Revista de Filosofía* 5 (1943): 211–36.

Carreras y Artau, Tomás, and Joaquín Carreras y Artau. *Historia de la filosofía española: filosofía cristiana de los siglos XIII al XV*. 2 vols. Madrid: Real Academia de Ciencias Exactas, Físicas y Naturales, 1939–43.

Carruthers, Mary. *The Craft of Thought: Meditation, Rhetoric, and the Making of Images, 400-1200*. New York: Cambridge UP, 1998.

Cartagena, Alfonso de. *Libros de Tulio: De senetute y De los ofiçios*. Ed. María Morrás. Alcalá de Henares: U de Alcalá de Henares, 1996.

– *El* Oracional *de Alonso de Cartagena: edición crítica (comparación del Manuscrito 160 de Santander y el Incunable de Murcia)*. Ed. Silvia González-Quevedo Alonso. Valencia: Albatros Hispanófila, 1983.

– *La Rethórica de M. Tullio Cicerón*. Ed. Rosalba Mascagna. Naples: Liguori, 1969.

Carvalho, Joaquim de. "Sobre a erudição de Gomes Eannes de Zurara." *Estudos sobre a Cultura Portuguesa do século XV*. Vol. 1. Coimbra: Universidade de Coimbra, 1949. 1–241.

Carvalho Homem, Armando Luís de, and Isabel Beceiro Pita. "Rey y 'totalidad nacional' en la obra de don Duarte: En torno a los conceptos de prudencia y consejo." *Hispania: Revista Española de Historia* 67 (2007): 929–44.

Casanova, Emili. "Recorregut per la llengua d'Ausiàs March (1397–1458)." *Ausiàs March i el món cultural del segle XV*. Ed. Rafael Alemany Ferrer. Alicante: U d'Alacant, Institut Interuniversitari de Filologia Valenciana, 1999. 135–72.

Casas Rigall, Juan. *Agudeza y retórica en la poesía amorosa de cancionero*. Santiago de Compostela: U de Santiago de Compostela, 1995.

– "El enigma literario del trovador Macías." *El Extramundi y los Papeles de Iria Flavia* 6 (1996): 11–45.

Cascardi, Anthony J. "Afterword: The Subject of Control." *Culture and Control in Counter- Reformation Spain*. Ed. Anne J. Cruz and Mary E. Perry. Minneapolis: U of Minnesota P, 1991. 231–54.

– *The Subject of Modernity*. Cambridge: Cambridge UP, 1992.

Cassian, John. *The Conferences*. Trans. Boniface Ramsey, OP. New York: Paulist Press, 1997.

Castillo Vegas, Jesús Luis. "Aristotelismo político en la Universidad de Salamanca del siglo XV: Alfonso de Madrigal y Fernando de Roa." Recio and Cortijo Ocaña, *Critical Cluster*, 39–52.

– "El humanismo de Alfonso de Madrigal, el Tostado, y su repercusión en los maestros salmantinos del siglo XV." *Cuadernos Abulenses* 7 (1987): 11–21.

Castro Lingl, Vera. "The Constable of Portugal's *Sátira de infelice e felice vida*. A Reworking of Rodríguez del Padrón's *Siervo libre de amor*." *Revista de Estudios Hispánicos* 32.1 (1998): 75–100.

Cátedra, Pedro M. *Amor y pedagogía en la Edad Media (Estudios de doctrina amorosa y práctica literaria)*. Salamanca: U de Salamanca, Secretariado de Publicaciones, 1989.

– ed. *Cancionero del Marqués de Santillana*. Transcribed by Javier Coca Senande. Salamanca: U de Salamanca, 1990.

Charland, Louis C. "Moral Undertow and the Passions: Two Challenges for Contemporary Emotion Regulation." *Emotion Review* 3.1 (2011): 83–91.

Chas Aguión, Antonio. *Amor y corte. La materia sentimental en las cuestiones poéticas del siglo XV*. A Coruña: Toxosoutos, 2000.

Cheyette, Fredric L. *Ermengard of Narbonne and the World of the Troubadours*. Ithaca, NY: Cornell UP, 2001.

Cicero. *Cicero on the Emotions: Tusculan Disputations 3 and 4*. Trans. and ed. Margaret Graver. Chicago: U of Chicago P, 2002.

– *De Officiis*. Trans. Walter Miller. Loeb Classical Library 30. London: William Heinemann, 1913.

– *On Obligations*. Trans. P.G. Walsh. Oxford: Oxford UP, 2000.

– *On Old Age. On Friendship. On Divination*. Trans. William Armistead Falconer. Loeb Classical Library 154. Cambridge, MA: Harvard UP, 1923.

– *Tusculan Disputations*. Trans. J.E. King. Loeb Classical Library 141. Cambridge, MA: Harvard UP, 2001.

Cingolani, Stefano Maria. "Joan Roís de Corella o la interioritat de la moral." *Revista de Catalunya* 120 (1997): 83–98.

Cocozzella, Peter. "Ausiàs March's *Imitatio Christi*: The Metaphysics of the Lover's Passion." *Romance Languages Annual* 6 (1995): 428–33.

– *Text, Translation, and Critical Interpretation of Joan Roís de Corella's* Tragèdia de Caldesa, *a Fifteenth-Century Spanish Tragedy of Gender Reversal: The Woman Dominates and Seduces Her Lover*. Lewiston, NY: Edwin Mellen P, 2012.

Coderch, Marion. *Ausiàs March, les dones i l'amor*. Valencia: Institució Alfons el Magnànim –Diputació de València, 2009.

Coleman, Janet. "The Individual and the Medieval State." *The Individual in Political Theory and Practice*. Ed. Janet Coleman. Oxford: Clarendon, 1996. 1–34.

Copeland, Rita. *Rhetoric, Hermeneutics, and Translation in the Middle Ages: Academic Traditions and Vernacular Texts*. Cambridge: Cambridge UP, 1991.

Corpus del Nuevo diccionario histórico (CDH). Instituto de Investigación Rafael Lapesa de la Real Academia Española, 2013. http://web.frl.es/CNDHE.

Corriente, Federico. *Romania arabica: Tres cuestiones básicas: arabismos, "mozárabe" y "jarchas."* Madrid: Trotta, 2008.

Cortijo Ocaña, Antonio. "*De amicitia, amore et rationis discretione*. Breves notas a propósito de Boncompagno da Signa y el *Siervo libre de amor*." *Revista de poética medieval* 16 (2006): 23–52.

– *La evolución genérica de la ficción sentimental de los siglos XV y XVI: Género literario y contexto social*. London: Tamesis, 2001.

– "Notas sobre El Tostado *De amore*." Recio and Cortijo Ocaña, *Critical Cluster*, 67–83.

– "La Orden de Venus en el *Comentario* de Hernán Núñez: dignidad humana y conducta amorosa." *Dicenda: Cuadernos de Filología Hispánica* 29 (2011): 103–19.

Covarrubias Orozco, Sebastián de. *Tesoro de la lengua castellana o española*. Ed. Antonio Bernat Vistarini, Ignacio Arellano, and Rafael Zafra. Madrid: Vervuert, 2006.

Coy, José Luis. "La estructura del *Rimado de palaçio*." *Hispanic Studies in Honor of Alan D. Deyermond: A North American Tribute*. Ed. John S. Miletich. Madison: Hispanic Seminary of Medieval Studies, 1986. 71–82.

Cuesta, Luisa. "La edición de las obras del Tostado, empresa de la corona española." *Revista de Archivos, Bibliotecas y Museos* 56 (1950): 321–34.

Culler, Jonathan. "Lyric, History, and Genre." *The Lyric Theory Reader: A Critical Anthology*. Ed. Virginia Jackson and Yopie Prins. Baltimore: Johns Hopkins UP, 2013. 63–77.

– *Theory of the Lyric*. Cambridge, MA: Harvard UP, 2015.

Cullmann, Oscar. *Christ and Time: The Primitive Christian Conception of Time and History*. Trans. Floyd V. Filson. Philadelphia: Westminster Press, 1950.

Dagenais, John. "Genre and Demonstrative Rhetoric: Praise and Blame in the *Razos de trobar* and the *Doctrina de compondre dictats*." *Medieval Lyric: Genres in Historical Context*. Ed. William D. Paden. Urbana: U of Illinois P, 2000. 242–54.

Dante. *Inferno*. Trans. Robert Hollander and Jean Hollander. New York: Doubleday, 2000.

Davies, Mark, and Michael Ferreira. *Corpus do Português: 45 million words, 1300s–1900s*. https://www.corpusdoportugues.org.

Derrida, Jacques. *The Politics of Friendship*. Trans. George Collins. London: Verso, 2005.

Descartes, René. *The Passions of the Soul*. Trans. Stephen H. Voss. Indianapolis: Hackett, 1989.

Dewey, John. "The Theory of Emotion." *Psychological Review* 1.6 (1894): 553–69; 2.1 (1895): 13–32.

Deyermond, Alan. "Baena, Santillana, Resende and the Silent Century of Portuguese Court Poetry." *Bulletin of Hispanic Studies* 59 (1982): 198–210.

– "The Love Poetry of King Dinis." *Florilegium Hispanicum: Medieval and Golden Age Studies Presented to Dorothy Clotelle Clarke*. Ed. John S. Geary, Charles Faulhaber, and Dwayne E. Carpenter. Madison: Hispanic Seminary of Medieval Studies, 1983. 119–30.

– *Tradiciones y puntos de vista en la ficción sentimental*. Mexico City: U Nacional Autónoma de México, 1993.

Dias, Aida Fernanda. *História crítica da literatura portuguesa I: A Idade Média*. Lisbon: Verbo, 1998.

Di Camillo, Ottavio. *El humanismo castellano del siglo XV*. Trans. Manuel Lloris. Valencia: Fernando Torres, 1976.

Diccionario de Autoridades (1726–1739). Real Academia Española. http://web.frl.es/DA.html.

Dionísio, João. "D. Duarte, leitor de Cassiano." PhD diss., U de Lisboa, 2000.

Dixon, Thomas. *From Passions to Emotions: The Creation of a Secular Psychological Category*. Cambridge: Cambridge UP, 2003.

Dolz-Ferrer, Enric S. "'Ficçiones, digo': letra y alegoría de la 'Estoria de dos amadores' en el contexto del *Siervo libre de amor*." *Proceedings of the Ninth Colloquium*. Ed. Andrew M. Beresford and Alan Deyermond. London: Department of Hispanic Studies, Queen Mary and Westfield College, 2000. 121–34.

Duarte, D. *Leal conselheiro o qual fez dom Eduarte Rey de Portugal e do Algarve e senhor de Cepta*. Ed. Joseph M. Piel. Lisbon: Livraria Bertrand, 1942.

Duby, Georges. *The Three Orders: Feudal Society Imagined*. Trans. Arthur Goldhammer. Chicago: U of Chicago P, 1982.

Egginton, William. "Gracián and the Emergence of the Modern Subject." *Rhetoric and Politics: Baltasar Gracián and the New World Order*. Ed. Nicholas Spadaccini and Jenaro Taléns. Minneapolis: U of Minnesota P, 1997. 151–69.

Eiximenis, Francesc. *Regiment de la cosa pública*. Ed. Daniel de Molins de Rei. Barcelona: Barcino, 1927.

Ermengaud, Matfre. *Le Breviari d'Amor*. Vol. 5. Ed. Peter T. Ricketts. Leiden: Brill, 1976.

Espadaler, Antoni M. "Sobre el poema XXIII d'Ausiàs March." *Homenatge a Antoni Comas*. Barcelona: Facultat de Filologia, U de Barcelona, 1985. 121–31.

Faraudo de Saint-Germain, Lluís. *Vocabulari de la llengua catalana medieval*. Ed. Germà Colón Domènech. Institut d'Estudis Catalans. http://www.iec.cat/faraudo/.

Faulhaber, Charles. *Latin Rhetorical Theory in Thirteenth and Fourteenth Century Castile*. Berkeley: U of California P, 1972.

Fenollar, Bernat, Joan Escrivà, and Joan Roís de Corella. *Lo passi en cobles*. Ed. Marinela Garcia Sempere. Alacant and Barcelona: Institut Interuniversitari de Filologia Valenciana and Publicacions de l'Abadia de Montserrat, 2002.

Fernández, Enrique. *Anxieties of Interiority and Dissection in Early Modern Spain*. Toronto: U of Toronto P, 2015.

Fernández Gallardo, Luis. "Alonso de Cartagena y el humanismo." *La corónica* 37.1 (2008): 175–215.

Fernández Vallina, Emiliano. "El tratado *De optima politia* del Tostado: una visión singular en el siglo XV hispano sobre las formas políticas de gobierno." *Anuario Filosófico* 45.2 (2012): 283–311.

Ferreira, Ana Paula. "Telling Woman What She Wants: The *Cantigas d'amigo* as Strategies of Containment." *Portuguese Studies* 9 (1993): 23–38.

Ferrer, Francesc. *Obra completa*. Ed. Jaume Auferil. Barcelona: Barcino, 1989.

Flood, Gavin. *The Ascetic Self: Subjectivity, Memory and Tradition*. Cambridge: Cambridge UP, 2004.

Folger, Robert. *Escape from the Prison of Love: Caloric Identities and Writing Subjects in Fifteenth-Century Spain*. Chapel Hill: U of North Carolina P, 2009.

– *Images in Mind: Lovesickness, Spanish Sentimental Fiction and* Don Quijote. Chapel Hill: U of North Carolina P, 2002.

Foucault, Michel. "About the Beginning of the Hermeneutics of the Self: Two Lectures at Dartmouth." *Political Theory* 21.2 (1993): 198–227.

– *The Hermeneutics of the Subject: Lectures at the Collège de France 1981–1982*. Ed. Frédéric Gros. Trans. Graham Burchell. New York: Picador, 2005.

– "Technologies of the Self." *Technologies of the Self: A Seminar with Michel Foucault*. Ed. Luther H. Martin, Huck Gutman, and Patrick H. Hutton. Amherst: U of Massachusetts P, 1988. 16–49.

Fraisse, Jean-Claude. *Philia: La notion d'amitié dans la philosophie antique*. Paris: J. Vrin, 1974.

Francomano, Emily C. *Wisdom and Her Lovers in Medieval and Early Modern Hispanic Literature*. New York: Palgrave Macmillan, 2008.

Fuster, Joan. *Ausiàs March*. Valencia: Eliseu Clement, 1982.
– "Joan Roís de Corella." *Pont Blau* 22 (1954): 242–3.
– "Lectura de Roís de Corella." *Obres completes*. Vol. 1. Barcelona: Edicions 62, 1968. 285–313.
Galvez, Marisa. *Songbook: How Lyrics Became Poetry in Medieval Europe*. Chicago: U of Chicago P, 2012.
Gama, José. "Análise das paixões no *Leal Conselheiro* – A sensibilidade e o modo de ser português." *Revista Portuguesa de Filosofia* 47.3 (1991): 387–405.
– *A filosofia da cultura portuguesa no* Leal conselheiro *de D. Duarte*. Lisbon: Fundação Calouste Gulbenkian and Junta Nacional de Investigação Científica e Tecnológica, 1995.
Garcia, Michel. *Obra y personalidad del Canciller Ayala*. Madrid: Alhambra, 1983.
García, Santiago. "La competencia hebraica de Alfonso de Madrigal." Recio and Cortijo Ocaña, *Critical Cluster*, 85–98.
Garcia Sempere, Marinela. "Algunes connexions entre l'obra religiosa i l'obra profana de Joan Roís de Corella: L'*Oració* i la prosa mitològica *La història de Leànder i Hero*." *Estudis sobre Joan Roís de Corella*. Ed. Vicent Martines. Alcoi: Marfil, 1999. 169–81.
Gascón Vera, Elena. *Don Pedro, Condestable de Portugal*. Madrid: Fundación Universitaria Española, 1979.
Gaunt, Simon. *Love and Death in Medieval French and Occitan Courtly Literature: Martyrs to Love*. Oxford: Oxford UP, 2006.
– "A Martyr to Love: Sacrificial Desire in the Poetry of Bernart de Ventadorn." *Journal of Medieval and Early Modern Studies* 31.3 (2001): 477–506.
Gerli, E. Michael. "La 'Religión del Amor' y el antifeminismo en las letras castellanas del siglo XV." *Hispanic Review* 49.1 (1981): 65–86.
– "Toward a Poetics of the Spanish Sentimental Romance." *Hispania* 72.3 (1989): 474–82.
– "Toward a Revaluation of the Constable of Portugal's *Sátira de infelice e felice vida*." *Hispanic Studies in Honor of Alan D. Deyermond: A North American Tribute*. Ed. John S. Miletich. Madison: Hispanic Seminary of Medieval Studies, 1986. 107–18.
Gimeno Casalduero, Joaquín. "Pero López de Ayala y el cambio poético de Castilla a comienzos del XV." *Hispanic Review* 33.1 (1965): 1–14.
Girón-Negrón, Luis M. *Alfonso de la Torre's* Visión Deleytable: *Philosophical Rationalism and the Religious Imagination in 15th Century Spain*. Leiden: Brill, 2001.
Glosa castellana al "Regimiento de príncipes" de Egidio Romano. Ed. Juan Beneyto Pérez. 3 vols. Madrid: Instituto de Estudios Políticos, 1947.
Gomes, Rita Costa. *The Making of a Court Society: Kings and Nobles in Late Medieval Portugal*. Trans. Alison Aiken. Cambridge: Cambridge UP, 2003.
Gómez-Bravo, Ana María. "*Decir canciones*: The Question of Genre in Fifteenth-Century Castilian *Cancionero* Poetry." *Medieval Lyric: Genres in Historical Context*. Ed. William D. Paden. Urbana: U of Illinois P, 2000. 158–87.
– "Retórica y poética en la evolución de los géneros poéticos cuatrocentistas." *Rhetorica* 17.2 (1999): 137–75.

– *Textual Agency: Writing Culture and Social Networks in Fifteenth-Century Spain.* Toronto: U of Toronto P, 2013.

Gómez Moreno, Ángel. *El* Prohemio e carta *del marqués de Santillana y la teoría literaria del s. XV.* Barcelona: PPU, 1990.

– "La *Qüestión* del Marqués de Santillana a don Alfonso de Cartagena." *El Crotalón* 2 (1985): 335–63.

González Maeso, David. "Alonso de Madrigal (Tostado) y su labor escrituraria." *Miscelánea de Estudios Árabes y Hebraicos* 4 (1955): 143–85.

Gracián, Baltasar. *El héroe. El discreto. Oráculo manual y arte de prudencia.* Ed. Luys Santa Marina. Barcelona: Planeta, 2001.

Green, Otis H. "Courtly Love in the Spanish *Cancioneros.*" *The Literary Mind of Medieval & Renaissance Spain.* Lexington: UP of Kentucky, 1970. 40–92.

Grieve, Patricia E. *Desire and Death in the Spanish Sentimental Romance (1440–1550).* Newark, DE: Juan de la Cuesta, 1987.

Grondin, Jean. *Introduction to Philosophical Hermeneutics.* Trans. Joel Weinsheimer. New Haven, CT: Yale UP, 1994.

Gross, Daniel M. *The Secret History of Emotion: From Aristotle's* Rhetoric *to Modern Brain Science.* Chicago: U of Chicago P, 2006.

Gwara, Joseph J., and E. Michael Gerli, eds. *Studies on the Spanish Sentimental Romance, 1440–1550: Redefining a Genre.* Woodbridge: Tamesis, 1997.

Haidu, Peter. "Making It (New) in the Middle Ages: Towards a Problematics of Alterity." Review of Paul Zumthor, *Essai de poétique médiévale. Diacritics* 4.2 (1974): 2–11.

– *The Subject Medieval/Modern: Text and Governance in the Middle Ages.* Stanford, CA: Stanford UP, 2004.

HarperCollins Study Bible: New Revised Standard Version, with the Apocryphal/Deuterocanonical Books. Ed. Wayne A. Meeks. New York: HarperCollins, 1993.

Harpham, Geoffrey Galt. *The Ascetic Imperative in Culture and Criticism.* Chicago: U of Chicago P, 1987.

Harré, Rom. "An Outline of the Social Constructionist Viewpoint." *The Social Construction of Emotions.* Ed. Rom Harré. Oxford: Basil Blackwell, 1986. 2–14.

Hart, Thomas R. "The *cantigas de amor* of King Dinis: *em maneira de proençal*?" *Bulletin of Hispanic Studies* 71.1 (1994): 29–38.

– *En maneira de proençal: The Medieval Galician-Portuguese Lyric.* London: Department of Hispanic Studies, Queen Mary and Westfield College, 1998.

– "New Perspectives on the Medieval Portuguese Lyric." *Estudos portugueses: homenagem a Luciana Stegagno Picchio.* Lisbon: Difel, 1991. 69–78.

Hartnett, Daniel. "The Marqués de Santillana's Library and Literary Reputation." *Self-Fashioning and Assumptions of Identity in Medieval and Early Modern Iberia.* Ed. Laura Delbrugge. Leiden: Brill, 2015. 116–43.

Harvey, Ruth. "Courtly Culture in Medieval Occitania." *The Troubadours: An Introduction.* Ed. Simon Gaunt and Sarah Kay. Cambridge: Cambridge UP, 1999. 8–27.

Hauf, Albert. *D'Eiximenis a Sor Isabel de Villena: aportació a l'estudi de la nostra cultura medieval.* Barcelona: Publicacions de l'Abadia de Montserrat, 1990.

Haywood, Louise M. "Lyric and Other Verse Insertions in Sentimental Romances." *Studies on the Spanish Sentimental Romance (1440–1550): Redefining a Genre*. Ed. Joseph J. Gwara and E. Michael Gerli. London: Tamesis, 1997. 191–206.

Heidegger, Martin. *Plato's* Sophist. Trans. Richard Rojcewicz and André Schuwer. Bloomington: Indiana UP, 1997.

Herrero, Javier. "The Allegorical Structure of the *Siervo libre de amor*." *Speculum* 55.4 (1980): 751–64.

Heusch, Carlos. "Entre didacticismo y heterodoxia: vicisitudes del estudio de la ética aristotélica en la España escolástica (siglos XIII y XIV)." *La corónica* 19.2 (1990–91): 89–99.

Hillman, James. *Emotion: A Comprehensive Phenomenology of Theories and Their Meanings for Therapy*. Evanston, IL: Northwestern UP, 1972.

Història de la literatura catalana. Literatura medieval (II): Segles XIV–XV. Ed. Lola Badia. Barcelona: Enciclopèdia Catalana, Barcino, and Ajuntament de Barcelona, 2014.

Holmes, Olivia. *Assembling the Lyric Self: Authorship from Troubadour Song to Italian Poetry Book*. Minneapolis: U of Minnesota P, 2000.

Isidore of Seville. *Etymologies of Isidore of Seville*. Ed. and trans. Stephen A. Barney et al. West Nyack, NY: Cambridge UP, 2002.

Jaeger, C. Stephen. *Ennobling Love: In Search of a Lost Sensibility*. Philadelphia: U of Pennsylvania P, 1999.

Jauss, Hans Robert. *Toward an Aesthetic of Reception*. Trans. Timothy Bahti. Minneapolis: U of Minnesota P, 1982.

Johnston, Mark. "Scholastic Psychology as a Literary Tradition in Ausias March." *Romance Notes* 19 (1979): 383–7.

Kantorowicz, Ernst H. *The King's Two Bodies: A Study in Mediaeval Political Theology*. Princeton, NJ: Princeton UP, 1985.

Kaplan, Gregory B. "*Tractado que fizo el obispo*: la contribución pre-renacentista de Alfonso Fernández de Madrigal a la evolución de la novela sentimental." *eHumanista* 4 (2004): 13–21.

Kassier, Theodore L. "*Cancionero* Poetry and the *Celestina*: From Metaphor to Reality." *Hispanófila* 56 (1976): 1–28.

Kay, Sarah. "Grafting the Knowledge Community: The Purposes of Verse in the *Breviari d'amor* of Matfre Ermengaud." *Neophilologus* 91 (2007): 363–73.

– *Parrots and Nightingales: Troubadour Quotations and the Development of European Poetry*. Philadelphia: U of Pennsylvania P, 2013.

– *Subjectivity in Troubadour Poetry*. Cambridge: Cambridge UP, 1990.

Kent, Bonnie. *Virtues of the Will: The Transformation of Ethics in the Late Thirteenth Century*. Washington, DC: Catholic U of America P, 1995.

Kent, Dale. *Friendship, Love, and Trust in Renaissance Florence*. Cambridge, MA: Harvard UP, 2009.

Kinkade, Richard P. "Pero López de Ayala and the Order of St. Jerome." *Symposium* 26.2 (1972): 161–80.

Knuuttila, Simo. *Emotions in Ancient and Medieval Philosophy*. Oxford: Oxford UP, 2004.

Kohut, Karl. "Der Beitrag der Theologie zum Literaturbegriff in der Zeit Juans II. von Kastilien: Alonso de Cartagena (1384–1456) und Alonso de Madrigal, genannt El Tostado (1400?–1455)." *Romanische Forschungen* 89 (1977): 183–226.

– "La teoría de la poesía cortesana en el *Prólogo* de Juan Alfonso de Baena." *Actas del Coloquio Hispano-Alemán Ramón Menéndez Pidal: Madrid, 31 de marzo a 2 de abril de 1978*. Ed. Wido Hempel and Dietrich Briesemeister. Tübingen: Niemeyer, 1982. 120–37.

Lacarra Lanz, Eukene. "*Siervo libre de amor*, ¿autobiografía espiritual?" *La corónica* 29.1 (2000): 147–70.

Lang, Henry R. *Cancioneiro Gallego-Castelhano: The Extant Galician Poems of the Gallego-Castilian Lyric School (1350–1450)*. New York: Charles Scribner's Sons, 1902.

Lapesa, Rafael. "La lengua de la poesía lírica desde Macías hasta Villasandino." *Romance Philology* 7 (1953): 51–9.

– "Poesía de cancionero y poesía italianizante." *De la Edad Media a nuestros días: Estudios de historia literaria*. Madrid: Editorial Gredos, 1967. 145–71.

Lawrance, J.N.H. "Nuño de Guzmán and Early Spanish Humanism: Some Reconsiderations." *Medium Aevum* 51 (1982): 55–85.

– "On Fifteenth-Century Spanish Vernacular Humanism." *Medieval and Renaissance Studies in Honour of Robert Brian Tate*. Ed. Ian Michael and Richard A. Cardwell. Oxford: Dolphin Book, 1986. 63–79.

– "The Spread of Lay Literacy in Late Medieval Castile." *Bulletin of Hispanic Studies* 62 (1985): 79–94.

Leclercq, Jean. *The Love of Learning and the Desire for God: A Study of Monastic Culture*. Trans. Catharine Misrahi. New York: Fordham UP, 1982.

Le Goff, Jacques. *The Birth of Purgatory*. Trans. Arthur Goldhammer. Chicago: U of Chicago P, 1984.

Lida de Malkiel, María Rosa. "La hipérbole sagrada en la poesía castellana del siglo XV." *Revista de filología hispánica* 8 (1946): 121–30.

– "Juan Rodríguez del Padrón: Vida y obras." *Nueva Revista de Filología Hispánica* 6.4 (1952): 313–51.

Lírica trobadoresca del segle XV: Joan Basset i altres poetes inèdits del Cançoner Vega-Aguiló. Ed. Pere Bohigas. Valencia and Montserrat: Institut de Filologia Valenciana and Publicacions de l'Abadia de Montserrat, 1988.

Liuzzo Scorpo, Antonella. *Friendship in Medieval Iberia: Historical, Legal and Literary Perspectives*. London: Ashgate, 2014.

Lledó-Guillem, Vicente. "El rechazo del neoplatonismo en Ausiàs March." *Neophilologus* 88 (2004): 545–57.

Lloret, Albert. *Printing Ausiàs March: Material Culture and Renaissance Poetics*. Madrid: Centro para la Edición de los Clásicos Españoles, 2013.

Llull, Romeu. *Obra completa*. Ed. Jaume Turró [Torró]. Barcelona: Barcino, 1996.

López de Ayala, Pero. *Libro rimado de Palacio*. Ed. Kenneth Adams. Madrid: Cátedra, 1993.

Lorenzo Gradín, Pilar. "*Adversus Deum*. Trovadores en la frontera de la *cantiga de amor*." *Estudios de literatura medieval en la Península Ibérica*. Ed. Carlos Alvar. San Millán de la Cogolla: Cilengua, 2015. 861–78.

Machado, José Pedro, ed. *Dicionário etimológico da língua portuguesa*. 3 vols. Lisbon: Confluência, 1967–73.

Madrigal, Alfonso de. *Breuiloquyo de amor e amyçiçia sobre vn dicho platonyco*. Real Biblioteca del Monasterio de San Lorenzo de El Escorial, h.II.15. ff. 1r-163r.

– *Breve forma de confesión: Villa mayor de Mondoñedo (1495)*. Ed. Ignacio Cabano Vázquez and Xosé María Díaz Fernández. Santiago de Compostela: Xunta de Galicia, 1995.

– *Brevyloquyo de amor e amiçiçia*. Ed. Nuria Belloso Martín. Cuadernos de Anuario Filosófico 15. Pamplona: Servicio de Publicaciones de la U de Navarra, 2000.

– *Commentaria in Genesim*. Venice: Sessa, 1596.

– *El gobierno ideal (De optima politia)*. Ed. Nuria Belloso Martín. Pamplona: U de Navarra, 2003.

– *Libro intitulado las catorze questiones del Tostado*. Burgos: Juan de Junta, 1545.

Manrique, Jorge. *Poesía*. Ed. Jesús-Manuel Alda Tesán. Madrid: Cátedra, 1981.

Maravall Casesnoves, José Antonio. *El concepto de España en la Edad Media*. 4th ed. Madrid: Centro de Estudios Constitucionales, 1997.

March, Ausiàs. *Ausiàs March: A Key Anthology*. Ed. and trans. Robert Archer. Sheffield: The Anglo-Catalan Society, 1992.

– *Ausias March: Selected Poems*. Ed. and trans. Arthur Terry. Austin: U of Texas P, 1976.

– *Poesies*. Ed. Pere Bohigas. Revised by Amadeu-J. Soberanas and Noemí Espinàs. Barcelona: Barcino, 2005.

March, Jaume. *Obra poètica*. Ed. Josep Pujol. Barcelona: Barcino, 1994.

March, Pere. *Obra completa*. Ed. Lluís Cabré. Barcelona: Barcino, 1993.

Martín, Oscar. "Allegory and the Spaces of Love." *Diacritics* 36.3–4 (2006): 132–46.

Martinengo, Alessandro. "Un aspetto del tradizionalismo ispanico: La 'canzone a citazioni' attraverso il tempo." *Studi mediolatini e volgari* 11 (1963): 161–77.

Matthews, Ricardo. "Song in Reverse: The Medieval Prosimetrum and Lyric Theory." *PMLA* 133.2 (2018): 296–313.

Mattoso, José. "Revoltas e revoluções na Idade Média portuguesa." *Naquele Tempo: Ensaios de História Medieval*. Lisbon: Círculo de Leitores, 2009. 409–25.

McGuire, Brian Patrick. *Friendship and Community: The Monastic Experience, 350–1250*. Ithaca, NY: Cornell UP, 2010.

McNamer, Sarah. *Affective Meditation and the Invention of Medieval Compassion*. Philadelphia: U of Pennsylvania P, 2010.

Mena, Juan de. *Obras completas*. Ed. Miguel Ángel Pérez Priego. Barcelona: Planeta, 1989.

Mendoza, Fray Íñigo de. *Cancionero*. Ed. Julio Rodríguez-Puértolas. Madrid: Espasa-Calpe, 1968.

Menocal, María Rosa. *The Arabic Role in Medieval Literary History: A Forgotten Heritage*. Philadelphia: U of Pennsylvania P, 1987.

Meyer, Michel. *Philosophy and the Passions: Toward a History of Human Nature*. Trans. Robert F. Barsky. University Park: Pennsylvania State UP, 2000.

Miguel-Prendes, Sol. *Narrating Desire: Moral Consolation and Sentimental Fiction in Fifteenth-Century Spain*. Chapel Hill: U of North Carolina P, 2019.

– "Reimagining Diego de San Pedro's Readers at Work: *Cárcel de amor*." *La corónica* 32.2 (2004): 7–44.

Moi, Toril. "Desire in Language: Andreas Capellanus and the Controversy of Courtly Love." *Medieval Literature: Criticism, Ideology and History*. Ed. David Aers. New York: Palgrave Macmillan, 1986. 11–33.

Molas, Joaquim. "Un poema inèdit de Lluís Icart." *Estudis Universitaris Catalans* 26 (1984): 131–47.

Monroe, James T. "*Zajal* and *Muwashshaha*: Hispano-Arabic Poetry and the Romance Tradition." *The Legacy of Muslim Spain*. Ed. Salma Khadra Jayyusi. Vol. 1. Leiden: Brill, 1992. 398–419.

Montaigne, Michel de. "Of Friendship." *The Complete Essays of Montaigne*. Trans. Donald M. Frame. Stanford, CA: Stanford UP, 1958. 135–44.

Monteiro, João Gouveia. "Orientações da cultura de corte na 1.a metade do século XV." *Vértice* 5 (1989): 89–103.

Montero, Ana M. "'¿Durmiendo con el enemigo?': La reina Isabel de Portugal en la obraliteraria de su hermano Don Pedro, condestable de Portugal. Ficción e historia." *Erebea* 4 (2014): 173–98.

– "A New Reading of *Sátira de infelice e felice vida* by don Pedro, Constable of Portugal: The Influence of Seneca's *On Clemency*." *La corónica* 41.2 (2013): 105–34.

Morreale, Margherita. "Los 'Gozos' de la Virgen en el *Libro* de Juan Ruiz." *Revista de Filología Española* 63.3–4 (1983): 223–90 and 64.1–2 (1984): 1–69.

Morris, Colin. *The Discovery of the Individual, 1050–1200*. London: SPCK, 1972.

Morrison, Karl F. "Framing the Subject: Humanity and the Wounds of Love." *Studies on Medieval Empathies*. Ed. Karl F. Morrison and Rudolph M. Bell. Turnhout, BE: Brepols, 2013. 1–58.

Moya García, Cristina, ed. *Mosén Diego de Valera: entre las armas y las letras*. Woodbridge: Tamesis, 2014.

Murphy, James J. *Rhetoric in the Middle Ages: A History of the Rhetorical Theory from Saint Augustine to the Renaissance*. Tempe: Arizona Center for Medieval and Renaissance Studies, 2001.

Nascimento, Aries Augusto de. "As livrarias dos príncipes de Avis." *Biblos* 69 (1993): 265–87.

Nieto Soria, José Manuel. "Del rey oculto al rey exhibido: un síntoma de las transformaciones políticas en la Castilla bajomedieval." *Medievalismo: Boletín de la Sociedad Española de Estudios Medievales* 2 (1992): 5–27.

– *Iglesia y génesis del estado moderno en Castilla (1369–1480)*. Madrid: Editorial Complutense, 1993.

Nirenberg, David. "Figures of Thought and Figures of Flesh: 'Jews' and 'Judaism' in Late-Medieval Spanish Poetry and Politics." *Speculum* 81.2 (2006): 398–426.

– "The Politics of Love and Its Enemies." *Critical Inquiry* 33.3 (2007): 573–605.

Pacheco, Maria Cândida Monteiro. "Para uma antropologia situada: o *Leal conselheiro* de Dom Duarte." *Revista Portuguesa de Filosofia* 47.3 (1991): 425–41.

Pagden, A.R.D. "The Diffusion of Aristotle's Moral Philosophy in Spain, ca. 1400–ca. 1600." *Traditio* 31 (1975): 287–314.

Pedro, Constable of Portugal. *Sátira de infelice e felice vida. Obras completas do Condestável.* Ed. Luís Adão da Fonseca. Lisbon: Fundação Calouste Gulbenkian, 1975. 1–175.

– *Tragédia de la insigne reina doña Isabel.* Ed. Carolina Michaëlis de Vasconcelos. Coimbra: Imprensa da U, 1922.

Pedro, Duke of Coimbra, and Frei João Verba. *Livro da vertuosa benfeytoria.* Ed. Adelino de Almeida Calado. Coimbra: U de Coimbra, 1994.

Penna, Mario, ed. *Prosistas castellanos del siglo XV.* Vol. 1. Madrid: Atlas, 1959.

Peraino, Judith A. *Giving Voice to Love: Song and Self-Expression from the Troubadours to Guillaume de Machaut.* Oxford: Oxford UP, 2011.

Perea Rodríguez, Óscar. *La época del* Cancionero de Baena*: los Trastámara y sus poetas.* Baena: Centro de Documentación Juan Alfonso de Baena, 2009.

Pérez de Guzmán, Fernán. *Floresta de philósophos.* Ed. Raymond Fouché-Delbosc. *Revue hispanique* 11 (1904): 5–154.

Pérez Priego, Miguel Ángel. *Estudios sobre la poesía del siglo XV.* Madrid: UNED, 2012.

Pérez Rosado, Miguel. "Una sección de la *Floresta de philósophos.*" *La corónica* 24.1 (1995): 153–72.

Piera, Montserrat. "Writing, *Auctoritas* and Canon Formation in Sor Isabel de Villena's *Vita Christi.*" *La corónica* 32.1 (2003): 105–18.

Pierce, Joanne M. "Medieval Christian Liturgy." *Oxford Research Encyclopedia, Religion.* Oxford: Oxford UP, 2019. https://oxfordre.com/religion.

Pinet, Simone. "Babel historiada: un episodio del *Libro de Alexandre.*" *Literatura y conocimiento medieval. Actas de las VIII Jornadas Medievales.* Ed. Lillian von der Walde Moheno, Concepción Company, and Aurelio González. Mexico, DF: U Nacional Autónoma de México, U Autónoma Metropolitana, and Colegio de México, 2003. 371–89.

– *The Task of the Cleric: Cartography, Translation, and Economics in Thirteenth-Century Iberia.* Toronto: U of Toronto P, 2016.

Polín, Ricardo. *Cancioneiro galego-castelán (1350–1450):* Corpus *lírico da decadencia.* Sada, A Coruña: Edicios do Castro, 1997.

Pujol, Josep. "Amor i desmemòria. Notes per a la interpretació del poema X d'Ausiàs March." *Ausiàs March: Textos i contextos.* Ed. Rafael Alemany Ferrer. Valencia: Institut Interuniversitari de Filologia Valenciana, Departament de Filologia Catalana (U d'Alacant), Publicacions de l'Abadia de Montserrat, 1997. 297–320.

Ramírez i Molas, Pere. "Ausiàs March: el saber del sentiment." *Ausiàs March: Textos I contextos.* Ed. Rafael Alemany Ferrer. Valencia: Institut Interuniversitari de Filologia Valenciana, Departament de Filologia Catalana (U d'Alacant), Publicacions de l'Abadia de Montserrat, 1997. 321–41.

– *La poesia d'Ausiàs March: Anàlisi textual, cronologia, elements filosòfics.* Basel: J.R. Geigy, 1970.

Recio, Roxana. "La propiedad del lenguaje: poeta y poesía según Alfonso de Madrigal, El Tostado." Recio and Cortijo Ocaña, *Critical Cluster*, 145–62.

Recio, Roxana, and Antonio Cortijo Ocaña, eds. *Critical Cluster: Alfonso Fernández de Madrigal, El Tostado. La corónica* 33.1 (2004): 7–162.

– "Alfonso de Madrigal 'El Tostado': un portavoz único de la intelectualidad castellana del siglo XV." Recio and Cortijo Ocaña, *Critical Cluster*, 7–15.

Reddy, William M. *The Navigation of Feeling: A Framework for the History of Emotions*. Cambridge: Cambridge UP, 2001.

Rennert, Hugo Albert. *Macias, O Namorado: A Galician Troubadour*. Philadelphia: Avil Print, 1900.

Resina, Joan Ramon. "Iberian Modalities: The Logic of an Intercultural Field." *Iberian Modalities: A Relational Approach to the Study of Culture in the Iberian Peninsula*. Ed. Joan Ramon Resina. Liverpool: Liverpool UP, 2013. 1–19.

Rico, Francisco. "La clerecía del mester." *Hispanic Review* 53.1–2 (1985): 1–23 and 127–50.

– "Imágenes del Prerrenacimiento español: Joan Roís de Corella y la *Tragèdia de Caldesa*." *Estudios de literatura española y francesa, siglos XVI y XVII: homenaje a Horst Baader*. Ed. Frauke Gewecke. Frankfurt/Main: Vervuert, 1984. 15–27.

– *El pequeño mundo del hombre: varia fortuna de una idea en las letras españolas*. Madrid: Castalia, 1970.

Rico, Maria João Toscano. "A projecção da obra de João Cassiano na Península Ibérica: elenco de testemunhos e edição de textos inéditos." *Euphrosyne* 40 (2012): 123–48.

Riquer, Martí de. *Història de la literatura catalana*. Vol. 3. 2nd ed. Barcelona: Ariel, 1980.

Robinson, Cynthia. *Imagining the Passion in a Multiconfessional Castile: The Virgin, Christ, Devotions, and Images in the Fourteenth and Fifteenth Centuries*. University Park: Pennsylvania State UP, 2013.

Rocabertí, Bernat Hug de. *The* Gloria d'Amor *of Fra Rocabertí: A Catalan Vision-Poem of the 15th Century*. Ed. H.C. Heaton. New York: AMS Press, 1966.

Rodríguez del Padrón, Juan. *Obras Completas*. Ed. César Hernández Alonso. Madrid: Editora Nacional, 1982.

– *Siervo libre de amor*. Ed. Enric Dolz. *Anexos de la Revista Lemir*, 2004.

Rodríguez-Puértolas, Julio. "Mosén Diego de Valera: ideología y poesía." *Mosén Diego de Valera y su tiempo*. Cuenca: Ayuntamiento de Cuenca and Instituto Juan de Valdés, 1996. 15–46.

Rohland de Langbehn, Regula. "Power and Justice in *Cancionero* Verse." *Poetry at Court in Trastamaran Spain: From the* Cancionero de Baena *to the* Cancionero general. Ed. E. Michael Gerli and Julian Weiss. Tempe, AZ: Medieval and Renaissance Texts and Studies, 1998. 199–219.

– *La unidad genérica de la novela sentimental española de los siglos XV y XVI*. London: Department of Hispanic Studies, Queen Mary and Westfield College, 1999.

Roís de Corella, Joan. *Obres completes I: obra profana*. Ed. Jordi Carbonell. Valencia: Albatros, 1973.

Rojas, Fernando de. *La Celestina: Comedia* o *Tragicomedia de Calisto y Melibea*. Ed. Peter E. Russell. Madrid: Castalia, 2001.

Romeu i Figueras, Josep. "Dos poemes de Joan Roís de Corella: 'A Caldesa' i 'La sepultura.'" *Estudis en memòria del professor Manuel Sanchis Guarner: estudis de llengua i literatura catalanes*. Vol. 1. Valencia: U de València, 1984. 299–308.

Rorty, Amélie Oksenberg. "From Passions to Emotions and Sentiments." *Philosophy* 57.2 (1982): 159–72.

Rosenwein, Barbara H. *Emotional Communities in the Early Middle Ages*. Ithaca, NY: Cornell UP, 2006.

– *Generations of Feeling: A History of Emotions, 600–1700*. Cambridge: Cambridge UP, 2016.

Round, Nicholas G. "Renaissance Culture and Its Opponents in Fifteenth-Century Castile." *Modern Language Review* 57.2 (1962): 204–15.

Rubio, Josep E. "De Llull a March: Memòria, enteniment, voluntat." *Ausiàs March (1400–1459): Premier poète en langue catalane*. Ed. Georges Martin and Marie-Claire Zimmermann. Paris: Séminaire d'études médiévales hispaniques de l'université Paris 13, 2000. 115–22.

– "Les tres potències de l'ànima en la poesia d'Ausiàs March." *Boletín de la Real Academia de Buenas Letras de Barcelona* 44 (1993–94): 143–67.

Ruiz, Juan, Arcipreste de Hita. *Libro de buen amor*. Ed. Alberto Blecua. Madrid: Cátedra, 2003.

Ruiz, Teófilo F. *Spain's Centuries of Crisis: 1300–1474*. Malden, MA: Blackwell, 2007.

– "Unsacred Monarchy: The Kings of Castile in the Late Middle Ages." *Rites of Power: Symbolism, Ritual, and Politics since the Middle Ages*. Ed. Sean Wilentz. Philadelphia: U of Pennsylvania P, 1999. 109–44.

Russell, Peter E. "Las armas contra las letras: Para una definición del humanismo español del siglo XV." *Temas de* La Celestina *y otros estudios: Del* Cid *al* Quijote. Barcelona: Ariel, 1978. 207–39.

Russo, Sara. "La transmisión de la 'Querella de amor' del Marqués de Santillana. Estado de la cuestión, problemas y perspectivas." *Dicenda. Cuadernos de Filología Hispánica* 30, Núm. Especial (2012): 31–45.

Ryder, Alan. *The Wreck of Catalonia: Civil War in the Fifteenth Century*. Oxford: Oxford UP, 2007.

Sánchez de Arévalo, Rodrigo. *Suma de la política*. Ed. Juan Beneyto Pérez. Madrid: Consejo Superior de Investigaciones Científicas, Instituto "Francisco de Vitoria," 1944.

Sánchez de Badajoz, Garci. *Cancionero de Garci Sánchez de Badajoz*. Ed. Julia Castillo. Madrid: Editora Nacional, 1980.

San Pedro, Diego de. *Cárcel de amor. Arnalta y Lucenda. Sermón*. Ed. José Francisco Ruiz Casanova. Madrid: Cátedra, 2004.

– *Obras completas, II: Cárcel de amor*. Ed. Keith Whinnom. Madrid: Castalia, 1971.

– *Obras completas, III: Poesías*. Ed. Dorothy S. Severin and Keith Whinnom. Madrid: Castalia, 1979.

Santillana, Íñigo López de Mendoza, marqués de. *Poesías completas*. Ed. Maxim P.A.M. Kerkhof and Ángel Gómez Moreno. Madrid: Clásicos Castalia, 2003.

Sant Jordi, Jordi de. *Poesies*. Ed. Aniello Fratta. Barcelona: Barcino, 2005.

Santoro, Fernando. "Saudade." *Dictionary of Untranslatables: A Philosophical Lexicon*. Ed. Barbara Cassin. Trans. Steven Rendall et al. Trans. ed. Emily Apter, Jacques Lezra, and Michael Wood. Princeton, NJ: Princeton UP, 2014. 929–31.

Saraiva, António José. *O crepúsculo da Idade Média em Portugal*. Lisbon: Gradiva, 1998.

Sarbin, Theodore R. "Emotion and Act: Roles and Rhetoric." *The Social Construction of Emotions*. Ed. Rom Harré. Oxford: Basil Blackwell, 1986. 83–97.

Saugnieux, Joël. *Berceo y las culturas del siglo XIII*. Logroño: Instituto de Estudios Riojanos, 1982.

Schiff, Mario. *La bibliothèque du Marquis de Santillane*. Paris: Bouillon, 1905.

Schleiermacher, Friedrich. Hermeneutics and Criticism *and Other Writings*. Ed. and trans. Andrew Bowie. Cambridge: Cambridge UP, 1998.

The Secreto de los secretos*: A Castilian Version*. Ed. Philip B. Jones. Potomac, MD: Scripta Humanistica, 1990.

Seneca. *Moral and Political Essays*. Ed. and trans. John M. Cooper and J.F. Procopé. Cambridge: Cambridge UP, 1995.

– *Moral Essays I: De Providentia, De Constantia, De Ira, De Clementia*. Trans. John W. Basore. Loeb Classical Library 214. London: William Heinemann, 1928.

Serés, Guillermo. "Don Pedro de Portugal y el Tostado." In *Actas del III Congreso de la Asociación Hispánica de Literatura Medieval: Salamanca, 3 al 6 de octubre de 1989*. Ed. María Isabel Toro Pascua. Salamanca: Biblioteca Española del Siglo XV, 1994. 975–82.

– "Ficción sentimental y humanismo: La *Sátira* de Don Pedro de Portugal." *Bulletin Hispanique* 93.1 (1991): 31–60.

Serra i Baldó, Alfons. "Els 'Goigs de la Verge Maria' en l'antiga poesia catalana." *Homenatge a Antoni Rubió i Lluch: miscellània d'estudis literaris, històrics i lingüístics*. Barcelona: Estudis Universitaris Catalans, 1936. 367–86.

Serrano, Luciano. *Los conversos D. Pablo de Santa María y D. Alfonso de Cartagena*. Madrid: C. Bermejo, 1942.

Severin, Dorothy S. *An Electronic Corpus of 15th Century Castilian* Cancionero *Manuscripts*. http://cancionerovirtual.liv.ac.uk/.

– "Juan Rodríguez del Padrón, Parodist: *Los siete gozos de Amor*." *Juan Rodríguez del Padrón: Studies in Honour of Olga Tudorică Impey. I: Poetry and Doctrinal Prose*. Ed. Alan Deyermond and Carmen Parrilla. London: Department of Hispanic Studies, Queen Mary and Westfield College, U of London, 2005. 75–83.

– "The *Sepultura de Macías* by San Pedro – But Which San Pedro?" *Medieval and Renaissance Spain and Portugal: Studies in Honor of Arthur L-F. Askins*. Ed. Martha E. Schaffer and Antonio Cortijo Ocaña. Woodbridge: Tamesis, 2006. 301–8.

Silleras-Fernández, Núria. *Chariots of Ladies: Francesc Eiximenis and the Court Culture of Medieval and Early Modern Iberia*. Ithaca, NY: Cornell UP, 2015.

Silva Maroto, Pilar. "El *Retablo de los Gozos de María* de Jorge Inglés." *Boletín del Museo del Prado* 30.48 (2012): 6–23.

Simó Santonja, Vicente-Luis. *Doctrinas internacionales de Alonso de Madrigal "El Tostado."* Ávila: Excma. Diputación Provincial de Ávila, 1959.

Sinkewicz, Robert E., ed. and trans. *Evagrius of Pontus: The Greek Ascetic Corpus*. Oxford: Oxford UP, 2003.

Smith, Nathaniel B. "Medieval and Renaissance in Catalan Courtly Literature." *Court and Poet: Selected Proceedings of the Third Congress of the International Courtly Literature Society, Liverpool, 1980*. Ed. Glyn S. Burgess. Liverpool: Francis Cairns, 1981. 297–307.

Sobrequés Vidal, Santiago, and Jaume Sobrequés i Callicó. *La guerra civil catalana del segle XV*. 2 vols. Barcelona: Edicions 62, 1987.

Sobrer, Josep Miquel. "The Architecture of Ausiàs March's First Death Song (Poem 92)." *Hispanic Review* 60.3 (1992): 267–84.

– "Ausiàs March, the Myth of Language, and the Troubadour Tradition." *Hispanic Review* 30.3 (1982): 327–36.

– *La doble soledat d'Ausias March*. Barcelona: Quaderns Crema, 1987.

Solomon, Michael. *The Literature of Misogyny in Medieval Spain: The* Arcipreste de Talavera *and the* Spill. Cambridge: Cambridge UP, 1997.

Sorabji, Richard. *Emotion and Peace of Mind: From Stoic Agitation to Christian Temptation (The Gifford Lectures)*. Oxford: Oxford UP, 2000.

Spence, Sarah. "Rhetoric and Hermeneutics." *The Troubadours: An Introduction*. Ed. Simon Gaunt and Sarah Kay. Cambridge: Cambridge UP, 1999. 164–80.

Stone, Gregory B. *The Death of the Troubadour: The Late Medieval Resistance to the Renaissance*. Philadelphia: U of Pennsylvania P, 1994.

Taylor, Barry. "Old Spanish Wisdom Texts – Some Relationships." *La corónica* 14.1 (1985): 71–85.

Tejada, Francisco Elías de. "Ideologia e Utopia no 'Livro da Virtuosa Benfeitoria.'" *Revista Portuguesa de Filosofia* 3.1 (1947): 5–19.

Terry, Arthur. "Introspection in Ausiàs March." *Medieval and Renaissance Studies in Honour of Robert Brian Tate*. Ed. Ian Michael and Richard A. Cardwell. Oxford: Dolphin Book, 1986. 165–77.

– "'Per la mort és uberta la carrera': Una lectura d'Ausiàs March, poema 92." *Ausiàs March (1400–1459): Premier poète en langue catalane*. Ed. Georges Martin and Marie-Claire Zimmermann. Paris: Séminaire d'études médiévales hispaniques de l'université Paris 13, 2000. 231–41.

– *Three Fifteenth-Century Valencian Poets*. London: Department of Hispanic Studies, Queen Mary and Westfield College, 2000.

Tillier, Jane Yvonne. "Passion Poetry in the *Cancioneros*." *Bulletin of Hispanic Studies* 62 (1985): 65–78.

Toduricǎ Impey, Olga. "La poesía y la prosa del *Siervo libre de amor*: ¿'aferramiento' a la tradición del *prosimetrum* y de la convención lírica?" *Medieval, Renaissance and Folklore Studies in Honor of John Esten Keller*. Ed. Joseph R. Jones. Newark: Juan de la Cuesta, 1980. 171–87.

Tomassetti, Isabella. "Los *Salmos penitenciales* de Diego de Valera: entre cortesía y parodia." *Aspectos actuales del hispanismo mundial: Literatura – Cultura – Lengua*. Vol. 1. Ed. Christoph Strosetzki. Berlin: De Gruyter, 2018. 262–73.

– "Sobre la tradición ibérica de los decires con citas: Apuntes para un estudio tipológico." *Actas del VIII Congreso Internacional de la Asociación Hispánica de Literatura Medieval: Santander, 22–26 de septiembre de 1999, Palacio de la Magdalena, Universidad Internacional Menéndez Pelayo*. Ed. Margarita Freixas, Silvia Iriso Ariz, and Laura Fernández. Vol. 2. Santander: Asociación Hispánica de Cultura Medieval, 2000. 1707–24.

– "Tra intertestualità e interpretazione: i '*decires* a citazioni' del *Cancioneiro Geral* di Garcia de Resende." *Rivista di filologia e letterature ispaniche* 1 (1998): 63–100.

Torre y Franco-Romero, Lucas de. "Mosén Diego de Valera: Su vida y obras (Continuación)." *Boletín de la Real Academia de la Historia* 64 (1914): 249–76.

Torró, Jaume. "Ausiàs March no va viure en temps d'Ovidi." *Estudis de filologia catalana. Dotze anys de l'Institut de Llengua i Cultura Catalanes, Secció Francesc Eiximenis.* Barcelona: Publicacions de l'Abadia de Montserrat, 1999. 175–99.

– "El mite de Caldesa: Corella al *Jardinet d'orats.*" *Atalaya* 7 (1996): 103–16.

– ed. *Sis poetes del regnat d'Alfons el Magnànim*. Barcelona: Barcino, 2009.

– "Una cort a Barcelona per a la literatura del segle XV." *Revista de Catalunya* 163 (2001): 97–123.

Torroella, Pere. *Obra completa.* Ed. Francisco Rodríguez Risquete. 2 vols. Barcelona: Barcino, 2011.

Tratado de la comunidad. Ed. Frank Anthony Ramírez. London: Tamesis, 1988.

Trigg, Stephanie. "Introduction: Emotional Histories – Beyond the Personalization of the Past and the Abstraction of Affect Theory." *Exemplaria* 26.1 (2014): 3–15.

Triste deleytaçión: An Anonymous Fifteenth Century Castilian Romance. Ed. E. Michael Gerli. Washington, DC: Georgetown UP, 1982.

Turner, Denys. *Eros and Allegory: Medieval Exegesis of the* Song of Songs. Kalamazoo, MI: Cistercian Publications, 1995.

Turner, Jonathan H., and Jan E. Stets. *The Sociology of Emotions.* Cambridge: Cambridge UP, 2005.

Valera, Diego de. *Doctrinal de príncipes. Prosistas castellanos del siglo XV.* Vol. 1. Ed. Mario Penna. Madrid: Atlas, 1959. 173–202.

– *Exortación de la pas. Prosistas castellanos del siglo XV.* Vol. 1. Ed. Mario Penna. Madrid: Atlas, 1959. 77–87.

Vallín, Gema. "Villasandino y la lírica gallego-portuguesa." *Cancioneros en Baena. Actas del II Congreso Internacional* Cancionero de Baena. *In Memoriam Manuel Alvar.* 2 vols. Ed. Jesús L. Serrano Reyes. Baena: Ayuntamiento de Baena, 2003. 2: 79–85.

Vanderford, Kenneth Hale. "Macías in Legend and Literature." *Modern Philology* 31.1 (1933): 35–63.

Vaquero, Mercedes. "Cultura nobiliaria y biblioteca de Fernán Pérez de Guzmán." *Revista Lemir* 7 (2003): 1–116.

Varela, José Luís. *La transfiguración literaria.* Madrid: Prensa Española, 1970. 3–51.

Verderber, Suzanne. *The Medieval Fold: Power, Repression, and the Emergence of the Individual.* New York: Palgrave, 2013.

Vilanova, Arnau de. *Tractat sobre l'amor heroic (Tractatus de amore heroico).* Ed. Michael McVaugh. Trans. Sebastià Giralt. Barcelona: Barcino, 2011.

Villena, Enrique de. *Tratado de la consolación.* Ed. Derek C. Carr. Madrid: Espasa-Calpe, 1976.

Viterbo, Joaquim de Santa Rosa de. *Elucidário das palavras, termos, e frases, que em Portugal antigamente se usaram, e que hoje regularmente se ignoram: obra indispensável para entender sem erro os documentos mais raros e preciosos que entre nós se conservam.* 2 vols. facsims. Ed. Mário Fiúza. Porto: Livraria Civilização, 1962–65.

Vitz, Evelyn Birge. *Medieval Narratives and Modern Narratology: Subjects and Objects of Desire.* New York: New York UP, 1992.

Vives, Juan Luis. *The Passions of the Soul: The Third Book of* De Anima et Vita. Trans. Carlos G. Noreña. Lewiston, NY: Edwin Mellen Press, 1990.

Wack, Mary Frances. *Lovesickness in the Middle Ages: The "Viaticum" and Its Commentaries.* Philadelphia: U of Pennsylvania P, 1990.

Walters, D. Gareth. "The Reader Misled and Empowered: Expectation, Ambiguity and Deception in Three Poems of Ausiàs March." *Bulletin of Hispanic Studies* 74 (1997): 41–60.

Warner, Marina. *Alone of All Her Sex: The Myth and the Cult of the Virgin Mary.* Oxford: Oxford UP, 2016.

Weiss, Julian. "Álvaro de Luna, Juan de Mena and the Power of Courtly Love." *MLN* 106.2 (1991): 241–56.

– "Las *fermosas e peregrinas ystorias*: sobre la glosa ornamental cuatrocentista." *Revista de literatura medieval* 2 (1990): 103–12.

– "Introduction." *Poetry at Court in Trastamaran Spain: From the* Cancionero de Baena *to the* Cancionero General. Ed. E. Michael Gerli and Julian Weiss. Tempe, AZ: Medieval and Renaissance Texts and Studies, 1998. 1–16.

– "Memory in Creation: The Context of Rojas's Literary Recollection." *Bulletin of Hispanic Studies* 86 (2009): 150–8.

– *The* Mester de Clerecía*: Intellectuals and Ideologies in Thirteenth-Century Castile.* Woodbridge: Tamesis, 2006.

– "On the Conventionality of the *Cantigas d'amor.*" *La corónica* 26.1 (1997): 225–45.

– *The Poet's Art: Literary Theory in Castile c. 1400–60.* Oxford: Society for the Study of Mediæval Languages and Literature, 1990.

– "'¿Qué demandamos de las mugeres?': Forming the Debate about Women in Late Medieval Spain (with a Baroque Response)." *Gender in Debate from the Early Middle Ages to the Renaissance.* Ed. Thelma S. Fenster and Clare A. Lees. New York: Palgrave, 2002. 237–81.

Weissberger, Barbara F. "'Deceitful Sects': The Debate about Women in the Age of Isabel the Catholic." *Gender in Debate from the Early Middle Ages to the Renaissance.* Ed. Thelma S. Fenster and Clare A. Lees. New York: Palgrave, 2002. 207–35.

Whinnom, Keith. *Spanish Literary Historiography: Three Forms of Distortion.* Exeter: U of Exeter P, 1967.

– *The Spanish Sentimental Romance, 1440–1550: A Critical Bibliography.* London: Grant & Cutler, 1983.

– "Towards the Interpretation and Appreciation of the *Canciones* of the *Cancionero general* of 1511." *Medieval and Renaissance Spanish Literature: Selected Essays.* Ed. Alan Deyermond, W.F. Hunter, and Joseph T. Snow. Exeter: U of Exeter P, 1994. 114–32.

Wilhite, Valerie M. "Instructing the Court: Raimon Vidal's Pedagogy for the Courtly *Joglar.*" *Courtly Arts and the Art of Courtliness: Selected Papers from the Eleventh Triennial*

Congress of the International Courtly Literature Society, University of Wisconsin-Madison, 29 July–4 August 2004. Ed. Keith Busby and Christopher Kleinhenz. Cambridge: D.S. Brewer, 2006. 755–70.

Zambrano, María. *La confesión: género literario*. Madrid: Siruela, 1995.

– *El hombre y lo divino*. Madrid: Fondo de Cultura Económica de España, 2007.

Zimmermann, Marie-Claire. *Ausiàs March o l'emergència del jo*. Barcelona: Publicacions de l'Abadia de Montserrat, 1998.

– "Metàfora i destrucció del món en Ausiàs March." *Actes del Cinquè Col·loqui Internacional de Llengua i Cultura Catalanes (Andorra, 1–6 d'octubre de 1979)*. Ed. Jordi Bruguera and Josep Massot. Barcelona: Publicacions de l'Abadia de Montserrat, 1980. 123–50.

Zinato, Andrea. *Macías: l'esperienza poetica galego-castigliana*. Venice: Cafoscarina, 1996.

Zumthor, Paul. *Langue et techniques poétiques a l'époque romane (XIe–XIIIe siècles)*. Paris: C. Klincksieck, 1963.

– *Toward a Medieval Poetics*. Trans. Philip Bennett. Minneapolis: U of Minnesota P, 1992.

Zwartjes, Otto. *Love Songs from al-Andalus: History, Structure, and Meaning of the* Kharja. Leiden: Brill, 1997.

Index

Note: Parenthetical title after name entry indicates fictional character in that work.

Toronto Iberic

1 Anthony J. Cascardi, *Cervantes, Literature, and the Discourse of Politics*
2 Jessica A. Boon, *The Mystical Science of the Soul: Medieval Cognition in Bernardino de Laredo's Recollection Method*
3 Susan Byrne, *Law and History in Cervantes'* Don Quixote
4 Mary E. Barnard and Frederick A. de Armas, eds., *Objects of Culture in the Literature of Imperial Spain*
5 Nil Santiáñez, *Topographies of Fascism: Habitus, Space, and Writing in Twentieth-Century Spain*
6 Nelson Orringer, *Lorca in Tune with Falla: Literary and Musical Interludes*
7 Ana M. Gómez-Bravo, *Textual Agency: Writing Culture and Social Networks in Fifteenth-Century Spain*
8 Javier Irigoyen-García, *The Spanish Arcadia: Sheep Herding, Pastoral Discourse, and Ethnicity in Early Modern Spain*
9 Stephanie Sieburth, *Survival Songs: Conchita Piquer's* Coplas *and Franco's Regime of Terror*
10 Christine Arkinstall, *Spanish Female Writers and the Freethinking Press, 1879–1926*
11 Margaret Boyle, *Unruly Women: Performance, Penitence, and Punishment in Early Modern Spain*
12 Evelina Gužauskytė, *Christopher Columbus's Naming in the* diarios *of the Four Voyages (1492–1504): A Discourse of Negotiation*
13 Mary E. Barnard, *Garcilaso de la Vega and the Material Culture of Renaissance Europe*
14 William Viestenz, *By the Grace of God: Francoist Spain and the Sacred Roots of Political Imagination*

15 Michael Scham, Lector Ludens: *The Representation of Games and Play in Cervantes*
16 Stephen Rupp, *Heroic Forms: Cervantes and the Literature of War*
17 Enrique Fernandez, *Anxieties of Interiority and Dissection in Early Modern Spain*
18 Susan Byrne, *Ficino in Spain*
19 Patricia M. Keller, *Ghostly Landscapes: Film, Photography, and the Aesthetics of Haunting in Contemporary Spanish Culture*
20 Carolyn A. Nadeau, *Food Matters: Alonso Quijano's Diet and the Discourse of Food in Early Modern Spain*
21 Cristian Berco, *From Body to Community: Venereal Disease and Society in Baroque Spain*
22 Elizabeth R. Wright, *The Epic of Juan Latino: Dilemmas of Race and Religion in Renaissance Spain*
23 Ryan D. Giles, *Inscribed Power: Amulets and Magic in Early Spanish Literature*
24 Jorge Pérez, *Confessional Cinema: Religion, Film, and Modernity in Spain's Development Years, 1960–1975*
25 Joan Ramon Resina, *Josep Pla: Seeing the World in the Form of Articles*
26 Javier Irigoyen-García, *"Moors Dressed as Moors": Clothing, Social Distinction, and Ethnicity in Early Modern Iberia*
27 Jean Dangler, *Edging toward Iberia*
28 Ryan D. Giles and Steven Wagschal, eds., *Beyond Sight: Engaging the Senses in Iberian Literatures and Cultures, 1200–1750*
29 Silvia Bermúdez, *Rocking the Boat: Migration and Race in Contemporary Spanish Music*
30 Hilaire Kallendorf, *Ambiguous Antidotes: Virtue as Vaccine for Vice in Early Modern Spain*
31 Leslie Harkema, *Spanish Modernism and the Poetics of Youth: From Miguel de Unamuno to* La Joven Literatura
32 Benjamin Fraser, *Cognitive Disability Aesthetics: Visual Culture, Disability Representations, and the (In)Visibility of Cognitive Difference*
33 Robert Patrick Newcomb, *Iberianism and Crisis: Spain and Portugal at the Turn of the Twentieth Century*
34 Sara J. Brenneis, *Spaniards in Mauthausen: Representations of a Nazi Concentration Camp, 1940–2015*
35 Silvia Bermúdez and Roberta Johnson, eds., *A New History of Iberian Feminisms*
36 Steven Wagschal, *Minding Animals in the Old and New Worlds: A Cognitive Historical Analysis*
37 Heather Bamford, *Cultures of the Fragment: Uses of the Iberian Manuscript, 1100–1600*
38 Enrique García Santo-Tomás, ed., *Science on Stage in Early Modern Spain*

39 Marina Brownlee, ed., *Cervantes'* Persiles *and the Travails of Romance*
40 Sarah Thomas, *Inhabiting the In-Between: Childhood and Cinema in Spain's Long Transition*
41 David A. Wacks, *Medieval Iberian Crusade Fiction and the Mediterranean World*
42 Rosilie Hernández, *Immaculate Conceptions: The Power of the Religious Imagination in Early Modern Spain*
43 Mary Coffey and Margot Versteeg, eds., *Imagined Truths: Realism in Modern Spanish Literature and Culture*
44 Diana Aramburu, *Resisting Invisibility: Detecting the Female Body in Spanish Crime Fiction*
45 Samuel Amago and Matthew J. Marr, eds., *Consequential Art: Comics Culture in Contemporary Spain*
46 Richard P. Kinkade, *Dawn of a Dynasty: The Life and Times of Infante Manuel of Castile*
47 Jill Robbins, *Poetry and Crisis: Cultural Politics and Citizenship in the Wake of the Madrid Bombings*
48 Ana María Laguna and John Beusterien, eds., *Goodbye Eros: Recasting Forms and Norms of Love in the Age of Cervantes*
49 Sara J. Brenneis and Gina Herrmann, eds., *Spain, World War II, and the Holocaust: History and Representation*
50 Francisco Fernández de Alba, *Sex, Drugs, and Fashion in 1970s Madrid*
51 Daniel Aguirre-Oteiza, *This Ghostly Poetry: Reading Spanish Republican Exiles between Literary History and Poetic Memory*
52 Lara Anderson, *Control and Resistance: Food Discourse in Franco Spain*
53 Faith Harden, *Arms and Letters: Military Life Writing in Early Modern Spain*
54 Erin Alice Cowling, Tania de Miguel Magro, Mina García Jordán, and Glenda Y. Nieto-Cuebas, eds., *Social Justice in Spanish Golden Age Theatre*
55 Paul Michael Johnson, *Affective Geographies: Cervantes, Emotion, and the Literary Mediterranean*
56 Justin Crumbaugh and Nil Santiáñez, eds., *Spanish Fascist Writing: An Anthology*
57 Margaret E. Boyle and Sarah E. Owens, eds., *Health and Healing in the Early Modern Iberian World: A Gendered Perspective*
58 Leticia Álvarez-Recio, ed., *Iberian Chivalric Romance: Translations and Cultural Transmission in Early Modern England*
59 Henry Berlin, *Alone Together: Poetics of the Passions in Late Medieval Iberia*